HARD TOMATOES, HARD TIMES

The Original Hightower Report, Unexpurgated, of the
Agribusiness Accountability Project on the Failure
of America's Land Grant College Complex
and Selected Additional Views of the Problems
and Prospects of American Agriculture
in the Late Seventies

Forewords by Professor Harry M. Scoble
and Senator James Abourezk

SCHENKMAN BOOKS INC.
Rochester, Vermont

AGRIBUSINESS ACCOUNTABILITY PROJECT
TASK FORCE ON THE LAND GRANT COLLEGE COMPLEX

Director: Jim Hightower
Research Coordinator: Susan DeMarco
Legal Research: Valerie Kantor
Research Staff: Toby Edelman, Al V. Krebs, Helen Lichtenstein, Susan Sechler, Kathryn Seddon
Research Assistants: Jeanne Dangerfield, Cyma Heffter, Sandra Moore, Virginia Richardson

The work of the Task Force on the Land Grant College Complex was an activity of the Agribusiness Accountability Project, which is a non-profit, non-partisan, public-interest research organization based in Washington, D. C.

Library of Congress Cataloging in Publication Data
Main entry under title:

Hightower, Jim.
    Hard Tomatoes, Hard Times.

    "(Report of) Agribusiness Accountability Project, Task Force on the Land Grant College Complex."
    Includes bibliographical references.
    1. Agricultural colleges--United States. 2. Agricultural research--United States. 3. Agricultural industries-- United States. 4. State universities and colleges--United States. 5. Agricultural extension work--United States. I. Agribusiness Accountability Project. Task Force on the Land Grant College Complex.
II. Title.
S533. H5133 1978   338.1'0973   78-9002
ISBN 0-8467-0516-8

Contents

AGRICULTURAL COLLEGES

Any type of survey in depth of the agricultural situation demands focusing on our agriculture colleges, as they are and have been the seedbed that nourishes our agricultural talent. Close inspection of these institutions does not put much joy in the heart of the investigator.

Behind these hallowed walls lies an almost unbelievable chaos. You learn that the term colleague means the S.Ò.B. down the hall, that the caste system is the accepted way of life, that tenure, paycheck, and career are the most important things in their life, that they are the most rested group you will ever meet, that they are without responsibility as they are "experimental," which in turn excuses them from being objective. Yet they treat subjectivity as if it were subversiveness.

And when a farmer finally screws up enough courage to personally call on one of these public servants, he invariably leaves more confused and disillusioned than when he arrived, feeling in his heart that, perhaps, he should have spent this day sweeping down cobwebs in the hoghouse. At least he would have rid himself of cobwebs rather than have acquired them.

Ira Dietrich, Poor Damn Janeth

Foreword to 1978 Edition
by Harry M. Scoble

Hard Tomatoes, Hard Times was a collective research product of the Agribusiness Accountability Project, as were also Martha M. Hamilton's *The Great American Grain Robbery & Other Stories,* etc. The Agribusiness Accountability Project is one of several score new-type political research projects generated in the turbulent politics of the 1960's. (Others of this type that come immediately to mind are the North American Congress on Latin America (NACLA); the Radical Education Project of Students for a Democratic Society (REP/SDS), part of which has evolved into the Union of Radical Political Economists (URPE); the Interfaith Corporate Responsibility Project which has researched American investments in southern Africa; and the Council on Economic Priorities (CEP) which initially researched and publicized U.S. military R&D of bio-chemical warfare techniques.)

Some of these organizations were tax-exempt or sought such status from the Treasury Department. The full political history of how many of these were "legally" harassed out of existence by the Special Services Staff of Mr. Nixon's IRS, by Mr. Hoover's FBI, and so on, remains to be documented. Regardless, almost all of these new action-oriented social research agencies shared two common characteristics. First, almost every one of them operated on a true shoe-string: near-starvation pay (by the conventional material standards of the better educated elements of this society) for the one or tiny handfuls of more-than-fulltime activist-researchers, a hole-in-the-wall office (without "a Bigelow on the floor"), a telephone, a typewriter, and a beat-up mimeograph machine. Davids all, yet seeking to slay Goliath — or at least to significantly change his behavior. And to do so with facts.

This was the second shared attribute: the energetic search for a factually-grounded understanding of the American political economy as a prerequisite for popularly-directed political change. Such facts

viii   HARD TOMATOES, HARD TIMES

are not easy to come by when the research centers in on the sources
and techniques of power — the modern American business corporation, in short — in a society that proclaims itself democratic; the facts
are especially difficult to discover when the power-holders control
the definition of such inherently expansive (and self-protective)
politico-legal doctrines as "national security" and "executive privilege," "proprietary information" and "lawyer-client privilege." Mr.
Hightower and his associates are to be congratulated for having
undertaken their careful research on how "the tax-paid, land grant
complex has come to serve an elite of private, corporate interests in
rural America. . . ."

Hard Tomatoes is a relevant book. "Relevant" is a word, along
with the more recent (and misspelled) "dialog," that has been grossly
overworked by both pols and "professional educators"; nonetheless, the student rebels of the 1960's had a valid point — in their
demand for relevance in higher education — if by that we understand them to have insisted that what was taught and researched,
perhaps most especially in the *social* sciences, be true (in the sense
of factually accurate), non-trivial, and useful. So defined, *Hard
Tomatoes, Hard Times* is relevant in its focus on higher education
and agricultural research/teaching as one significant independent
variable contributing to social change in America; change, that is to
say, which is man-made, not just man-affecting, and thereby potentially controllable in a truly democratic fashion.

Some social scientists have spoken of "the seamless web" of social
causation; others more recently have written in terms of "ideas whose
time has come." Such phrases, howsoevermuch elegant appearing,
are more pedantic propaganda than scientific explanation: they obfus-
cate and mystify far more than they clarify. Hightower helps us to
understand the socio-economic causes of, and the predictable impact
of, "America's Land Grant College Complex" in its major contribution to a revolution in the agricultural sector. The industrialization
of American agriculture — and by that one means the three inter-
twined processes of mechanization, automation, and concentration
of both ownership and managerial-control of productive assets — has
since World War II shoved, not merely pushed, millions of American
citizens (including yet hardly limited to the Mississippi Delta blacks)
into the urban centers of the nation. In the Keynesian-cushioned
post-war era, it is our metropolitan centers which have provided a
last-chance this side of suicide, symbolic or actual.

Additionally, do we wish to understand — and thereby gain the potential for democratically controlling — the role, influence, impact of the federal government itself in promoting a mindless R&D which, in turn, triggers the perverted logic that what can in fact be done technologically must therefore seek and find a commercially-profitable application? The historical tendency toward concentration of economic power in what so many scholars choose to call "a post-industrial society" is somewhat less than inevitable. How long can we ignore the evidence before us, yet still retain a chance to determine our own future while permitting an equal option to our progeny, that technology is never neutral in relation to the distribution of effective power in a society?

Some democratic theorists have spoken in terms of two central values, those of "political equality" and of "rule by the numerical majority." Others, bending under the perceived impact of inhospitable social trends (i.e., the tendencies toward urbanization, industrialization, and rationalization in modern mass societies plus, of course, the unavoidable constraints of an unsought Superpower status with reference to foreign and "defense" policies), have employed a more relaxed definition. They accept the logic of Michels' "iron law of oligarchy" (while at the same time politely rephrasing it in terms of "the active minority" tendency in all human groups, or of a "political elite" being inevitable, functional, and thus desirable), yet claim that the essence of democracy is retained by various legal mechanisms — in particular, the general electoral process and the two-party system in the United States — which are said to have the effect of rendering that political elite representative, responsive, and accountable. With regard to either operationalization of that basic political concept. Hightower raises to the threshold of public consciousness the central political and ethical dilemma of our times: technology requires — one might say "is" — bureaucracy, yet bureaucracy is inherently anti-democratic.

Hard Tomatoes . . . also helps us to recall that, when poverty and hunger were (cyclically) rediscovered in the United States in the early 1960's, it was not the federal government — executive departments or congressional committees — which produced the evidence. It was private individuals and organizations, economists and medical researchers in particular. And, perhaps demonstrating that the conventional analytic distinction between "foreign" and "domestic" policies is artificial and, for small-d democrats, self-defeating, one should note that at the 1974 FAO-sponsored World Food Conference in Rome the U.S. political elite — represented primarily by

USDA and State Department personnel — stridently denied that American food was being employed as "a political weapon." (The claim rings false in light of the fact that this nation's official policies, for far more than a decade and indeed back to "The Occupation" in the cases of Germany and Japan, have been to promote the consumption of meats — most particularly grain-fed beef — as a key ingredient of West European and Japanese diets. Recall: it takes approximately nine pounds of grain to produce one pound of beef.) A telephone call to the Agribusiness Council (ABC) in New York City will produce a firm and politely grudging response that no universities or foundations are involved at all, that ABC is made up solely of large agribusiness corporations (which, regrettably, are unidentifiable over the telephone because people would "jump right on our members' backs for jobs"), and that a Mr. Henry J. Heinz — the one who is the son of the founder and the father of the present Republican Senator from Pennsylvania, in fact — is the chairman and was the founder of the ABC in 1967. The wholly-owned government corporation, the U.S. Overseas Private Investment Corporation, earmarked $750,000 for controlling our "preinvestment survey" to the ABC.

Ever since mankind turned from hunting and gathering to agriculture, food has always been a political weapon of the strong against the weak. If this is so, then the critical political question is simply, who shall utilize this power-resource and for what purposes? It may be reading too much into his work, nevertheless I do not think it impermissible to infer that Hightower's answer is that a democratic society could and should employ its surplus-food exports in order to foster democratic regimes. Or, in the liberal Democratic chic of today, to promote "human rights."

Hard Tomatoes, Hard Times also carefully documents what some have termed "the technological imperative" which, despite the defeat of the SST and the arresting of the ABM deployment, is with us today in current debates over the cruise missile. But it also presents nice case-studies of both the politicization of higher education and of "interest group liberalism" gone mad. In the 1960's, conservative faculty and administrators, trustees and alumni cautioned the student dissidents that they were politicizing the university (and that this was morally wrong, and/or it was dangerously self-destructive in that universities were alleged to be fragile institutions, and/or it would lower the high quality of the outputs produced by such institutions). Not so! As Hightower demonstrates with the land-grant colleges of agriculture and the associated agricultural experiment stations and state extension services, the ag schools have since before Woodrow Wilson's administration increasingly served only the interests of agribusiness. In this sense they have always been politicized, just as it is true more broadly that the higher-education elite has generally, and faithfully, served purposes defined by the combined governmental and economic elite.

Doctors and only AMA-type doctors dictate what the tax-supported medical schools do (and do not do). Equally so for agribusiness control — it is far more than mere "influence" — of the agriculture schools. As U.S. multinational agribusiness corporations, for instance, have moved pineapple culture out of The Hawaiis (because Anglo-American property law and the hidden hand of the market dictate a "higher use" for their lands there) and into The Philippines and Kenya, the ag schools have assisted them. In like manner, the agricultural engineers invent and fabricate new machines, on taxpayers' money and time, which will put some of those same taxpayers — both individual farmers and migrant laborers — permanently out of work. Yet these ag-engineers serve no constituency broader than those corporate entities with sufficient capital to utilize a "new technology" whose scale is at once both supra-human and anti-human. Meanwhile, the agricultural economists and other ag-planners are not required — by law, professional ethics, or common decency — to submit "social and economic impact" statements honestly assessing the probable consequences of what they and their agricultural-engineering colleagues are doing.[1] This precisely illustrates "the higher immorality" of an unrepresentative, non-responsive, and unaccountable political elite that the late C. Wright Mills sought to document and publicize more than two decades ago.

Since Franklin Roosevelt's New Deal, every "agricultural adjustment act" from 1938 on has invoked the preservation of "the small,

[1] What is missing is not intelligence but rather the proper conjunction of both political power and values to put such intelligence to use. The American value system has "improved" somewhat since the 1960's, in the sense that the environmental-ecology movement's values have been added to an earlier American credo almost exclusively related to economic growth *per se*. Our operative values remain badly skewed, if not as fully inverted as previously, since we do not seem to strive to accord equal protection to humans even of the fellow-citizen sort. This may reflect a communications technology problem. (That is, it is relatively easy to fly a helicopter close enough so that the newsman can photograph the "hunter" clubbing the baby seal to death; but how does one photograph the destruction of a man or woman's livelihood and ego?)

family-sized farm" as the justification for the detailed programs and activities of the main titles of the legislation. Some public policy analysts, however, have gone beyond the rhetoric of the statutory preambles; in doing so, their research has quite consistently revealed that approximately 80 percent of the benefits (such as crop subsidies have been allocated to the top 20 percent of income-recipients in agriculture. It remains to be demonstrated — substantively, not merely procedurally or in rhetoric, image and style — just how much better the new Democratic Administration will be.

To return to the research of James Hightower and his associates in the Agribusiness Accountability Project, there remains a concluding note. A new "processing" tomato (known as UC-82) is now going into commercial production. In fact, an account in the *New York Times,* March 8, 1977, indicates that the probabilities of overproduction, by that fateful year 1984, are so high that the agricultural-engineering researchers are already happily at work evaluating the potentiality of quick-frozen tomatoes; and they are testing a new snack-food (which will probably appear in a pretty metal container) in the form of tomato chips. Thus do the white-collar educational allies of major business corporations automatically ensure their own continued fruitful employment, with no visible evidence of concern for the fact that their hard tomatoes create very hard times indeed for other human beings. My students in an undergraduate course in American Politics: Current Problems and Controversies" remain fascinated by these phonemena — even in Chicago.

Foreword to 1973 Edition
by U. S. Senator James Abourezk

Over a hundred years ago this country opened up its frontiers by investing our public resources in people. We granted homesteads to anyone willing to work the land, gave land to communities for schools, awarded public land for the extension of railroad transportation into the countryside, and established land grants for states that would create colleges of agriculture. The focus of that investment was on people, and that focus gave rise to strong agricultural development and a strong rural America.

If our leaders had as much vision today as they did then, our rural policy would still enable people to live and work prosperously on the farms and in the towns and small cities across the country. Thirty or forty years ago, however, we turned from that policy and instead focused the public investment in rural America on corporate structures and food systems, rather than on people. The shift has proven costly. Farmers and small town merchants have been forced out of business, workers and professionals have had to move elsewhere to find jobs and clients, communities and towns have been broken up and abandoned — and an entire rural culture is disappearing.

A farmer recently told me:

> We would like to have our kids stay in the hometown areas, and a lot of them would like to stay. But what would they do here? There's less and less chance in farming. Small businessmen have all they can do to make a living for themselves, so they can't pay much. Smart kids go on to school. They'd like to come back to their own community or some other small community. But there aren't enough good jobs there. Out of 110 kids graduated from high school with my boys six years ago, only seven stayed here. Four others are in other small communities. The rest all went to the big city — quite a few left the state for even bigger cities.

The cities, in turn, are choking on these people. As rural urban migrants they come looking for jobs that do not exist, and they are in need of services that overburdened cities are incapable of delivering. To date, 73 percent of the American people live on less than 2 percent of the American land. By the year 2000, we will have an additional 75 million people in this country. Where shall they live? What shall they do?

These are questions properly directed at America's land grant colleges. As *Hard Tomatoes, Hard Times* makes clear, these multi-million dollar, public institutions have the legislative mandate and the tax resources to participate in the solution. They are research and development agencies intended to benefit the public. It is only fair to ask for a public accounting of their work.

As a Senator representing thousands of farmers and other rural people, I know the importance of agricultural research, education and extension. Throughout my years in public office, I have supported these programs, and I consider myself today a good friend of land grant colleges.

Hard Tomatoes, Hard Times is also a good friend of those colleges. It is precisely the kind of document that long-established institutions need every now and again to help them shake off the crust, re-examine their mission and ultimately do a better job of serving the public. Land grant colleges, dating back to the Morrill Act of 1863, should have had this tough, demanding book hurled at them long before now.

It is obvious that much good has come out of land grant colleges. No one doubts this, nor is anyone out to dismantle an institution that is so soundly conceived. But neither can their glaring faults and failures be doubted, and those of us who are supporters of these colleges will do them little good by refusing to face that fact.

You do not have to be a U. S. Senator or dean of a college of agriculture to know that there are real problems in rural America. But far too much of the money, time and intellect of land grant researchers is diverted away from those real problems. Rutgers University is trying to make spinach taste like potato chips; University of California researchers, having genetically, chemically and mechanically altered the tomato, now want to flavor it artificially; at Virginia Polytechnic Institute, two researchers are working on techniques to thaw a frozen turkey.

What about the skyrocketing cost of farm technology, the poor bargaining position of farmers, the nutritional impact of agribusiness methods, the absence of a rural health delivery system, the rising rate of crime on the farms, the need for cooperative marketing systems, the misery of farm worker housing, the tragedy of tractor deaths and hundreds of other very real and very immediate problems that consumers and rural people are struggling with every day, with miniscule or no assistance from their land grant institution?

Those people and those problems are what the land grant mission is all about. There is no need for new legislation or new funding. Agricultural research, education and extension were created quite specifically to deal with the needs of rural people and consumers. But there is a troubling tendency by too many top land grant officials to wash their hands of that responsibility. In response to the point that the cost and necessity of farm mechanization is a staggering burden to thousands of farmers, the chancellor of one land grant college said coldly, "They can go out of business." The national association representing land grant colleges offered this weak apology:

> Great agricultural achievements are not accomplished without some side effects, and the accusation that the land grant colleges and universities have been taken over by the great food conglomerates and have driven the little farmer out of business tend to overlook the dazzling array of abundant foods this cooperation has made available.

And we know where the secretary of agriculture, Earl Butz, is on the issue: "Adapt or die," he said.

That attitude simply is unacceptable. The resources of our land grant institutions are too valuable and the history of those institutions is too proud to allow such a distortion of the land grant mission. There are thousands of good people within those colleges and there is enormous potential there. America needs those people.

Hard Tomatoes, Hard Times is a useful, timely and important book. It is forcing public officials and land grant college officials to take a long-overdue, hard look at the impact of agricultural research, education and extension. Both a political and an academic debate on the role of land grant colleges have been set in motion by this book, and that debate ultimately will reorient the focus of those institutions.

Hard Tomatoes, Hard Times is aimed primarily at two audiences with special potential to make a difference in the way the colleges operates and for whom it operates. The first of these audiences is the land grant community itself, specifically students and those professors and scientists who share some of the Project's concern that the land grant effort is misdirected. In these people exists the potential to expand the vision of the colleges, to alter curricula and press for new expertise on the faculties, to weaken the corporate ties and generally to open up the institution to the research and extension needs of other interests. Such people are present on practically every land grant campus, and publication of this book has emboldened, embarrassed and otherwise encouraged many of them to be more outspoken and insistent on changes. The other primary audience for which the report was written is that diverse constituency of farmers, farm workers, small town businessmen, consumers, environmentalists and other whose needs and aspirations either are ignored or directly opposed by the land grant colleges. They have the potential to bring into the colleges organized and very specific demands for redirection.

These constituencies have disparate interests in agriculture and there is no need to dwell on the obvious fact that their narrow interests often conflict at specific points. There are too many efforts to play these interests against each other. The present secretary of agriculture seems to delight in that exercise, suggesting that the consumer is the enemy of the farmer, wildly characterizing environmentalists as "extremists" demagoging about the Caesar in his salad, saying that organic farming would mean starvation for 50 million Americans, calling on hard pressed farmers to break up the strike of hard pressed dock workers, and otherwise trying to play people against one another.

But it is my view that these people have more common interests than differences, and that those common interests are much more fundamental. At the very least, they share a common recognition that corporate domination of agriculture is not in the best interests of any of them. If the enormous power of corporate agribusiness is ever to be countered, and if people oriented policies are ever to exist in agriculture and rural America — and they must — these constituencies will have to come together more and more for common action.

The land grant colleges can make an important contribution to the revitalization of rural America. They clearly have the legislative mandate, the expertise and the tax resources to help devise agricultural policies and rural programs which put the needs of common people above the needs of an agribusiness elite. Having that capacity, they have the responsibility. Those of us who are genuine friends of these colleges must work to hold them to that responsibility.

Hard Tomatoes, Hard Times has focused public attention on this important issue. Congress has been awakened by this book, and land grant appropriations can expect a tougher going over than in the past. But if there is to be long lasting change in the focus of the colleges, if this public institution is to turn away from its preoccupation with private interest and devote itself to the needs of the people and community, the fight will have to be carried by those who now stand on the outside, with all the support that can be generated among the people oriented forces within the land grant community.

Preface

This preliminary report is an independent examination of America's land grant college-agricultural complex, focused on the work of colleges of agriculture, agricultural experiment stations and state extension services. The message of the report is that the tax-paid, land grant complex has come to serve an elite of private, corporate interests in rural America, while ignoring those who have the most urgent needs and the most legitimate claims for assistance.

The report has no destructive aims. It is the objective of the Task Force to provoke a public response that will help realign the land grant complex with the public interest. In a recent speech on re-ordering agricultural research priorities, the director of Science and Education at the U.S. Department of Agriculture (USDA) said that, "the first giant steps are open discussion and full recognition of the need."[1] this report is dedicated to that spirit.

The Task Force recognizes that "public interest" is not something that is carved on stone tablets. Rather it is the variable result of a process, not a particular set of goals and values. Public interest is only served when all legitimate interests are assured a reasonable chance to be heard on a particular issue and to compete for scarce resources. The president of the National Farmers Union expressed this well in an address on the subject of land grant research:

> If we have learned one thing in America it is that implementation of the democratic ideal requires democratic participation. Our young people talk much of participatory democracy. Minorities demand the right to take part in decisions that affect their lives. When planners do not represent the public, the program is not likely to represent the public interest.[2]

[1]Ned Bayley. "Agricultural Research: Arrows in the Air." Speech before Division of Agricultural Chemistry, American Chemical Society. New York, N.Y. September 10, 1969, p. 15. Available from United States Department of Agriculture (USDA) Office of Information.

[2]Tony T. Dechant. Address before National Association of State Universities and Land Grant Colleges (NASULGC). Chicago, Illinois. November 11, 1969, p. 9. Available from National Farmers Union, Denver, Colorado.

This examination of America's land grant college complex is not intended to be a total rejection of that agricultural system. In fact, there is much to commend its efforts. Conceptually, and even to some extent structurally, it is designed to reach people, particularly to assist rural Americans in their work and in their lives. There are many individuals within this agricultural complex who are at work every day in an earnest application of the historical concepts of the land grant colleges.

For the most part, information contained in the report is taken from public information produced by the system itself, from reports in the agricultural press and from interviews with people involved in the land grant complex.

This preliminary report is the product of research that has been underway for about six months through the Agribusiness Accountability Project's "Task Force on the Land Grant College Complex." In addition to research conducted in Washington and by correspondence, the Task Force effort included research on the campuses of the University of California, Cornell University, University of Florida, Iowa State University, University of Maryland, Michigan State University, North Carolina State University, Purdue University, and Texas A & M University.

The Agribusiness Accountability Project particularly appreciates the cooperation given this research effort by officials in USDA and by officials and staff at the campus level of the land grant complex.

Hard Tomatoes, Hard Times

Introduction

The Obvious Failure

Although agriculture has been and will continue to be the economic and social base of rural America, our rural population is becoming largely a nonfarm one. By 1980, only one rural resident in seven or eight may live on a farm. It is generally agreed that it is neither socially desirable nor economically feasible to try to arrest or even slow down this trend. *(emphasis supplied)*

—*USDA, NASULGC 1966*[1]

Although the land grant college complex[2] was created to be the people's university, to reach out to serve the various needs of a broad rural constituency, the system has, in fact, become the sidekick and frequent servant of agriculture's industrialized elite.

Agriculture's preoccupation with scientific and business efficiency has produced a radical restructuring of rural America, and consequently of urban America. There has been more than a "green revolution"[3] out there—in the last thirty years there literally has been a social and economic upheaval in the American countryside. It is a protracted, violent revolution, and it continues today. The land grant college com-

[1]USDA and National Association of State Universities and Land Grant Colleges. (NASULGC). "A National Program of Research for Agriculture." Report of a study sponsored jointly by USDA and NASULGC for submission to the Senate Committee on Appropriations (October 1966), p. 158.

[2]As used throughout this report, "land grant college complex" denotes three inter-related units, all attached to the land grant college campus:

A. Colleges of Agriculture, created in 1862 and 1890 by two separate Morrill Acts.
B. State Agricultural Experiment Stations, created in 1887 by the Hatch Act for the purpose of conducting agricultural and rural research in cooperation with the Colleges of Agriculture.
C. Extension Service, created in 1914 by the Smith-Lever Act for the purpose of disseminating the fruits of teaching and research to the people of the countryside.

[3]The "green revolution" is the popular label for the increased productivity that has come from hybrid crops, agricultural chemicals, and farm mechanization.

plex has been the scientific and intellectual progenitor of that revolution.

At least since World War II, the land grant colleges of this country have put their tax supported resources almost solely into efforts that primarily have worked to the advantage and profit of large corporate enterprises, particularly the huge corporate farms and ranches, the vertically-integrated and conglomerate corporations in agricultural production, the seed, feed, chemical, credit, machinery and other "in-put" industries, and the processing, packaging, marketing, distributing, retailing, exporting and other "out-put" industries.

The basis of land grant teaching, research, and extension work has been that "efficiency" is the greatest need in agriculture. Consequently, this agricultural complex has devoted the overwhelming share of its resources to mechanize all aspects of agricultural production and make it a capital-intensive industry; to increase crop yield per acre through genetic manipulation and chemical application; and to encourage "economies of scale" and vertical integration of the food process. It generally has aimed at transforming agriculture from a way of life to a business and a science, transferring effective control from the farmer to the business executive and the systems analyst.

On the one hand, this focus on scientific and business efficiency has led to production (and over-production) of a bounty of food and fiber products, and, not incidentally, it certainly has contributed to the enrichment of an agribusiness few.

On the other hand, there have been far-reaching side effects of the land grant college's preoccupation with the "green revolution." As statistics indicate, and as visits to the countryside make clear, rural America is crumbling. Not just the family farm, but every aspect of rural America is crumbling—schools, communities, churches, businesses and way of life.

RURAL AMERICA IN CRISIS: OFF THE LAND AND INTO THE CITIES

—47.1 percent of the farm families in this country have annual incomes below $3000.

—More than half of the farms in the country have sales of less than $5,000 a year; together, this majority of farmers accounted for only 7.8 percent of farm sales.

—Since 1940, more than 3 million farms have folded, and farms continue to fold at a rate of 2,000 a week.

—The number of black farm operators fell from 272,541 in 1959 to 98,000 in 1970.

—For the first time since the nation was settled coast to coast, about a hundred years ago, the farm population has fallen below 10 million.

—During the 1960's, the proportion of farm people over 55 years of age rose by a third, while the proportion of those under 14 years of age declined by half.

—Hired farm workers in 1970 averaged an income of $1,083 if they did farm work only, while those who also did some nonfarm work averaged an income of $2,461.

—Fourteen million rural Americans exist below a poverty income, with millions more clinging just on the edge of poverty.

—Independent, small-town businesses are closing at a rate of more than 16,000 a year.

—132 rural counties have no doctor.

—30,000 rural communities are without central water systems; 30,000 are without sewer systems.

—2.5 million substandard houses are occupied by rural families; that is 60 percent of the bad housing in America.

—64 percent of all rural counties lost population during the sixties.

—Entire rural communities are being abandoned.

—Since 1940, 30 million people have left their rural homes for urban areas, and this migration continues at a rate of 800,000 a year.

—More than 73 percent of the American people live now on less than two percent of the land.

RESPONSE OF THE LAND GRANT COLLEGE COMPLEX

Despite the obvious need, the land grant college complex, which is the public's primary investment of intellectual and scientific resources in rural America, has failed to respond. Lauren Soth, a close ally of land grant colleges and an editor of the Des Moines *Register and Tribune*, bemoaned this fact in a recent article:

> The land-grant universities continue to devote the overwhelming portion of their research and educational funds to the promotion of agricultural technology and the service of the highest income farmers. They have not yet given anywhere near the attention in either research of education to the problems of the bypassed poor farmers and bypassed

rural communities that their numbers justify—to say nothing of help on the basis of need.[4]

In fiscal year 1969, a total of nearly 6,000 scientific man-years were spent doing research on all projects at all state agricultural experiment stations.[5] Based on USDA's research classifications, only 289 of those scientific man-years were expended specifically on "people-oriented" research. That is an allocation to rural people of less than five percent of the total research effort at the state agricultural experiment stations.

The other 95 percent has been concentrated on projects that steadily are creating an automated, integrated and corporatized agriculture. The primary beneficiaries are agribusiness corporations. These interests envision rural America solely as a factory that will produce food, fiber and profits on a corporate assembly line extending from the fields through the supermarket checkout counters.

There is great wealth to be made from rural America. Consumers spent $118 billion for food in 1971. In fact, agriculture is the biggest industry in the country—bigger than the automobile industry, the defense industry, or the electronics industry. With 4.5 million workers in 1969, agriculture employs more people than the combined total of the transportation, steel and automobile industries. One out of every nine dollars in the Gross National Product is accounted for by the food industry.

But that money is not staying in rural America. Only a third of the consumer's food dollar is pocketed by farmers, and the independent family farmers are getting a small portion of that. The rest of it flows to the cities, with a major chunk going to corporate headquarters in New York, in Atlanta, in Nashville, in Kansas City, in Chicago, in Houston, in Denver, in San Francisco and in other urban centers of agricultural power.

Increasingly, agricultural production is vertically integrated, markets are concentrated and dinner is prepackaged by corporate America. IT&T serves up Gwaltney ham and Wonder Bread. The turkey comes from Greyhound Corporation's Armour division. Dow Chemical brings the lettuce, while Tenneco provides fresh fruits. Count on Boeing for the potatoes and American Brands for Motts apple sauce. Coca Cola serves orange juice and, for dessert, there are strawberries from Purex.

Agribusiness corporations such as Ralston Purina, Del Monte,

[4]Lauren Soth. "The End of Agrarianism: Fission of the Political Economy of Agriculture." *American Journal of Agricultural Economics*, vol. 52, no. 5 (December 1970), p. 655.

[5]USDA Science and Education Staff. "Inventory of Agricultural Research, fy 1969 and 1970," table IV-D-O, vol. II (October 1970), p. 250.

Tropicana and Safeway are taking control of agricultural production, reducing farmers to contract laborers. Commodity after commodity is being grown under vertically integrated contract, including 95 percent of the broilers, 75 percent of processed vegetables, 70 percent of citrus, 55 percent of turkeys, 40 percent of potatoes and 33 percent of fresh vegetables.[6] Those percentages are increasing every day as corporate power takes hold of rural America, expropriating power and profits.

Profits and power are not all that go to the cities. People go, too. They go unwillingly and they go unprepared. Ironically, they are the waste products of an agricultural revolution largely designed within a land grant college complex originally created to serve them. Today's urban crisis is a consequence of failure in rural America. The land grant college complex cannot shoulder all the blame for that failure, but no single institution—private or public—has played a more crucial role.

The land grant complex has been eager to work with farm machinery manufacturers and with well-capitalized farming operations to mechanize all agricultural labor, but it has accepted no responsibility for the farm laborer who is put out of work by the machine. The complex has worked hand in hand with seed companies to develop high-yield seed strains, but it has not noticed that rural America is yielding up practically all of its young people. The complex has been available day and night to help nonfarming corporations develop schemes of vertical integration, while offering independent, family farmers little more comfort than "adapt or die."[7] The complex has devoted hours to create adequate water systems for fruit and vegetable processors and canners, but 30,000 rural communities still have no central water system for their people. The complex has tampered with the gene structure of tomatoes, strawberries, asparagus and other foods to prepare them for the steel grasp of the mechanical harvestors, but it has sat still while the American food supply has been laced with carcinogenic substances.

It is remarkable that this imbalance continues year after year, while rural America crumbles and urban America seethes, without any public figure taking a hard look at the investment. It is indicative of national leadership's general failure in rural America that this society continues to pour billions of dollars into the land grant complex without questioning the total impact of the expenditure.

[6] Don Paarlberg. "Future of the Family Farm." Address before Milk Producer's Federation, November 30, 1971. (USDA), p. 10.

[7] Statement by Dr. Earl L. Butz, former dean of the College of Agriculture at Purdue University, currently U.S. secretary of agriculture. Quoted in The *Record Stockman*, March 10, 1955.

In 1966, USDA and land grant spokesmen said: "It is generally agreed that it is neither socially desirable nor economically feasible to try to arrest or even slow down this trend (of a steadily declining farm population)."[8] Who "generally agreed" on this? Did they check with the one million more farmers expected by USDA to fold between now and 1980?[9] What about tens of thousands of small-town businessmen who will have to board up their stores as those farmers pull out?[10] There would not likely be general agreement among the residents of the rural towns that will wither and die, nor by the millions of people who will be rural refugees in alien cities.

Yet, no one in a position of leadership questioned this basic assumption of land grant college policy. In the five years since that statement, half a million farms have gone out of business[11] and some three to four million people have migrated from their rural homes.[12] But the land grant college complex apparently does not perceive this as a crisis. If those four million people leaving rural America had been four million corn-borers entering rural America, the land grant community would have rung all alarms, scurried into the labs and rushed out with an emergency action program to meet the "crisis."

The American public has a right to expect better from the land grant college complex. The total complex—the colleges of agriculture, the agricultural experiment stations and the state extension services—receive annually an appropriation that is approaching three quarters of a billion tax dollars, including federal, state and county appropriations. The public has a right to expect that those intellectual and scientific resources be more than a subsidy for corporate agribusinesses.

The land grant colleges must get out of the corporate board rooms, they must get the corporate interests out of their labs, and they must draw back and reassess their preoccupation with mechanical, genetical and chemical gadgetry. The complex must, again, become the people's

[8]USDA-NASLUGC, op. cit., p. 158.

[9]The Washington Post. "Study Sees Huge Drop in Number of Farms," July 12, 1971.

[10]This figure is an estimate based on a National Farmers Union study that showed one small town businessman closing for every six farmers that folded. Thus, if a million farms fold by 1980, some 166,000 small businesses could be estimated to close in the same period.

[11]USDA Statistical Reporting Service. "Trend to Fewer and Larger Farms Continues." Press release from Washington, D.C. office, January 12, 1972. Number of farms in 1966 was 3,239,000; number of farms in 1972 estimated to be 2,831,000—a decline of 508,000 farms in five years.

[12]Based on a non-metropolitan to metropolitan area migration rate that has fluctuated roughly between 600-800 thousand people a year during the 1960's.

university—it must be redirected to focus the preponderance of its resources on the full development of the rural potential, helping to make the American countryside a place where millions of people can live and work in dignity.

I

An Overview
of the Land Grant College Complex

An institution is to be opened for the good it can do; for the people it can serve; for the science it can promote; and for the civilization it can advance.

— *William Oxley Thompson, 1912*[1]

To understand the land grant complex today requires a look at what it promised to be when it was created. The complex that has become a handmaiden of corporate agribusiness began as an institution of the people.

HISTORICAL PERSPECTIVE

1862 was a landmark year for agriculture. In that one year, Congress enacted (1) the Homestead Act, which opened up the "trans-Mississippi" West to settlement by providing 160 acres of public land free to anyone who would settle his quarter-section and cultivate it for at least five years; (2) legislation creating the Department of Agriculture, although it would not be elevated to cabinet status until 1889; and (3) the Morrill Land Grant Act, providing an endowment of public land (or its monetary equivalent) to each state that would earmark the income from this endowment for the establishment and support of agricultural and mechanical colleges.

Each of these acts partially was the product of the "Westerners," who lived in the section of the country that is today's Mid-West and still is considered the farm belt—Ohio, Indiana, Illinois, Michigan, Wisconsin, Iowa and Minnesota. Farmers were the majority and the dominant economic class there, and they generally had their way

[1]Edward Danforth Eddy. *Colleges for Our Land and Time.* (New York: Harper Brothers, 1956), p. 269.

8

politically. The West was the most democratic section of the country at the time, but as historian T. Harry Williams put it, "It was a capitalistic, property-conscious, middle-class kind of democracy."[2] This was the democracy of the small capitalist versus the Eastern aristocracy of concentrated wealth and the plantation aristocracy in the South.

The Morrill Acts of 1862 and of 1890, the Hatch Act of 1887, and the Smith-Lever Act of 1914, are the legislative foundations of today's land grant college complex—teaching, research and extension (see Appendix A for a more thorough presentation of these and other land grant laws). In the context of the times, each of these land grant functions was designed to serve a majority of rural Americans and to meet a wide range of rural needs. It was not intended in any of these acts that the complex would be the servant primarily of the most affluent agricultural enterprises or that the system would focus narrowly on any one particular thrust in agriculture.

Morrill Act of 1862   The Morrill Act recognized both that the common man could make good use of university education and that science was coming to farming. Like the agrarians who pressed for their creation, these "people's universities" were to be democratic and pragmatic—as Lauren Soth wrote, "The tillers of the soil were going to have their own colleges and their own departments of agriculture."[3]

At the time of enactment of the Morrill Act, America was a very rural country, and farming was the domain of the little man. Rural territory accounted for 80 percent of the 1860 population of 31,443,321.[4] Out of 4,009,000 farms that existed in the United States about this time, 97 percent were under 260 acres, with only 29 farms in the entire country as large as 1,000 acres.[5] In 1860, 59 percent of the total labor force was engaged in agriculture.[6]

This was the general setting when U.S. Representative Justin Smith Morrill, a Whig from Vermont, introduced legislation for land grants in the late 1850's. In 1859, legislation was approved by Congress over some objections. Critics called it a raid on the Treasury and warned that it would lead to land speculation (which later proved a justified concern). President Buchanan vetoed the bill for several reasons, ranging from cost to states' rights. In 1861, with the South no longer

---

[2] T. Harry Williams, Richard N. Current, and Frank Friedel. *A History of the United States, to 1876* (New York: Alfred A. Knopf, 1960), p. 469.

[3] Lauren Soth, *op. cit.*, p. 663.

[4] U.S. Bureau of the Census. *Historical Statistics of the United States* (Washington, D.C., 1960), p. 14.

[5] *Ibid.*, p. 279.

[6] *Ibid.*, p. 74.

in Congress and the nation at war, Morrill again introduced his legislation, which was passed in 1862 and sent to President Lincoln. Facing re-election and needing support in his native Mid-West, a hotbed of anti-war sentiment, Lincoln signed the Act.

Writing a century later, Henry Brunner of the U.S. Office of Education noted that the legislation itself and Representative Morrill's statements made it clear that the purpose embodied in the Act included "a protest against the then characteristic dominance of the classics in higher education" and "a desire to develop, at the college level, instruction relating to the practical activities of life."[7]

Hatch Act of 1887   In their early years, the land grant institutions primarily were trade schools, focusing on the rudiments of farming and offering such courses as "How to Plow." But the colleges clearly had a mandate to teach the "science of agriculture," and they took the leadership in bringing new ideas, methods and techniques to the people of rural America.

By the mid-1880's, some 40 land grant institutions existed, and the administrative heads of these colleges already had come together in a loose association. Their first cooperative action was a campaign for passage of the Hatch Act of 1887, which authorized federal funds for direct payment to each state that would establish an agricultural experiment station in connection with its land grant college. In this legislation, Congress first codified the mandate of the land grant colleges to meet the needs of a broad constituency. It directed the research stations to:

> conduct original and other researches, investigations, and experiments bearing directly on and contributing to the establishment and maintenance of a permanent and effective agricultural industry of the United States, including researches basic to the problems of agriculture in its broadest aspects, and *such investigations as have for their purpose the development and improvement of the rural home and rural life and the maximum contribution by agriculture to the welfare of the consumer.* (emphasis supplied)[8]

By 1890, the colleges were full-fledged educational institutions and had outgrown their ability to operate from endowment income. State support was inadequate to make up the difference. Justin Morrill, now a Senator from Vermont, was ready with a second Morrill Act,

[7]Henry S. Brunner. *Land-Grant Colleges and Universities: 1862-1962* (Washington, D.C.: U.S. Office of Education, 1962, 1966), p. 3.

[8]Hatch Act of 1887, section 2.

this one to provide an annual appropriation, apportioned by formula, to support teaching at the colleges. This second Act made one other addition to the system—it provided money for creation of land grant colleges for blacks.

Colleges of 1890: The Deep, Dark Secret   In 1862, at the time of the first Morrill Act, 90 percent of America's black population was in slavery.[9] The land grant colleges that developed were white bastions, and even after the Civil War, blacks were barred from admission both by custom and by law. When the second Morrill Act was passed in 1890, primarily to obtain more operating money for the colleges, Congress added a "separate but equal" provision authorizing the establishment of colleges for blacks. Seventeen southern and border states took advantage of the Act, creating institutions that still are referred to euphemistically as "colleges of 1890."

The black colleges have been less than full partners in the land grant experience. It is a form of institutional racism that the land grant community has not been anxious to discuss. From USDA, resource allocations to these colleges are absurdly discriminatory—Peter Schuck of the Center for Study of Responsive Law, reports that "Of the approximately $76,800,000 in USDA funds allocated to these schools, about 99.5% went to the sixteen white land grant colleges; the 1890 colleges received a grand total of $383,000 (or 0.5%)."[10] As shown in Figure 1, less than one percent of the research money distributed by Cooperative State Research Service (CSRS) to those sixteen states in 1971 went to the black colleges.

This disparity is not by accident, it is by law. The Hatch Act of 1887 provides that federal research money "shall be divided between such institutions as the legislature of such State shall direct." The McIntyre-Stennis Act, authorizing money for forestry research, gives the power of designation to the governor of each state. The Smith-Lever Act, authorizing funds for extension, also turns the money over to the college selected by the state legislature. Senator Smith himself left little room for doubt concerning the interpretation of these provisions: "We do not . . . want the fund if it goes to any but the white college."[11]

[9]William Payne. "The Negro Land-Grant Colleges." *Civil Rights Digest*. Vol. 3, No. 2 (Spring 1970), p. 12.

[10]Peter H. Schuck. "Black Land-Grant Colleges: Separate and Still Unequal" (unpublished paper), February 1972, p. 8. Available from Center for Study of Responsive Law, 1156 Nineteenth Street, N.W., Washington, D.C., 20036.

[11]Quoted in Schuck. *Ibid.*, p. 9.

FIGURE 1

CSRS Distribution of Funds to Colleges of 1890 and
to Predominantly White Institutions in the Same States

State	Institution	FY 1970	FY 1971
Alabama	Alabama A&M*	$ 18,396	$ 18,396
	Auburn University	1,766,049	1,962,179
Arkansas	Arkansas A&M & Normal*	16,980	16,980
	Univ. of Arkansas	1,486,634	1,644,956
Delaware	Delaware State*	12,413	12,413
	Univ. of Delaware	547,929	605,855
Florida	Florida A&M*	14,946	14,946
	Univ. of Florida	1,070,418	1,205,759
Georgia	Fort Valley State*	18,836	18,836
	Univ. of Georgia	1,918,117	2,138,902
Kentucky	Kentucky State*	19,080	19,080
	Univ. of Kentucky	. 1,858,134	2,078,901
Louisiana	Southern University*	16,251	16,251
	Louisiana State Univ. &		
	Louisiana Tech	1,337,213	1,487,282
Maryland	Univ. of Md., Eastern Sh.*	14,231	14,231
	Univ. of Md., Coll. Park	962,558	1,082,689
Mississippi	Alcorn A&M*	18,751	18,751
	Mississippi State Univ.	1,830,043	2,048,632
Missouri	Lincoln Univ.*	18,239	18,239
	Univ. of Missouri	1,718,465	1,950,328
North Carolina	North Carolina A&T*	22,424	22,424
	North Carolina St. U.	2,564,966	2,882,386
Oklahoma	Langston Univ.*	15,956	15,956
	Oklahoma State Univ.	1,229,335	1,359,792
South Carolina	South Carolina State*	17,143	17,143
	Clemson University	1,501,523	1,677,593
Tennessee	Tennessee State Univ.*	19,256	19,256
	Univ. of Tennessee	1,908,060	2,127,860
Texas	Prairie View A&M*	21,991	21,991
	Texas A&M Univ. &		
	Stephen F. Austin St.	2,445,273	2,728,487
Virginia	Virginia St. College*	18,107	18,107
	Virginia Polytech. Inst.	1,702,819	1,901,628
Total	Colleges of 1890[1]	$ 283,000	$ 283,000
	Predominantly white[2]		
	Institutions	$25,847,536	$28,883,229

1. Funds from Public Law 89–106.
2. Hatch and McIntire-Stennis Act funds.
* Denotes colleges of 1890.

SOURCE: USDA, CSRS.

In 1971, USDA suffered a belated twinge of conscience and accepted a proposal from Representative Frank Evans that $12.6 million be appropriated directly to the black colleges for research and extension. Once the money was appropriated, however, USDA adopted a scheme of "coordination" whereby the white land grant colleges still were in charge of the resources of the black colleges. As Peter Schuck put it in a letter to Secretary Clifford Hardin:

> The core of the new procedure is a "research coordinating committee." Obviously, no responsible person can be against the coordination of research, and the 1890 colleges are no exception. But the RCC, as established by the CSRS guidelines, is less a device for coordinating research between autonomous institutions than an instrument for the effective control by the 1862 colleges of the research funds intended by Congress for the 1890 colleges.[12]

Of course, twelve million dollars, even if under the full control of the black institutions, does not begin to approach the enormous need. If whites in rural America are in trouble, blacks are facing disaster. The median income for black farm families was $3,027 in 1970, compared to $7,016 for white farm families. The number of black-operated farms fell from 559,980 in 1950 to an estimated 98,000 in 1970. During the decade of the 1960's, black people left the sixteen southern states at an annual rate of 140,000—1.4 million for the decade.[13]

These people need the attention of a land grant complex that is attuned to their needs. But the system does not respond—a hundred years after the first Morrill Act, and 82 years after the second Morrill Act, the system will not let go of even a few million dollars to help the black people in rural America. It is more than their secret; it is their shame.

Smith-Lever Act of 1914   In 1914, the third major component of the land grant complex was added—the extension service. The Smith-Lever Act of that year authorized Federal apropriations and brought some national coordination to a network of state extension staffs that had been operating for several years. The extension movement was a reflection of an obvious need to take the teachings of the college and the research of the experiment stations directly into the rural areas for the benefit of the people there. The colleges had been attempting some of this work on their own almost from the start of their existence.

[12]Peter H. Schuck. Letter to Secretary of Agriculture Clifford M. Hardin, October 14, 1971.

[13]All figures from National Sharecroppers Fund. "Rural Black Economic Development: A Position Paper" (unpublished, 1972), pp. 4 and 6. Available from NSF, 1346 Connecticut Avenue, N.W., Washington, D.C., 20036.

The extension principal was to go to people where they were, to help them solve problems that they were facing in their work, in their homes and in their communities. As Representative Lever explained to the House in his report on the extension legislation, the extension agent "must give leadership and direction along all lines of rural activities—social, economic and financial."[14]

The People's Universities   The rationale for making a public investment in agriculture was to help the little man in rural America; the benefits of research were to be widespread among the farming class. During public discourse leading toward passage of the Hatch Act, advocates for the legislation were quite clear on this point:

> The farmer's work is not big business, they argued, and he needs the assistance of the government where business and commerce do not.[15]

Had it been made clear at the outset that the land grant complex was going to become a subsidy for corporate agribusiness, and that the complex would help to eliminate farmers and leave a majority of rural Americans in crisis, it is not likely that it would have been created. The land grant complex, as it is known today, has wandered a long way from its origins.

From the start, the land grant college complex was a scientific undertaking, and its prime supporters were farm groups and individual farmers who "saw their way to prosperity in improved technology."[16] As enacted by Congress and as initially established, the complex was to bring the benefits of science to all farmers and to all rural Americans.

In practice, the colleges quickly established close working relationships with the most productive and wealthiest class of farmers. Those who did not actively seek out the assistance of the system did not receive its assistance. In 1911, the dean of the College of Agriculture at Cornell University wrote:

> We are now in the midst of a process of the survival of the fit. Two opposite movements are very apparent in the agriculture of the time: certain farmers are increasing in prosperity, and certain other farmers are decreasing in prosperity. The former class is gradually occupying the land and extending its power and influence . . . notwithstanding that this is the very time when agricultural colleges and experiment stations and governmental departments have been expanding knowledge and extending their influence. The fact is, that all these agencies relieve first

[14]Report of the Joint USDA-NASULGC Study Committee. *A People and a Spirit.* (Ft. Collins, Colorado: Colorado State University, November 1968), p.18.
[15]Eddy, *op cit.*, p. 96.
[16]Soth, *op. cit.*, p. 664.

the good farmers. They aid first those who reach out for new knowledge and for better things. The man who is strongly disadvantaged by natural location or other circumstances, is the last to avail himself of all these privileges . . . The failure of a great many farmers may be less a fault of their own than a disadvantage of the conditions in which they find themselves. It is fairly incumbent on the state organization to provide effective means of increasing the satisfaction and profit of farming in the less-fortunate areas as well as in the favorable ones . . .[17]

The dean was right, but unheeded. In the same year, the Association of American Agricultural Colleges and Experiment Stations sanctioned what already was practice by noting that "It is undoubtedly the duty of our institutions to render service to industry."[18] They have been faithful to that "duty" ever since. During the depression of the 30's, the complex accepted an invitation to assist government in the development of public policy in agriculture, and that completed the three-way alliance between agricultural science, agribusiness and government. That is the alliance that exists today.

THE EXTENT OF TODAY'S LAND GRANT COMPLEX

"The Land-Grant Colleges," wrote a historian of the system, "have developed from institutions which were little more than trade schools."[19] Today it is an extensive educational and research system involving much more than agriculture. There are 69 land grant universities (see Appendix B), enrolling 1.5 million students[20] and offering degrees in practically every discipline and profession. These universities include the minimal-agricultural curriculum of Massachusetts Institute of Technology, the multiversity system of the Univeristy of California and the urban focus of Federal City College.

Within that extensive university system is the agricultural complex that is the focus of this report—the colleges of agriculture, the agricultural experiment stations and the state extension services.

This land grant agricultural complex is huge, intricate and expensive. Figure 2 offers one example (Purdue University) of the extent of that complex as it exists on campuses today. Over the past few years, the land grant college complex has tapped the public treasury each year for 500 to 700 million dollars (see Figures 3 and 4).

[17]Liberty Hyde Bailey. Quoted in Gould Colman. *A History of the New York State College of Agriculture*, (1962).

[18]Eddy, *op. cit.*, p. 115.

[19]*Ibid.*, p. 280.

[20]Table supplied by NASULGC. "Number and Percent of Enrollment in Institutions of Higher Education . . . by 4-year, 4-year Public, and Land Grant Colleges: Aggregate United States, Fall 1970."

FIGURE 2

The Agricultural Complex

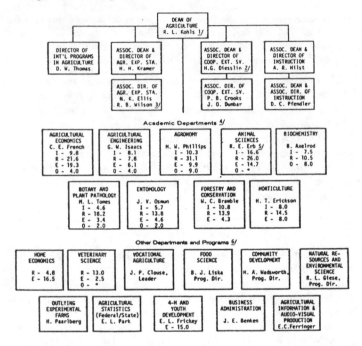

1. All activities of various offices and departments dealing with instruction, research, extension and international programs are responsible through appropriate directors.

2. Field forces of Extension are directly responsible through this office.

3. In charge of market services and regulatory activities. Liaison with Lt. Gov. as Commissioner of Agriculture for services at Purdue. Personnel of State Chemist, Egg Board, etc. are attached to the Experiment Station and in academic departments, and report through this office.

4. F.T.E. data for permanent professional personnel only (1971–72). I - instruction, R - research, E - extension, O - other appointed personnel (usually U.S.D.A., LARS, regulatory). Graduate instructors and post-doctoral personnel not included. Vacancies included. *In these departments, regulatory and diagnostic personnel not enumerated.

5. Interim department head.

6. Home Economics and Veterinary Science are departments in Agriculture for research, extension and regulatory activities only. Faculties of Program Directors are from academic departments.

FIGURE 3

Tax Funds Appropriated for the LGC System,* by Funding Source, 1969

Federal Taxes:		
Colleges of Agriculture	14,349,719	
Experiment Stations	89,015,000	
Extension Service	80,762,000	
Total Federal		184,126,719
State Taxes:		
Colleges of Agriculture	**	
Experiment Stations	134,254,000	
Extension Service	106,326,281	
Total State		240,580,281+
County Taxes:		
Colleges of Agriculture	0	
Experiment Stations	0	
Extension Service	50,287,525	
		50,287,525
TOTAL		474,994,525***

*These are funds for the Division of Agriculture within all land grant colleges — including the colleges of agriculture, the agricultural experiment stations and the extension services.

**No federal agency or other source available to this Task Force had this figure, but traditionally the states have provided the overwhelming share of instructional funding, so it can be expected that this figure would be at least double the $14 million federal contribution.

***This total is understated considerably because it does not include state money appropriated for instruction (see note above), nor does it include funds derived from the use of appropriations. For example, land grant colleges derived $4,221,607 in 1969 from investment of their original Morrill endowment, and they derived another $15,718,000 from sales of products originating from their tax-supported enterprises.

SOURCES: Colleges of Agriculture figures taken from U.S. Office of Education, Bureau of Higher Education. "Statistics on Condition of Land-Grant Funds — 1969 Report." April 22, 1970.

Experiment Station figures taken from USDA. Science and Education Staff. "Inventory of Agricultural Research, by 1969 and 1970." Volume II. October 1970.

Extension Service figures taken from USDA. Extension Service. "Source of Funds allotted for Cooperative Extension Work . . . for Fiscal Year Ending June 30, 1969."

FIGURE 4

Proposed Federal Appropriations for the LGC System, FY 1973

Colleges of Agriculture	$ 2,600,000
Experiment Stations	78,778,000°
Extension Service	168,101,000
	$249,479,000°

°This figure does not include "other Federal" funds appropriated to other Federal agencies for research that subsequently is contracted out to the experiment stations. In 1969, these funds totalled $27.6 million, and it can be expected that they would total at least that much and probably more in fy 1973.

source: The Budget of the United States Government, FY 1973. Appendix, pp. 125, 127 and 440.

Investment of tax dollars in the total land grant complex continues to rise. As shown in Figure 3, the Federal investment in 1969 came to $184,126,719. As shown in Figure 4, the Federal share has jumped 35 percent in the fiscal year 1973 budget, where $249,479,000 is proposed for the land grant functions of teaching, research and extension.

Other tax support has shown similar increases. The extension service funding, for example, rose from a level of $237.4 million on 1969 to $331.9 million in 1971, reflecting a 23 percent increase in state support and a 19 percent increase in county support.[21] While official figures are not available, it can be estimated that the land grant complex in 1972 is the recipient of something like 650 million tax dollars appropriated from Federal, state and county governments.[22]

But even this appropriated sum is not the full measure of tax support for the land grant complex, for it does not reflect the enormous assets of the system, purchased in earlier years with tax money and used today. Although accurate figures are not available, it is clear that the public's total land grant college investment comes to several billion dollars in any given year, paying for everything from test tubes to

[21]USDA. Cooperative Extension Service. "Amount and Percent of CES Funds Available to States . . . by Source, From FY Beginning July 1, 1914." Form MU-34 (2-71).

[22]This estimate assumes a total federal appropriation in the neighborhood of $275-300 million (including "other federal"), a total state appropriation in the neighborhood of $300-325 million (including "instructional support"), and a county appropriation in the neighborhood of $50-75 million. That gives a range of $625-700 million.

experimental farms, from chalk to carpeting in the dean's office.[23]

Thousands of people are involved in this system. In 1969, professionals, technicians and other workers totalled more than 16,000 man-years of work at the agricultural experiment stations throughout the country.[24] In 1971, the extension services had 15,482 professional employees,[25] a support staff of 10,000 and 11,000 program aides, not to mention an estimated 1,000,000 volunteers.[26]

Colleges of agriculture are the primary producers of agricultural professionals in the country. The colleges enrolled more than 52,000 undergraduates and 16,000 graduate students of agriculture in 1970.[27] Degrees are available in a vast array of subjects—from agribanking to entomology, from agricultural engineering to bakery management.

Farmers no longer are the main focus or product of this educational process—the National Association of State Universities and Land Grant Colleges (NASULGC) reported that only 8.9 percent of nearly 10,000 graduating seniors in 1969 chose to enter farming.[28] College curricula today are directed more and more toward the in-put and out-put businesses of agriculture. As Secretary of Agriculture, Earl Butz said, "At Purdue University, as is true at every agricultural college in the United States, they are engaged in training farm boys and farm girls to take jobs in agribusiness."[29] In a special survey of this year's graduating class, *Feedstuffs*[30] found that 12 percent of the undergraduates and only two percent of the graduate students intended to go into farming or ranching. On the other hand, they found that 24 percent of the undergraduates and 20 percent of the graduates intended to

---

[23]Admittedly, this is the crudest of estimates. The total public investment in the land grant system either is not known, not reported or not available in a usable form. No one in USDA or in HEW would hazard a guess. If such a figure were available, it would include in any given year public monies used for (1) salaries, wages and related expenses for teaching, research and extension; (2) administrative costs of operating the system; (3) capital outlays for equipment, and facilities; and (4) current book value of the plant—classrooms, farms, laboratories, equipment, libraries, livestock and so forth,

[24]USDA, Science and Education Staff, *op. cit.*, Table IV-A-9, p. 242.

[25]USDA, Cooperative Extension Service (CES). "Number of Cooperative Extension Agents, 1971."

[26]USDA, CES. "Extension Service, USDA: Functions, Objectives and Responsibilities" (May 1971), p. 3.

[27]NASULGC. *Proceedings*. Report of the 84th Annual Convention of NASULGC, (1970), pp. 119-121. Available from NASULGC, One Dupont Circle, Washington, D.C., 20036.

[28]*Ibid.*, p. 125.

[29]U.S. Senate. Committee on Agriculture and Forestry. "Nomination of Earl Lauer Butz," (Hearing, November 17, 1971. GPO, Washington, D.C., p. 6.

[30]*Feedstuffs: The Weekly Newspaper for Agribusiness* (January 17, 1972), p. 1.

join agribusiness firms. The remainder of the graduating class intended to enter the military, or pursue graduate study, education, government service of other work. *Feedstuffs* reported that, in terms of overall interests in agriculture:

> 41.9 percent of their graduates found the sales area most appealing; 13.8 percent leaned toward marketing; 5.2 percent toward administration; 15.4 percent toward technical research and service (primarily graduate degree holders); 18 percent toward production (primarily engineering students); and 5.9 percent toward some other aspect of agribusiness employment.

The land grant complex today is massive. It reaches into every state, plus Puerto Rico and the District of Columbia, and it has a presence in practically every rural county in America. It is a rich complex, both in terms of money and in terms of intellectual resources. It is a complex with an enormous potential to serve the people of this country. Certainly, it is a resource that rural America desperately needs. But the land grant college complex is a failure. Nowhere is that failure more striking than in the research component.

II

Hard Tomatoes, Hard Times:
Another View of
Land Grant College Research

Today's advances are based on yesterday's research. Right now more scientists are working on investigations related to agriculture than ever before. And this progressive accumulation of knowledge can only accelerate the farm revolution. [1]
—*Dr. George Irving, former director,*
Agricultural Research Service, USDA

It is practically impossible to talk with anyone in the land grant college complex or to read anything about the complex without getting a mindful of the staggering achievements wrought by agricultural research. From the Secretary of Agriculture right down to the most junior instructor of agricultural economics, the entire land grant community enthusiastically recites the litany:

—The farmer today is able to produce food and fiber for himself and 45 others, up from the 11 others that he could provide for in 1940.

—Because of the farmer's increasing productivity, millions of other Americans are freed from farming and able to pursue other occupations.

—The consumer receives an abundant and steady supply of more food products than ever before.

—Because of the farmer's productivity, the American consumer pays a mere 16 percent of his disposable income on food, the lowest rate in the world.

[1] Quoted in Jules B. Billard. "The Revolution in American Agriculture," *National Geographic.* Vol. 137, no. 2 (February 1970), p. 169.

—As the producer of America's agricultural abundance, the farmer is the major contributor toward a favorable balance-of-payments position for his country.

—American agricultural technology and know-how stand as a final bulwark against world-wide famine.

Every one of those points can be concealed.[2] There is no doubt that American agriculture is enormously productive and that agriculture's surge in productivity largely is the result of mechanical, chemical, genetical and managerial research conducted through the land grant college complex. The land grant community has every right to boast of its achievements along these lines.

But the question is whether the achievements outweigh the failures, whether benefits are overwhelmed by costs. In short, land grant college research is not the bargain that has been advertised.

In computing food prices, USDA does not add on the enormous social and cultural costs that also are products of the agricultural revolution. That cost is passed on first to the millions of humans who have been wasted by that revolution and secondly, to the consumer, whose higher taxes must help to pay for those victims. One need only drive the backroads of rural America (or walk the streets of any urban ghetto) to see the obvious failure. The rural poor, the independent family farm, the small-town business and the small towns cannot draw their proper share of research attention, Effectively, most rural Americans have been abandoned by their land grant institutions. And there is at least very serious doubt that the consumer, in whose name all this has been done, is better off with the assembly-line food that results.

The public investment today is being misspent. The indictment was delivered by Tony Dechant, president of National Farmers Union:

> Agricultural research is systematically irrelevant. It is fragmented. It evades issues. It is, ultimately, corrupt of purpose. It has too often been research for its own sake, in which disciplines vie with one another. It has too often ignored the physical, economic and social environment that is the substance of competent disciplines. It has too often failed to serve the public interest, or has done so only incidentally.[3]

[2] Of these points, the most questionable one is that the farm revolution is accountable for reducing the food share of the consumer dollar to 16 percent. The Bureau of Labor Statistics reports that a family with a $12,700 income spends 24.5% of its disposable income for food, families with $9,000 incomes spend 27.2% and families earning $6,300 a year spend about 30.5% on food.

[3] Tony T. Dechant, *op. cit.*, p. 2-3.

A NATIONAL OVERVIEW OF AGRICULTURAL RESEARCH

The federal government is involved in agricultural research primarily through two USDA agencies:

(1) Cooperative State Research Service (CSRS) is the main Federal link to the 53 state agricultural experiment stations (SAES)[4] and administers federal money that is appropriated for distribution to those stations (see Appendix D.) USDA estimates that CSRS will distribute a total of $82 million to SAES in fiscal year 1972.[5]

(2) Agricultural Research Service (ARS) is USDA's in-house research component, conducting agricultural research at its own facilities and through contracts with SAES (see Appendix E). USDA estimates that ARS will expend a total of $195 million for research in fiscal year 1972.[6]

But USDA is not the only source of public money for agricultural research. The states make the major investment, working through their SAES, and other federal agencies also contract with SAES for research. Fiscal year 1969 is the latest one for which figures are available on these investments, totalling $134 million from the states and $28 million from other federal agencies.[7] Thus, assuming a fiscal year 1972 USDA research expenditure of $277 million, and assuming that the state and "other federal" categories have shown at least a modest increase in the three fiscal years since 1969,[8] the total public investment in agriculture research will be half a billion dollars this year. That includes state and all federal expenditures for agricultural research. It generally is estimated that private industry and private research groups spend another half billion for agricultural research.

This is no small operation and it is growing more extensive each year. In a 1969 symposium on "Resource Allocation In Agricultural Research" a perspective was offered on the extent of the research network in this country:

> Nationally, agricultural research at state stations and in the U.S. Department of Agriculture laboratories concerns some 10,500 scientists in about

[4]Two states, New York and Connecticut, have two state agricultural experiment stations. All other states, plus Puerto Rico, have one each.

[5]*The Budget of the United States Government,* Fiscal Year 1973. Washington, D.C.: USGPO, 1972), Appendix, p. 125.

[6]*Ibid.,* p. 116.

[7]"Other federal agencies" include grants from the Agency for International Development, Atomic Energy Commission, Department of Defense, National Academy of Science. National Institutes of Health and National Science Foundation.

[8]In fy 1970, non-federal funds at SAES were $246 million, up from $170 million in fy 1969. It is likely that state funds accounted for at least $200 million of that 1970 total.

20,000 different projects. Of this total public effort, 58 percent is performed by the state experiment stations and 42 percent by USDA. The federal agency provides 27 percent of the funds used by state experiment stations and about half of the total public funds in agricultural research.[9]

According to a USDA inventory in 1969, the cost of supporting one scientist, working full-time, was $51,400.[10]

FIGURE 5

FY 1969 National Total of State Agricultural Experiment Station Funds and a Very Rough Estimate of FY 1972 National Totals

Source of Funds	FY 1969	FY 1972
CSRS:		
Hatch Act	39,249,000	49,587,000
Regional Research Funds	10,282,000	13,619,000
Forestry (McIntire-Stennis)	2,825,000	4,672,000
Contracts and Grants	1,316,000	12,500,000
Other CSRS	18,000	NA
Total CSRS Research	53,681,000	80,378,000
Other USDA:		
Contracts, Grants and Cooperative Agreements	7,749,000	10,000,000
Other Federal:	27,576,000	35,000,000
State Appropriations:	134,254,000	200,000,000
Product Sales at SAES:	15,718,000	16,000,000
Private Industry:	12,236,000	12,000,000
Other Non-tax:	7,519,000	8,000,000
Total SAES Research Funds	$258,743,000	$361,000,000

SOURCE: USDA. Science and Education Staff. "Inventory of Agricultural Research, FY 1969 and 1970." Vol. II. October 1970, p. 244. FY 1972 estimates based on FY 1973 Budget figures, interviews with land grant officials and educated guesses.

[9]Phillip J. Tichenor and Vernon W. Ruttan. "Resource Allocation in Agricultural Research: The Minnesota Symposium" (University of Minnesota: Agricultural Experiment Station, 1969), pp. 4-5.

[10]U.S. House of Representatives, Committee on Appropriations. "Agriculture-Environmental and Consumer Protection Appropriations for 1972." Hearings. 92nd Congress, 1st session. Part 2, p. 551. (Referred to hereafter as House Agricultural Appropriations Hearings, 1972.)

A majority of agricultural research is conducted at land grant colleges, through the agricultural experiment stations. Figure 5 shows a detailed breakdown of total research money available in 1969 to all experiment stations, along with this Task Force's educated guess as to what those figures are in 1972.

What is purchased with this research expenditure? What did society buy in 1969 with a quarter billion dollars, 5,955.9 scientific man-years and 19,965 projects? The answer is, "more revolution." Overwhelmingly, agricultural research continues to be committed to the technological and managerial needs of the largest-scale producers and of agribusiness corporations, and it continues to omit those most in need of research assistance.

USDA's inventory of agricultural research is broken down into nine "Research Problem Areas":

1. Insure a stable and productive agriculture for the future through wise management of natural resources

2. Protect forests, crops and livestock from insects, diseases and other hazards

3. Produce an adequate supply of farm and forest products at decreasing real production costs

4. Expand the demand for farm and forest products by developing new and improved products and processes and enhancing product quality

5. Improve efficiency in the marketing system

6. Expand export markets and assist developing nations

7. Protect consumer health and improve nutrition and well-being of the American people

8. Assist rural Americans to improve their level of living

9. Promote community improvement including development of beauty, recreation, environment, economic opportunity, and public services.

In 1969, areas 1, 2, and 3 accounted for 68 percent of the total research expenditures at SAES, with areas 4, 5 and 6 receiving another 17 percent. Left over was only 15 percent of the resources to put into the "people-oriented" areas, numbers 7, 8 and 9.[11]

But there is less than meets the eye in these "people" areas. An examination of research categories within those areas reveals that they

[11]USDA, Science and Education Staff, *op. cit.*, pp. 247-248.

include research on the farm subsidy program, on wildlife and fish biology and habitat, on culture and protection of ornamentals and turf, on forestland recreation and on trees to enhance the rural and urban environment.

FIGURE 6

SMY of "People Oriented" Research at All SAES — FY 1969

Research Classification Category		Allocation of SMY
Food and Nutrition:		
Food consumption habits	11.5	
Food preparation	12.4	
Human nutrition	93.5	
Sub-total		117.4
Improve Levels of Living:		
Clothing and textile care	15.0	
Family financial		
management	16.0	
Sub-total		31.0
Community Improvement:		
Rural poverty	17.1	
Economic potential of		
rural people	9.8	
Communications among		
rural people	18.3	
Adjustment to change	25.6	
Rural income improvement	17.9	
Rural institutional		
improvement	45.3	
Sub-total		134.0
Housing:		
Rural housing		6.5
Total SMY of "people oriented" research		288.9
Total SMY of all research at SAES		5,955.9
Percent of SAES research that is people oriented		4.8%

SOURCE: USDA. Science and Education Staff. "Inventory of Agricultural Research, FY 1969 and 1970." Volume II. Table IV-D-O, pp. 247–248. October 1970.

In fact, as shown in Figure 6, less than five percent of the scientific man-years in 1969 were expended within research categories that appear to be concerned with people, and even some of those are questionable.

There is an enormous disparity between the SAES research investment in people and its investment in technology and systems. Some of the contrasts are striking:

—1,129 scientific man-years (smy) on improving the biological efficiency of crops, and only 18 smy on improving rural income

—842 smy on control of insects, diseases and weeds in crops, and 95 smy to insure food products free from toxic residues from agricultural sources

—200 smy on ornamentals, turf and trees for natural beauty, and a sad seven smy on rural housing

—88 smy on improving management systems for livestock and poultry production, and 45 smy for improving rural institutions

—68 smy on marketing firm and system efficiency, and 17 smy on causes and remedies of poverty among rural people.

It is this distorted allocation of resources that led Lauren Soth to refer to agricultural research as "Probably the most backward area of the USDA Land Grant College system."[12] The disparity of focus is so dramatic that there even has been some grumbling within the land grant community. Admitting that his remarks might be interpreted as "an act of heresy," Dr. Don Paarlberg, then of Purdue University and now USDA's Director of Agricultural Economics, drew this unusually candid parallel in 1968:

> Many years ago in England the industrial revolution resulted in dislocations and social problems that were largely ignored. It has become common to criticize the leaders of that day for their callousness. It may be appropriate to ask whether we who promote today's agricultural revolution may in time come under similar indictment.[13]

One can imagine that his remarks were greeted by silence; certainly they were not greeted by action.

[12]Lauren Soth. "The Obsolete Dream Machine," *The Nation* (May 31, 1971), p. 689.

[13]Don Paarlberg. "Some Implications of Industrialization of the Food Sector of the U.S. Economy." In: *Agricultural Organization in the Modern Industrial Economy.* NCR-20-68. Department of Agricultural Economics and Rural Sociology. (Columbus, Ohio: Ohio State University, 1968), p. 17.

A TAX-PAID CLINIC FOR AGRIBUSINESS

The original rationale for public support of agricultural research was that farming was not big business.[14] That has changed. Agriculture today is the country's biggest business, and it is an industry that is dominated by relatively few huge-scale producers and by giant processing, marketing and exporting corporations.

Expressing concern that rural people should receive more attention from land grant colleges, University of Maryland chancellor, Dr. C. E. Bishop, wrote that "to continue on the road we have been traveling will likely lead us into the role of publicly subsidized consultants to the corporate farms and marketing firms of the future."[15] The future is now. The experiment stations at land grant colleges exist today as tax-paid clinics for agribusiness corporations, while others who need publicly supported research either benefit only incidentally, are not served at all, or actually are being harmed by land grant research.

Land grant researchers are preoccupied with machinery, chemicals, systems and other gadgetry designed to assist agribusiness and to eliminate the human element from farming. The research focus is warped by the land grant community's fascination with technology, integrated food processes and the like. Efficiency is the goal, not people. Consider a bit of future shock from Dr. George Irving, who offered this vision in a 1970 interview with *National Geographic:*

> It isn't difficult to visualize agricultural plots several miles long and a hundred feet wide. Equipment straddling the strip will roll on tracks or paved runways, swinging around at the end to work the adjacent plot without a wheel-touch compacting the soil in the cultivated areas.
>
> Weather control may tame hailstorm and tornado dangers. Atomic energy may supply power to level hills or provide irrigation water from the sea. Satellites and airplanes overhead will transmit readings enabling a farmer to spot diseases breaking out in his crops more surely than he could by walking through the fields.
>
> Sensors buried in the soil will tell him when his plants need water, and automated irrigation systems will bring it to them. He may have at hand chemical means of speeding or slowing crop growth to bring harvests to market at optimum times. *Such things sound fantastic, but already they exist in pilot form or in the research stage.*[16] (emphasis supplied)

It is through mechanization research that land grant colleges are coming closest to Irving's ideal of automated agriculture. It is also

[14]Eddy. *op. cit.*, p. 96.

[15]C. E. Bishop. "The Urbanization of Rural America," *Journal of Farm Economics,* Vol. II (December 1967), 999-1008.

[16]Billard. *Op. cit.*, pp. 184-185.

in mechanization research that one can draw a relatively sharp line between who is helped and who is hurt by land grant college research.

Mechanization   Without making any deliberate effort to dig out mechanization projects, the Task Force came across land grant college research to mechanize the harvest of:

1. Apples (Virginia Polytechnic Institute, Cornell University)
2. Asparagus (Rutgers University, Michigan State University)
3. Beans (Cornell University)
4. Blueberries (North Carolina State University, University of Arkansas, University of Maine)
5. Boysenberries (University of Florida, Ohio State University, Cornell University, North Carolina State University)
6. Cabbage (University of Florida, Ohio State University, Cornell University, North Carolina State University)
7. Citrus (University of Florida)
8. Coffee (University of Hawaii, University of Puerto Rico)
9. Cucumbers (North Carolina State University)
10. Grapes (Cornell University)
11. Lettuce (Cornell University, University of Arizona)
12. Nuts (University of California)
13. Olives (University of California)
14. Onions (Texas A&M University, University of Idaho)
15. Peaches (University of Georgia)
16. Peanuts (Auburn University)
17. Pickles (Michigan State University)
18. Potatoes (University of Maine)
19. Prunes (University of California)
20. Red Raspberries (Washington State University)
21. Strawberries (University of Arkansas, University of Illinois, Iowa State University, Louisiana State University, Oregon State University
22. Sweet Potatoes (Virginia Polytechnic Institute)
23. Tea (University of Florida)
24. Tobacco (University of Maryland, North Carolina State University
25. Tomatoes (University of California, University of Florida, Purdue University).

In addition to this work on the harvest, there also were projects to mechanize thinning of lettuce (Ohio State University), thinning of peaches (Texas A&M University) and pruning of grapes (Cornell University).

Mechanization means more than machinery for planting, thinning, weeding and harvesting. It also means improving on nature's design; *i.e.*, breeding new food varieties that are better adapted to mechanical harvesting. Having built machines, the land grant research teams found it necessary to build a tomato that is hard enough to survive the grip of mechanical "fingers"; necessary to redesign the grape so that all the fruit has the good sense to ripen at the same time; and necessary to restructure the apple tree so that it grows shorter, leaving the apples less distance to fall to its mechanical catcher. Michigan State University, in a proud report on "tailor-made" vegetables, notes that their scientists are at work on broccoli, tomatoes, cauliflower, cucumbers, snapbeans, lima beans, carrots and asparagus.[17]

If it cannot be done by manipulating genes, land grant scientists reach into their chemical cabinet. Louisiana State University has experimented with the chemical "Ethrel" to cause hot peppers to ripen at the same time for "once-over" mechanical harvesting; scientists at Michigan State University are using chemicals to reduce the cherry's resistance to the tug of the mechanical picker; and a combination of ferric ammonia citrate and erythorbic acid is being used at Texas A&M to loosen fruit before machine harvesting.

Once harvested, food products must be sorted for size and ripeness. Again, land grant college engineers have produced a mechanical answer. North Carolina State University, for example, has designed and developed an automatic machine "which dynamically examines blueberries according to maturity." The University of California and other colleges have scientists at work on machinery that will sort tomatoes.[18]

Genetically redesigned, mechanically planted, thinned and weeded, chemically readied and mechanically harvested and sorted, food products move out of the field and into the processing and marketing stages—untouched by human hands.

This assembly line process is the product of research conducted at state agricultural experiment stations and funded by billions of tax dollars. Not only has the land grant college complex produced this mechanization "package" (machines, new plants and chemicals), but that complex actually has been the initiator and chief promoter of agricultural mechanization.

Who is helped by this research and development? More significantly, who is hurt?

[17]Michigan State University, Agricultural Experiment Station. " 'Tailor-Made' Vegetables," *Michigan Science in Action* (June 1970), p. 3.

[18]The examples above are taken from the 1970 and 1971 annual reports of the respective institutions.

It is agribusiness that is helped. In particular, the largest-scale growers, the farm machinery and chemical in-put companies and the processors are the primary beneficiaries. Big business interests are called upon by land grant staffs to participate directly in the planning, research and development stages of mechanization projects. The interests of agribusiness literally are designed into the product. No one else is consulted.

Obviously, farm machinery and chemical companies are direct beneficiaries of this research, since they can expect to market products that are developed. Machinery companies such as John Deere, International Harvester, Massey-Ferguson, Allis-Chalmer and J. I. Case almost continually engage in cooperative research efforts at land grant colleges. These corporations contribute money and some of their own research personnel to help land grant scientists develop machinery; in return, they are able to incorporate technological advances in their own products. In some cases they actually receive exclusive license to produce and market the machinery.

Even a farm machinery company not involved directly in land grant research will profit directly from the resulting increase in machinery use. With more and more crops being mechanized, there is more and more machinery to be sold. As one article put it:

> All of this adds up to a $3.8 billion-a-year bumper sales crop for the nation's 1,600 farm-machinery makers, especially for the handful of big, "full-line" manufacturers that together account for nearly two-thirds of all equipment sales.[19]

Large-scale farming operations, many of them major corporate farms, also are directly in line to receive the rewards of mechanization research. In the first place, these are the farms that hire the overwhelming percentage of farm labor; they thus have an economic incentive to mechanize. Secondly, these are the massive farms, spreading over thousands of acres. This scale of operation warrants an investment in machinery. Thirdly, they are heavily-capitalized producers, including processing corporations, vertically-integrated in-put industries and conglomerate enterprises. Such farming ventures are financially able and managerially inclined to mechanize the food system.

Mechanization has been a key element in the cycle of bigness: enough capital can buy machinery, which can handle more acreage, which will produce greater volume, which can mean more profits, which will buy more machinery.

Mechanization of fruits and vegetables has focused first on crops used by the processing industries. Brand name processors such as

[19]*Time.* "Toward the Square Tomato," (August 18, 1967), p.78.

Del Monte, Heinz, Hunt, Stokely Van-Camp, Campbell's and Green Giant are direct beneficiaries of mechanization research. Many of these corporations have been directly involved in the development of mechanization projects. In addition to the food breeding aspects of mechanization, processors and canners have benefitted also insofar as mechanization has been able to lower costs of production and insofar as the resulting savings have been passed on to them. Of course, many food processors are also growers either growing directly on their own land, or growing indirectly, controlling the production of others through contractual arrangements.

Then there are the victims of mechanization—those who are directly hurt by research that does not consider their needs. If mechanization research has been a boon to agribusiness interests, it literally has been a bane to millions of rural Americans. The cost has been staggering.

Farm workers have been the earliest victims. It is outrageous that those who have been brutalized so badly by mechanization have been used as the excuse for mechanization. Again and again there are references in land grant research materials to the scarcity, unreliability and cost of farm labor as the factor requiring mechanization. In fact, mechanization has been the force that has eliminated farm jobs.

There are comments throughout the printed materials of the land grant complex indicating that they have been at work on mechanization for years—"since the 1930's."[20] As with the tomato harvestor, land grant scientists sometimes boast that they initiated research long before there was a labor shortage and long before farmers saw a need for extensive mechanization.

The truth is that mechanization is perceived as an essential, tactical step within the land grant community's broad strategy of making agriculture strictly efficient. By initiating and promoting mechanization, land grant scientists and economists were asserting their brand of far-sighted leadership. The land grant community was able to see back in the 50's that an exploited laboring class was "unstable" and that the day finally would come when exploitation of those workers no longer would be a tenable position. Farm worker exploitation is inefficient, especially with a mechanical alternative right at hand. Why mess with a union, make payroll deductions and wrestle with a whole range of worker problems when you can turn to machinery?

The turn to machinery has a snowball effect. As one crop is mechanized, there is less work in the area; as two or three crops are mechanized, there is not enough work in the area to make a living,

[20]USDA, NASULGC Joint Task Force. "A National Program of Research for Farm Labor and Mechanization" (September 1968), p. 1.

so the farm worker hits the road. Then there is a "scarcity of labor," so other crops are mechanized. In the 1960's, there arose a farm worker union and serious efforts to legislate an end to the most blatant farm worker exploitation. This assertion of farm worker dignity was met with a rush to mechanize as completely as possible.

"The machine cost $10,000, but I saved almost enough to pay for it," said a Georgia peach grower.[21] "A new asparagus harvester can take care of 6 acres per hour, doing the work of 400 hand laborers," noted an item in *The American Farmer* magazine.[22] "A mechanical harvester for fresh market onions has been developed by the Texas Agricultural Experiment Station. . . . More than 2 million man hours of stoop labor are required to harvest the present onion crop in Texas," reported Dr. Roy Lovvorn to the Congress.[23]

It is not just harvest jobs that are being eliminated. A joint NASULGC-USDA task force reported that "additional labor reductions on deciduous and small fruits and tree nuts are anticipated through improved pruning, thinning, harvesting and handling techniques." They went on to point out that labor requirements in white potato production have been reduced "through mechanization of tillage, seeding, pest control and harvesting."[24]

Again and again the message is hammered home—machines either exist or are on the way to replace farm labor. There were 4.3 million hired farm workers in 1950. Twenty years later, that number has fallen to 2.5 million, As a group, those laborers averaged $1,083 for doing farm work in 1970,[25] making them among the very poorest of America's employed poor. The great majority of these workers were hired by the largest farms, which are the same farms moving as swiftly as possible to mechanize their operation. The 1968 NASULGC-USDA task force on farm labor and mechanization research noted that "the greater increase in farm output per unit of labor indicate(s) that about a third less labor will be used in 1980 than in 1967."[26]

This is a fair representation of the land grant community's concern with farm workers. There literally has been nothing personal in the land grant community's effort over the last 30 years to replace men

[21]Billard, *op cit.*, p. 18.

[22]*The American Farmer* (February 1972), p. 18.

[23]U.S. House of Representatives, Committee on Appropriations *Hearings*, "Department of Agriculture Appropriations for 1971," 91st Congress, 2nd session, Part 2, p. 367.

[24]USDA, NASULGC. "Farm Labor and Mechanization," *op. cit.*, p. 4.

[25]USDA, Economic Research Service. "The Hired Farm Working Force of 1970," *Agricultural Economic Report No. 201* (March 1971), p. 5.

[26]USDA, NASULGC. "Farm Labor and Mechanization," *op. cit.*, p. 2.

with machines and chemicals. Those workers are considered only as "units" or "inputs," no different than the machinery that replaces them. It is not that researchers have it in for farm workers; chances are that they just do not know any.

The NASULGC-USDA task force commented coldly that "labor was viewed as a physical rather than a sociological resource." The task force determined that the goals of mechanization research would be to:

> (1) reduce farm labor requirements and improve efficiency in the production of crops and livestock through mechanization, and (2) through systems analysis, combine that set of production and marketing practices with land, labor, capital, and management inputs that will optimize income from the production of crops and livestock.[27]

The task force recommended a 75 percent increase over ten years in scientific man years of research conducted on mechanization of fruit, vegetable and field crop production. It recommended an increase of 84 percent in research man years allotted to systems analysis related to mechanization.[28]

Farm workers have not been compensated for jobs lost to mechanization research. They were not consulted when that research was designed, and their needs were not a part of the research package that resulted. They simply were left to fend on their own—no retraining, no effort to find new jobs for them, no research to help them adjust to the changes that came out of the land grant colleges. Corporate agribusiness received a machine with the taxpayer's help; farm workers were put out of a job with the taxpayer's help, and those workers are not even entitled to unemployment compensation.

The victimization of farm workers and their families is a heavy cost that must be added to the price of mechanization research.

Independent, family farmers—at least those who have sales under $20,000 a year (which includes 87 percent of all U.S. farms)[29]—also have been victimized by the pressure of mechanization, and their needs also have been largely ignored by the land grant colleges.

USDA's director of Science and Education, Dr. Ned Bayley, has spoken about a group of farmers who have "been on the treadmill of technological change so long that they are frustrated about the past and the present, and apprehensive of the future."[30] Dr. Bayley is

[27]USDA, NASULGC. "Task Force on Research for Farm Labor and Mechanization," *op. cit.*, p. 2.

[28]*Ibid.*, p. 3.

[29]USDA, Economic Research Service. "Our 31,000 Largest Farms," *Agricultural Economic Report No. 175* (March 1970) Table 2, p. 4.

[30]Bayley, *op cit.*, p. 5.

speaking of farmers making less than $10,000 in sales, but what he says of them is just as true of those making sales of $20,000 a year and undoubtedly is true of the majority of those independent farmers with sales up to $100,000 a year:

> They accept new technology as a requirement for survival. Much of it is ill-adapted to their types of operation, to their own farming skills, to their business experience. The purchase of new machinery and the adoption of new practices often force them to over-capitalize their operations, bleed their assets, and mortgage their future returns. They find themselves in a cost-price squeeze, unable to expand their scale of operations to yield sufficient gross income to make a decent living. And they see no prospects of relief.
>
> These are intelligent hardworking people. At the recent Listening Conferences of the secretary of agriculture and his staff, these people let it be known that they *want* to farm. Alternative ways of life are second best for them. . .
>
> When we ask what agricultural research has done for this group of farmers, the answer comes back: "very little." In fact, the overall impact of agricultural research has threatened their survival. Research which, through the development of new knowledge, is supposed to give people *more* acceptable choices, has actually *reduced* the choices for this group of farmers. We have narrowed their choices to two: either get *with* the new production efficiency technology as we are developing it, or get *out* of farming business. These are not very inspiring alternatives.[31]

The rapidly-increasing cost of farming, in combination with the perennially low farm prices, is driving farmers off the land. Mechanization is a major contributor to that skyrocketing cost of doing business. Tractor prices range from about $7,000 for a small one to $36,000 for huge crawler tractors. A tractor is useless without the plows, rakes, harrows and other essential attachments. Those cost extra, and dearly. Harvesting equipment is tremendously expensive: for example, a cotton picker costs $26,000 to $30,000 and a tomato harvester runs $23,000. More sophisticated pieces, with electronic sensors and other gadgets developed by land grant scientists, simply are out of the question for all but the very well-heeled. Operator of his own 600-acre Nebraska farm, Elmer Zeis told a newspaper interviewer about these costs:

> You can't get a piece of small equipment for under $1,000. The combine I bought this fall cost $20,000; I pay all that and use it one month out of the year. Then I have to trade a piece or two each year just to keep current.[32]

Zeis estimated that he had $50,000 tied up in machinery and another $25,000 in storage buildings and bins.

[31]*Ibid.*, p. 5.
[32]*Daily News*, Mount Union (Pennsylvania), December 22, 1971.

Representative Jamie Whitten, chairman of the House agricultural appropriations subcommittee, noted that in 1971 "the average investment per farm was in excess of $70,000."[33] He pointed out that it takes "about as much money to start a farm as to start a bank, and about as much nerve as to rob a bank."

The fact is that the land grant colleges are expending their resources on mechanization that primarily is useful to the highest income growers, focusing attention exclusively on those producers with the necessary acreage, capital and management to achieve economies of scale. At best, that means that land grant college research benefits are geared to the needs of no more than 13 percent of the country's farmers—those with annual sales above $20,000.[34] More realistically, mechanization research at land grant colleges is designed to meet the specifications of the largest producers, that 1 percent of American farms with annual sales of $100,000 or more.

It is in this one percent that America's massive, corporate farms are established. These are the "farmers" who are welcome in the land grant research labs. They bring grants and equipment to those labs, but, more importantly, they also bring a shared vision of assembly-line food production. In turn, they get research to implement that vision. These huge growers are more than clients of the land grant system; they are colleagues.

Designed to the specifications of the largest-scale producers, mechanization has not been much of a blessing to those who are lacking capital, acreage or management capabilities. Small and medium-scale farmers, making annual sales under $20,000, simply are not able to make much use of $25,000 harvesting equipment. Even the great majority of large-scale farmers, with sales ranging to $100,000 a year, have not been well-served by the mechanization research of land grant colleges. For the independent operator, mechanization is too expensive, it is uneconomical on his limited acreage, and it causes a bookkeeping nightmare for the family. Despite this harsh reality, land grant colleges relentlessly preach the necessity for more machinery, frequently sounding a little too much like salesmen:

[33]House Agriculture Appropriations Hearings, 1972. *Op. cit.*, pp. 328-329.

[34]"Our 31,000 Largest Farms," *op. cit.* The last reported census of agriculture is 1964. The 1969 census has yet to be published. The breakdown of farms by size and sales, according to the 1964 census was:

Category by Size of Sales	% of Farms	% of Sales 1964
1. Largest ($100,000 or more)	1.0	24.2
2. Large (20,000-$99,999)	11.7	38.7
3. Medium ($15,000-$19,999)	30.8	29.2
4. Small (less than $5,000)	56.5	7.8
	100.0%	100.0%

After analyzing 1,000 farmers, Purdue's Howard Doster believes most farmers should lean toward the over-equipped side.[35]

The mechanization research of land grant colleges either is irrelevant or only incidentally adaptable to the needs of some 87 to 99 percent of America's farmers. The public subsidy for mechanization actually has weakened the competitive position of the family farmer. Taxpayers, through the land grant college complex, have given corporate producers a technological arsenal specifically suited to their scale of operation and designed to increase their efficiency and profits. The independent, family farmer is left to strain his private resources to the breaking point in a desperate effort to clamber aboard the technological treadmill.

Mechanization has not been pressed by the land grant colleges as an alternative, but as an imperative. The fact that his corporate and well-to-do neighbors are rushing pell mell into agricultural technology means that the independent operator must either "adapt or die," as the current Secretary of Agriculture put it.

The point is that land grant colleges have left them to "die." It is not that mechanization research is designed intentionally to force a majority of America's farmers off the farm, but that the research is *not* designed to help those farmers "adapt" and stay on the farm. The taxpayer has developed total mechanization systems for agribusiness, but has abandoned the independent farmer, leaving him to adjust as best he can.

Like the farm worker, the average farmer is not invited into the land grant laboratories to help design mechanization research. If he were, that research "package" would include machines useful on smaller acreages, it would include assistance to develop cooperative ownership systems, it would include efforts to develop low-cost and simpler machinery, it would include a heavy emphasis on new credit schemes, and it would include special extension to spread knowledge about the purchase, operation and maintenance of machinery. In short, there would be a deliberate and major effort to extend mechanization benefits to all, with an emphasis on at least maintaining the competitive position of the family farm in relation to agribusiness corporations. These efforts do not exist, or exist only in a token way. Mechanization research has left the great majority of farmers to "get big" on their own, or to get out of farming altogether.

With land grant college research assisting their corporate competitors and largely ignoring their own needs, family farmers are being forced to get out. Since 1940, a majority of America's farmers gave up their land. There were 6.4 million farms in 1940. Thirty years and a revolution

[35] "Too Much Equipment or Too Little?" *Successful Farming*, February 1972. p. 23.

later, there are under 2.8 million farms. USDA benignly predicts that another million farms will go under by 1980. Technological "advances" are cited as the principal force contributing to fewer and bigger farms. The literature of land grant colleges and experiment stations makes clear that these public institutions do not intend to stand in the way of those one million farm families pulling out of rural America. The land grant community rationalizes this massive displacement by boasting that their technological revolution has liberated folks from the farm. "Because only one person in 43 is needed to produce food," said Agricultural Secretary Clifford Hardin, "others can become doctors, teachers. shoemakers, janitors—even Secretaries of Agriculture."[36] That must be cold comfort to those who happen to like farming.

That is not to say that there is no concern within the land grant community. Dr. Paarlberg, speaking at a 1968 symposium on "Agricultural Organization in the Modern Industrial Economy," urged the community to shift its focus away from a preoccupation with production efficiency and technology:

> I think we should reorient our research, working more on agricultural adjustment, rural poverty, and world agricultural development. The invention of new institutional forms that would help more family farms to survive the technological revolution, and the development of new ways to help farmers preserve their decision-making role seem to me priority items for research and policy.[37]

1969 research allocations at all state agricultural experiment stations reveal that a total of 283.2 scientific man years[38] were engaged in Dr. Paarlberg's research categories of "agricultural adjustment, rural poverty, and world agricultural development," while 3,288 scientific man years[39] were allotted to production efficiency research on fruits, vegetables, field crops, livestock and poultry. In short, there may be occasional expressions of concern, but there is no change. The technological revolution will roll on, and it will continue to roll over a majority of the people in rural America.

As farms collapse, small town businesses follow, and small towns begin to die. Rural America is changing radically, irrevocably and for the worse. All America is affected. It is not demonstrated anywhere

[36]Clifford M. Hardin. Quoted in Billard, *op. cit.*, p. 152.

[37]Paarlberg, *op. cit.*, p. 17.

[38]USDA, Science and Education Staff, *op. cit.*, pp. 247-248. To figure "adjustment, poverty and world agriculture," SMY were added for RPA numbers 506, 507, 510, 807, 808, 316, 603, 802, 803, 804, 806, 907, 908 and 801.

[39]*Ibid.*, pp. 247-248. To figure "efficiency," SMY were added for all RPA numbers within the following Program Elements: 12-6121, 12-6122 and 12-6123.

that the public wanted or expected these changes to come from its tax investment in mechanization research.

The land grant community would insist that all of its research is targeted toward the consumer, that he is the ultimate beneficiary. Considering the cost of mechanization research, that assertion is at least questionable. It is true that the consumer enjoys an abundance of a wide variety of food products, and that he enjoys those products at a relatively cheap market price. But the connection between the price of tomatoes and the tomato harvester is a bit strained. Assuming that there are cost savings on mechanized production, and assuming that the producer's savings are passed on to the processor or marketer, it is unlikely that the savings comes intact from there to the consumer. The consumer is not a primary beneficiary, he is not consulted by the land grant community when the research project is designed, and at best he enjoys the benefits of that research only after it has passed through the fine sieve of "trickle-down."

To this must be added the cost that the consumer pays for mechanization. The assembly line is neither gentle nor particularly concerned with quality. That is not to say that mechanized production equals bad food; it is to say that mechanical and systems efficiency gives up something in quality. Mechanized crops are bred for the machine, not for the consumer. Mechanized crops require sizable doses of chemicals to regulate their growth. Mechanized crops are harvested, sorted and packaged by machine. All of this raises unanswered questions of inferior taste and nutritional quality. The genetical and chemical aspects of mechanization raises unanswered questions of carcinogenic effects. And chemicals raise unanswered questions of ecological impact. If the consumer was intended to be the primary beneficiary of mechanization research, these questions would have been an integral part of the research package.

If economies of scale, integrated food systems and assembly-line efficiency are products of mechanization research at land grant colleges, so are hard tomatoes and hard times. There have been many untabulated costs of land grant research, and those costs make clear that tax-paid mechanization has not been the bargain many have claimed. Indeed, in terms of wasted lives, depleted rural areas, choked cities, poisoned land and maybe poisoned people, mechanization research has been a bad investment. It can be a good investment. It is not that mechanization is wrong, but that it has been wrongly applied. The land grant college community, working too intimately with its agribusiness colleagues, is accountable for that failure.

Serving the Agricultural In-put and Out-put Firms   Agricultural research has strayed a good ways from the farm. It is a rare experiment station report today that does not state at the outset that agriculture has changed, now requiring research to meet the needs of a vast agribusiness complex located off the farm:

> Many persons consider agriculture to be farming only—nothing more. However, the modern concept is that agriculture also includes the farm input industries, which supply goods and services used by farmers for production, and the marketing industries, which perform the many operations necessary to make farm products available to consumers. The former include the production and distribution of farm machinery, fertilizers and other agricultural chemicals, livestock feed, petroleum products, and many other commodities, as well as services such as credit, insurance, accounting, and research. The latter include marketing facilities and business firms such as country receiving and buying agencies, processing firms, and wholesale and retail food businesses. Modern farming depends on both the input and marketing businesses, which in turn require productive and efficient farming.[40]

There is a vital need for research that will help farmers get better and cheaper production in-puts, and there certainly is a need today for a major research emphasis to help all farmers deal more effectively with the marketing phase of agriculture. But much of the publicly supported research coming out of the land grant complex is focused strictly on the needs of the in-put and out-put industries and is not linked to the farmers. In fact, too much of the research is assisting corporate agribusiness at the expense of the farmer.

Three assumptions are made here. First, if there is to be research for firms that surround the farmer, benefits of that research should flow back to the farmer. Secondly, no public money should be expended on research that principally serves the financial interests of agricultural in-put and out-put corporations. They may be a part of modern agriculture, but they also are very big business and capable of doing their own profit-motivated research. Finally, anything that is good for agribusiness is *not* necessarily good for agriculture, farmers and rural America.

There is no way to measure precisely the extent to which land grant colleges exist as research "service stations" for these corporations. There are several categories under which experiment station research for in-put and out-put firms might fall, but they can give only the roughest estimate of the nature of that research. In fy 1969, the total expenditure of scientific man years within these categories was 610.3 (see Figure 7), but that does not indicate what proportion was expended primarily for farmers and what proportion went primarily to agribusiness firms.

[40]Cornell University and Agricultural Experiment Station. *Eighty-third Annual Report*, (Ithaca, New York: June 30, 1970), p. 9.

FIGURE 7

FY 1969 Allocation of Scientific Man Years to Research Categories
That Include Research for Agribusiness Input and Output Firms

Research Categories		Allocation of SMY
Fruits and Vegetables Marketing and Distribution Efficiency Research		
New & improved fruit & vegetable produce	102.1	
Quality maintenance in marketing fruits and vegetables	53.3	
Physical & economic efficiency in marketing fruits and vegetables	18.0	173.3
Field Crops Marketing & Distribution Efficiency Research		
New & improved food, products from field crops	33.0	
New & improved feed, textile & industrial products from field crops	21.7	
Quality maintenance in marketing field crops	24.7	
Physical & economic efficiency in marketing field crops	14.3	93.8
Livestock and Poultry Marketing and Distribution Efficiency Research		
New & improved meat, milk, and egg products	107.9	
New & improved products from wool, hides, skins and animal fats	1.0	
Quality maintenance in marketing animal products	38.4	
Physical & economic efficiency in marketing livestock	48.0	195.2
Forest Products Marketing Research		
Development of markets & more efficiency marketing of timber products	8.3	
Improvement of grades & standards of forest products	3.0	
Supply, demand & price analysis forest products	3.7	15.0
Forest Products Utilization Research		
New & improved forest products	41.5	41.5
Marketing Firm and Efficiency Research		
Improvement of grades & standards	12.8	
Development of domestic markets for farm products	18.8	
Marketing firm & systems efficiency	35.2	66.7
Foreign Market Development Research		
Expansion of foreign markets for U.S.	13.3	13.3
Food Nutrition Research		
Food choices, habits & consumption	11.5	11.5
TOTAL SMY		610.3

SOURCE: USDA, Science and Education Staff. "Inventory of Agricultural Research, FY 1969, 1970." Vol. II (October 1970), pp. 247–248.

However, a reading of annual reports and other land grant college literature offers clear evidence that these institutions are being used as tax-paid clinics for agribusinesses.

The processor receives a great deal of attention from research scientists and economists at land grand colleges. At the New York Agricultural Experiment Station at Geneva, the college has built a two-story factory and equipped it with ovens, dehydrators, high-speed freezers and other apparatus to simulate private processing plants and test new processing methods. From research labs around the country come projects such as these to assist the processing corporations:

—Dairy technologists at Ohio State University found that plastic coated paper cartons were satisfactory for storage of packaged cream products, thus presenting the processors with a 50 percent cost saving over the foil-lined cartons that had been used.

—VPI scientists studied factors affecting the quality and shelf-life of pre-cooked, dehydrated sweet potato flakes.

—University of Wisconsin researchers have developed a process for making mozarella cheese in 5½ minutes, compared to the usual time of four hours. The flavor of the final product is reported to be "mild, but satisfactory for the normal uses."

Supermarkets, too, find shopping a convenience at land grant colleges. Cornell University; in cooperation with the National Association of Food Chains, made a study in 1970 of the gross margins, expenses and profits of U.S. food chains. Purdue University has used public money for a research project on "selling strategy in the food industry." Also at Purdue, the Department of Agricultural Economics is at work on display modules for supermarkets:

> This involves the actual development of a retail display at the point of final assembly at the processor level. For example, half gallons of milk are loaded into the conventional metal containers, one side of which has been eliminated. These metal containers are stacked on dollies which are then rolled into trucks, and upon delivery at the retail supermarket are rolled directly into the retail display. The same is happening in regard to eggs and bakery items. You can anticipate the labor saving potential of such activities.[41]

These efforts for the processors and retailers might be useful projects, and way down the road there might even be a small trickle of benefits for the farmer. But the primary target and major beneficiary is corporate

[41]Letter to Agribusiness Accountability Project from Professor Eric Oesterle, Department of Agricultural Economics, Purdue University (February 4, 1972).

agribusiness. Involved here are major brand names—huge businesses. If these firms find such research useful, they should do it themselves, not ask the public to pay for it. If there is a small overflow of benefits to the farmer, the corporation can write it off to good will.

The most distressing examples of land grant college research for agribusiness are those that work against the farmer. Chief among these are projects to assist vertical integration of agriculture—a system whereby the in-put and out-put industries usurp from the farmer control of production. Vertical integration is a key component in the land grant college community's effort to achieve total food systems, with one corporation maintaining effective control of a crop from seed to supermarket. Vertical integration of the broiler industry was effected during the sixties by such feed corporations as Ralston Purina, and the impact was devastating to thousands of independent poultry producers. [42] Ralston Purina and others are moving now toward vertical integration of the hog industry. Given the experience of broiler raisers, it is easy to understand the chagrin of hog producers today when they learn that their tax dollars are being expended at land grant colleges for these projects:

—Vertical coordination in the hog industry. (Purdue)

—Economic evaluation of alternative forms of vertical coordination in the livestock meat industry. (Auburn)

—Development of an integrated procurement and production control system for feed manufacturers. (Purdue)

Throughout the land grant system, research projects such as these are underway, designed principally to increase the profits of the corporate in-put and out-put industries surrounding agriculture. A 1969 Minnesota symposium on resource allocation in agricultural research stated that the "essential rationale" for investing tax dollars in agricultural research is that "publicly supported units are less constrained by the need to relate research expenditures to their ability to capture the economic gains from the research they perform. [43] These examples of research underway indicate that the land grant colleges are not as constrained as might be thought. Through the research efforts of these institutions, the public is subsidizing corporate profits.

[42]Harrison Wellford. "Poultry Peonage," draft manuscript of *Sowing the Wind,* to be published in 1972. Chapter 6. Copyright 1971 by Center for Study of Responsive Law, Washington, D.C.

[43]Tichenor and Ruttan, *op. cit.,* p. 4.

Agricultural Technology and The Consumer: Food Gadgetry   A great deal of agricultural research involves tampering with nature's plan, using the sciences of genetics and chemistry. In large part, this research stems from the land grant community's faith in technology and fascination with gadgetry. Michigan State University spends 20 percent of its vegetable breeding effort on the development of a seedless cucumber. One suspects that the effort is made simply because "the seeds are there." Just as the military-industrial complex always is producing new weaponry, land grant scientists always are developing new and different foods. They do it because it is something that they are able to do, and it is something for which there is money.

The major impetus for food engineering has come from the desire to eliminate labor by mechanizing the harvesting and processing phases of agriculture. "In some cases," reported *Time* magazine in 1967, "new machinery will dictate the size and kind of food that Americans will eat."[44] *Time* might be surprised at the number of cases. From asparagus to zuchini, from hard strawberries to pear-shaped tomatoes, food is being reshaped by land grant colleges so that it will be compatible with some machine. The central position of mechanization was illustrated by the recommendations of the USDA-NASULGC task force on fruit research, reported in 1969:

> The impact of harvest mechanization is of such magnitude that all fruit crops should now be planted, using appropriate varieties, coupled with modification in culture, plant densities, and training to accommodate machine harvest. All fruit research should be conceived and designed so that mechanization is a built-in component.[45]

In fy 1969, research at state agricultural experiment stations included 243 scientific man years allocated to "new and improved" fruit, vegetable, field-crop, meat, milk and egg products.[46] There are hundreds of food items today on the typical supermarket shelf. Most of those items were not there as recently as 1950, and, as *National Geographic* reported, "more are taking shape in laboratories and experimental kitchens.[47] Of course, many of these products have been useful both to the consumer, who had something new to eat, and to the farmer, who developed a new market or expanded an old one. But much of this research raises two fundamental questions: (1) are the colleges engaged in "selling" the consumer on products that he neither wants

[44]*Time, op. cit.*, p. 83.

[45]USDA-NASULGC. "A National Program of Research for Fruit," (February 1969), pp. 5-6.

[46]USDA, Science and Education Staff, *op. cit.*, pp. 247-248.

[47]Billard, *op. cit.*, p. 180.

nor needs; and (2) if there are profits to be made on these new food products, shouldn't the research be financed privately? Consider these samples:

—Michigan State University has developed a green cauliflower by crossing broccoli with the standard, white cauliflower.

—At VPI, eight separate studies were conducted to determine if people would like apple and grapefruit juice blended.

—Ohio State University is at work to develop new products from sauerkraut.

—Agricultural Research Service has worked with several SAES over the last 30 years to develop 232 new fruit and nut varieties, including 37 peaches, 35 strawberries and 29 blueberries.

Research scientists appear to be burdened by the same imagination that characterized the automobile designers of the 1950's, those who added the massive grills, strips of chrome and sweeping fins to the cars of that period. It is not likely that the consumer particularly wants a green cauliflower; it is likely, however, that the consumer would choose that such food products be researched and developed privately, not with his tax dollars.

Another aspect of selling the consumer is "knowing" him. There are many projects that analyze consumer behavior. Typically these involve consumer surveys to determine what influences the shopper's decision-making. If this research is useful to anyone it is food marketers and advertisers, and reports on this research make clear that those firms are the primary recipients of the results. The corporations who benefit from this research should pay for it and conduct it themselves.

The consumer is not just studied and "sold" by land grant research; he also is fooled. These public laboratories have researched and developed food cosmetics in an effort to confirm the consumer's preconceptions about food appearances, thus causing the consumer to think that the food is "good." Chickens have been fed the plant compound Xanthophyll to give their skin "a pleasing yellow tinge," and several projects have been undertaken to develop spray-on coatings to enhance the appearance of apples, peaches, citrus and tomatoes. Cosmetic research that is underway at land grant colleges includes the following projects:

—Iowa State University is conducting packaging studies which indicate that color stays bright longer when bacon is vacuum-packed or sealed in a package containing carbon dioxide in place of air, thus contributing to "more consumer appeal."

—Because of mechanical harvesting, greater numbers of green tomatoes are being picked; scientists at South Carolina's agricultural experiment station have shown that red fluorescent light treatment can increase the red color in the fruit and can cause its texture and taste to be "similar to vine-ripened tomatoes."

—Cornell University is at work on a project concerned with the red color in apples.

—Kansas State University Extension Service, noting that apples sell on the basis of appearance rather than nutrition, urged growers to have a beautiful product. To make the produce more appealing, mirrors and lights in supermarkets' produce cases were cited as effective selling techniques.

Sold, studied and fooled by his tax-supported researchers, there finally is evidence that the consumer actually is harmed by food engineering at land grant colleges. The issues here are food quality and human health. — What are the short and long-range impacts of the wide array of chemicals and hormones applied at various stages of the food process? These substances are not added for the benefit of the consumer; they are added either to eliminate labor or to speed-up nature's timetable. In either case, it is agribusiness that profits and the consumer who loses.

Land grant scientists in recent years have expended much of their energy on the development of chemicals and hormones that can be applied to fruits and vegetables as a ripening agent. Mechanical harvesting is the mother of invention in this case, requiring both that crops "mature uniformly" for once-over picking and that they be picked "green," in order to withstand the bruising grasp of machinery.

Chemical ripening agents are sprayed on the plants in the field, causing the commodity to mature faster and at a uniform rate. The food then is mechanically harvested while green, and another application of the chemical might be added to cause the product to ripen artificially while in storage, in transit, or even in the grocery bin. One such substance, Ethrel, currently is the subject of a great deal of land-grant attention. Its chemical designation is 2-chloroethyl-phosphonic acid, and its function is to stimulate the plant to produce ethylene, which is the plant's own ripening agent. Michigan State University is experimenting with Ethrel as a means of "reducing the fruit removal force of cherries for facilitating mechanical harvesting." The University of California is applying it to canning tomatoes to ripen them uniformly for harvest.

Louisiana State University has experimented extensively with Ethrel, primarily in an effort to ripen peppers grown for the processing industry. The chemical has been applied as a spray "to ripen the fruit on the plant and as a post-harvest dip to ripen fruit in storage." In one pepper experiment, the scientists reported that "two days after spraying Ethrel at 6,000 ppm (air temperature 95 degrees F.) the plants were completely defoliated."[48] Another test was conducted on hot sauce made with Ethrel treated peppers—"Ethrel resulted in a considerable increase in the carotenoid pigments of the ripe peppers, thus improving sauce color."[49] The advantages to the industry are clear: Ethrel shows great promise as an aid to mechanical harvesting; green fruit that previously was discarded now can be· "ripened" in storage; and Ethryl gives the hot pepper sauce a better color. Advantages to the consumer are less obvious, but land grant scientists continue their research:

> At present, Ethrel is not recommended for use since this material has not been cleared for a commercial label. However, Ethrel is being used experimentally with other crops such as tomatoes and pecans.[50]

In some cases, land grant researchers are applying ethylene gas to ripen fruit. Ethylene is a plant hormone that functions as a ripening agent. By experimenting with this substance, fruit scientists at the University of California at Davis brought small, green figs to full size and ripeness in seven days—58 days sooner than naturally-ripened figs. It is not certain that figs or any fruits come through this intensely concentrated "ripening" fully matured. In fact, there has been testimony that ethylene gassed tomatoes are of lower quality, "with less vitamin A and C and inferior taste, color and firmness."[51] The allegation is not that ethylene itself has a negative impact on the tomato,· but that the artificial ripening process does not mature them in the same sense that vine ripened tomatoes mature. Ethylene turns them red, but it is not to be mistaken for sunshine and nature's own way.

Land grant researchers do not confront this question of quality impact, choosing instead to dwell on the benefits that food engineering offers agribusiness. The University of Florida, for example, recently has developed a new fresh market tomato (the MH-1) for machine harvesting. In describing the characteristics that make this tomato so desirable for machine harvest, the University pointed to "the thick walls, firm flesh, and freedom from cracks."[52] It may be a little tough

---

[48]John E. Love, James F. Fontenot and Joe W. White. "Ripening Hot Peppers with Ethrel," *Louisiana Agriculture*. Vol. 14, no. 4 (Summer 1971), pp. 14-15.

[49]*Ibid.*, p. 15.

[50]*Ibid.*, p. 15.

[51]Richard A. Frank. Submission to USDA on behalf of several consumer groups in regard to a proposed rule, "Tomatoes Grown in Florida, Proposed Import Regulations," (January 14, 1972), p. 3.

[52]Agricultural Experiment Station, Institute of Food and Agricultural Sciences, University of Florida. "Florida MH-1," Circular S-212, (Gainesville: September 1971), p. 7.

for the consumer, but they can't please everyone. The MH-1, which will eliminate the jobs of thousands of Florida farm workers who now hand-pick tomatoes for the fresh market, also is designed to be harvested green and to be "ripened" in storage by application of ethylene gas.

The use of mechanization and chemicals to eliminate field labor is well known. Much less well known is the movement of these forces into food processing plants. The rationale is the same: eliminate labor, thus creating a savings to the processors. But labor may not be the only ones harmed by this move. The consumer may have serious questions to ask. More and more, chemicals are playing a role in the processing phase. Ohio State University reports that "chemical peeling of tomatoes with wetting agents and caustic soda reduces labor by 75 percent and increases product recovery." One wonders if the consumer will recover. Lovers of catfish might be distressed to know that this tasty meat now is being skinned chemically for commercial packaging. Mississippi State University scientists have been busy developing chemical solutions for catfish processors and offer this report on skinning methods:

> Exposure time 1.5 to 2.0 minutes in from nine to eleven percent boiling sodium hydroxide solutilized the skin so that is was readily rinsed off. The best overall treatment was two minutes in the hot lye bath followed by a rinse in ambient temperature water followed by a three minute dip in two percent acetic acid solution.

The report claimed that there was "no change in pH or product flavor," but the next paragraph noted that,

> Since no storage tests have been conducted on chemically skinned catfish, processors are urged to evaluate the method carefully before making commercial application.[53]

Consumers might also want to evaluate the method carefully.

Then there is meat. Land grant college research has played a key role in the development of integrated meat systems that have successfully brought huge quantities of beef, pork, lamb and poultry to American dinner tables. Land grant scientists, economists, and management and marketing experts have all assisted corporations in the creation of mass production centers, where livestock and poultry are closely confined, constantly fed to achieve a standard weight, and slaughtered for quick sale. Again, the effort is to short-circuit nature's design by accelerating "maturity." Profits flow to the agribusiness firms that own the production centers. Increasingly these owners are major feed companies, supermarket chains and even oil conglomerates. The consumer

[53]Mississippi Agricultural and Forestry Experiment Station. "83rd Annual Report." June 30, 1970, p. 46.

is benefitted by an abundance of meat, but, as one writer put it, "Americans buy at high prices, cook poorly, and eat in incredible quantities the lowest quality meat possible.[54] He offered this view of chicken:

> It is factory raised, indoors and immobile, chemically fed; and while I think the birds reach a kind of forced, physiological maturity, the only flavor they have is what will be absorbed from the cardboard and plastic wrappings they're presented in.[55]

Perhaps to compensate for the taste that they have taken out of meat, land grant scientists have added a cabinet-full of drugs. These are given to livestock and poultry to ward off diseases and infections (many of which are the result of being jammed side by side in feeding pens), to contribute to the final appearance of the meat product, and to enhance the "maturation" of the animal.

A drug additive used for the latter purpose is an artificial hormone named diethylstilbestrol, also known as stilbestrol or DES. It is mixed with feed to increase the efficiency and rate at which cattle convert feed into pounds of beef.

DES is a product of land grant college research, and its wide use is a product of land grant college promotion. Iowa State University proudly reports that "the discovery of how to use this hormone in cattle feeds was made by the Iowa Experiment Staton."[56] The specific research program that developed Stilbestrol lasted about two years, but projects on growth regulators had been going on for years before that. The research at ISU was funded by state tax dollars.

A patent on DES was obtained in 1956 by the Iowa State Research Foundation. ISRF awarded an exclusive license to Eli Lilly drug company to manufacture and market DES, which it does under the registered trademark "Stilbosol." There was no competitive bidding for the license—the Foundation chose Lilly because it thought that company "was big enough to do the job and was ethical."[57] Under the terms of the licensing agreement, ISU receives a 5 percent royalty on net sales of DES (85 percent of that royalty on net sales goes to the Foundation, while the other 15 percent goes to the inventor). Since 1956, DES has produced a royalty of $2.9 million for ISU, which means that the taxpayer has helped Eli Lilly and Company to sales of $58 million.

[54]Vance Bourjaily. "Eight Months on Full Feed," *Harpers Magazine*, (March 1972), p. 74.

[55]*Ibid.*, p. 75.

[56]Iowa Agricultural and Home Economics Experiment Station. "A Better Iowa Through Research," (undated), no p.

[57]Dan Griffin, Iowa State Research Foundation, telephone interview with Susan DeMarco, AAP Task Force, February 29, 1972.

Referring to DES as their "star performer," ISU promoted the drug throughout the country—now it is fed to about three-fourths of the 40 million cattle slaughtered annually.[58] ISU reports that a "thimbleful of stilbestrol in a ton of feed makes cattle gain 15 percent faster at a 10 percent saving in feed per pound of grain." Harrison Wellford of the Center for Study of Responsive Law, states that DES "adds $90 million annually to the profits of cattle growers."[59]

But diethylstilbestrol is more than effective and profitable for agribusiness. It also is extremely dangerous to consumers. There is strong clinical evidence that the drug is carcinogenic in man. Twenty-one countries have banned the use of DES as a threat to public health, and both Sweden and West Germany have banned the import of American beef because of the possibility of DES residues. The Consumer and Marketing Service of USDA, charged with regulating the use of such additives, condemns any meat in which DES residues are detected.

But the consumer is hardly well-protected. The method of taking DES out of cattle is to ask the producers and feed-lot operators to cease feeding the drug seven days before slaughter. The idea is that the DES will be excreted naturally during that period. The consumer is forced to take his chances that this drug withdrawal will take place. As back-up protection the consumer is left with USDA's regulatory mechanism. Wellford points out the folly of putting much faith in the inadequate sampling techniques employed there: "even though a pound of meat is found to contain no DES, residues up to 14 times the amount found carcinogenic in some strains of mice could be present without being detected."[60]

Land grant scientists, in their eagerness to serve agribusiness and to promote agricultural efficiency, have sacrificed the well-being of the consumer. DES is a dramatic and efficient gadget for fattening steers quickly, but where is the compensating research to insure that food quality is not lost? More to the point, where is the research to assure that the consumer literally will not choke on the profits of agribusiness? DES is an example of land grant research at its worst—it is at once a service to industry and a disservice to consumers.

In their efforts with food gadgetry, in their work for the in-put and out-put industries and in their mechanization research, land grant colleges and state agricultural experiment stations exist primarily as tax-paid clinics for agribusiness. Land grant college research is directed toward those private interests that least need assistance, while it ignores or works against the interests of those who desperately need help.

[58]Wellford. *Op cit.*, p. V-26.
[59]*Ibid.*, p. V-26.
[60]*Ibid.*, p. V-30.

The advantage is all on one side—agribusiness, millions; folks, zero. It is an outrageous allocation of public resources.

LIES, LIP SERVICE AND HOGWASH:
LAND GRANT COLLEGE RESEARCH FOR RURAL PEOPLE AND PLACES

"Evaluation of national and state research in agriculture," wrote the USDA-NASULGC task force on rural development, "reveals that far too little attention has been given to the development of rural people and places." The task force then offered a concise paragraph on the enormous problem and the needs stating dramatically that the "backdrop for current and projected research is a scene of national crisis—serious, urgent, of great magnitude."[61]

Since that task force reported its findings and recommendations in November of 1968, about a million farm workers have disappeared, some 300,000 independent family farmers have left the land, perhaps 50,000 small town businessmen have closed up shop, entire rural areas have shrivelled economically if not literally and about 2.4 million people have moved from their rural homes into urban centers. This continuing American tragedy is due in part to the failure of land grant college research—failures of omission as well as failures of commission. In people-oriented research, the land grant college community has not put its money where its mouth is.

Despite the rhetoric of exigency, research allocations for rural development and family living (which are USDA's categories for "people" research) are ludicrously small. In fact, as shown in Figure 8 allocations of scientific man years to research for rural people and places actually were lower in 1969 than they were when the task force trumpeted its concern in 1966!

The sad truth is that research to help rural Americans is only of secondary importance to the land grant community. Departments of rural sociology are treated as stepchildren of the system. Rural sociologists are considered to be something less than "scientists," and the departments generally find themselves on the short end of the stick when the budgets are divided. The Department of Sociology and Anthropology at Iowa State University, for example, expended $50,558.29 in fiscal year 1971.[62] That represented a mere one percent of the unrestricted funds that were expended by the College of Agriculture that year. Sociology's $50,000 at ISU compared with $565,000

[61]USDA-NASULGC. "A National Program of Research for Rural Development and Family Living" (November 1968), p. 8.

[62]See Appendix of this report. These expenditures are taken from Iowa State University of Science and Technology, *Financial Report* (Ames, Iowa: November 1971), Schedule B-2-b, p. 24.

FIGURE 8

Scientific Man Years of Research for Rural Development and
Family Living Conducted at SAES, 1966, 1969

Research Problem Areas	1966 SMY at SAES	1969 SMY at SAES	Recommended[*] 1972	1977
703 — Food Choices, Habits & Consumption	8	11.5	9	14
704 — Home & Commercial Preparation of Food	14	12.4	22	30
708 — Human Nutritional Well-being	103	93.5	189	223
705 — Selection & Care of Clothing and Household Textiles	18	15.0	24	32
801 — Housing Needs of Rural Families	11	6.5	27	31
802 — Family Decision Making and Financial Management	20	16.0	42	54
803 — Causes and Remedies of Poverty Among Rural People	11	17.1	46	63
804 and 907 — Improvement of Economic Opportunities for Rural People	42	27.7	131	153
805 — Communication Processes in Rural Life	17	18.3	27	37
806 — Individual & Family Adjustment to Change	28	25.6	53	61
908 — Improvement of Rural Community Institutions & Services	29	45.3	52	69
Total SMY Allocated to "People" Research	301	288.9	602	767

[*]These are allocations that were recommended by the 1968 task force. They indicate how meager the commitment really was in comparison to the rhetoric. Even if the 1972 goal of 602 SMY had been achieved, it would have been only about 8% of the total research conducted at SAES.

SOURCES: USDA, Science and Education Staff. "Inventory of Agricultural Research, fy 1969 and 1970." October 1970, pp. 247-248 and USDA-NASULGC. "A National Program of Research for Rural Development and Family Living." November 1968, pp. 5, 28 and 29.

for Animal Science, $332,000 for Agronomy, $237,000 for Agricultural Economics, $184,000 for Forestry and $138,000 for Dairy and Food Industry.

Many agricultural colleges do not even have departments of rural sociology, choosing instead to place that discipline within the departments of agricultural economics. That literally is cooping the chickens with the fox, since strict business efficiency is the stern message of the economist, and rural folks their chief victims.

The products of rural sociology match the meager investment made in them. At Iowa State University, out ot 274 research articles prepared in 1969-1970 by members of the experiment station staff, only one was in rural sociology.[63] The 1970 report of the Texas Agricultural Experiment Station notes that they have adopted a research project system which provides "the necessary coordination to insure that the most important priority problems are being investigated and to prevent costly and unnecessary duplication."[64] There is not much danger of duplication in Rural Sociology and Family Life, which totalled four of the 489 active research projects listed. That also leaves little room for doubt about the priorities at Texas A&M. With 28 projects in soil science, Texas A&M researchers are concerned more about the land itself than they are about the people who are being forced to leave it.

An analysis of specific land grant college research projects on rural people and places reveals that commitment to these needs is even less than appears on the surface. The low percentage of scientific man years, the pitiful departmental budgets and the handful of projects do not begin to plunge the depths of the bankruptcy that exists within this research.

In the first place, much of that research is not for rural people at all; it is for agribusiness. Consider "Research Problem Area 801: Housing Needs of Rural Families." The implication of that category is that research is underway to assist those millions of rural families living in "substandard" houses—a bureaucratic euphemism that includes tarpaper shacks, mud huts and even abandoned buses. The fact of that research focus is something else. Professor Don F Hadwigger, of the Political Science Department at Iowa State University, analyzed the 71 projects that were on-going at state agricultural experiment stations under RPA 801 during calendar year 1970. Those projects totalled 65.2 man years. 39.6 man years—*60 percent of the total*—were

[63]ISU. "1969-1970 Annual Report," (Ames, Iowa: August 1970), pp. 9-17.
[64]The Texas Agricultural Experiment Station. *Impact: Agricultural Research in Texas—1970* (Texas: College Station, 1971), p. 73.

concerned with technical aspects of physical construction on houses.[65]

Thus, the major share of rural housing research was not directed to those who live in them, but to those who profit from the construction and maintenance of houses—architects, builders, lumber companies and service industries. "One may postulate," wrote Dr. Hadwigger, "that economies achieved in the construction of houses will be passed along to the consumer, though that proposition was not tested or even touched upon in any rural housing research project." Noting that "the spirit and intent of much research is industry-oriented," Dr. Hadwigger pointed to this project description:

> Use of automated and more complex sawmill machinery is increasing demand for operations research to provide information for decision making in forest product industries. Benefits of operation research analysis are useful to an existing plant, and are extremely valuable in evaluating invest-ment in both horizontal and vertical integration and in new plant facilities.[66]

According to Dr. Hadwigger, "most projects endeavored to improve the use of wood, and often were specifically aimed at increasing the use of wood in low-income or other housing."[67] Included was a project that tested the effect of foot traffic wear on wood floor surfaces, and another one that undertook law searches designed to facilitate the marketing of lumber. It is not that such research should not be done, but (1) that it should be done by lumber corporations and others that profit from the research, and (2) it most certainly should not be classified as housing research for rural families.

Another 18 percent of the man years were allocated to projects concerned with wood parasites. That compared with seven-tenths of one man year expended for research projects that included a concern with independent housing for elderly persons, acceptability of new housing designs for low income people and promotion of self-help housing organizations. Dr. Hadwigger wondered, "Is the lack of this kind of research by USDA and CSRS in rural housing due to lack of interest on the part of researchers, or lack of qualified researchers to undertake projects of this nature, lack of resources, or simply lack of priority for rural social phenomena?"[68] The answer is yes.

Perhaps worse than the fact that agribusiness research is masquerad-ing as "people" research is the fact that the great percentage of the

[65]Don F. Hadwigger. "Analysis of Research Projects of USDA and Agriculture Experi-ment Stations for calendar year 1970, Categorized under RPA 801 (Housing)," unpub-lished paper (Ames, Iowa: Political Science Department, Iowa State University, January 1972), p. 5.

[66]*Ibid.*, p. 7.

[67]*Ibid.*, p. 6.

[68]*Ibid.*, p. 5.

research actually focused on people is irrelevant and demeaning. The premise of people research conducted by the land grant community is that the people somehow are inadequate. "Factors contributing to the low level of achievement," wrote a USDA-NASULGC task force, "are inadequacies in: educational preparation, occupational choices, business ability, employable skills, effective use of their personal and financial resources, and the effectiveness with which they adjust to social and economic change."[69]

It is curious that the land grant community can pour billions of tax dollars into public assistance for giant agribusiness corporations without once questioning their need or making moral judgments about their worthiness, but when the system hands out a research token to rural people it must come with a condescending smugness about their condition. Again and again, the point is made that industry needs help because it cannot do its own research and because it is affected by external factors. People, however, are responsible for their own condition. For one, public research assistance is an investment; for the other, that assistance is welfare.

Unlike service to agribusiness, research on people and places in rural America is not geared to action. Projects tend to be irrelevant studies of characteristics, and they tend to stem more from curiosity than a desire to change conditions. Dr. Ned Bayley, head of Science and Education as USDA, spoke of research for low-income farmers and farm workers in this manner: "Only recently have we turned some of our social science studies in their direction—mostly to enlighten ourselves as to who they are and what sort of existence they lead."[70]

If he reads the sociology research reports of land grant colleges, he will not be much enlightened:

> —A Cornell study found that "employed homemakers have less time for housekeeping tasks than non-employed homemakers."

> —Mississippi State University researchers discovered "that families in poverty are not of a single, homogeneous type."

> —The University of Nebraska is at work on a study of "factors affecting age at marriage."

> —A Cooperative Regional Research study unveiled two findings of such significance that Dr. Roy Lovvorn included them in CSRS' 1970 presentation to Congress: "the rural population is dichotomous in racial composition" and "pre-retirement family incomes have a direct bearing upon economic expectations for retirement."

[69]USDA-NASULGC. "A National Program of Research for Rural Development and Family Living" (November 1968), p. 1.

[70]Bayley, *op. cit.*, p. 8.

—Back at Mississippi State, researchers concluded that "the better educated young individuals are able to recognize and take advantage of economic opportunities attainable through migration."

—University of Nebraska researchers surveyed football coaches in the state and got 60 percent agreement "that introduction of a federally sponsored school breakfast program would benefit the nutritional health of teenage athletes."

It is not difficult to come across this kind of sociological bullshit. In fact, such projects appear to form the bulk of rural sociology research. For the most part, it is useless poking into the behavior and life styles of rural people.

In December of 1971, Cooperative Research Information Service reported 91 projects in their RPA 803, "Causes and Remedies of Poverty Among Rural People." 41.3 man years were involved in those projects. Half of those projects, using 60 percent of the man years, can be categorized as studies that simply analyze the poor. These people have been analyzed to death, yet project after project intrudes into their lives to ask the same, tired questions, leaving the people no better off. The following are typical projects in this category.

—University of Missouri project to "determine the typologies of poverty among rural people within selected areas of Missouri and nearby States through the study of family socio-economic status, family ties to local institutions, family participation in governmental and other programs, and amenability to assistance programs!"

—A University of Tennessee project to "Determine for young adults in rural areas relationship of education to migration, relation of migration pattern to occupational selection and level of living, and motives for migration and non-migration"!

—A Southern University project to "Develop and analyze the relationships between income levels and personal characteristics affecting income earning capacity for farm and non-farm rural persons"!

—A University of Kentucky project to "Study the personal stability and social adjustments of Eastern Kentuckians, the relationship of selected variables (including current socio-economic and cultural changes) to their mental health, and their perception of mental health and illness"!

There were only 20 projects, involving 8.1 man years, that were focused on rural people from a programmatic perspective. Rather optimistically labeled "Paths Out of Poverty," a University of Maryland project typifies the research approach: "Analyses will be made of the problems of families in poverty and of the resources, social action programs, and institutional patterns needed to assist families to climb out of poverty in contrast with existing organizational and community programs and ethos milieus." The remaining 25 projects, representing 8.5 man years, ranged from a Washington State University study of "Educational Aspirations of Farm Boys and Girls" to a Louisiana State University study of "Agribusiness Careers."

Occasionally, rural sociology research actually is injurious to rural people. Texas A&M researchers, for example, found in a survey of East Texas youth that many of them had changed their life aspirations and expectations in late adolescence, with about half of them becoming "less 'realisitic'—they changed to higher goals." The research report concluded that "More attention should be given to intensive vocational guidance during the later part of the high school experience than is now the case, at least in rural areas."[71] In short, stifle aspirations rather than assist in meeting them. One wonders how long that researcher would last if he were to suggest that agribusiness be content with hand-harvested onions rather than aspiring to a mechanical harvester.

Land grant college research for rural people and places is a sham. Despite occasional expressions of concern from land grant spokesmen, a look at the budgets and research reports makes clear that there is no intention of doing anything about the ravages of the agricultural revolution. The focus will continue to be on corporate efficiency and technological gadgetry, while the vast majority of rural Americans—independent family farmers, farm workers, small town businessmen and other rural residents—will be left to get along as best they can, even if it means getting along to the city. If they stay in rural America, a rural sociologist will come around every now and then to poke at them with a survey.

AN IDLE BRAIN IS THE DEVIL'S WORKSHOP

There are some land grant research projects that boggle the mind. Michigan State University's creation of green cauliflower and seedless cucumbers is a bit much, but it just is not in the same league with Cornell University's effort on the critical issue of how hard to squeeze the grapefruit in the supermarket:

> Should you squeeze a product firmly or softly to determine its freshness, such as is commonly done with bread and some fruits? By using a universal testing machine, scientists have determined that a gentle squeeze, or more scientifically, a small deformation force, is much more precise in

[71]The Texas Agricultural Experiment Station. *Impact, op. cit.,* p. 66.

comparing textural differences than a firm squeeze or large deformation force.[72]

The only thing softer than the fruit are the minds of the people who spent time, energy and money on such a project. One wonders whether they had their heads caught in the universal testing machine just as a large deformation force was applied.

Cornell is not alone in its willingness to take on questionable projects, but it has been a leader. Scientists there accepted a $1,200 grant from Superior Pet Products, Inc. in 1970 to conduct studies on cleaning teeth in dogs. Extension veterinarians at Iowa State University came up with a disease tracking plan that involved tagging every new-born pig with the owner's social security number.

With the problems of agriculture and rural America well in hand, many land grant researchers have turned to new challenges offered in the sports world. The Mississippi Agricultural and Forestry Experiment Station has focused some attention an golf, testing herbicides on putting greens in one test and determining in another project that "golf superintendents should aerify bermuda grass putting greens three times annually, and vertical mow at three to four week intervals."[73] Farmers will be glad to know that.

Farmers in Alabama and Pennsylvania undoubtedly will be pleased to learn that some of their tax dollars allocated to agricultural research at Auburn University and Pennslyvania State University have been used to study the "heat-retaining properties" of Astroturf and other artificial coverings for football fields.[74] Never mind that many Alabama and Pennsylvania farmers are having a tough time retaining their own property.

The University of Wisconsin has turned to camping for a research challenge. Researchers there explored the critical question of satisfaction with camping, comparing the camper's aspirations to the perceived reality of his camping experience. Campers and rural Americans everywhere will applaud the finding that "fellowship is part of the camping experience."

It is Purdue University, however, that would have to be voted the standout performer among the land grant colleges that have taken up sports. The department of agronomy at Purdue has spent years and untold tax dollars for research and extension on athletic turfs, particularly football fields and golf courses. Just recently, Purdue agronomists developed and are promoting "Prescription Athletic Turf

[72]Geneva (New York) Experiment Station. *Annual Report* (1967).

[73]Mississippi Agricultural and Forestry Experiment Station, *op. cit.*, p. 17.

[74]Alabama Agricultural Experiment Station System. "Active Research Projects, Main Station," (Auburn, Alabama: Auburn University, January 1971), p. 4.

System" (PAT) as an alternative to artificial turf. Including suction pumps to withdraw water, electric heating cables to thaw soil and a powered insulation cover to conserve soil heat, the PAT system is capable of producing "that uniform, firm, safe turf, plus the TV look needed."[75] Complete installation instructions are included. "So, play ball!" exults a Purdue University report on their new system.[76]

The 1971 Midwest Regional Turf Conference offered an insight into the extent to which Purdue University is committed to the services of country clubs and football teams.[77] Practically every presentation at the conference focused on golf and football, including such topics as:

—Ideas that promote golf

—Going the extra mile in athletic field care

—Needs of golf course architects today

—Ball mark, bounce and roll

—Report on U-3 fairways

—Injuries and athletics today

—Taxes and serving golfers.

Dr. William H. Daniel is a turf grass specialist in Purdue's department of agronomy. He also is the executive secretary of the Midwest Regional Turf Foundation, which co-sponsors the annual turf conference at Purdue. The foundation bills itself as "a non-profit organization supporting turf research and education." The president and vice president of the foundation represent country clubs in Cleveland, Ohio and Louisville, Kentucky, while the treasurer is Charles L. Rhykerd of Purdue's agronomy department. There are seven directors of the foundation: five from country clubs and two from golf course equipment corporations. It is a case where the industry and the university are the same, spending tax dollars to make the ball bounce better out at the country club.

Cornell University's fruit squeezer aside, there may be some need to conduct this kind of research, but it is not a proper undertaking for land grant colleges. These researchers are playing around with games while rural America falls apart. It is a tragic perversion of the land grant mission, and it is evidence that the system is incapable of monitoring itself.

[75] "Proceedings of the 1971 Midwest Turf Conference." (Lafayette, Indiana: Department of Agronomy, Purdue University, 1971), p. 29.

[76] Purdue University. "Agronomy Notes" (July-August, 1971), p. 20.

[77] "Proceedings of the 1971 Midwest Turf Conference," *op. cit.*

AGRICULTURAL RESEARCH SERVICE:
IN-HOUSE IMITATION OF SAES

There is another major research operation within USDA that should
be considered a part of the land grant complex—the Agricultural
Research Service (ARS). Not only is its money, facilities and personnel
interwoven with those of the state agricultural experiment stations,
but it is practically impossible to recognize any difference in their
work products. In every aspect, ARS research is just more of the
same.

ARS was created in 1953 to give the Federal government its own
mechanism, directly under its control, to conduct agricultural research
that is national in scope and to fill-in research gaps left by the work
of the experiment stations. Until the establishment of the Animal and
Plant Health Service in 1971, ARS also had regulatory responsibilities
for control of plant and animal diseases and pests.

With a staff of more than 14,000 people, research facilities in 220
localities and 1970 research expenditures of $158 million, ARS is no
small undertaking. But there is nothing unique or creative about ARS
research, nothing that distinguishes it from the land grant college effort.
Its research focus over the years makes ARS a full partner with land
grant colleges in the agricultural revolution, deserving a full share
of both the credit and the blame for the products of that revolution.
ARS research, like SAES research, is focused primarily on the physical
and biological sciences, working "to improve efficiency at all stages,
from farm production through marketing and processing."[78] As shown
in Figure 9, ARS categorizes its research efforts under four headings:
Farm, Utilization, Marketing, and Nutrition and Consumer Use. There
are no surprises in the focus of that research—the usual emphasis
on commodities, yield and engineering totalled 91 percent of the
research dollars and man years. Marketing research received 6 percent,
while nutrition and consumer use lagged behind with 3 percent of
the resources.

Putting ARS research into the same categories used for SAES reveals
that the efforts virtually are identical. 1969 was the last year for which
ARS figures are broken down into USAD's various Research Problems
Areas (RPA). ARS projects under the three RPA's of "food and nutrition," "improve levels of living" and "housing," totalled a mere 71
scientific man years, 2 percent of the total of 3,045 smy expended
that year.[79] That compared with 210 smy for "improvement of biological

[78]Horace L. Puterbough. "An Application of PPB in the Agricultural Research Service."
In Walter Fishel, ed. *Resource Allocations in Agricultural Research.* (Minneapolis:
University of Minnesota Press, 1971), p. 318.
[79]USDA, Science and Education Staff, *op. cit.,* pp. 19-20.

FIGURE 9

ARS Research Obligations and Man-Years by Program, FY 1970

Program	Obligation	% of Total	Man-Years	% of Total
Farm Research:				
Animal Science	$ 10,513,600		407.1	
Veterinary Sciences	16,037,700		938.3	
Plant Science	34,359,800		1,609.0	
Entomology	20,421,900		951.9	
Soil and Water Conservation	19,120,500		983.2	
Agricultural Engineering	7,375,700		338.7	
Total, Farm Research	$107,829,200	(68%)	5,228.2	(71%)
(Basic)	(43.5%)			
(Applied)	(54.6%)			
(Development)	(1.9%)			
Utilization Research and Development:				
Northern	8,372,300		383.9	
Southern	9,716,700		357.6	
Eastern	8,866,900		317.2	
Western	8,213,400		391.9	
Southeastern	1,263,200		41.0	
Total, Utilization R&D	$ 36,432,500	(23%)	1,491.6	(20%)
(Basic)	(50.0%)			
(Applied)	(35.8%)			
(Development)	(14.2%)			
Marketing Research:				
Market Quality	6,670,000		308.8	
Transportation and Facilities	2,736,500		112.9	
Total, Marketing Research	9,406,500	(6%)	421.7	(6%)
(Basic)	(35.2%)			
(Applied)	(52.5%)			
(Development)	(12.3%)			
Nutrition and Consumer Use Research:				
Human Nutrition	2,961,200		109.5	
Consumer and Food Economics	1,742,300		66.0	
Total, Nutrition and Consumer Use Research	$ 4,703,500	(3%)	175.5	(3%)
(Basic)	(64.3%)			
(Applied)	(34.8%)			
(Development)	(.9%)			
Total Research, FY 1970	$158,371,700	(100%)	7,317.0	(100%)

SOURCE: USDA. ARS. "Estimated Obligations, Man-years, and Number of Projects for Research, by Division, Fiscal Year 1970." October 29, 1971.

efficiency of field crops," 118 smy for "new and improved fruit and vegetable products," and 203 smy for "livestock and poultry marketing and distribution efficiency." A breakdown of ARS' scientific man years of research into 54 fields of science showed sociology with 1 smy, psychology with 0.5, education-communications with 0.8, economics with 31.2 and anthropology with 0.5. The other 3,011 smy were allocated to the crop sciences and to engineering.[80]

There is nothing different about ARS. Its scientists and administrators are full-fledged members of the land grant community and there is constant interchange between ARS and the campuses. About a fifth of ARS research is done either by ARS personnel located at land grant colleges or by land grant researchers working under ARS contracts. An examination of ARS "applied" research makes clear that these scientists too are focused almost solely on efficiency and gadgetry, with primary concern for the very largest producers, the processors and other agribusiness interests. Following are some examples of this research, taken from ARS' fy 1972 budget presentation to the House of Representatives.[81]

—ARS engineers have worked on a "completely computerized checkout system" for food stores. The system can be expected to create "retailing efficiencies" by "eliminating the labor of price marking and price changing, eliminating the labor of physically checking the shelves for merchandise replacement and of filling out order sheets, better control of inventories, and managing the store more effectively through the use of the detailed data made available."

—ARS scientists have developed a process for removing a tomatoe's natural wax, thus making it easier for tomato canners to peel tomatoes. In a test of the method conducted by a commercial firm, processed yield was increased 17.5 percent, waste disposal was reduced 40 percent, lye cost were reduced 67 percent and, "as a general statement, the quality was much improved." The use of the method "returned $870,000 to the packer after he had deducted the equipment cost." ARS reported that a number of other canning companies are considering the use of the method next year.

—ARS engineers have developed a mechanical unloading device for use by poultry processing plants, thus eliminating three laborers. The machine "removes the coops from the trucks,

[80]*Ibid.*, p. 12.

[81]"House Agricultural Appropriations Hearings, 1972," *op. cit.*, pp. 194-223. These specific examples are from pp. 222, 214 and 221.

destacks them, and places them on the conveyor with no labor except one person to push the buttons that operate the machine." ARS estimated that the equipment should save processors in excess of $1,500,000 annually.

In addition to conducting its own research, ARS also makes research grants, contracts and cooperative agreements with land grant colleges, foundations, corporations and private individuals. Called "extramural" research, these arrangements totalled $8,031,600 in fy 1970.[82] This fund not only has helped agribusiness, but it has allowed agribusiness to help itself. 1970 contracts include $149,850 to General Mills for work on the treatment of industrial and municipal waste waters; $200,000 to B. F. Goodrich for studies of selected starch reinforced rubbers; and $89,000 to Ralston Purina for limited commercial-scale preparation of cottonseed protein isolates.[83] Recipients in previous years have included such agribusiness interests as Cargill, National Canners Association and General American Transportation Corporation.

Other corporations, private research foundations, trade associations and corporate consultants received grants to work on projects that would profit them or their clients. Out of $2,610,500 granted to non-public concerns, not one dime went to a farm worker organization, a consumer group, a farmer cooperative, a small town businessman's association or a public interest organization concerned with the needs of people in rural America.

Corporate agribusiness can expect to be served by ARS, but rural people can expect to fare no better in-house than they do out on the campuses.

HARD TOMATOES, HARD TIMES

Land grant college research is agribusiness research. Projects are designed with agribusiness interests in mind, frequently with agribusiness participation. Whether the need is an irrigation system, a new shaped tomato, a plan for vertical integration, a chemical solution for processing vegetables, a new food product or an electronic checkout system for supermarkets, land grant researchers stand ready and able to assist, irrespective of other interests in rural America.

The great majority of rural Americans are strangers to these public laboratories that were created to serve them. When research does not ignore them, chances are it will work against them. If they do

[82]USDA, ARS. "Summary, Research Obligations by Inhouse and Extramural, Fiscal Years 1969 and 1970 (October 29, 1971).

[83]USDA, ARS. "Research and Marketing Act Contracts and Grants (P.L. 85-934 and P.L. 89-106)—Fiscal Year 1970" (Undated).

get help, it comes either in the form of a meager trickle that has been carefully sluiced and strained upstream, or in the form of irrelevant and demeaning sociological probes into their personal habits.

Consumers, too, are abused by research that sacrifices taste and maybe nutrition to an agribusinessman's desire to eliminate labor and to rush nature. The consumer may get a steady supply of relatively cheap food, but he also is getting a good dose of chemicals. Land grant colleges produce promotional literature on the cheapness of food today, but there are not many slick brochures on the carcinogenic impact of the agricultural revolution.

While rural towns shrivel and megalopolis becomes hopelessly congested, land grant researchers are using tax dollars to concoct managerial schemes and to design technological systems that will send millions more packing off to the cities. Tax dollars buy new tinker toys for agribusiness, misery for migrants, death for rural America and more taxes for urban America. All in the name of efficiency.

Except for agribusiness, land grant college research has been no bargain. Hard tomatoes and hard times is too much to pay.

That does not mean a return to hand plows. Rather it means that land grant college researchers must get out ot the comfortable chairs of corporate board rooms and get back to serving the independent producer and the common man of rural America. It means returning to the historic mission of taking the technological revolution to all who need it, rather than smugly assuming that they will be unable to keep pace. Instead of adopting the morally bankrupt posture that millions of people must "inevitably" be squeezed out of agriculture and out of rural America, land grant colleges must turn their thoughts, energies and resources to the task of keeping people on the farm, in the small towns and out of cities. It means turning from the erroneous assumption that big is good, that what serves Ralston Purina serves rural America. It means research for the consumer rather than for the processor. In short, it means putting the research focus on people first—not as a trickle-down after thought.

This change in focus will not happen simply because it should happen. Change will come only if those interests now being abused by land grant research begin to make organized demands on the system. If independent family farmers, consumers, small town businessmen, farm workers, environmentalists, farmer cooperatives, small town mayors, taxpayers' organizations, labor unions, big city mayors, rural poverty organizations and other "outsiders" will go to the colleges and to the legislatures, changes can occur. These interests need not go hand in hand, but they all must go if land grant college research ever is to serve anyone other than the corporate elite.

III

Making Research Policy

We tried to change the direction of research while I was in the Department of Agriculture, away from strict production research and in the direction of facilitating adjustment. About all that happened was that we succeeded in renaming a few projects, getting the word "adjustment" inserted in the titles, with no real change in the nature of the studies.

—Don Paarlberg, 1968[1]

Current research policy is the same as it was thirty years ago, if not earlier. It remains based on the concept of making two blades of grass grow where only one grew before. Land grant research has carried that concept to an extreme, producing blade after blade, finally overproducing blades, but rushing pell mell toward the production of still more blades. Working hand in hand with in-put and out-put industries, land grant colleges have pressed efficiency and yield research with such single mindedness that they have run right over the vast majority of farmers in the country, virtually eliminated agricultural labor, left rural America a disaster area, gorged urban America with the waste products of "progress," and sold the consumer an abundance of food that is bred and produced for profit rather than taste or nutrition.

USDA-NASULGC STUDY OF 1966

The Senate report accompanying the fiscal year 1966 agricultural appropriations recommended,

. . . that the Secretary of Agriculture give immediate consideration to the establishment of an appropriate Research Review Committee comprised

[1]Paarlberg, *op cit.*, p. 16.

equally of representatives of the land-grant experiment stations, departmental research activities, affected producer organizations, and with appropriate industry representation to examine fully each and every line of agricultural research conducted by the Department and by the State Experiment Stations.[2]

The result of that mandate was *A National Program of Research for Agriculture*, sponsored jointly by USDA and the National Association of State Universities and Land Grant Colleges and submitted to Congress in October of 1966.

This report represents an effort by the land grant community to define its research goals, to classify its research, to appraise the effectiveness of its research, to project future research needs and to recommend resources necessary to meet the needs during the next decade.[3] It was, as Bayley put it, "the first time that the USDA research agencies and the State Experiment Stations, with the cooperation of industry, had worked together on an intensive, total research evaluation and planning effort."[4] It was a stab at making broad research policy for the next 10 years.

The recommendations are pedantic and predictable. The very structure of the task force assured that this will be so. As a member of the USDA-SAES task force wrote in a critique of the study, "some system should have been devised to better insulate the task force from the conventional thinking within the department."[5] There were twelve members of the task force, all from USDA and SAES. In addition, five technical panels were asked to review the work of the task force. Of the 92 members on those panels, only 16 came from outside USDA or the academic community. Of those, 12 represented agribusiness, including such corporations as Peavey Company Flour Mills, Weyerhauser Company, Ralphs Grocery and the Kern County Land Company, as well as National Cotton Council of America, American Forestry Association and National Canners Association. The only non-corporate outsiders were from the Tennessee Valley Authority, USDA's Staff Economists Group and the U.S. Weather Bureau's Laboratory for Environmental Data Research—not exactly folks.

As shown in Figure 10, the recommendations of the task force are less than exciting. Every category gets an increase, but there is no substantial shift in research focus. For example, it is recommended

---

[2]USDA, NASULGC. *A National Program of Research for Agriculture, op. cit.*, p. i. (Also see Senate Report No. 156, 89th Congress, 1st session, Committee on Appropriations (April 9, 1956), pp. 3-4.)

[3]*Ibid.*, p. 5.

[4]Bayley. "Allocation of Resources to Agricultural Research" *op. cit.*, pp. 1-2.

[5]J. C. Williamson, Jr. "Some Criticism of the Procedure and Report" in Fishel, *op. cit.*, p. 297.

FIGURE 10

Scientist-man-years in SAES–USDA Program by Research Goal for FY 1965 and Recommended for FY 1972 and 1977

Research Program Goal	% of total program by year	0	1000	Scientist-man-years 2000	3000	4000	5000
I Resource conservation and use	1965: 13 1972: 12 1977: 13						
II Protection of forests, crops, and livestock	1965: 21 1972: 21 1977: 21						
III Efficient production of farm and forest products	1965: 30 1972: 26 1977: 26						
IV Product development and quality	1965: 17 1972: 15 1977: 14						
V Efficiency in the marketing system	1965: 6 1972: 5 1977: 5						
VI Expand export markets and assist developing countries	1965: 2 1972: 5 1977: 5						
VII Consumer health, nutrition, and well-being	1965: 4 1972: 5 1977: 5						
VIII Raise level of living of rural people	1965: 2 1972: 4 1977: 3						
IX Improve community services and environment	1965: 5 1972: 7 1977: 8						

SOURCE: USDA-NASULGC. *A National Program of Research for Agriculture.* October 1966. Figure 4, p. 12.

that research to raise the level of living of rural people be increased over ten years to get 3 percent of the attention, rather than the 2 percent of total SMY that it was receiving in 1965. After ten years, four categories of production and marketing efficiency (II, III, IV and V) still would be getting two-thirds of the research attention.

There is a great deal of rhetoric in the report about the need to commit more resources to people-oriented research, but a glance at the research recommendations exposes the emptiness of that rhetoric. When it comes down to the hard matter of allocating scientific man years, "people" are left holding the same empty bag they came in with. That misoriented research policy remains in force today. Bayley, in a 1971 address, noted that "the long range study continues to be the basic planning document for our national research program."[6]

RESEARCH FADS

Land grant college research policy may not be susceptible to just plain people, but it does respond to volatile shifts in the public's perception of issues. In the mid-1960's,, for example, America's inner cities were aflame, put to the torch by thousands of alienated, frustrated and poor people who earlier had been forced out of rural America by the onslaught of agricultural "efficiency." The land grant community rushed forward with plans to send the extension services into the city, stressing the value that 4-H clubs could be there.

Late in the 1960's, America discovered hunger and malnutrition among its people, many of them in the rural areas. Fast as a fire truck, the land grant community was on the spot with a special nutrition aide program to tell poor people how to use government food programs and how to cook the food they received. In the late 1960's and early 1970's, public attention has been focused on destruction of the environment. The land community currently is front and center with a recitation of concern and a display of research projects designed to save the good earth. Now comes rural development and organic food. The literature of the system currently is filled with the intention of the land grant community to do better by rural towns and people and with their plans for research on non-chemical pest control.

Apparently it is some sense of guilt that compels the community to rush forward with a show of concern. After all, where has the land grant complex been while rural Americans were struggling into the cities by the hundreds of thousands, while the rural poor were left hungry and malnourished and while America's environment steadily deteriorated to its present disastrous state? These are land grant chick-

[6]Bayley. "Allocation of Resources to Agricultural Research," *op.cit.*, pp. 12-13.

ens coming home to roost. During the 1972 agricultural appropriation hearings, Representative William Scherle wondered aloud about the depletion of the rural population:

> Isn't it strange that some methods were not devised during those last 20 or 30 years that would have given some solid attention to maybe reinstituting reasons why these people should stay on the farms. . . . With all the knowledgeable men we have had in the Department of Agriculture down through the years, and the intelligence that seems to abound, isn't it strange that more attention was not given to this problem that everybody could foresee down through the years.[7]

The land grant community never shifts resources to meet these needs. The system will posture toward reform, almost in a pose of apology, but it will not actually undertake reform. The evidence is in the allocation of dollars and man years. Despite that evidence, the land grant community keeps up its pretensions. Roy L. Lovvorn assured the Senate agricultural appropriations subcommittee, that a new "depth of competence" exists now at land grant colleges "for meeting the broader spectrum of problems needing research in rural areas." Rather than dwell on the precise nature and extent of that competence, he pointed to name changes:

> The parent institutions and the colleges of agriculture also have changed names to reflect new or redirected missions. Seventeen colleges of agriculture, as they were named 15 years ago, now carry titles such as College of Agriculture and Environmental Sciences, Institute of Food and Agricultural Sciences, or College of Agriculture and Life Sciences. Experiment stations have been renamed Agricultural Research and Development Center or Agricultural and Life Sciences Research Division.[8]

THE POLICY-MAKING APPARATUS

Within the broad guidelines of the 1966 report, short-range research policy is the product of the annual budgeting process, itself the product to a series of consultations and reviews among USDA and land grant officials.

The substance of the research budget is determined by the Agricultural Research Policy Advisory Committee (ARPAC), which is an in-house committee reporting directly to the secretary of agriculture. As shown in Figure 11, ARPAC members are taken from USDA and the land grant community and, in fact *are* the agricultural research establishment. The committee meets at least twice a year "to develop

---

[7]House Agriculture Appropriations Hearings, (1972) *op cit.*, p. 398.

[8]U.S. Senate, Committee on Appropriations. "Agriculture-Environmental and Consumer Protection Appropriations, Fiscal Year 1972." 92nd Congress, 1st session (Washington, D.C.: USGPO, 1971), part 1, p. 366.

FIGURE 11

Membership of the Agricultural Research Policy Advisory Committee

---

Cochairmen:
  Director of Science and Education, U.S. Department of Agriculture
  A President of a Land Grant College or University, to serve for a four
    year term

Members:

  Federal:
    Administrator, Agricultural Research Service, USDA
    Administrator, Cooperative State Research Service, USDA
    Administrator, Economic Research Service, USDA
    Administrator, Farmer Cooperative Service, USDA
    Administrator, Federal Extension Service, USDA
    Deputy Chief for Research, Forest Service, USDA
    Administrator, Statistical Reporting Service, USDA

  State:
    Member, Division of Agriculture, Executive Committee of the Na-
      tional Association of State Universities and Land Grant Colleges
      (NASULGC)
    Chairman, Experiment Station Committee on Organization and Policy
      (ESCOP) of NASULGC
    Chairman, Association of State Colleges and University Forestry Re-
      search Organizations (ASCUFRO)
    One State Agricultural Experiment Station Director from each of the
      four regions to serve four year staggered terms

  Ex-Officio (non-voting)
    USDA and SAES Cochairmen, ARPAC Research Program and Fa-
      cilities Subcommittee
    Director of Agricultural Economics, USDA
    Director, National Agricultural Library, USDA
    Director, Planning Evaluation and Programming Staff, USDA
    A representative from each of the following:
      National Agricultural Research Advisory Committee
      Bureau of the Budget
      Office of Science and Technology
      Agricultural Research Institute
      Agricultural Research Board, National Academy of Sciences

USDA members will be appointed by the Secretary of Agriculture.

State members will be appointed by the President of the National Association of State Universities and Land Grant Colleges.

Ex-officio members will be appointed by the appropriate person in those
organizations.

SOURCE: "Agricultural Research Policy Advisory Committee." Secretary's Memorandum No. 1657. June 16, 1969, USDA, pp. 2–3.

recommendations for policy with respect to planning, evaluating, coordinating and supporting unified long-range agricultural research programs and delineating the appropriate areas of responsibility of Federal and State agencies in carrying out these programs.[9]

The only outsider sitting in on sessions of ARPAC is one ex-officio member from the National Agricultural Research Advisory Committee (NARAC), which is a creature of agribusiness (see Chapter VI). As of October 1971, the NARAC representative to ARPAC is J. W. Stiles of Agway, Inc. In the minutes of the ARPAC meeting of October 6-7, 1970 Mr. Stiles is recorded speaking twice, both times advocating agribusiness concerns.[10] No other outside voices intrude in these top-level. decision making sessions.

As shown in Figure 12, ARPAC is structured to receive the advice of three groups: the scientific community, the land grant and USDA research establishment, and the "public". The scientific community has its input through the Agricultural Research Institute of the National Academy of Sciences. This channel is supposed to involve the broader scientific community. In practice it has been little more than another channel for agricultural scientists from the land grant community.[11] The land grant and USDA establishment is comprised of top officials of NASULGC and of USDA's research agencies. These people literally are ARPAC, so their impact on policy is direct. Finally, the "public" is expected to have its influence on research policy through regional workshops that report to the agribusiness-dominated NARAC.

the regional workshop concept was devised in 1969 and approved at the September 19, 1969 meeting of NARAC. The idea was to replace existing advisory committees with regional workshops that would seek broad based participation, including major commodity groups, agribusiness, consumers and other public interests. These workshops were to:

> provide a forum for agriculture, industry, and consumers to present for consideration by the Department and the universities their views on the important problems of their region which are limiting effective production, marketing and use of agricultural and forestry products, and which adversely effect (sic) the physiological, economic and social environment of our homes and communities.[12]

[9]Clifford M. Hardin. "Agricultural Research Policy Advisory Committee," Secretary's Memorandum No. 1657 (USDA: June 16, 1969), p. 2.

[10]Agricultural Research Policy Advisory Committee. "Summary of Meeting, October 6-7, 1970." (Washington, D.C.: USDA), pp. 9-10.

[11]Ned Bayley. Interview with Agribusiness Accountability Project (Washington D.C.: February 2, 1972).

[12]National Agricultural Research Advisory Committee. "Minutes of 87th Meeting, September 19, 1969" (Washington, D.C.: USDA), p. 3.

FIGURE 12

Research Advisory Structure (for both in-house and LGC agricultural research)

Legislature

OMB (Office of Management and Budget)

Office of Secretary

NAS
(National Academy
of Sciences)

ARPAC
(Agricultural Research
Policy Advisory Committee)

*NASULGC** (8)
(agricultural division)

USDA (8)
(agency administrators)

NARAC
(National Agricultural
Research Advisory
Committee)

*Agricultural
Research
Institute*

Ex-Officio (8)
(other government officials — non-voting)

Regional Workshops
(open to National
Trade and Professional
Associations)

Input from
subject matter
scientists

Input from
LGC and USDA
"establishment"

Input from
the "public"

*NASULGC meets independently with OMB.

72

Three NARAC members, including the representatives from Agway and Peavey Company Four Mills, were selected to help organize these workshops.

Two regional workshops were held in 1971, one in the northeast and another in the south. For the southern workshop, invitations were extended to more than a hundred national trade and professional associations, only 12 of which could be considered non-agricultural groups. Attendance records at the northeast workshop reveal that agribusiness interests were dominant. No workshops have been held in any other region of the country. According to established procedure, these workshops reported to NARAC, which was to "assemble, sift, and appraise the problems reported by the workshops and make its recommendations as to implementation and priority to the USDA and the National Association of State Universities and Land Grant Colleges."[13]

These workshops did not work out satisfactorily even for USDA. Dr. Lloyd Davis, director to USDA's Science and Education Staff, reported that officials there were "disappointed that a greater range of participants had not been involved."[14] As a result, USDA presently is considering a restructuring of the workshop format to include better participation from other rural and consumer organizations.

In addition to consultations with scientists and others on research substance, ARPAC also consults closely with those who wield power. Federal budgeting power is vested in the Office of Management and Budget (OMB), which is a part of the Executive Office of the President. OMB must approve agricultural research requests, placing them in context of the overall, federal budget. ARPAC members hold private consultations with OMB well in advance of drawing the budget, and an OMB official serves on ARPAC as an ex-officio member. Also, very private sessions are held with staff members of the congressional appropriations subcommittees to determine in advance what looks feasible politically. Particular attention is given to the feelings of Representative Jamie Whitten, who is chairman of the House agricultural appropriations subcommittee and whose word is law at USDA. Based on all of these inputs, ARPAC determines broad research priorities for the year and draws a budget to implement those priorities.

Decisions on research policy are made from the top down, but decisions on specific research projects generally are made from the bottom up. Obviously, the two are closely related: broad policy determines what will be submitted as a project, and projects in the aggregate help determine future policy.

[13]*Ibid.*, p. 4.
[14]Lloyd Davis. Telephone interview with Agribusiness Accountability Project (Washington, D.C.: March 7, 1972.)

Development of a specific research proposal is a relatively informal process, usually initiated at the local level either by a researcher or by an outside interest. Assume that an outside interest decides that it would be useful if asparagus grew to the same height. He would visit a college of agriculture and explain his need to a horticulturalist. If the scientist agreed that the proposal seemed worthwhile, he would talk with other scientists, the head of the horticulture department and perhaps with scientists and interests off campus about feasibility, methodology, cost and other relevant matters. In consultation with these people, he would draw up a research proposal for submission to the head of the experiment station or the dean of agriculture. At that level, it would be decided whether the project fit the college's research agenda for that year and whether funding should come from federal, state, private or a combination of sources.

It is in this climate of informality that agribusiness flourishes. Anybody can walk in off the street and attempt to initiate their project, but agribusiness (1) shares the philosophical perspective of the land grant community, (2) has cultivated close relationships with the community, (3) brings project suggestions that the community knows it can handle and already is inclined to do, (4) comes with cash in hand, and (5) strides in with the full richness and prestige of the corporate world. They are "our kind of people," or at least the kind of people that the land grant community would like to be. After a while, it all hardens into a very tight bond—not corrupt, merely cozy. Over at the college, agribusiness is "just one of the boys."

NATIONAL ASSOCIATION OF STATE UNIVERSITIES AND LAND GRANT COLLEGES

Shepherding the land grant community along is NASULGC, which traces its history almost as far back as the land grant colleges themselves. The association dates back to 1885, when the several land grant officials of the time came together at the call of the U.S. commissioner of agriculture. By 1887, they had undertaken their first lobbying effort (passage of the Hatch Act) and had constituted themselves as the Association of American Agricultural Colleges and Experiment Stations. The association has been directly involved since in initiating or shaping every piece of legislation that has affected the land grant complex.

Membership in NASULGC consists of 49 state universities and 69 land grant colleges. Every state, the District of Columbia and Puerto Rico have land grant colleges represented in the association. Headquartered in Washington, D.C., the NASULGC staff handles secretarial chores for its membership, publishes and distributes a newsletter, convenes an annual convention, engages in public education on issues of interest to its membership and serves generally as a Washington representative for its membership.[15] It is a sizable operation, with 1970 receipts of $394,349, including $277,335 from membership dues and $93,500 in grants from Ford Motor Company Fund, Olin Corporation Charitable Fund, U.S. Steel Foundation, American College Testing Program, Sears Roebuck Foundation, Burlington Industries Foundation, International Business Machines Corporation and W. K. Kellogg Foundation.

The National Association is the home of the land grant establishment. Their particular corner of the association is the division of agriculture, composed of all deans of agriculture, all heads of state experiment stations and all deans of extension. When the division gets together, it is the entire land grant complex getting together, The agricultural division wields a great deal of power within the association. Several years back, NASULGC made an effort to reorganize, replacing an existing system of divisions with more manageable councils. They succeeded everywhere but in agriculture, which remains today as the only division in the association. The division has several committees, including its own legislative committee, Experiment Station Committee on Organization and Policy (ESCOP), Extension Committee on Organization and Policy (ECOP) and Resident Instructional Committee on Organization and Policy (RICOP), which boasts its own agribusiness subcommittee.

The agricultural division's ties to USDA are extensive. In fact, USDA's administrative apparatus for land grant research, CSRS, was created in 1961 at the direction of the secretary of agriculture, primarily because it "had been strongly recommended by the land-grant colleges and . universities."[16] There also are strong blood ties between NASULGC's division of agriculture and USDA. Dr. Roy Lovvorn, administrator of CSRS, is a former chairman of ESCOP, CSRS even serves as something of an administrative arm to the Division of Agriculture. The administrator of CSRS sits as an ex-officio member of ESCOP, and CSRS provides a tax-paid recording secretary to assist in taking and distributing the minutes of ESCOP meetings.

It is in the determination of research priorities and budgets that NASULGC's Agricultural Division is most significant, The division places eight members on the 24-member ARPAC, which is USDA's official mechanism for budgeting research. But the division's influence is much more direct. Representatives of the division meet separately with the Office of Management and Budget to work out the budgeting framework; then they meet separately with USDA research officials.

[15]NASULGC. "Proceedings of the NASULGC 84th Annual Convention, November 8-11, 1970, Washington, D.C.," p. 18.

[16]USDA, ERS, Agricultural History Branch. *Century of Service* (1962), p. 409.

The division also makes visits on Capitol Hill prior to presentation of the final budget.

Individual land grant colleges do not send representatives to testify before Congress on budget matters. That function is handled by NASULGC's Division of Agriculture, through its legislative committee. Every year, the division appears before both the House and Senate agricultural appropriations subcommittees, presenting testimony on behalf of colleges of agriculture, experiment stations and state extension services. It is a united front, as Dr. Orville Bentley, Dean of Illinois' College of Agriculture and chairman of the Division of Agriculture's Legislative Committee, explained to the Senate subcommittee on agricultural appropriations in 1972:

> This budget request that we are presenting and justifying this afternoon came about through a rather lengthy process of recommendations for budget increases made by directors of the extension service, the experiment stations and those responsible for the Forestry Research Programs.
>
> These proposals were reviewed and passed on by the division associated and approved by the National Association of State Universities and Land Grant Colleges and transmitted to the Secretary of Agriculture for his consideration in presenting budget requests on behalf of these joint Federal-State programs.[17]

For all practical purposes, this country's agricultural research policy is the policy of NASULGC's agricultural division. In terms of broad policy, NASULGC was a full partner with USDA in the planning and preparation of the 1966 report, *A National Program of Research for Agriculture*. In terms of annual priorities, the division dominates the deliberation of ARPAC, In terms of budgets, the division meets with OMB even before going to USDA, then exerts the amassed prestige of the entire land grant system in testimony before Congress. In terms of administration, the division is represented on practically every advisory committee and is involved almost daily in informal consultations.

It is not that there is conspiracy or corruption here, Rather it is that the product is so dull, the inevitable result of narrow participation in the decision-making process. Just one example of that narrowness is the failure of the division even to include the 16 black land grant colleges as full participants in its decision-making, The black colleges have existed since 1890 but were not admitted into the association until 1954 and did not have their own office until 1968. Consider this exchange between Dr. Bentley and Representative Frank Evans during NASULGC testimony in 1972:

[17]"Senate Agricultural Appropriations for 1972," *Hearings, op. cit.,* part 2, p. 2144.

MR. EVANS . . . I was looking over the groups represented and I was looking over your statement and find examples that you have given of the new demands of technology and all. I wondered, these things that you point out in your statement are of equal interest to the land-grant colleges of 1890. Do you have representatives here of those colleges?

MR. BENTLEY. They are not here.

MR. EVANS. Why is that?

MR. BENTLEY. Well, as to the 1890, we can speak about that in a little while, At present time, I think the best way to asnwer is by telling you the status of discussions involving the 1890 institutions. There is a committee within the division of agriculture and land grant colleges that has met on several occasions with representatives from the 1890 institutions working out an arrangement for representation on the various committees and functions of the division of agriculture in this association. This is progressing very nicely and I am very pleased to report this to you.

MR. EVANS. When did this begin?

MR. BENTLEY. This has been going on for about a year.[18]

Eighty-two years after their creation, the black land grant colleges still are not an integral part of a decision making process that directly determines their existence. Congresswoman Evans, in something of an understatement, had the last word: "It seems to me awfully late." If even staid, black administrators of land grant institutions cannot pierce the isolation of the division of agriculture, what is the hope of such outsiders as family farmers, farm workers, the rural poor, consumers and other interests that need a say in research policy?

THE CONGRESSIONAL ROLE

Presumably, the public's interest in land grant policy would be taken care of in Congress. The land grant system largely is the creation of Congress, rather than the executive branch. In fact, the system is remarkable for the lack of presidential attention that it has received. The Morrill Acts, the Hatch Act, and the Smith-Lever Act all are the products of congressional initiatives, and even today the president asserts almost no leadership on land grant college matters. Policy is made by the land grant community and their USDA colleagues. The only presidential involvement has been to make sure that the agricultural research budget falls within the guidelines of the total federal

[18]"House Agricultural Appropriations for 1972," *Hearings, op. cit.*, part 7, p. 330.

budget and to issue an occasional proclamation in praise of the work of the land grant colleges.

Congress, on the other hand, holds hearings each year on the appropriations request for agricultural research. It is here that the public might expect some serious questioning of research focus and some assertion of other than private interests. It does not happen.

The research budget requests fall under the jurisdiction of the House and Senate subcommittees on Agriculture-Environmental and Consumer Protection Appropriations. USDA officials are heard, then there is testimony from members of Congress and "other interested individuals and organizations." Hearings continue for several days; the hearing record runs several volumes and thousands of pages. The agricultural appropriations subcommittees consider the land grant complex in the separate budget presentations of CSRS, ARS and the Extension Service. Federal appropriations for instruction at land grant colleges are made to the Department of Health, Education and Welfare and thus fall under another jurisdiction.

Public witnesses appearing before the agricultural subcommittees overwhelmingly represent agribusiness interests. Technically, anyone can testify, but it is industry that has the resources to maintain Washington representatives and to fly witnesses in and out of the Capitol for a day of testimony. There are dozens of agribusiness lobbyists in Washington, ranging from the full-scale operation of the American Farm Bureau Federation to covies of Washington "lawyers" retained to look out for the special interests of practically every corporate name in agriculture.

The few Washington organizations representing the interests of farmers, sharecroppers, small businesses, the poor, minorities, consumers, environmentalists and other people do not have the resources and staff to deal effectively with the agricultural research budget or have failed to perceive their self-interest in that budget. Tax-exempt, public interest groups are prohibited by law from lobbying and cannot appear to testify on appropriations unless invited to do so by the committee. On the House side, the committee chairman has adopted the position that anyone is welcome to testify, but he will not invite witnesses. There is, however, a curious inconsistency there, for NASULGC testifies each year in the House, even though it is a tax-exempt organization.

Hearings on agricultural research budgets, then, are left pretty much to the land grant community, buttressed by its agribusiness colleagues. The appropriations process falls far short of being a careful, substantive scrutiny. In fact, it is little more than a chance for special interests to press for particular research projects or facilities. Just a few examples from the 1972 Senate hearing record are the National Grain and Feed Association pitching for more money for the U.S. Grain Marketing Research Center in Kansas, the American Seed Trade Association asking generally for more money in the state agricultural research stations, Food Merchandisers of America, Inc. wanting more money for "wholesaling and retailing research," National Restaurant Association seeking research dollars for food distribution, National Cotton Council submitting a special multi-million dollar package for research on "cotton cost-cutting," and Society of American Florists looking for additional research for their industry.[19]

In addition to these interests, there is a lengthy parade of senators coming in or submitting letters in support of research projects and facilities of interest to the agricultural industry in their states. These appearances and submissions range from Senator Bellmon appearing with three constituents asking for pecan weevil research to former-Senator Smathers writing on behalf of the American Horse Council for "medical and production research in the equine industry." The involvement of these senators is not substantive. They simply are serving constituent interests. But their involvement lends a special sense of legitimacy to industry research requests. As Chairman Gale McGee assured a witness for the Georgia Peach Council, "I must say you have not only the understanding of the committee here, but you have the effective power of your senator (Talmadge) who gets through in very meaningful ways."[20]

There are hundreds of pages of testimony on the land grant complex each year, but no tough questioning of how those resources are being used. Out of a thousand pages of senate testimony from non-departmental witnesses in 1972, the only note of disharmony was struck by Senator Gaylord Nelson, who submitted a statement in opposition to continuing work on the fire ant control program of ARS. On the House side, only Congressman Frank Evans raised doubts about the workings of the complex, in particular the failure to deal equitably with the black land grant institutions. With 2,000 farm families leaving the land each week, with some 800,000 people a year being forced out of rural America and with all the other stark evidence of rural failure, it seems that some representative of the people would probe a bit into the nature and impact of the land grant complex.

Even obvious questions go unasked. In its 1972 budget presentation to the House subcommittee, CSRS included a table showing distribution of their money by research program areas. It showed $1,425,000

[19]"Senate Agricultural Appropriations for 1972," *Hearings, op. cit.*, part 2, examples throughout the Volume.
[20]*Ibid.*, p. 1400.

expended for "research on natural beauty" while only $278,000 spent on housing research. [21] Two-thirds of the bad housing in this country is in rural areas, but none of the representatives thought to question this obvious distortion of research priorities. In that same table, $715,000 was allocated to "research to improve levels of living." Aside from the sheer miserliness of that expenditure, no member of the subcommittee thought to ask what CSRS had bought with that money. An analysis of specific projects in that category reveals that it would have been a question worth asking.

There are two research problem areas involved in the "levels of living" category—"Selection and Care of Clothing and Household Textiles" and "Individual and Family Decision Making." [22] Projects for clothing and textiles totalled $170,222 and overwhelmingly were focused on problems of the clothing and textile industries. A few examples will suffice:

—Clothing and social acceptability of adolescents (University of Nevada)

—Consumer satisfaction with permanent press shirts (Texas A&M University)

—Location and distribution of methylene crosslinds in formaldehyde-treated cellulose (Cornell University)

—Clothing buying practices of young adult women (South Dakota State University)

—Developmental aspects of clothing awareness (University of Nebraska).

Projects under family decision making were not geared to industry, but amounted to the same old sociological hogwash. $543,877 was wrapped up in projects such as:

—Identification of dimensions or complexity in household tasks. (Cornell University)

—Relationship of cash receipts to family expenditures and savings. (Ohio State University)

—Decision making in families as influenced by husbands' and wives' interest values. (Mississippi State University)

—(Again) Clothing and social acceptability of adolescents. (University of Minnesota)

[21]"House Agricultural Appropriations for 1972," *Hearings, op. cit.*, part 2, p. 524.
[22]Information that follows on these Research Problem Areas is taken from CRIS printouts made available to the Agribusiness Accountability Project by CSRS.

—Components in effectiveness and satisfaction with the managerial role of homemaking. (Ohio State University)

—Density, elaboration and use of dwelling space and socialization
of preschool children—phase I. (Michigan State University)

The point is that this stuff is being passed off as research for people,
and the Congress of the United States is accepting it without question.
Except for Chairman Whitten and maybe one or two others, all of
whom share the land grant community's fascination with integration
and automation of agriculture, the Congress really plays no role in
shaping agricultural research policy. The liberals on the subcommittees
generally ignore the research presentations—for example, in the 1972
Senate hearings, neither Senator Mansfield nor Senator Inouye were
even present for consideration of the CSRS or ARS budgets, while
Senator Proxmire showed up only one day, and then it was to express
concern about cutting back on production research and to oppose termi-
nation of a tobacco research program at the University of Wisconsin.
Congressional hearings on agricultural research budgets have been
reduced to just another forum for agribusiness, and the subcommittee
themselves act as rubber stamps for policy already determined by
others.

In part, congressional failure to act responsibly on land grant budgets
is the result of general inattention to rural America. There are few
rural congressmen today and there is little press or media focus on
rural issues. Rural America is a remote place to many congressmen.
Rather than do the hard work of understanding and coping with its
needs, the tendency is to follow the lead of Chairman Whitten, to
accept the views of agribusiness lobbyists and to go along with the
"expertise" of USDA and the land grant community.

Over the years since World War II, Congress has appropriated billions for land grant research, but congressmen have failed utterly to
ask any hard questions about the relationship between those billions
and the millions of people pouring out of the countryside. Urban congressmen particularly have failed to see that their blind votes for those
appropriations have been instrumental in creating misery, despair and
violence in their own central cities.

Congress has relinquished its responsibility and authority to narrowly
focused officials at USDA and within the land grant community. Like
spokesmen of the military-industrial complex, these officials and their
allies come to the Capitol at appropriations time to assure a docile
Congress that its investment in agricultural hardware is buying
"progress" and that rural pacification is proceeding nicely.

TWO BLADES OF GRASS

Isaac Newton, the first U.S. commissioner of agriculture, wrote in 1863 that "It should be the aim of every young farmer to do not only as well as his father, but to do his best; 'to make two blades of grass grow where but one grew before.' "[23] A hundred and nine years later, the land grant complex still is dedicated to the same old stuff, though it is sold now under an agribusiness label. As Lauren Soth has written, "If there was ever an example of a good thing over-done, this is it."[24] As a result, today's farming father either is vertically integrated or in trouble, and his son is looking to the city. Isaac Newton would not be pleased.

It is time that this country's agricultural research policy was changed. This is not an argument against technology, productivity or efficiency; rather it is an argument that technology, productivity and efficiency should be humanized. Agricultural progress need not mean that millions of people are forced out of work, that rural America must crumble or that food must taste like it came off an assembly line. Isaac Newton did not mean to grow two blades of grass *and* kill off 2,000 farmers a week. Progress can be measured differently than in corporate profits—it can be measured by how many people are assured good and honest work to do, by how food tastes and how good it is for you, and by how healthy and prosperous rural America is, offering a realistic alternative to megalopolis. It is essential that this society end its subsidy of corporate agribusiness and begin to invest its land grant resources in people.

But the present decision-making apparatus is hardly conducive to the massive changes that must occur. That apparatus must be shaken, and other interests must become dominant in shaping land grant research policy. That means that those interests must come out fighting, that the "unbought" element within the land grant community must come out of hiding and that people-oriented congressmen must come out of their deep slumber.

[23]Quoted in T. Swann Harding. *Two Blades of Grass* (Norman: University of Oklahoma Press, 1947), p. ix.
[24]Soth. "The End of Agrarianism." *Op. cit.*, p. 665.

IV

The Failure of Research

When I said we were going to have upwards of a million fewer farmers by 1980, that didn't mean necessarily that I approved of that. I simply was reporting what is going to happen. I think it is inevitable.
— Earl L. Butz, Secretary of Agriculture[1]

Earl Butz and his life-long colleagues in the land grant college complex are more than reporters. Their work for the last 30 years and more has been devoted to the creation of an automated, integrated and corporatized agriculture. They are directly accountable for the results from which they now step back and shrug off as "inevitable." There will be a million fewer farmers by 1980 for the same reason that there are three million fewer farmers today than in 1945: because Earl Butz and company will not lift a finger to prevent it. The issue is not inevitability. The issue is irresponsibility.

Land grant colleges have become closed communities. The administrators, academics and scientists, along with USDA officials and corporate executives, have locked themselves into an inbred and even incestuous complex, and they are incapable of thinking beyond their self-interest and traditional concepts of agricultural research.

"I think that you have a big job," admonished Congressman Jamie Whitten at the 1972 CSRS budget hearing. "I think we had better forget the rural development research and move ahead on the things that we know how to do."[2] The land grant community needs little encouragement from Chairman Whitten to plod along with the same old stuff that is their forte, ignoring the real work that needs to be done in rural America.

[1] Earl L. Butz. *NBC Meet The Press.* Vol. 15, 49 (Washington, D.C.: Merkle Press, Inc., December 12, 1971), p. 2.

[2] "House Agricultural Appropriations for 1972," *Hearings, op. cit.,* part 2, p. 564.

Such plodding is the inevitable result of being closed off to the rest of the world. Researchers are trained in a traditional manner, so they operate that way and are not encouraged to do otherwise. Then they train others. There also is the fact that land grant research successfully has increased productivity, so there is a tendency to try to replicate success, sticking with the kind of concrete research that they know how to do, without questioning whether it is research that they *should* do. Not least is the influence of money. The land grant community follows dollars, and both public and private funds are bonded securely to traditional research areas. Corporations and trade associations are well organized, willing to give research grants and always prepared at appropriations time to make a show of strength to direct public money toward their vested interests in research. Then there is the "rat hole" syndrome—so much has been poured into this research that there simply "must" be something worthwhile there, something that warrants still more funding.

People have not gotten much out of that system. Too often, the land grant community deliberately has thwarted efforts to help rural people. One example is Cornell University's treatment of migrant farm workers employed for Cornell's College of Agriculture as harvest laborers on its 200-acre fruit farm in upstate New York. Conditions were less than ideal at the Cornell migrant labor camp. The potential of embarrassment dawned on Cornell officials in 1968 (they had owned the camp since 1960), and a meeting was convened to discuss "what Cornell might do to relieve itself of any onus attached to being an employer of migrant workers.[3]"

One of those attending was Dr. William H. Friedland, then a professor in Cornell's School of Industrial and Labor Relations. At this and subsequent meetings, he urged officials to undertake a study of the conditions of migrant workers in New York and to demonstrate means of self-help, using the Cornell farm as one of the demonstration sites. He drew up a specific research proposal and attached a price tag of $10,432. Dr. Friedland was given preliminary approval and was preparing to implement the plan when, suddenly, he learned that it had been scuttled in the College of Agriculture. In a letter to the comptroller of Cornell University, Friedland expressed considerable disappointment:

> I can only conclude that the decision to abort the project stems from the traditional concerns that the College of Agriculture has with its traditional clientele. . . . In concern for the sensitivities of this clientele, black and Puerto Rican agricultural workers have again been ignored.[4]

[3] "The Aborting of Demonstration 1970." Memorandum from William H. Friedland to Arthur Peterson, Cornell University comptroller (June 10, 1969), p. 2.

[4] *Ibid.*, p. 4.

With a total operating budget of $41 million for fy 1969, it seems that the College of Agriculture could have spared $10,000 to do something for those who work in New York agriculture. In 1971, there was a national exposé of the Cornell migrant situation. Rather than respond positively to the obvious needs of their workers, Cornell officials closed the camp, mechanized their fruit farm and washed their hands of the workers. "We're going to be the hell out of the thing," blurted the Dean of Agriculture, Charles Palm.[5] And they were. A few days later, the bulldozers were called in and the camp was levelled.

Such blatant abuse is not the norm in the land grant complex, but it does indicate the extreme to which the land grant mentality can and will be carried. The community is so closed off that it no longer considers rural people, or any interests other than industrial, to be legitimate constituents.

Land grant college research is science for sale. Research is undertaken with a very clear understanding of who will profit, but without the slightest concern for those who will be hurt. It is research that effectively is accountable to none but private interests, and ultimately it is corrupt of purpose.

The greatest failing of land grant research is its total abdication of leadership. At a time when rural America desperately needs leadership, the land grant community has ducked behind the corporate skirt, mumbling apologetic words like "progress," "efficiency" and "inevitability." Overall, it is a pedantic and cowardly research system, and America is less for it.

[5] *Cornell Daily Sun*, February 11, 1971, p. 1.

V

The Land Grant College Community:
The Old School Ties

Agricultural education has become a rock of "the Establishment"—indeed it is an establishment in itself, which means privilege, favoritism, "papa knows best" and "preserve the system" at any cost. The inventiveness and daring of the leaders of the original farm education system have been subordinated to conventionality and "getting along."

Lauren Soth, "The Obsolete Dream Machine." [1]

One cannot look very long at the land grant college complex before being struck by the fundamental sameness that pervades. Texas A&M might have a particular interest in cattle, while North Carolina State is more concerned with tobacco, but the basic thrust and the motivating forces do not change much from campus to campus. Fifty states have not produced even one or two maverick colleges.[2] Practically everyone within the land grant community seems to perceive the world with a single mind, to act from common assumptions and to speak with one voice. It is a case where the whole simply is not greater than the sum of its parts.

The land grant college community includes more than those who are on campus: administrators, faculty, researchers and extension agents. In addition, the community also includes officials of the National Association of State Universities and Land Grant Colleges (NASULGC), the Cooperative State Research Service and other USDA officials, various local and national advisory structures, private agricultural and research foundations and agribusiness clients of the system. It is a close-knit bunch.

[1] Lauren Soth. "The Obsolete Dream Machine," *op. cit.*, p. 688.

[2] With the single exception of Federal City College, which was created in the District of Columbia to respond to the urban needs of a predominantly black population. It is significant that this creative use of the Morrill Acts came from outside the land grant community, primarily from the efforts of Senator Wayne Morse.

THE COMMUNITY REPRODUCES ITSELF

The community is inbred and rather tightly drawn. That may not be unusual for any long-lived system, but it nevertheless is holding back a creative response to the needs of millions of people in rural America. Out of this closeness and inbreeding, there has grown a way of doing business and a rather rigid set of in-house attitudes. It is difficult for fresh air, much less a fresh idea, to pierce the chumminess of it all.

Those who run the land grant college complex are themselves creatures of it. Figure 13 shows that of 51 college of agriculture deans:[3]

—47 received their undergraduate degree from a land grant college,

—51 received at least one graduate degree from a land grant college,

—45 taught at a land grant college,

—17 had been administrators at a land grant college, and

—14 had been with the extension service.

The pattern holds true for the rest of those on the land grant campus. Of 26 directors of state extension services listed in biographical sources, 26 had come up through extension ranks, and all state directors of agricultural experiment stations were products of that research system.[4]

In some cases, a sizeable percentage of a land grant college's staff is homegrown. At Purdue University, for example, the 1970-71 faculty and professional staffs of the College of Agriculture, the extension service and the agricultural experiment station totaled 787 people. 280 of those, or 36 percent of the total, received their bachelors degree from Purdue. 192 staff members (24 percent) had received at least one advanced degree from Purdue.[5]

The perspective of the land grant community is narrowed even more by the fact that the educational and career orientation of its members overwhelmingly are toward pure science, toward engineering and toward commodities—not toward people.

The old school ties extend well beyond the campus. In fact, those ties reach right into the agencies of government charged with overseeing the land grant complex. Federal investments in agricultural research

---

[3] *Who's Who in America 1970-71*. Vol. 36, (Chicago: Marquis) and *American Men of Science—Physical and Biological*. 11th Edition. (New York: Bowker, 1967).

[4] *Ibid*.

[5] Purdue University. "Faculty and Staff Roster 1970-71," pp. 1-28.

and extension are administered by men who are products of the land
grant complex, who have spent their lifetimes within that community
and who systematically confer with their land grant colleagues on all
matters relating to the federal investment in their institutions.

Dr. Roy L. Lovvorn, administrator of the Cooperative State Research
Service, epitomizes the nature and extent of this in-grown community:
BS in agronomy from Auburn University; AM in agronomy from University of Missouri; PhD in agronomy from University of Wisconsin; county
extension agent in Missouri; agronomist at North Carolina State University's; (NCSU) agricultural experiment station; professor and director
of instruction, School of Agriculture, NCSU; head of weed investigation, Agricultural Research Service (USDA), Beltsville, Maryland;
director of research, School of Agriculture, NCSU; acting dean, School
of Agriculture, NCSU; chairman of NASULGC's Experiment Station
Committee on Organization and Policy; and administrator, CSRS.[6]

One can try to make too much of these old school ties. It is not
unusual for officials of any institution to be products of the system
they oversee. But if it is usual, it is not necessarily desirable. In the
case of the land grant college community, inbreeding has led to
exclusivity, and that has distorted the work of the land grant complex.
The point regarding Lovvorn and his colleagues is not conflict of interest
or abuse of position, but narrowness.

THE COMMUNITY ORGANIZES ITSELF

Obviously there are strong, informal ties among the individuals
within the land grant community. They have been each other's teachers
and students, they work side by side every day, they read each other's
books, they join the same societies, they attend professional meetings
together, they serve on in-house committees and they even throw
dinners to honor each other.

But there also is a formal coming-together of the community. Almost
from the beginning of the land grant experience there has been an
association of those involved.[7] The organization survives intact today,
under the name of the National Association of State Universities and
Land-Grant Colleges (NASULGC). Throughout its history, NASULGC
has been the paternal figure of the community:

The present day finds (NASULGC) a valuable forum for discussion and

[6] Information contained in biographical sketches issued by USDA's Office of Information and from biographical data made available to the Task Force by Lovvorn.

[7] Eddy, op. cit., p. 108.

FIGURE 13

Some Indicators of Inbreeding Within the Land Grant College System

Land Grant Official	Rec'd LGC Undergrad Degree		Rec'd LGC Graduate Degree		Taught at LGC		Served as an LGC Administrator		Served on Staff of an Ag. Exp. Station		Served on Staff of Extension Service	
	no.	%	no.	%	no.	%	no.	%	no.	%	no.	%
69 Land Grant Presidents and Chancellors	29	42	40	58	45	65	66	94	5	7	2	3
51 Deans of Colleges of Agriculture	47	92	51	100	45	88	17	33	28	55	14	28
50 Directors of Ag. Experiment Stations	34	68	43	86	44	88	32	64	50	100	8	16
26 Directors of State Extension Services	24	92	25	96	18	69	16	62	6	23	26	100

SOURCE: *Who's Who in America 1970–71*, Vol. 36. (Chicago: Marquis) and *American Men of Science — Physical and Biological*, 11th ed. (New York: Bowker, 1967).

exchange of opinion, a clearing-house for all matters of importance to the member institutions and a strong voice for their concerns.[8]

All land grant colleges are members of NASULGC.[9] Its Division of Agriculture is the most powerful bloc within the organization. The elite of the land grant community serve as officers and sit on committees of NASULGC. The association acts as spokesman for the entire community. When the USDA budget comes up each year, it is NASULGC—not individual colleges, experiment stations or extension services—that works with the Office of Management and Budget and that makes the official land grant presentation before Congress.

As outlined in more detail in Chapter III, federal officials consult regularly with NASULGC on all policy matters affecting the land grant system. The association is a formal part of USDA's research budgeting process, and it serves on advisory committees throughout the federal government. When the Senate Appropriations Committee called for a report on agricultural research priorities, it was conducted and submitted jointly by USDA and NASULGC.[10] From the campus up, and from USDA down, the land grant college community comes together at NASULGC.

This systematic ordering of land grant opinion through NASULGC has the logic of any "united front" approach. But there already exists a remarkable sameness to the attitudes and opinions of the land grant community. To funnel that through the additional screening mechanism of NASULGC is to intimidate minority viewpoints and to stifle creativity. The inevitable product is the monotonous uniformity of today's land grant system. It is stable, but stagnant.

AGRIBUSINESS INGRATIATES ITSELF

Agribusiness is the one "outside" element that has been welcomed into the land grant community. For all practical purposes agribusiness corporations must be considered part of that community today. To a large extent, agribusiness firms bought their way into the community, bringing grants for research and scholarships,[11] as well as lending political influence to increase the taxpayer's investment in the land grant system. But to a larger extent, agribusiness was welcomed into the

[8] *Ibid.*, p. 254.

[9] The information on NASULGC that is contained in this section was obtained from *Proceedings* of recent NASULGC annual conventions and from interviews conducted with the Washington staff of NASULGC.

[10] USDA, NASULGC. "A National Program of Research for Agriculture," October, 1966.

[11] See Chapter VI of this report for a discussion of these grants.

community because its attitudes and objectives were shared by the land grant communities. Agribusiness corporations wanted help with their new chemical, with their hybrid seed, with their processing facility, or with their scheme for vertical integration. The scientists, engineers and economists of the land grant community had both the tools and the inclination to deal with those needs.

Agribusiness quickly established itself as more than a wealthy client. Particularly at the campus level, corporations play a major role in establishing research priorities. They have their impact formally through service on research advisory committees, but they have their greatest impact informally through research investments and through close working relationships with research staff. The joint NASULGC-USDA task force told of this relationship in their study of agricultural research:

> Industry provides support to both SAES and USDA research in the form of grants, equipment, material, and space. Industry personnel also serve an important role in advising and participating in program formation at public institutions. Thus, in numerous ways, industry aids in carrying out research, as well as in guiding the programs of others.[12]

THE COMMUNITY SERVES ITSELF

As in the military-industrial complex, the land grant college community offers an opportunity for a good deal of cross-pollination from campus to government to agribusiness.

Corporate executives sit on local and national advisory committees relating to the work of the land grant complex, and they shape that work much more extensively and effectively through informal relationships on campus. Corporations make a sizeable investment in teaching, research and extension work, and they are repaid amply in (1) research products, (2) graduates prepared to work in agribusiness, and (3) legitimacy for their commercial products. Land grant officials and staffs, on the other hand, work hard to meet the requests of agribusiness, while many are on corporate retainers and a few actually hold seats on corporate boards of directors. It is a sharing process that raises serious questions of conflict of interest and of intellectual and scientific integrity.

The striving student in today's college of agriculture can look forward to a wide array of opportunities for advancement within the land grant community. While still an undergraduate, he can begin his upward mobility by serving as an intern with one of many participating corpora-

---

[12] USDA-NASULGC, *op. cit.*, p. 201.

tions. As a graduate student, he might continue to work with agribusiness, while also serving as a teaching assistant at the college of agriculture. With advanced degree in hand, he can join the faculty or the research staff and probably develop a consulting relationship with one or more agribusiness firms. Then he might take a position with a corporation, spending part of his time as informal liaison to the land grant college. After a stint in agribusiness, he could move back onto campus, though at a higher level, and work his way into an administrative post, all the while maintaining his consulting relationships. From his administrative post, he could play an active role in NASULGC, serving on one of its committees and maybe appearing on a NASULGC panel testifying before Congress. He might be named to a federal task force or advisory committee and launch himself into a mid-level policy position within USDA. From there, he is in a position to locate a deanship, which can be parlayed either into a seat on an agribusiness board, and appointment to a major USDA post, a selection as president of some land grant college, or a taste of any of the other delicious fruits that are available at the top of the land grant community.

A Double Jump on Checkerboard Square   Such a scenario is not far-fetched. One need look no further than the present and immediate-past secretaries of agriculture to find its basis in fact.

As shown in Figure 14, Earl Lauer Butz has spent his life shifting back and forth between campus, government and agribusiness. He has used Purdue University as his base of operations, going on and off that payroll five times since 1933. At Purdue, Butz was an undergraduate, a graduate student, a graduate fellow, an instructor, an assistant professor, an associate professor, a professor, head of the agricultural economics department, dean of agriculture, dean of continuing education and vice president of the Purdue Research Foundation.

At the time of his nomination by President Nixon to be Secretary of Agriculture, Butz was almost doubling his $35,000 a year Purdue salary by serving on corporate boards. He was getting $12,000 a year from Ralston Purina, $10,000 from International Minerals and Chemical Corporation (IMC), $4,800 from Stokely Van-Camp and $2,000 from Standard Life Insurance Company. He also was collecting dividends from stock he owns in these corporations.[13]

Neither Butz nor the president of Purdue University saw any conflict of interest in the dean of agriculture serving on the boards of agribusiness giants that did business with Purdue and with other colleges

[13] U.S. Senate, Committee of Agriculture and Forestry. "Nomination of Earl Lauer Butz," *Hearings,* pp. 208-10, and Nick Kotz. "Butz An Agribusiness Man," *The Washington Post,* November 14, 1971, p. A10.

FIGURE 14

Professional Vitae of Earl Lauer Butz

1932 —Received BSA degree in Animal Husbandry, Purdue University
1932-33—Worked on his father's farm
1933-35—Graduated Fellow in Agricultural Economics, Purdue University
1935-37—Research Fellow, Federal Land Bank
1937 —Received PhD degree in Agricultural Economics, Purdue Univ.
1937-38—Instructor, Agricultural Economics, Purdue University
1938-42—Assistant Professor, Agricultural Economics, Purdue Univ.
1942-46—Associate Professor, Agricultural Economics, Purdue Univ.
1943-44—Research Fellow, Brookings Institute
1944-45—Research Fellow, National Bureau of Economic Research
1946-54—Professor and Head of Agricultural Economics, Purdue Univ.
1946-65—Lecturer, School of Banking, University of Wisconsin
1950-58—Lecturer, Graduate School of Banking, Rutgers University
1951 —Elected to the Board of Directors, Standard Life Insurance
        Company of Indiana
1954-57—Assistant Secretary of Agriculture, USDA
        —Board of Directors, Commodity Credit Corporation, USDA
1955-56—Chairman, US Delegation to UN Food & Agriculture
        Organization
1957-67—Dean of Agriculture, Purdue University
1958 —Elected to Board of Directors, Ralston Purina Company
1961 —Elected to Board of Directors, International Minerals and
        Chemical Corporation
1966 —Elected to Board of Directors, J. I. Case Company
1967 —Unsuccessful candidate for Republican gubernatorial
        nomination, Indiana
1968-71—Dean of Continuing Education, Purdue University
        —Vice President, Purdue Research Foundation
1969 —Appointed to President Nixon's Task Force on Foreign Aid
1970 —Elected to Board of Directors, Stokely Van-Camp, Inc.
1971 —Appointed US Secretary of Agriculture

The following positions were held by Dr. Butz, but correct dates are
not known:
        —Board of Trustees, Farm Foundation
        —Board of Directors, Foundation of American Agriculture
        —Advisory Committee on Agricultural Credit, American
          Bankers Association
        —Advisory Committee, US Export-Import Bank
        —Lecturer, Life Officers Investment Seminar, University
          of Chicago

SOURCES: *Who's Who in America*. Marquis. Vol. 36. 1970–1971.
American Men of Science — Physical and Biological. 11th Ed. New York, 1967.
USDA Press Release. No. 3746–71. November 11, 1971.
U.S. Senate. Agriculture and Forestry Committee. Hearings "Nomination of
Earl Lauer Butz." 92nd Congress, 1st Session. USGPO. November 17, 18 and
19, 1971, p. 4.
International Minerals and Chemical Corporation. Press Release. Oct. 20, 1961.

of agriculture throughout the country. Frederick L. Hovde, president of Purdue University at the time that Butz accepted his agribusiness directorships, wrote that:

> This arrangement is not uncommon for the American university professor. Good professors often consult or serve commercial concerns in the area of their expertise. It is felt that this kind of practical contact with the industrial and commercial world often enables professors to be better teachers and researchers. [14]

On his application to Purdue for permission to serve on Ralston Purina's board, Butz wrote that "this connection with one of the large agricultural business is quite useful in developing background information and contacts for Purdue's expanding program for training students in agribusiness." He also noted that "contacts are made at these (board) meetings with top agribusiness leaders that are useful from the standpoint of both Continuing Education and fund raising." [15] On his application for service with Stokely Van-Camp, Butz remarked that "contacts made here are helpful in connection with the development program at Purdue University." [16]

Perhaps Dean Butz and President Hovde missed the question. It is not only a matter of what this corporate-campus brings into the classroom, but of what is taken into the boardroom. On that issue, no one is talking. From Dr. Butz's applications for permission to join these agribusiness boards, the reader would think that the total commitment involved only ten and a half days a year for board meetings. [17] But IMC's Chairman of the Board suggested in a 1961 *Forbes* magazine article that a good deal more is expected from the $10,000 a year that the corporation pays to each of its board members: "We want to attract not only good names, but also men who will spend time on our problems," Chairman Ware said. "I'll tell you this, we expect to get our money's worth out of these men." [18] As administrative head of Purdue's tax-supported research facility, Butz was in a position to earn his pay from an agricultural chemical corporation that regularly has research projects underway at land grant colleges, including Purdue.

Butz's predecessor as secretary of agriculture is his successor at Ralston Purina. Clifford Morris Hardin also is a product of the land grant complex and a full-fledged member of the land grant com-

---

[14] U.S. Senate. "Nomination of Earl Lauer Butz," *op. cit.*, p. 211.
[15] *Ibid.*, p. 209.
[16] *Ibid.*, p. 210.
[17] *Ibid.*, pp. 208-210.
[18] *Forbes.* "Underpaid Brass?" vol. 88, no. 9 (November 1, 1961), p. 13.

munity.[19] He has a BS, MS, and PhD from Purdue University, where he was a student of Earl Butz. He taught at Purdue, University of Wisconsin and Michigan State University. At Michigan State, Hardin rose through the ranks to become chairman of the agricultural experiment station and finally, dean of agriculture. In 1954, he was named chancellor of the University of Nebraska, where he remained until chosen by President Nixon in 1969 to be secretary of agriculture.

In 1960, Hardin served as president of NASULGC, and in 1961 he was chairman of NASULGC's executive committee. He also has been a Farm Foundation fellow (1939-1940), a trustee of Bankers Life Insurance Company (1958-1969), on an advisory committee of the W.K. Kellogg Foundation (1960-1961), chairman of the Omaha branch of the Federal Reserve Bank of Kansas City (1962-1967), a trustee of the Rockefeller Foundation (1960-1969), and a director of Behlen Manufacturing Company, which is an agribusiness corporation manufacturing grain storage equipment (1964-1969).

After serving less than three years as Secretary of Agriculture, Hardin gave way to his old mentor, Earl Butz. Hardin, in turn, became vice chairman of Ralston Purina and took Butz's seat on the board of directors.

The land grant community takes care of its own.

[19] The biographical information on Hardin in this section is taken from *Congressional Directory: 92nd Congress, First Session.* (Washington, D.C.: USGPO, 1971), p. 526.

VI

Agribusiness-Agrigovernment:
The Ties That Bind

> *Agricultural supply businesses, the greatest beneficiaries of this public investment in more agricultural technology, keep cheering the "ag" colleges on—providing funds for research which the colleges are glad to accept. The power of decision over what kinds of research to do is thus in some measure given over to special interests.*
> Lauren Soth, "The End of Agrarianism"[1]

The bow on the agribusiness-agrigovernment relationship is tied on the land grant campuses. It is here that business executives, government officials, and university professors and researchers come together for implementation of their common vision of an integrated and automated agriculture. College and corporate officials sit on each other's boards of directors, consult and advise each other and do little favors for each other. The ties are extensive, and they bind the relationship securely.

SOILING THE TILL: AGRIBUSINESS GRANTS FOR LAND GRANT RESEARCH

Money is the web of the tight relationship between agribusiness interests and their friends at the land grant colleges. It is not that a huge sum of money is given: industry gave $12 million directly to state agricultural experiment stations for research in fy 1969. Rather it is that enough money is given to influence research done with public funds.

Referring to the "creeping industrialization" of the agricultural experiment stations, Robert Rodale noted back in 1954 that,

> Industrial grants lead the colleges and experiment stations into lines of commercial research at the expense of other fields of study which may not promise as much financial success. Why, for example, should a college

[1]Lauren Soth, "The End of Agrarianism," *op. cit.*, p. 666.

look for ways to fight insects naturally when the chemical companies
are willing to pay for research on insecticides?[2]

Bert Evans, an extension economist at the University of Nebraska,
made the same point about the failure of land grant colleges to extend
information on community issues: "Commercial interests have no direct
interest in increasing your knowledge about, for example, schools and
roads as they have a direct interest in increasing your knowledge about
fertilizer application rates and new crop varieties."[3]

Industry money goes to meet industry needs and whims, and these
needs and whims largely determine the research program of land grant
colleges. A small grant for specific research is just good business. In
the first place, the grant is tax-deductible either as an educational
contribution or, if the research is directly related to the work of the
corporation, as a necessary business expense.[4] Secondly, the grant
will draw more scientific attention than its value warrants. One scientist
will consult with another, graduate assistants and other personnel will
chip-in some time and overhead expenses cannot be figured precisely.
If the project is at all interesting, it will be picked up and carried
on by someone working under a public budget or assigned to someone
working on a PhD. Finally, not only is the product wrapped and delivered to the corporation, but with it comes the college's stamp of
legitimacy and maybe even an endorsement by the scientist who conducted the research. If it is a new product, the corporation can expect
to be licensed, perhaps exclusively, as the producer and marketer.
Everything considered, it amounts to a hefty return on a meager
investment.

There is a long list of satisfied, corporate customers. As would
be expected, half of industry's research contributions to state agricultural experiment stations in fiscal year 1969 went to just four categories:
insect control, weed control, plant and animal biology and biochemical
efficiency.[5] Appendix C offers a breakdown of total industrial grants
by Research Problem Area.

Prime contributors are chemical, drug and oil corporations. Again
and again the same names appear—American Cyanamid, Chemagro,
Chevron, Dow Chemical, Esso, Eli Lilly, Geigy, FMC-Niagara, IMC
Corporation, Shell, Stauffer, Union Carbide and The Upjohn Company

[2]Robert Rodale. "Who Pays for Agricultural Research?" *Organic Gardening and Farming* (January 1954), pp. 18-19.
[3]Bert M. Evans. "Agri-business and the Rural Community of the Future." (Unpublished address) *National Rural Life Convention*, St. Cloud, Minnesota, August 11,1968,
p. 8.
[4]Telephone Interview with Exempt Organizations Office, Internal Revenue Service,
February 28, 1972.
[5]USDA, Science and Education Staff. *Op. cit.*, table IV-A-9, p. 242.

are just a few of the giants that gave research grants to each of three colleges checked (University of Florida, North Carolina State University and Purdue University). Chemical, drug and oil companies invested $227,158 in research at Florida's Institute of Food and Agricultural Sciences, accounting for 54 percent of research sponsored there by private industry in 1970.[6] At North Carolina State University, 35 chemical companies accounted for 25 percent of the experiment station's "commercial agreements" in 1970.[7] At Purdue University, 27 percent of the private research support come from 20 chemical companies, 6 drug companies and 2 oil companies.[8] (See Appendix F for a complete listing of private research grants made to Purdue University in fiscal year 1970.)

The grants are not particularly large. Chemical, drug and oil corporation grants to Purdue University, for example, averaged only $1,888, ranging from a low of $250 to a high of $20,000. What can that buy? For one thing it buys very specific research, usually pegged directly to the sponsor's line of business. Many grants are given for testing a company's chemical. Chemagro Corporation, for example, gave $500 to University of Florida for "testing of Chemagro 7375, an experimental nematicide." There are dozens of these kinds of grants. A favorable land grant test can lend a great deal of legitimacy to the corporation's product, inclining corporate executives to smile on that researcher and remember him the next time a grant is pondered. Except for being told that such things go on, there is no way of knowing if that happens, but the potential for such conflict of interest certainly is very strong.

In fact, many land grant research facilities begin to look like laboratories for the chemical industry. At the University of California, where chemical companies contributed just over $600,000 in the three-year period 1969-1971, a member of that entomology department was moved to comment on "individuals that are more loyal to the insecticide companies than to the University or the growers":

> There seems to be a trend developing that I don't think should continue.
> Men that retire from jobs with chemical corporations take jobs in universities if for no other reason than to give their ideas credence by using a university letterhead.[9]

[6]University of Florida. Division of Sponsored Research. "IFAS 'Sponsored Research' By: Sponsoring Agency, Company and Foundation," July 1, 1969-July 30, 1970.

[7]North Carolina State University, School of Agriculture and Life Sciences. *Annual Report* (Raleigh: North Carolina, 1970), pp. 60-63.

[8]Purdue University, Agricultural Experiment Station. *1970 Annual Report* (Lafayette, Indiana), pp. 26-30.

[9]D. L. Dahlsten. Confidential Memorandum to Dr. R. F. Smith, head of entomology, University of California at Berkeley. "Subject: Pesticide Companies and University Employees," February 2, 1971, p. 1. For full text of the memorandum, see appendices.

If the chemical corporations have bought into land grant research, what happens to the interests of consumers, the environmentalists, the organic farmers and the farm workers who are badly served by the continuing emphasis of pesticides and other chemicals? Some of the most toxic chemicals are products of land grant experimentation and development, just as land grant colleges also have produced some of the strongest language in defense of the widespread use of these chemicals. Secretary of agriculture Earl Butz sat on the board of directors of International Minerals and Chemical Corporation at the same time that he served as vice president of the Purdue Research Foundation, channeling industry grants into Purdue labs and Purdue research back to industry. In fact, IMC was one of the corporations doing business with Purdue. In 1971, with chemical companies investing some $50,000 in Purdue research, Dr. Butz was offering such industry lines as "Caution must be exercised that we don't go overboard in our hysteria to clean up the environment and make everything absolutely safe."[10]

Texas A&M University assisted Union Carbide Corporation with experimental work on its insecticide, Temik, which Harrison Wellford described as "one of the most poisonous chemicals ever developed for general use in the United States."[11] Dr. Frederick W. Plapp, an A&M entomologist, chastised his colleagues for going along with Union Carbide on this insecticide:

> I feel that materials with such high toxicity are not safe to use even in the laboratory. As an entomologist I am distressed that the profession has acquiesced so supinely in the development of such a toxic chemical.[12]

In praising Temik before the Senate agricultural appropriations subcommittee, the National Cotton Council was able to note that the insecticide "was given extensive screening and evaluation at the University of California through the support of Cotton Producers Institute."[13] In fiscal year 1970, both the University of Florida and North Carolina State University listed grants from Union Carbide to test Temik on various crops.

Where does Union Carbide end and the land grant college begin? It is difficult to find the public interest in that tangle. These ties to industry raise the most serious questions about the subversion of scientific integrity and the selling of the public trust. If grants buy corporate

---

[10]Earl L. Butz. "Man and His Environment—Crisis or Challenge," *Proceedings of the 1971 Midwest Turf Conference, op. cit,.* p. 5.

[11]Wellford, *op. cit,.* p. VIII-9.

[12]Ibid., p. VIII-11

[13]U.S. Senate, Committee on Appropriations. "Department of Agricultural Appropriations for 1971," *Hearings,* 91st Congress, 2nd session, part 2, pp. 1332-1333.

research, do they also buy research scientists and agricultural experiment stations?

A VEIL OF SECRECY: UNIVERSITY RESEARCH FOUNDATIONS

At least twenty-three land grant colleges have established foundations to handle grants and contracts coming into their institutions for research. These quasi-public foundations are curious mechanisms, handling large sums of money from a wide array of private and public donors, but under practically no burden of public disclosure.

The first of these foundations was created in 1930 as a private, nonprofit organization at Purdue University. There are two original founders of the Purdue Research Foundation (PRF): David Ross, a wealthy inventor who served on Purdue's board of trustees, and Joshiah K. Lilly, of the drug company, Eli Lilly. That tie between industry and the campus is a relationship that continues today in the work of PRF.

The Foundation and Purdue University technically are separate. In fact, however, PRF is closely coupled with the University. As the PRF organization manual puts it, "there are no problems in the Foundation's dealings with the University administration because the administrative officers of the University are practically the same as the administrative officers of the Foundation."[14] As shown in Figure 15 Purdue University's top officials receive a portion of their salary from PRF.

PRF is in the business of buying, holding, renting and selling land, hustling research grants and contracts and handling patents and copyrights. Its sole client is Purdue University. PRF today holds assets of more than $25 million, including land valued at $4.5 million and corporate stock worth $5 million.[15]

Land is purchased by the Foundation, rented to the University or to private interests until the cost is recovered, then leased to the University for $1 a year. In this way, Purdue has been able to buy choice lands as soon as they become available, without having to wait for a state appropriation and without submitting the purchase to public review. Because the Foundation is free from public scrutiny, there are opportunities for speculative buying, and, when land is sold, the bother of open-bidding is avoided.

It is in research, however, that PRF is most useful to Purdue. The function of the foundation is to receive research proposals from all

[14]Purdue Research Foundation. "Organization and Purposes." September 1, 1968, p. 11.

[15]Purdue Research Foundation. "Return of Organization Exempt from Income Tax," Form 990, U.S. Department of the Treasury, Internal Revenue Service (Washington, D.C.), 1970.

FIGURE 15

Some 1970 Interlocks between Purdue University and
Purdue Research Foundation

Official	*University Position*	*Foundation Position*	*% of 1970 Salary From PRF*
Frederick Hovde	President	President	14
Earl L. Butz	Dean of Continuing Education	Vice President	33
F. N. Andrews	Vice President for Research and Dean of Graduate School	Vice President and General Manager	36
James R. Lowe	Assistant Secretary, Board of Trustees	Secretary	40
Winfield Hentschel	Investment Officer	Treasurer and Asst. Secretary	81

SOURCE: Purdue Research Foundation. "Return of Organization Exempt from Income Tax." Form 990. Internal Revenue Service. 1970. Schedule 5. And, PRF. "Organization and Purposes." September 1, 1968, p. 2.

departments in the University, to seek funding for these proposals and to manage any grants of contracts that develop. The research proposals are submitted to public and private funding sources in the name of the foundation and any grants or contracts that result are made to PRF. In turn, PRF grants the money to the researcher. In 1970, PRF paid out $12,191,819.73 in such grants, $2.7 million of which was from industry.[16]

In short, a funding source is giving money to a private research foundation, which then gives money to a public university to conduct research. By this shell game, industry-financed research can be undertaken without obligation to make public the terms of the agreement. The foundation need not report to anyone the names of corporations that are making research grants, the amounts of those grants, the purpose of those grants or the terms under which the grants are made. Except by traveling to the Internal Revenue Service in Washington, D.C. and wrestling with those people for a look at the 990 Form filed by all tax-exempt foundations, there is no way to know even how much total research money PRF funnels to Purdue University. PRF itself issues no public reports on any of its activities. As Winfield Hentschel, treasurer of PRF, put it to an interviewer, "we do not

[16]*Ibid.*

give out financial statements—there is no purpose to giving them out."[17]

The Foundation also handles patents for the University. When a corporation invests in research through the Foundation it is done normally with the understanding that the corporation will have first shot at a license on any patented process or product resulting from the research.[18] On research patents that do not result from corporate grants, the procedure for licensing is just as cozy. A list is drawn of "responsible" companies that might have an interest in the process or product, and the companies are approached one-by-one until there is a taker.[19]

There is no standard license at Purdue, each one is negotiated separately. Nor is there a standard rate of royalties, though it is policy that two-thirds of any royalties coming back to campus will go to PRF, with one-third going to the inventor.[20] Since PRF holds the patent and awards the license, the terms of the agreement, including the rate of royalty, are not public information. PRF Treasurer Hentschel estimated that patents held by the Foundation were returning royalties to Purdue of $20,000 to $30,000 a year."[21]

PRF officials reported that only 12 agricultural patents have been obtained since 1956. Of those, seven have been licensed to agribusiness firms (see Figure 16). It is interesting that four of those licenses have been granted to corporations with board members that coincidentally serve also as PRF members.[22] Also three licenses are for patented products invented by Dr. F. N. Andrews, who is vice president and general manager of PRF.

It is impossible for an outsider, denied all but the most basic information, to find his way through this maze of interlocks and closed doors. Why this veil of secrecy at public institutions? Is private gain accruing from the public investment? Who is determining the research program of land grant colleges? Why is there no open bidding on patent licenses? The public interest in research is not served when the public is screened from the activities of its own research institutions.

CLASSROOMS AND BOARDROOMS: DIRECT LINKS

Occasionally, one can get a direct look at the ties of agribusiness and land grant academics. There are a handful of land grant presidents

[17]Winfield Hentschel. Interview with Susan DeMarco. Lafayette, Indiana. November, 1971.

[18]R. L. Davis (Associate Director of Sponsored Research, PRF). Interview with Susan DeMarco. Lafayette, Indiana. November, 1971.

[19]*Ibid.*

[20]*Ibid.*

[21]Hentschel. *Op. cit.*

[22]Purdue Research Foundation. "Members," effective July 1, 1971.

FIGURE 16

Agricultural Patents Held by Purdue Research Foundation,
1956 to Present

U.S. Patent No.	Issued	Inventor	Patent Title	Licensee
2,763,935	9-25-56	F.N. Andrews* (with Whaley)	Determining depth of layers of fat and muscle on an animal body	Duncan Electric Company**
2,940,857	6-14-60	F.N. Andrews	Preservation of Silago	Commercial Solvents Corp.**
2,971,847	2-14-61	F.J. Babel & D.W. Mather	Creamed Cottage Cheese	A New York research found. incl. Borden, Inc.
3,083,533	6-12-62	E.W. Comings, H.A. McLain & J.E. Myers	Drying process for heat-sensitive materials	Swift & Company
3,196,019	7-20-65	F.N. Andrews & Martin Stob	Anabolic & estrogenic compound, & process of making it	Commercial Solvents Corp.**
3,326,187	6-20-67	R.M. Peart & C. Van Gilst	Automatic feeding system for animals	No licensee
3,348,909	10-24-67	Albright & Haug	Process for producing chlorine & nitrate	No licensee
3,362,828	1-68	W.M. Beeson & G. Thrasher	MSG pig creep feed	No licensee
3,374,772	3-26-68	F.M. Peart & C. Van Gilst	Nozzle for animal feeding system	No licensee
3,459,532	8-5-69	A.J. Ohlrogge T.J. Army	Soybean growth regulator	Internatl. Minerals & Chemical Corp.**
3,507,885	4-21-70	R.J. Whistler	Process of preparing cellulose sulfate & starch sulfate	Calco Company
(Public patent)		E.B. Williams & J. Janik	New & distinct variety of apple tree	n.a.

*Andrews is Vice President and General Manager of Purdue Research Foundation.

**Members of these corporate boards of directors also are members or directors of Purdue Research Foundation.

SOURCE: Listing prepared by Purdue Research Foundation, November 1971.

and college of agriculture deans who sit on the boards of agribusiness corporations. It works in the other direction too. Agribusiness executives sit on the boards of land grant colleges.

Other ties are less visible, but perhaps more significant. Corporate-campus links frequently surface in the industry press. For example, *The Packer* recently reported Dow Chemical's agricultural research director telling a Texas Agricultural Experiment Station group: "We have got to worry less about conflicts of interest and get together establish ground rules and testing standards and procedures . . ."[23] There also are occasional references in that press to former land grant academics joining corporate firms, and vice versa—*California Farmer* reported, for example, that,

> "Mr. Tomato," G. C. (Jack) Hanna, until recently with the University of California at Davis, has joined the research staff of Petoseed Co., Inc. at their Northern California Research Station at Davis. (A) long with work on other vegetable crops, Hanna is most famous for originating tomato varieties from which were developed the tomatoes now planted on over 95 percent of the commercial acreage in California and the Western States.[24]

It is generally acknowledged that many land grant researchers serve as consultants to agribusiness firms, some on long-term retainers. Purdue University's former president reported that "good professors often consult or serve commercial concerns in the area of their expertise."[25] Details of these relationships are hard to come by. Efforts were made at Purdue University and at University of Maryland to obtain a list of corporations with consulting ties to the staff of those colleges of agriculture and agricultural experiment stations. At both campuses, Task Force interviews were informed that the information was not compiled, that it existed only in the personnel files of the individual land grant staff members and that there was no outside access to those files. No one denies that these arrangements abound, but the public is denied access to information about them.

The most common direct link between the campus and the corporation is the advisory committee. On the one hand, land grant people often find themselves invited to serve on special groups established by industry. For example, the National Cotton Council created an industry committee on boll weevil eradication in 1969, and they named a six-man "technical subcommittee" that included three USDA representatives and three land grant college representatives. The make-up

[23]"Economic Patterns Force Chemical Firms to Limit Farm Chemical Search." *The Packer*, January 29, 1972.

[24]*California Farmer*. April 17, 1971.

[25]U.S. Senate. "Nomination of Earl Lauer Butz," *op. cit.*, p. 211.

of that subcommittee gave an authoritative ring to this comment by the Council on funding for their boll weevil eradication program: "The USDA, through ARS, CSRS, and the Federal Extension Service had indicated some significant support will be available.[26]

On the other hand, corporate executives are frequent participants on advisory committees relating to land grant college research. The University of Kansas has an Agricultural Council on Research and Education, whose members are selected from the following groups:[27]

> Kansas Fertilizer and Agricultural Chemical Council
> Kansas Banking Association
> Kansas Flour Milling Industry
> Kansas Formula Feed Industry
> Kansas Cooperative Council
> Kansas Livestock Association
> Kansas Interbreed Dairy Council
> Kansas Crop Improvement Association
> Kansas State Horticultural Society
> Kansas Poultry Association
> Kansas Association of Soil Conservation Districts
> Kansas Veterinary Medicine Association
> Agricultural Press, Radio and T.V.

Commenting on such groups and their impact on the allocation of research resources, Roland Robinson of CSRS wrote that:

> Many of the advisory groups, similar to those of the department of agriculture, are established along commodity and industry lines. Consequently, they are oriented toward traditional research needs. The rural non-farmer, the small farmer, the leaders of rural communities and the consumer are not usually represented on experiment-station advisory committees.[28]

The top rung on the advisory ladder is USDA's National Agricultural Research Advisory Committee (See Appendix G). This 11-member structure currently includes representatives from the Del Monte Corporation, the Crown Zellerbach Corporation, AGWAY, Peavey Company Flour Mills, the industry-sponsored Nutrition Foundation and the American Farm Bureau Federation.[29]

Most national advisory structures are dominated by land grant scien-

[26]U.S. Senate. "Department of Agriculture Appropriations for 1971, *op. cit.*, pp. 1333-1334.

[27]Floyd W. Smith, director, Kansas State University Agricultural Experiment Station. Letter to Agribusiness Accountability Project, December 14, 1971.

[28]Roland R. Robinson, "Resource Allocation in the Land-Grant Universities and Agricultural Experiment Stations." In Fishel, *op. cit.*, p. 243.

[29]USDA. Science and Education Staff. "National Agricultural Research Advisory Committee." January 1971.

tists and officials, but whenever an "outsider" is selected, chances
are overwhelming that the person will come from industry. Joint USDA-
NASULGC task forces, formed from 1965-1969 to prepare a national
program of agricultural research, were classic examples of this pattern.
Out of 32 task forces, 17 listed advisory committees containing non-
USDA, non-land grant people. All but one of the outside slots on
those seventeen committees were filled with representatives of
industry, including General Foods on the rice committee, US Sugar
on sugar, Quaker Oats on wheat, Pioneer Corn on corn, Liggett &
Myers on tobacco, Proctor & Gamble on soybeans and Ralston Purina
on dairy. Only on the "soil and land use" task force was there an
advisor representing an interest other than industrial, but even there
the National Wildlife Federation was carefully balanced by an advisor
from International Minerals and Chemical Corporation.[30]

Land grant colleges and agribusiness are related directly through
the graduation each year of thousands of students who are trained
to meet the needs of agribusiness and who are educated to accept
the futuristic vision of a programmed and automated agriculture. "We
don't teach Cotton Pickin' 102 anymore," beamed Dr. Ty Timm, director of Texas A&M University's agricultural economics department.[31]
Indeed they do not. A publication of that department reports that
"Today, 90 to 95 percent of the department's graduates who plan an
agricultural-related career go into agribusiness, with the remainder
choosing production agriculture."[32] Texas A&M has added two new
masters degrees in agriculture: Agribusiness Management and Agri-
Banking. Rutgers University has even coined the word "agrifactoring"
to demonstrate the industrialization of agriculture, redefining it in
terms of "the relationship of production agriculture to the food processing and distributing industries."[33]

Industry is quite pleased with this focus on their manpower needs.
In fact, industry invests thousands of dollars in scholarships and fellow-
ships to assure that the focus is maintained. For the past 24 years,
Ralston Purina has awarded $24,000 a year to six students who will
pursue graduate study in livestock and poultry production science.[34]
General Mills, Inc. frequently buys a full-page back-cover ad in *The
Southwestern Miller* to urge the baking industry's financial support

[30]USDA-NASULGC. "A National Program of Research for Soil and Land Use," April,
1969, p. v.

[31]Department of Agricultural Economics, Texas A&M University. "The Business of
Agribusiness at Texas A&M University" (College Station, Texas: 1971), p. 2.

[32]*Ibid.*, p. 3.

[33]New Jersey Agricultural Experiment Station, Rutgers University. *Search*, vol. 3,
No. 4, p. 4.

[34]"Purina Fellowship in 24th Year," *The Southwestern Miller*, December 21, 1971.

of "education for manpower." Here is a sample of copy from one of their recent ads:

> Through the years, industry-oriented schools like Kansas State University have furnished graduates who have become top executives in every facet of the industry.
>
> But every pool must be restocked and re-enriched, otherwise it plays out.
>
> Kansas State University, the future "breadstuffs center of the world," is unique in offering a degree in *advance bakery management* . . . along with its regular and proved studies in *milling and feed*. (italics and ellipsis theirs)
>
> For almost seventy years, Kansas State University has been training bright young men to become industry leaders. Endorsed, and in part supported by bakers' associations (ARBA, ABA) millers, feed manufacturers and private industry, today the school has 100 under-graduates and 50 graduate students preparing for careers in our industry.[35]

Agribusiness expends a great deal of energy and resources recruiting graduates of land grant colleges. Many corporations participate in intern programs designed to give promising students an early taste of the possibilities after graduation. A work-study program at Texas A&M works like this: "One boy attends classes at A&M for one semester while his team partner works in agribusiness. They reverse roles the next semester. In this way the students earn money, gain work experience, and acquire some insight into the elective courses they might wish to take."[36]

There is some evidence that land grant placement offices are not above steering the better students into the arms of favored corporations. At Cornell University, a recruiter for the National Farmers Organization (NFO) was denied access to resumes of alumni and graduating students. The placement system there, he was informed, requires that recruiting interests contribute a nominal sum, "whatever they feel it is worth," in order to list their job openings in a periodical distributed by Cornell's career center.[37] It was explained to Mr. Don Zmolek, the NFO recruiter, that the usual procedure was for a company representative to visit with the placement officers for a couple of days, expanding on the company's specific personnel needs, then Cornell placement officials would set up interviews for students that they considered appropriate for the positions. "The impression I got," reported

[35]*The Southwestern Miller*. January 1971, back cover

[36]"The Business of Agribusiness at Texas A&M University," *op. cit.*, p. 4.

[37]Transcript of tape recorded notes submitted to the Agribusiness Accountability Project by Mr. Don Zmolek, a recruiter for National Farmers Organization. February, 1972.

Mr. Zmolek, "is that in the posting of recruiting interviews—for example if NFO would come in or some other firm that is not in the best graces—it would get posted on the bulletin boards and there would be very little response from the students, particularly the top ones, the cream of the crop, because they have already been steered into the recruiting interviews with the selected companies and positions."[38] At North Carolina State University's placement office, Mr. Zmolek was greeted with much hostility and no interviews. He was told that there were no resumes whatsoever available to prospective employers. If the NCSU placement officials were hostile to NFO, the placement director apparently was on friendlier terms with agribusiness:

> On the wall were many photos taken at various companies of their facilities, out in different factories, where there were some sort of hospitality sessions for placement directors from around the country. And there were group photos where they apparently used tour and hospitality to sell the company to placement directors. Sort of like a trophy area in the office. There was obvious pride in all the companies that had taken him out. The pride in that sort of thing got to me a little.[39]

Educational ties to agribusiness extend far beyond commencement exercises. The campus is in constant use for agribusiness refresher courses and special educational programs. The "short course" is a system devised by the state extension services to reach non-students with knowledge that will be directly useful in their work or homes. It also is a system through which land grant colleges serve as agribusiness tutors. During 1970 and 1971, short courses at Iowa State University included:

—Iowa seed dealers field day

—turkey processors seminar

—Iowa fertilizer and agricultural chemical dealers conference

—organizational behavior for executives

—conference for laboratory personnel in food manufacturing plants

—future for frozen foods conference

—cattle feeders day.

Other programs, symposiums and conferences are designed specifically to meet the continuing education needs of agribusiness. Cornell University, in conjunction with the National Association of Food Chains, has developed a series of "home study courses" designed to

[38]*Ibid.*
[39]*Ibid.*

train retail food executives. In a *Supermarket News* ad for the courses, it was reported that more than 32,000 food industry employees have been enrolled, with A&P, Grand Union, Jiffy, Mayfair, Ralphs, Village Pantry and Winn Dixie among the more than 500 companies utilizing the courses. In addition to the courses themselves, there also are bonus benefits:

> Supplementary retail texts and seminars at your headquarters by Marketing Professors. Texts include, "Merchandising and Consumer Relations", "Retail Management", "Store Security", and (ready soon) "Consumer Relations for Retailers". Seminars for your company meetings by Cornell and Fordham University Professors.[40]

What can be made of these links—the boards of directors, the advisory committees and the educational relationships? The issue here is not conspiracy, but a community that has closed itself off from the needs of others. It is not that land grant colleges are tied to agribusiness, but that they are tied exclusively to it. A vast constituency—a majority of rural Americans, as well as environmental and consumer interests—stand outside this closed community and do not enjoy much of its warmth.

LITTLE FAVORS

The close relationship of land grant colleges and agribusiness has meant that each is available to perform little favors for the other. The most common assistance lent by agribusiness in behalf of its academic colleagues is to exert political influence at budget time. Ned Bayley noted in a recent speech that the moderate budget increases for agricultural research over the past few years "is testimony to the close federal-state-industry working relations and the efforts we have made together toward obtaining support for our programs."[41] The hearing record of practically any agricultural appropriation includes testimony, letter and telegrams from corporations and industry associations standing up in favor of increased money for some item of special interest to them and the land grant community. Just one recent example was the appearance of a representative from Borden, Incorporated's Aunt Jane pickle division testifying before the House agricultural appropriations subcommittee for "sufficient funds to increase the technical staff, laboratory equipment, and the facilities of the crops research division"

---

[40]Advertisement by Liggett and Myers Inc., "Do We Need the Famous Cornell Home Study Course?" *Supermarket News*, August 23, 1971.

[41]Ned Bayley. "Allocation of Resources to Agricultural Research: A Federal Viewpoint" USDA 3345-71, (Washington, D.C.: USDA, October 12, 1971), pp. 3-4.

of an ARS laboratory engaged in research on onions, carrots and processing cucumbers.[42]

In addition to the agribusiness support that appears on the public
record, there also is the usual array of industry lobbyists and Washington
representatives who make the rounds of Congress for support of some
special land grant facility or project. This is not high pressure stuff,
nor is there an effort to come and go unseen; it simply is a case of
agribusiness doing what it can to put federal money into the hands
of land grant researchers and academics who are prepared to do work
beneficial to the industry.

Land grant officials, in turn, do their share of back scratching for
agribusiness. In addition to research and educational services provided
on call, the land grant community also turns up rather frequently
as an "independent expert" to lend legitimacy to an agribusiness
viewpoint or action. The present secretary of agriculture, Earl Butz,
found many occasions to go to bat for agribusiness when he was dean
of Purdue University's college of agriculture. His article, "Don't Be
Afraid of Integration," was written while he was on the board of Ralston
Purina, which at the time was moving toward vertical integration of
the broiler industry. "The fact that an individual producer may surren-
der some of his managerial freedom and may transfer part of his risk-
taking to someone else is really a very small price to pay for the
advantages that flow out of an integrated system," wrote the dean.[43]
Since that article, thousands of chicken producers have been wiped
out or reduced to corporate cogs as a result of vertical integration
of their industry. They paid an awful price, while the advantages that
Dean Butz wrote about flowed to his corporate colleagues.

Utah State University offers a classic example of land grant willingness
to lend legitimacy to the special interest of agribusiness. At issue here
was a proposed increase in the federal fees charged to western cattle
ranchers who grazed their herds on Federal land. These lands were
being leased at a rate considerably below fair market value, working
to the competitive disadvantage of those ranchers who could not obtain
grazing permits and had to lease or purchase private land for grazing.
The American Farm Bureau Federation, a spokesman for large producers and agribusiness interests, lobbied very heavily against this
fee increase and testified against it at a 1969 House of Representatives
hearing.[44] Political pressure delayed the increase for a year, but the
higher fee was reinstituted in 1971.

[42]"House Agricultural Appropriations for 1972," *op. cit.*, part 7, p. 36.

[43]Earl Butz. "Don't Be Afraid of Integration," *Farmer's Digest*, Vol. 23 (August/Sep-
tember 1959), p. 20.

[44]U.S. House of Representatives, Subcommittee on Public Lands. "Review of Grazing
Fees," *Hearings*, 91st Congress, 1st Session, 1969, p. 203.

The Farm Bureau, through its research foundation, then entered into a contractural arrangement with the Utah State Agricultural Experiment Station to conduct a study on the economic impact to an increase in federal grazing fees. The study was "financed in part by the American Farm Bureau Research Foundation from funds contributed by ranchers in 11 Western States."[45] Authors of the study were Darwin B. Nielsen, associate professor of economics, and John P. Workman, assistant professr of range resources, both of Utah State University. The authors counseled with agricultural economists and range management personnel at the University of Arizona, Colorado State University, University of Idaho, Montana State University, University of Nevada, New Mexico State University, Oregon State University, Washington State University, and the University of Wyoming. Apparently the thinking was that if one land grant college could lend a degree of legitimacy, ten land grant colleges could lend absolute legitimacy.

The research was completed and a report issued in January of 1972. To the surprise of no one, it revealed that "scheduled increases in federal grazing fees on ranches in the western United States would adversely affect the income of ranches as well as the stability of the communities where ranching is a basic part of the economic structure."[46] The president of the Montana Farm Bureau Federation noted with some satisfaction that "this impartial research" would give the affected rancher "something he can use and talk with."[47]

Such favors are common. Cargill, Inc., a giant grain corporation based in Minneapolis, has joined with NASULGC to produce a motion picture extolling careers in agribusiness. Titled "Rewarding Careers in a Dynamic Industry," the script was developed by NASULGC and is available from its Washington office. *Southwestern Miller* reported that "the motion picture emphasizes a sophisticated agriculture—scientific, commercial farmers who understand technology, finance and marketing, use of computers, handling of grain with automated equipment, well equipped public and private laboratories and the use of the commodities market."[48]

The byline of land grant academia appears on article after article in support of mechanization, in defense of widespread application of chemicals, in advocacy of vertical integration or in apology for the ethic of bigness. Symposiums are held on land grant campuses across the country to put an academic sheen on agribusiness schemes. Land

[45]"Research Foundation Issues Report of Study of Federal Grazing Lands," *Farm Bureau News,* January 17, 1972.
[46]*Ibid.*
[47]Herb Kinnear. "A Montana Rancher Looks at Grazing Fees," *The American Farmer,* February 1972, p. 8.
[48]*Southwestern Miller,* February 17, 1970.

grant academics and officials are even paraded before congressional and administrative forums to offer their expertise in support of arguments put forward by agribusiness.

Integrity and credibility are the issues here. For whom do these public servants speak? Ties to agribusiness have become so pervasive that the question has to be asked. Is a land grant research report, an article of Congressional testimony going to be the product of independent and impartial thought, or will it continue to be a little favor, bought by agribusiness?

GETTING TOGETHER:
A PERSPECTIVE ON THREE AGRIBUSINESS FOUNDATIONS

Occasionally the land grant and agribusiness communities like to get together to think, to plan, to propagandize or maybe just to shoot the breeze. To make this both possible and respectable, several, non-profit, tax-exempt, educational foundations have been created. Some of these are corporate foundations, such as the Sears-Roebuck Foundation, International Harvester Foundation, American Oil Foundation, Central Soya Foundation, Swift and Company Foundation, W. K. Kellogg Foundation, Agway Foundation and the Moorman Company Foundation. Others are industry-wide. In the latter category are three that are particularly significant and that offer a good perspective on the nature of these gathering places.

Farm Foundation The Farm Foundation was established in 1933 and devotes its effort to "the development of leadership, personal responsibility, and sound economic thinking as a basis for the achievement of a satisfactory rural life."[49] Wesley McCune, in his 1956 book, *Who's Behind Our Farm Policy?*, wrote that the Farm Foundation is "one of the most elite and respectable meeting places of industrialists and agriculturists."[50]

Its 29 member board of trustees currently has four land grant college representatives: Dean Orville G. Bentley of Illinois' College of Agriculture, Dean Sherwood O. Berg of Minnesota's Institute of Agriculture, Chancellor C. E. Bishop of the University of Maryland and President W. Robert Parks of Iowa State University. In addition to these men, there are industrial representatives from such corporations as Burlington Northern, Deere and Company, Goodyear Tire and Rubber, Standard Oil of Indiana, Santa Fe Railway, International Harvester, Sears Roebuck, and Swift and Company.

The Farm Foundation is a granting agency, awarding money for

[49]Farm Foundation. *Annual Report 1970-71*, (Chicago, Illinois), p. 1.

[50]Wesley McCune. *Who's Behind Our Farm Policy?* (New York: Frederick A. Praeger, 1956), p. 149.

scholarships, research, publication, extension and teaching. It has an endowment fund of some $6 million, but it also supports its activities through tax-deductible contributions. In its 1970-71 annual report, the Farm Foundation listed the following 14 donors:

Agway Foundation
The Atchison, Topeka and Santa Fe Railway Company
John Deere Foundation
The Firestone Tire and Rubber Company
The B. F. Goodrich Fund, Inc.
First National Bank of Chicago Foundation
The Goodyear Tire and Rubber Company
International Harvester Foundation
International Minerals and Chemical Corporation
The Northern Trust Company
The Sears Roebuck Foundation
Standard Oil (Indiana) Foundation, Inc.
Swift and Company Foundation
WGN Continental Broadcasting Company.

Through the Farm Foundation, these corporations are closely tied to the land grant campuses. The foundation noted in its annual report that its "Board of Trustees early recognized that the foundation's limited funds could be used most effectively by working with and coordinating the work of other agencies. The agencies most closely involved with the Foundation program are the land grant universities and the U.S. Department of Agriculture."[51] The foundation works primarily through the land grant complex, having developed a closeness based on decades of working together: "Past relationships of the Foundation have created a climate of mutual trust as well as understanding and knowledge of the programs at the land-grant institutions."[52]

The Foundation is a key element in the agricultural advisory structure, having its own committees with land grant and USDA representatives, and, in turn, being given seats on public advisory committees. R. J. Hildreth, managing director of the foundation, demonstrated just how close the foundation is to the land grant complex when he was named a *member*—not an advisor—of the USDA-NASULGC task force on Rural Development and Family Living.[53] Out of 32 task forces, with hundreds of members, Hildreth was the only non-USDA, non-land grant person serving as a member.

It is not necessarily significant that a lot of corporate money is fun-

[51]Farm Foundation, *op. cit.*, p. 2.

[52]*Ibid.*, p. 5.

[53]USDA-NASULGC. "A National Program of Research for Rural Development and Family Living" (November 1968), p. iii.

neled through the foundation, but that the money is expended in strategic places. The foundation reports that it administered a $1,500 Sears Roebuck grant for workshops held "for the deans and directors of resident instruction in agriculture in the land grant colleges and state universities."[54] The foundation also worked with the deans to develop the workshop, which was held at Cornell University. In another activity, the foundation awarded ten scholarships of $200 each for enrollment of extension supervisors in a training course offered by Colorado State University. In 1968, the foundation helped to sponsor and plan a major land grant seminar on "Agricultural Organization in the Modern Industrial Economy," held at Ohio State University. Through these kinds of efforts, the foundation is investing in the upper level of the land grant community, gently working for "the development of leadership, personal responsibility, and sound economic thinking."

Foundation For American Agriculture   Another favorite huddle of agribusiness and academia is the Foundation for American Agriculture (FAA), incorporated in 1945 as a non-profit, educational institution. FAA represented a deliberate effort to bring agribusiness and farmers together, but its 30 man board of directors makes clear that agribusiness is in charge. Its directors include representatives of Armour and Company, Quaker Oats, E.I. du Pont, Peavey Company, Metropolitan Life Insurance Company, Safeway Stores, Bank of America, International Harvester, Sears Roebuck, Santa Fe, Swift and Company, Pfizer Inc., CPC International, Commercial Solvents Corporation and International Minerals and Chemical Corporation. "Cooperatives" are represented by three of the largest: Agway, Sunkist and Gold Kist. The American Farm Bureau Federation and the National Grange are the only farm groups represented.

The land grant community also has representation on the board of FAA: Dean Orville G. Bentley of Illinois' College of Agriculture, Dean Charles E. Palm of Cornell's College of Agriculture and, until his appointment as secretary of agriculture, Dean Earl Butz of Purdue University.

The work of the Foundation for American Agriculture primarily is directed toward increasing "understanding throughout rural and urban America of the role agribusiness plays in our total economy."[55] The Foundation presents a highly favorable "understanding" of that role.

Land grant colleges are a part of all this. In addition to serving on the board of the foundation, land grant academics write articles for it to publish, make addresses to its meetings and participate in its seminars, symposiums and other sessions.

[54]Farm Foundation, *op. cit.,* p. 35.
[55]Foundation for American Agriculture. Pamphlet published August 1971.

One sample of FAA's effort was a National Agribusiness Symposium at the University of Nebraska in 1969. The topic was "The Challenge of Preparing Agribusiness Manpower for the 1970's." The agribusiness and campus interlock at this session was summed up by FAA's Charles Dana Bennett in his expression of appreciation to those who had helped, particularly:

> . . . to the persistence of Dean Eldridge, the graciousness of Chancellor Hardin, the words of wisdom from that old China hand in the agribusiness syndrome, Herb Schaller formerly of the Pfizer Company and now of Purdue, to Dr. Joe Ackerman with whom and the Farm Foundation it's been a privilege to cooperate on various projects for a quarter of a century, and last, but far from least, to Hal Dean, Chairman of Ralston Purina, who made Keith Weber, Manager of their Educational Department, available to carry the tough, nitty-gritty, behind the scenes work absolutely essential to the holding of a successful meeting, a job Keith carried out flawlessly.[56]

That is the kind of clubiness among agribusinessmen and land grant academics that is fostered by the Foundation for American Agriculture.

The Nutrition Foundation, Inc.   The land grant community also lends prestige to foundations that blatantly serve industry. One such creature is The Nutrition Foundation, formed in 1941 by 15 companies in food and allied industries. Today, the Nutrition Foundation consists of 65 major food and chemical corporations, including such "nutritional" brands as Adolph's meat tenderizer, Allied Chemical Corporation, Beech-Nut, Coca Cola, Hershey, International Flavors and Fragrances, International Paper, Knox Gelatine, Eli Lilly, Monsanto, Nestle Company, and Pepsi Cola. Several Nutrition Foundation members have been called to task for nutritional, health or consumer abuse, including those from Armour, Campbell, Coca Cola, General Foods, General Mills, Kellogg, Eli Lilly, Monsanto and Quaker Oats.

The orientation of this agribusiness foundation is indicated in the introduction to its 1969-70 annual report:

> Not withstanding the high quality of the food supply, poor eating patterns and a lack of understanding of the basic principle of nutrition are prevalent among all socio-economic levels of the population.[57]

In short, despite the good work of the food manufacturers, folks just won't eat right. The report notes that "The Foundation is working closely with industry, federal and state agencies, and universities to

[56]"The Challenge of Preparing Agribusiness Manpower for the 1970's," *Proceedings of National Agribusiness Symposium.* (Foundation for American Agriculture, 1969), p. 3.

[57]The Nutrition Foundation. *1969-1970 Report*, New York, 1970, p. 13.

develop nutrition programs and materials to help establish good eating patterns for everyone."

The land grant college community participates in this sham. The 1969-70 report listed three land grant officials serving on the foundation's board of trustees: Dean Earl Butz of Purdue, Vice Chancellor Herbert E. Carter of the University of Illinois and Chancellor Emeritus Emil Mrak of the University of California, Davis, who also served on the Foundation's board of directors. Dr. George Irving, administrator of USDA's Agricultural Research Service at the time, also was listed as a trustee. In addition, two land grant college representatives were listed on the foundation's Nutrition Education Advisory Committee, and three land grant academics lent their names to the Scientific Advisory Committee.

THE TIES THAT BIND

In dozens of ways, agribusiness gets into the land grant college complex. It is welcomed there by administrators, academics, scientists and researchers who share the agribusinessman's vision of integrated, automated agriculture. Corporate executives sit on boards of trustees, purchase research from experiment stations and colleges, hire land grant academics as private consultants, advise and are advised by land grant officials, go to Washington to help a college or an experiment station get more public money for its work, publish and distribute the writings of academics, provide scholarships and other educational support, invite land grant participation in their industrial conferences and sponsor foundations that extend both grants and recognition to the land grant community.

Again and again, in these and many other ways, agribusiness corporations are making their presence felt and subtly are determining the work of the land grant complex. Taken individually, none of these ties appear terribly significant, but as they weave in and out and intertwine, they wrap up the land grant system pretty tightly for agribusiness. Being so preoccupied with their agribusiness colleagues, the land grant community has not had much time to give attention to the needs of such "outsiders" as the average family farmer, rural communities, the rural poor, farm workers, independent rural businessmen, minorities, the rural elderly, consumers and environmentalists.

As a fringe benefit, these agribusiness ties to the land grant complex are tax deductible. Whether the corporation buys research through a university foundation, buys manpower through scholarships, buys brainpower through a land grant symposium, or buys legitimacy through an agribusiness foundation, the expenditure is deductible from the corporation's income tax. In short, the public is extending a tax subsidy to agribusiness corporations to put them in a better position to reap even larger subsidies from land grant research, education and extension.

VII

Extension Service:
Strike Three

> *Up until ten years ago it was not socially acceptable for Extension*
> *to work with low-income farmers. National pressure is just beginning*
> *to make an impact at the county level.*
>   Federal Extension Service. November 10, 1971[1]

      The Extension Service (ES) is the outreach arm of the land
grant college complex. Its mandate is to go among the people of rural
America to help them "identify and solve their farm, home, and community problems through use of research findings of the Department
of Agriculture and the State Land Grant Colleges, and programs
administered by the Department of Agriculture."[2] Like its other partners in the land grant complex, the colleges of agriculture and the
agricultural experiment stations, Extension Service has not lived up
to its mandate for service to rural people:

    The focus of ES primarily is on rural "clients" who need it least,
    ignoring the obvious needs of the vast majority of rural Americans.

    The rural poor, in particular, are badly served by Extension, receiv-
    ing a pitiful percentage of the time of extension "professionals,"
    while drawing band-aid assistance from the highly-visible Nutrition
    Aides program and irrelevant attention from the 4-H program.

    The civil rights record of ES comes close to being the worst in
    government, even though the effectiveness of ES largely depends
    on its ability to reach minorities.

    Policy-making within ES fails to involve most rural people, and
    USDA has failed utterly to exercise its power to re-direct the
    priorities and programs of the state extension services.

[1]Interview with Charles Beer, Agricultural Production Staff, Federal Extension Service
by Sue DeMarco, November 10, 1971.
    [2]"House Agricultural Appropriations for 1972," *op. cit.*, part 2, p. 22.

HISTORICAL PERSPECTIVE

Extension work dates back to the founding of the land grant colleges. As early as 1863, "farmers institutes" were being held to demonstrate scientific farming methods, and many land grant colleges were holding short courses and lectures for farmers during the 1870's. Rutgers University, New Jersey's land grant campus, probably began the first formal extension service in 1891.[3] Recognizing that extension was an essential function of the land grant complex, congressional efforts were underway early in the 20th century to coordinate and codify the disparate efforts of several states. The effort culminated in 1914 with the passage of the Smith-Lever Act. As reported in *Colleges for Our Land and Time*, "The Smith-Lever Act did not create extension, but it gave nationwide recognition as well as firm financial basis to a work already valued and widespread."[4]

Extension Service was conceived as a vehicle by which practical information could be taken from the land grant colleges and the Department of Agriculture to the people in their local environment. The legislation did not limit the focus of the service, defining its clientele as "the people of the United States." Representative Lever, in his 1913 report to the House of Representatives, wrote that the extension agent "is to assume leadership in every movement, whatever it may be, the aim of which is better farming, better living, more happiness, more education and better citizenship."[5]

EXTENSION TODAY

$331 million tax dollars were available to the Extension Service in fiscal year 1971. The federal government appropriated 42 percent of that, while the states were good for 39 percent and the counties chipped in 18 percent. Since 1914, four and a half billion tax dollars have been plowed into extension work, with $2.7 billion of that being appropriated since 1952.[6] The service currently employs 15,482 professional extension employees, as well as some 10,000 support people and 11,000 program aides. ES officials estimate that more than 1,000,000 volunteers work in various aspects of the program.[7]

[3]Eddy, *op. cit.*, p. 139.

[4]*Ibid.*, p. 143.

[5]USDA-NASULGC, Extension Study Committee. "A People and A Spirit" (Fort Collins, Colorado: Colorado State University, November 1968), p. 18.

[6]USDA-FES. "Amount and Percentage of Cooperative Extension Funds Available to States and Puerto Rico, by Source, from Fiscal Year Beginning July 1, 1914," February 2, 1971.

[7]USDA, Extension Service. "Number of Cooperative Extension Agents," 1971 and, "Functions, Objectives and Responsibilities," May, 1971, p. 3.

What has extension done with that money and with that manpower? Like the other parts of the land grant complex, extension has been preoccupied with efficiency and production, a focus that has contributed much to the largest producers, but has also slighted the pressing needs of the vast majority of America's farmers, and ignored the great majority of other rural people. The service devotes more than half of its total work to just one quarter of the farmers in the country, those with sales of more than $10,000 annually. That leaves 2.4 million farmers—75 percent of the total according to ES figures—without the attention that their need and numbers warrant. Included are hundreds of thousands of marginal farmers, with "net incomes insufficient for levels of living acceptable even for rural areas."[8]

In a joint USDA-NASULGC report on extension in 1968, a great deal of concern was expressed for "farm unit fallout":

> This condition has characterized American agriculture during the 50's and 60's. Unless the individual operator is given some capability to maintain a competitive position, he will rapidly be forced out of any satisfactory position. This is not only an individual problem, it is significant to the vitality and nature of rural America.[9]

That concern would be more convincing if the failure in rural America was not so stark. There were 6 million farms in 1945; by 1971 the number had plummeted to 2.9 million—a "fallout" of half the farmers in the country.[10] During that same 26-year period, extension's annual budget skyrocketed from $38 million to $332 million—a 900 percent increase.[11]

Extension especially has failed these people. It is not the only institution that is responsible, but it must shoulder a special share of the burden, for it's specific function is to reach out to them, to search out their needs and to help them with pragmatic solutions. The reasons for this failure rest in structure and attitude.

ES is hailed by USDA as a model of federalism, with federal, state and local governments working together to deliver services to people. It is not what it is cracked up to be.

Federal supervision and control of Extension is broadly outlined in a "Memorandum of Understanding" with the land grant colleges, dating back to 1914.[12] It provides for "joint supervision" of extension

[8] "A People and A Spirit," *op. cit.*, p. 26.

[9] *Ibid.*, p. 13.

[10] U.S. Department of Commerce, Bureau of the Census. *Statistical Abstract of the United States*, 1971, table 924, p. 573.

[11] USDA-FES. "Amount and Percentage of Cooperative Extension Funds Available to States and Puerto Rico, by Source, from Fiscal Year Beginning July 1, 1914," February 2, 1971.

[12] "A People and A Spirit," *op. cit.*, p. 19.

programs by the states and the federal governments. In fact, however, the federal government exercises little control over state policies and even less control over individual agents. Today's extension agent is not a direct-line, federal employee. His responsibility is to his county and state. The Federal Extension Service is one of the weakest agencies in USDA, engaged in little more than ratification of decisions reached at the campus level.

The federal role need not be that weak. The federal administrator of Extension has the power of "final review" of all extension staff. Up to 1964, that power was rarely used. In 1964, it was administratively delegated to the several states.[13] The administrator also conducts a review of state programs and budgets, but it is a routine rather than a substantive review. In addition, the Smith-Lever Act authorizes the secretary of agriculture to withhold funds from any state misapplying them, and it gives him the power of approval of appointments of state extension directors, who are selected by the governing boards of the land grant colleges. These powers have been interpreted very strictly by federal officials, effectively leaving Extension administration in the hands of local officials.

There is an Extension Committee on Organization and Policy (ECOP) within NASULGC. Serving as a national advisory committee, ECOP is composed of the administrator of ES and 12 representatives elected from among state directors of Extension. ECOP is the primary element shaping national extension policy. The state directors are a tradition bound bunch; in a a 1968 survey, state extension directors favored "heavy emphasis on work with highly specialized farms and other commercial farms, cooperatives, farm product purchasers and processors, and county and community organizations." Only if there were to be a "significant expansion of resources" would they favor increased program activity with low-income farmers, rural non-farm and other low-income families[14]

In practice, extension policy is determined on a daily basis at the county level. Except for general oversight by state directors, the county agent is autonomous, as noted in "A People and A Spirit":

> Each local area may deviate and adapt its program thrusts toward local requirements, although the program must be conducted within limits set at the state level. This arrangement tends to blunt the sharp changes in objectives possible with changes in Federal, State, or local administration.[15]

[13]Telephone interview with Ralph Groenig, assistant administrator, Administrative Management, FES by Sue Sechler, AAP Task Force, March 1972.

[14]"A People and A Spirit," *op. cit.*, p. 32.

[15]*Ibid.*, p. 26.

The effect of that autonomy is to isolate extension work from shifts in public priorities. In fact, the county agent is left pretty much to his own instincts and to the inclinations of the local "establishment"—the two are rarely at odds. Only about a third of Extension's federal money is earmarked for a particular purpose, and it is unlikely that the state and county money comes with any more direction. That leaves a great deal of money to the discretion of the county agent, who consults a narrow group for advice on how to spend it.

The result is that things simply do not change much at the local level. The county agents just keep on with the same old stuff, day in and day out, preaching productivity and efficiency. One extension agent based at the University of Maryland described the problem:

> I got an invitation the other day to a conference on cooperatives for extension agents. I called up to find out if they were going to try and focus on how cooperatives could help all these guys who are still struggling—I mean, we're supposed to have all this expertise, and if we can't help them, who's going to? So, I called a few people and asked if the meeting was going to deal with the problems of the little guy or were we going to get the old "Southern States" success story again. It was the some old Southern State story.[16]

Another major influence on the work of extension is the fact that a large part of Extension's materials are determined by the research and knowledge that comes out of the facilities of the land grant colleges. "Since Extension is a part of each land-grant university," wrote the USDA-NASULGC Extension study committee in 1968, "it is subject to the policies, procedures and goals of that university in which it is a part." More specifically, "The capability of the university faculty influences the quality of the knowledge available for use by its Extension Service."[17]

It is a land grant version of "you are what you eat." On the one hand, extension people are full-fledged members of the land grant community, sharing the perspective and associations of that community. On the other hand, extension agents are involved in disseminating the products of land grant research and teaching. An example is the tobacco harvester and curing system developed by researchers at the University of Maryland. Because it is designed for use on the larger tobacco farms, and because of its expense, the harvester and

---

[16]Interview with M. Beider, Maryland University Extension Service by Sechler, AAP Task Force, March 19.
[17]"A People and A Spirit," op. cit., p. 20.

curing system is estimated to be useful for only about 30 percent of the tobacco farmers in Maryland.[18]

That machine is going to replace a great many tobacco workers, and it is going to work to the competitive disadvantage of 70 percent of Maryland's tobacco farmers, but there is no research underway at the University of Maryland even to evaluate this impact of the harvester. Extension will not have anything to say to that 70 percent, but at least the agents will have new equipment to show at their next Tobacco Field Day, an annual agribusiness event even in Maryland.

SERVING PEOPLE

In 1971, extension agents spent 16,983.6 man years on all activities, breaking down their work into the following allocations:[19]

4-H Youth	31.8 percent
Improving Farm Income	31.0 percent
Family Living	12.7 percent
Food and Nutrition	7.8 percent
Community Resource Development	7.0 percent
Marketing Supply & Distribution	4.2 percent
Pest. Ed. & Emer. Prep.	.8 percent
Environmental Protection	1.1 percent
Others (International, Recreation, Wildlife and Natural Beauty Forestry, Soil & Water Conservation)	3.6 percent

There is less in that for people than appears on the surface. 4-H receives the largest allocation of man years—a third of the total. This social club for youth exists as one of the sacred cows of the land grant world. Federal, state and local governments pour some $72 million

[18]According to USDA's most recent figures (1965) there are a total of 6,274 tobacco farms in Maryland. 3,700 of these were from 0-5 acres, 1,585 were from 5-10 acres; 1,275 were over 10 acres. In interviews with USDA, and Maryland Experiment Station officials, it was conceded that the harvester would not be practical for 3,700 of the farmers (over half) who grew under 5 acres. At the estimated price of $2,500 for the harvester, plus at least $7,000 for a tractor to pull it, the harvesting equipment would represent a sizeable portion of the 5-10 acre man's income. It was suggested that perhaps some of them would get together and buy one jointly, but there is no evidence that Maryland land grant officials intend to help the small growers make such a cooperative effort.

[19]Cooperative Extension Service. "Resources Expended by National Program Purposes, FY 1971, Professional Staff," 1971.

a year into this youth program, and another $30 million is added by industry and other private sources.[20]

The rationale for that money is always "enrollment." As NASULGC argued before Congress during consideration of the 1972 Extension budget, "an increase of $25 million would enable Cooperative Extension Service to reach an additional 1,000,000 youth."[21] Reach them with what? Why? The only answer given by NASULGC was that these youngsters then could help "solve critical problems relating to the quality of environment for all people," that there could be "special programs for the disadvantaged and minority groups," and that it would "help young people develop responsible citizenship attitudes and leadership capabilities through real-life learning experiences."[22]

Rural America is giving up large numbers of its young people because there is neither farm nor non-farm income opportunities for them there. 4-H, with $72 million, is responding to that by conducting litter cleanup days and awarding ribbons to everybody. "Poor Damn Janeth" is Ira Dietrich's literary character who has passed through her youth and now is at the door of opportunity, seeking a career in agriculture as a farmer:

Keeper: "Certainly you must have some evidence of capability with you to qualify you for admittance to the Land of Real."

Janeth: "I have my 4-H ribbons—see? Three purples, 26 blues, 19 reds, 15 whites, 11 pinks, and this brown one from 18th place from the Chicago International Stock Show."

Keeper: "Ribbons shmibbons—what good are they?"

Janeth: "Well, our 4-H leader said they would prove valuable in later life when we went out into the world on our own."

Keeper: "I wonder what he meant by that?"

Janeth: "I don't know, but that's what he said."[23]

The fact is that 4-H might be an adequate youth club, but it is not doing much that seriously promises to make a change in the rural plight. It is a frivolous diversion of 72 million tax dollars.

"Family Living" is a traditional category of extension work. It is the domain of the home demonstration agent and includes the sub-categories: family stability, housing, health, money management, con-

[20]"House Agricultural Appropriations for 1972," *op. cit.*, part 7, p. 346.
[21]*Ibid.*, p. 346.
[22]*Ibid.*, p. 346.
[23]Ira Dietrich. *Poor Damn Janeth.* (Madison: Bascom Housing Publishing Company, Inc., 1967), p. 168.

sumer competence, geriatrics and handicapped.[24] These are ameliorative efforts, designed to do what they can for people as they are, rather than change their situation. The 1971 report of the Texas Agricultural Extension Service offers an insight into the focus of these programs:

> Popular among the program topics explored in home demonstration clubs were these—"Choosing Home Cleaning Products," "Housing Alternatives for Retirement Living," "Consumer Decisions in Clothing," "Convenience Foods Versus Home-prepared Foods," and "What We Know about Mental Health."[25]

The two categories of "Improving Farm Income" and "Community Resources Development" appear to refer to work that would be useful to rural people, including the rural poor. These categories draw 31 percent and 7 percent respectively of extension man years. However, the service does not report these categories by audience served, so it is impossible to know how much of that assistance is going to whom and just whose incomes are being improved.

Dr. Chester Swank, of the Federal Extension Program and evaluation staff, reported that 37.3 percent of ES time is specifically aimed at low income people, with the major portion expended through nutrition and 4-H programs.[26] But when non-professional and volunteer time is removed from consideration, it is clear that Extension's professional staff does not waste much energy on the rural poor.

A check of the more detailed records of three states reveals that Dr. Swank's figure exaggerates the actual investment of Extension in low income people. The New York State Extension Service reports that only 9 percent of professional time is spent with low income people and that a mere 1 percent of their work on "Improving Farm Income" is directed toward the low income.[27] In Florida, work with the rural poor accounts for 5.3 percent of the state extension effort, over half of which is spent in the nutrition program.[28] The Indiana Extension Service spent the generous total of 1.26 percent of their professional time with low income homemakers and housing tenants.[29]

[24]"House Agricultural Appropriations for 1972," *op. cit.*, part 7, p. 344.

[25]"Texas Agricultural Extension Service Advances Progress," *Annual Report, 1971* (Texas A&M University), p. 42.

[26]Telephone interview with Dr. Chester Swank, Federal Extension Program and Evaluation Staff, November 29, 1971, by Susan DeMarco, AAP Task Force.

[27]Agricultural Policy Accountability Project, Cornell University. *New York State Cooperative Extension and the College of Agriculture.* Table 3A, N.Y.S. Cooperative Extension 1970-71 Total Effort, and 1971-72 Budget for Program Areas. (Unpublished report: 1972), p. 315.

[28]Florida Cooperative Extension. "Planned and Expended Time by State Purpose, F.Y. 1970."

[29]Purdue University, Purdue Extension Service. "Audience Type Hours Expended July-December 1970," computer printout provided by extension office, Purdue University.

The document, "Extension Service's Responsibility to Ranchers and Farmers with Gross FarmIncomes under $10,000," reports that three-fourths of the nation's firms fit into this category of "sub-level" income, and that one-third of these farms are expected to disappear in the next four or five years. Although this document demonstrates a grasp of the basic need, it does not report the percentage of extension time spent working with these farmers, nor does it report any details of actual extension services focused on their needs.

Mr. Dorris Rivers, with the Rural Development Staff of FES, acknowledged that only 500 of 15,482 extension agents were working in rural development—about three percent. He noted that it was *not* the purpose of these agents to help struggling farmers stay on the land. Rather, they were to move in with ameliorative assistance after extension's agri-production staff has determined that there is no way for an individual farmer or a group of farmers to make it. The rural development staff then is to do what it can to help "equip them for another environment" or to encourage industry to move into the area. It is difficult to get the state extension services to spend time on rural development, noted Rivers, because "they are uncomfortable with it and often lack the background necessary."[30]

Farm workers are among the poorest of this country's working poor. They are powerless, and they are ignored by practically every governmental program that could assist them. Extension is no exception. In Florida, for example, there is a large and growing farm worker population. Their needs are obvious. Yet, according to the Florida Cooperative Extension Service, 16 out of 100,000 man-days were spent in 1970 to help migrants—an allocation of 0.016 percent of ES time in Florida.[31]

Not only has Extension failed to allocate its resources to provide anywhere near adequate service to the rural poor, but the Service also has failed to make use of a special, earmarked fund deliberately established to serve these people. In 1955, an amendment was added to the Smith-Lever Act, creating a Special Needs Section:

> In determining that the area has such special need, the Secretary shall find that it has a substantial number of disadvantaged farms or farm families for one or more of the reasons heretofore enumerated. The Secretary shall make provisions for the assistance to be extended to include one or more of the following: (1) Intensive on-the-farm educational assistance to the farm family in appraising and resolving its problems; (2) assistance

[30]Interview with Dorris Rivers, deputy administrator, rural development, Federal Extension Service. November 8, 1971 by Susan DeMarco, AAP Task Force.

[31]Florida Cooperative Extension Service. "Planned and Expended Time by State Audience Type, Fiscal Year 1970."

and counseling to local groups appraising resources for capability of improvement in agriculture or introduction of industry designed to supplement farm income; (3) in cooperation with other agencies and groups in furnishing all possible information as to existing employment opportunities, particularly to farm families having underemployed workers; and (4) in cases where the farm family, after analysis of its opportunities and existing resources, finds it advisable to seek a new farming venture, the providing of information, advice and counsel in connection with making such change.[32]

A total of 10 percent, over and above the total funds available to the Cooperative Extension Service, can be made available for projects under this section to assist disadvantaged rural areas.

This money can only be obtained upon application from the 'state director of extension. The grants made under this section would be in addition to and not in substitution for the regular formula appropriations.

USDA reports that there have been no appropriations under this category.

SERVING MINORITIES

There is another contributing factor to Extension's failure to serve the small farmer, rural poor and farmworker—institutionalized racism. In evaluating USDA's civil rights compliance in the November 1971 document, *"One Year Later,"* the Federal Civil Rights Commission said:

> Improvements in the overall USDA Title VI program have been undermined by the grossly inadequate performance of the Extension Service, an agency whose program is fundamental to other agricultural programs. The Extension Service has consistently failed to discharge its Title VI responsibility to take forceful corrective action against non-complying recipients. Specifically, the Extension Service Compliance program has been marked by unparalleled procrastination in dealing with numerous State Extension Services which have failed even to file acceptable Title VI assurances. Seven years after the enactment of the Civil Rights Act of 1964, these noncomplying recipients continue to receive financial assistance from the USDA.[33]

Again, those who need assistance most are getting the least. In 1950, there were 560,000 black operated farms. Today there are only 98,000. In the same period, total black farm population fell from

[32]1955 Amendment to Hatch Act. 7 U.S.C., section 347a.

[33]U.S. Commission on Civil Rights. Federal Civil Rights Enforcement Effort. *One Year Later*. November 1971, pp. 130-131.

3,158,000 to 938,000. The average annual loss was 10.5 percent compared to 3.9 percent among the whites.[34]

USDA's own statistics show that those blacks who have remained on the farm fare less well than white farmers. 1970 median income figures show that white farm families can expect $7,016 per annum, whereas the black farm family could expect $3,037.[35]

Suits have been brought in three states against the Extension Service for overt and flagrant discrimination in hiring and service. In one decision, recently decided in Alabama against the Cooperative Extension Service, the court found that race discrimination was so pervasive and has so permeated the operations of the Alabama Extension Service that it felt compelled to issue a detailed decree which not only enjoined discrimination but also prescribed procedures for preventing future discrimination and for correcting the effect of past discrimination.[36]

In the process of investigation of the Alabama and Mississippi Extension Services, the Justice Department turned up some poignant statistics: of 67 county extension chairmen in Alabama, and of 83 chairmen in Misssissippi, none are black. In addition, despite the mandate to integrate, services are still not "cross racial". In Alabama, for example, 91 percent of the white agents' clients are white, 89 percent of the black agents' clients were black.[37]

SERVING AGRIBUSINESS

If the Extension Service is not comfortable with lower-income people and minorities, it does seem to be at ease in the company of agribusiness. Practically every state extension report points with pride to projects and demonstrations such as these:

> Texas extension agents assisted "a large East Texas poultry company" develop "drastic changes in egg gathering, handling and cleaning procedures and equipment adjustments." The grateful firm estimated that its gross income has "increased $1,040 per week."

> A 1972 California Extension Service conference on weeds focused on such topics as "A Bankers View of Weeds" and "What's New From Industry in Herbicides?"

> Michigan extension workers organized and conducted "Invest Tours," designed to introduce investors to the recreation and tourism potential of the state's upper peninsula.

[34]National Sharecroppers Fund, *op. cit.*, pp. 4, 6.
[35]*Ibid.*, pp. 4, 6.
[36]Strain vs Philpott. F.2D. (M.D. Ala.), filed September 1, 1971.
[37]*Ibid.*

Florida Extension conducted in-depth audits of both marketing and management firms in order to determine if the organizational structure and method of making decisions adequately carries out the overall objectives of the firm.

Agribusiness maintains the same close relations with Extension that it keeps with the colleges of agriculture and the experiment stations. In the annual report of the School of Agriculture and Life Sciences of North Carolina State University, for example, there is a listing of some 250 "Extension Service Cooperators," most of which are agribusiness corporations. A random selection of those are Allis Chalmers, American Cyanamid, Brown and Williamson Tobacco, Carnation, Chemagro, John Deere, Eli Lilly, Goodyear, IMC, Kraftco, Liggett and Myers, Montgomery Ward, Niagara Chemical, Proctor and Gamble, Ralston Purina, R. J. Reynolds, Sears Roebuck, Simplicity Pattern, S&H Green Stamps, Swift and Company, Tupperware, UniRoyal and Westinghouse Electric.

To an alarming degree, Extension agents are becoming salesmen for chemical companies. A recent article in *Farm Technology*, the magazine for county agents, offers this insight into corporate ties to Extension:

> We are impressed with the fact that much time is spent working closely with the industry agri-fieldmen and other company representatives. Nearly all states reported that this type of cooperation is increasing.

> A good example of this can be found in Arizona where weed specialists "hit the road" with the chemical company representatives and are involved in cooperative field tests and demonstrations.[38]

The Texas Extension Service reported a total of $139,869 from private contributors in 1970-1971. The bulk of that was from chemical companies, and the Service even maintained a separate Weed Control Demonstration Account.[39] Texas Extension reported that "twenty-five chemical companies supported weed control adaptive research and demonstrations during the year."

Farm Technology magazine reported on "The New Face of Agricultural Extension for the '70's," drawing on the comments of New Jersey's Extension Director:

> Gerwig made a statement that is particularly significant about today's extension workers. He said that all area agents in New Jersey are "on a first name basis" with chemical, plastic and fertilizer sales representatives

---

[38]*Farm Technology*. Vol. 27, no. 5 (Fall 1971), p. 16.

[39]Texas Agricultural Extension Service. "Annual Report of Gifts and Grants, September 1, 1970-August 31, 1971."

in their area. He added that cooperative demonstrations are held in many areas with materials furnished by agri-business concerns. Following this joint "result" meetings are held in cooperation with industry.[40]

In Florida, the extension service boasts of its salesmanship:

In cooperation with the Citrus Experiment Station and industry organizations, the Extension Service began a crash program in 1965 of selling chemical weed control to producers. In the four years from 1965 to 1969, grower acceptance of herbicides grew rapidly from zero acres to 350,000 acres under chemical weed control. . . . Grower meetings, seminars and printed materials have been used to promote acceptance of chemical controls.[41]

Like their research and teaching colleagues in the land grant complex, extension agents walk hand in hand with agribusiness. As in the case of the chemical industry, the agents frequently are focused so intently on corporate needs that they literally have become tax-supported extensions of agribusiness.

SERVING THE FARM BUREAU

No analysis of the Extension Service can ignore the long and continuing intimacy between it and the American Farm Bureau Federation.

The Farm Bureau, with a total membership of nearly two million families and local chapters in 2,800 counties, is the nation's largest, most powerful and affluent farm organization. Since its founding in 1909, the Bureau has become a four billion dollar business empire. And, as the self-proclaimed "spokesman for the American farmer," it speaks before government policy-makers on both agricultural and non-agricultural issues. It has consistently been one of the four or five most active lobbies in Washington. In *Dollar Harvest*,[42] a well-documented history of the Bureau, author Samuel Berger laid out these facts about the "farmer's spokesman":

1) The Farm Bureau has lobbied and spoken out against almost every ameliorative piece of social legislation since the New Deal: The War on Poverty program, medicare, federal aid to education, redevelopment, NLRB coverage for farm workers, and even price supports, the life-blood of the marginal farmer.

2) Through its various business enterprises, the Farm Bureau's membership has expanded to include at least 20 percent non-farm members, and yet it still claims to speak for the farmers. During the period from 1960-1970, the farm population shrank by five million people—during

[40]*Farm Technology, op. cit.*, pp. 13-14.
[41]IFAS, University of Florida. "Annual Report of Extension Work" 1969.
[42]Samuel R. Berger. *Dollar Harvest*. (Mass.: D. C. Heath and Co. 1971)

the same period, the Farm Bureau added nearly a million people to its roles. As one farmer wrote: "the Farm Bureau goes to Washington, D.C. and states they are talking for 2,500 farmers in my county. We have only 1,000 farmers, so just who are they talking for? It sure is not for me and a lot more just like me."

3) American agriculture has been built on the back of the farm worker, but they are not entitled to be full voting members of the Farm Bureau. Rather, they are only allowed a "non-voting associate" membership. Although the Bureau deals directly in procuring, housing and transporting migrant workers, it has consistently opposed legislation to improve their welfare, and it has violated the existing token regulations in its own camps. They also opposed "Freedom of Access" rights which gave farm workers and others the right to enter and leave work camps at free will.

4) Bureau cooperatives do volume business in selling feed, grain, fertilizer, and other equipment to the farmer member, although the prices are competitive with commercial sellers. The member does receive a certain amount of his cooperative purchases back in cooperative stock. But, more important to the low-income or marginal farmer, some Farm Bureau coops, have been loath to pay out dividends or to redeem shares, even upon death of the holder, using the money instead to capitalize.

5) The Farm Bureau may serve two masters—the "farmer" and agribusiness, but it *speaks* for agribusiness. It lines up with the food processor rather than the farmers and when it does line up with the farmer, it is the wealthy farmer.

The Extension Servicer's historical and current affiliation with this organization casts a deep shadow over its claim that it can never be part of the solution to the problems of rural America.

The multi-billion dollar Farm Bureau empire originated in humble origins. The individual chapters of the Farm Bureau come into existence as outgrowths of local farmer advisory committees, formed as a requirement of funding for the Extension Service. This early and significant co-mingling between the Farm Bureau and Extension still exists. The Bureau's growth can, in part, be attributed to the work of the extension agent, often to the exclusion of his other responsibilities.

The long range and as yet unsuccessful struggle to pry the two apart began in 1921 with a memorandum of separation signed by the president of the Farm Bureau and the head of the State Relations Board (predecessor of Federal Extension Service). The memorandum itself is a revealing document of the work of the county agents at that time. It stipulated that the county agents were to:

. . . perform service for the benefit of all the farming people of the country, whether members of the Farm Bureau or not . . . they will not themselves organize Farm Bureaus or similar organizations, conduct membership campaigns, solicit memberships, receive dues, handle Farm

Bureau funds, edit and manage the Farm Bureau publications, manage the business of the Farm Bureau, engage in commercial activities which are outside their duties as Extension agent.[43]

In the 1930's, the Farm Bureau-Extension Service linkages produced particularly blatant abuses:

. . . misuses of Extension franking privilege for pro-farm mailings; taking Farm Bureau dues directly out of AAA checks; and widespread recruitment of Farm bureau members by county agents.[44]

In 1945, a committee was appointed by Secretary Clinton Anderson and NASULGC to study the still-powerful connection between the Bureau and Extension Service. The committee concluded that "it is not sound public policy for Extension to give preferred service to any farm organization" and recommended that the formal operating relationship be discontinued. However, the committee went on to recommend that action on the matter be left up to the individual Farm Bureau and Extension leaders in each state. In 1947, a report described the extent of compliance:

. . . in nearly 400 counties in 13 states, the county agents were being paid at least in part by the Farm Bureau and were collecting Farm Bureau dues or keeping membership records . . . etc.[45]

In 1954, the bitter and intense feeling on the part of many individuals and other "non-bureau" farm groups was mounting. Perhaps more significantly, the Farm Bureau was faced with old state statutes that declared them "public institutions," because of their ties to the Extension Service. The Bureau found that these regulations now prohibited certain of their business activities, therefore, in many states, the statutes linking the two were repealed.

In 1964, in Illinois, a survey was made which showed that 60 percent of the farm advisors acknowledged that farmers thought of the Extension Farm Advisor's office as part of the Farm Bureau. The feeling was shared by 70 percent of the vocational agriculture teachers and 60 percent of the farmers themselves. The Extension Service in most states shared the same office space with the Farm Bureau—sometimes separated by partitions. The latest report released by the Federal Extension Service shows that the service rents offices from the Farm Bureau in 11 states. Of the more than $200 million spent on the Extension Service during fiscal year 1967, $3.8 million still come from private sources of which one million dollars came from the Illinois Farm Bureau alone.[46]

[43]*Ibid.*, p. 114.
[44]*Ibid.*, p. 115.
[45]*Ibid.*, p. 116.
[46]*Ibid.*, p. 126.

STRIKE THREE

Extension largely is irrelevant in today's rural America. The little good that it does manage to extend cetainly does not warrant an investment of 332 million tax dollars. Most rural Americans get little real help from that money and, even though agribusiness is able to use extension for its own profit needs, the Service is hardly a keystone in the plans of agribusiness. The fact is that Extension has deteriorated to the point that it is not much good to anybody, except maybe 15,000 extension agents who otherwise would have to look for work.

But Extension could be useful. It has a clientele that badly needs attention: independent family farmers, farm workers, small town businesses, small town government, non-farm rural people and others. Structurally, Extension is designed to reach these folks, reaching right down through the county agents and directly into the communities and homes of rural people. But that will mean getting out of the traveling salesmen's sample kit. It will mean a change in attitude at the top, and probably a change in personnel at the bottom. Such changes will not come from within.

VIII

Public Disclosure

Back in 1954 when Organic Gardening and Farming wanted to compare the amount of federal funds, state appropriations and industrial gifts which were available to state agricultural experiment stations, it was possible to turn to the "Report on the Agricultural Experiment Stations" issued every January by the Office of Experiment Stations.
That office doesn't exist any more, and finding the bare facts today is a bit more difficult, if not downright impossible in some cases.
Environment Action Bulletin[1]

Something in the neighborhood of three-quarters of a billion dollars is appropriated each year from national, state and county treasuries to support the teaching, research and extension of the land grant college complex. That complex is having an enormous impact on this country, yet, very little actually is known about it. One dramatic example is the fact that no one knows with any preciseness how much federal, state and local tax money is wrapped up in the complex.

ANNUAL REPORTS

The Morrill Act, the Hatch Act and the Smith-Lever Act all have specific provisions requiring annual reports on the land grant complex. The Hatch Act, for example, provides that "It shall be the duty of each of said (agricultural experiment) stations, annually, on or before the first day of February, to make to the Governor of the State or Territory in which it is located, a full and detailed report of its operations, including a statement of receipts and expenditures, a copy of which shall be sent to each of said stations, to the said Commissioners of Agriculture, and to the Secretary of the Treasury of the United States."[2] Most agricultural experiment stations comply with this direc-

[1]"Who Pays for Agricultural Research?" *Environment Action Bulletin*, January 9, 1971, p. 4.
[2]Hatch Act of 1887. 7 U.S.C., sections 334, 345.

134

tive, but not all. Oregon State Agricultural Experiment Station, for example, wrote that they do "not publish one in annual form nor does Oregon State University as it is one unit in a state system. The Extension Service also does not publish an annual report."[3]

But even having an annual report may not prove terribly enlightening:

> Some do not list all research projects, but merely list highlights.

> Some list research projects, but only by title, without even a brief description.

> Most do not include money figures with the individual projects, and very few reveal the source of the money.

> None contain any element of project continuity to show the total tax investment over the years in a particular investigation.

> Most contain only a very general financial breakdown, listing state, federal and "other" funds received and expended.

> Few offer any breakdown of industry contributions, naming the industry, the contribution and the project funded.

These are basic facts, but there is also *no* listing of more esoteric items, such as patents developed by the station and held by the college, or advisory structures surrounding the stations.

Most frustrating is any effort to obtain a national or regional picture from the annual reports. There is no uniformity of reporting—Purdue University's agricultural experiment station offers a relatively thorough breakdown of private contracts and grants, while the University of Wisconsin's annual report failed to give any financial breakdown at all. The *Environment Action Bulletin*, after attempting to determine how much money big business is pouring into agricultural research, observed in exasperation that "accountability seems to be a matter of conscience with each station."[4] The staff of the *Bullletin* concluded that "our office calculating machines couldn't help us compare one (report) with the other. We doubt whether a full-fledged computer could, given this sort of information."

CURRENT RESEARCH INFORMATION SYSTEM

CRIS, as it generally is known within the land grant community, represents the complex's effort to establish a computerized data bank

[3]Oregon State University. Letter to the Agribusiness Accountability Project from Mrs. Brenda Hood, administrative assistant to the president. December 27, 1971.

[4]"Who Pays for Agricultural Research?," *op. cit.*, p. 4.

on research projects. Inquiries to local experiment stations about their research are referred to CRIS in Washington. The service is not as efficient as one might hope. The greatest problem is obtaining up-to-date information. The service publishes an inventory of agricultural research, but the most recent inventory available now is the 1969-70 edition, and USDA is prepared to stand by the accuracy of only the 1969 figures in it.

There are numerous inadequacies in CRIS, not the least of which is the fact that information only is available regularly to USDA and land grant officials.[5] But the system remains the most authoritative and thorough source of information available on research projects. Only with a research classification print-out, for example, is it possible to perceive the reality of research budgets. For example, only by actually reading project descriptions within research categories can it be discovered that 60 percent of the research underway for "rural housing" really is directed toward the timber and homebuilding industries.

ELSEWHERE IN THE LAND GRANT COMPLEX

There are problems of public disclosure throughout the complex. For example, the Federal Extension Service collects information on the expenditure of county agents' time, but it is not gathered for the purpose of public release. FES considers it the prerogative of state extension services to release their own, more-detailed data. Even if all 50 states were to send their plan of work to an inquirer, it still would be impossible to get a national picture, since there is no uniformity of record keeping and disclosure. Florida and Indiana, for example, do not use the same categories of "audience served," nor do they even have the same number of categories. Even a simple matter like agent time spent is measured differently—Florida keeps records in man days, while Indiana uses man hours.

Deep within HEW, down the corridor to the Office of Education, through the Bureau of Higher Education and in the Division of College Support, an annual report is prepared, entitled "Statistics on Condition of Land-Grant Funds." It is a lackadaisical effort—a staff simply collecting forms sent to all land grant colleges and tabulating information from those that are returned. There is no enforcement power over the colleges, no serious review of the information supplied, just tabulation of what comes in. The mimeographed report, which is sent to

[5]The service is not authorized to charge for print-outs, so they are made available only to USDA and land grant officials. However, exceptions are made. Undoubtedly, members of Congress can obtain information from CRIS. Also, on special request by the Agribusiness Accountability Project, CSRS made available four print-outs.

all land grant colleges (but nowhere else), may or may not be accurate. Certainly the Division of College Support is unwilling to stand by the accuracy of the information, falling back on their role as simple reporters of whatever comes their way. The division does not know how the individual colleges arrive at their figures, nor does it know whether the colleges report all of their receipts and expenditures.

Also within HEW is the National Center for Educational Statistics, which collects more information than the Division of College Support. Unfortunately, that information is computerized and is not programmed to be broken out by land grant colleges. That makes it less than handy for those who want to know something about those colleges.

These are just among the many inadequacies that will confront any person interested in knowing what goes on in the land grant complex. Data is not supplied uniformly, it is not collected in a central location and it either is not reported or is reported in a form that cannot be easily obtained or understood. Even more significant is the fact that many fundamental questions go unasked and fundamental facts go unreported.

Millions of tax dollars annually are being spent by an agricultural complex that effectively operates in the dark. It is not that the land grant community deliberately hides from the public (though some of that goes on), but that the community makes no deliberate effort to reveal itself to the public. The farmer, the consumer, the rural poor and others with a direct interest in the work of the land grant complex can get no adequate picture of its work. Congress is no help; it does not take the time to probe the system, to understand it in detail and to direct its work in the public interest.

The land grant college complex has been able to get by with a minimum of public disclosure, and that has meant that the community has been able to operate with a minimum of public accountability.

IX

Conclusion And Recommendations

In their ability to serve the changing needs of a changing nation the Land-Grant Colleges and Universities have demonstrated their value.

Colleges for Our Land and Time[1]

America's land grant college complex has wedded itself to an agribusiness vision of automated, vertically-integrated and corporatized agriculture. It has accepted corporate agribusiness as an integral part of its community, applying some three-quarters of a billion tax dollars a year to help big business work its will in rural America.

The land grant community has done approximately nothing to extend the benefits of technology and management techniques to the vast majority of farmers and other rural Americans. These farmers, farm workers and small town residents are the source of rural America's strength. They are intelligent and hard working, and they clearly have the desire and the capacity to produce an abundance of good, nutritious food for the American consumer. USDA admits that the one and two man family farm is the most efficient that exists. Such people are a worthy investment—the true heirs to the egalitarian spirit and free enterprise ethic that spawned the land grant complex. But that complex has turned its back on these people and made its bed with corporate interests. It has been a deliberate choice—corporations over people.

There is nothing inevitable about the growth of agribusiness in rural America. While this country enjoys an abundance of relatively cheap food, it is not more food, not cheaper food and certainly not better food than that which can be produced by a system of family agriculture. And more than food rolls off the agribusiness assembly line: rural refugees, boarded up businesses, deserted churches, abandoned towns,

[1]Eddy. *Op. cit.*, p. 286.

broiling urban ghettos and dozens of other tragic social and cultural costs also are products of agribusiness. "The farmhouse lights are going out all over America," is the way it was put by Lee Staley, president of the National Farmers Organization:

> And every time a light goes out, this country is losing something. It is losing the precious skills of a family farm system that has given this country unbounded wealth. And it is losing free men.[2]

Had the land grant community chosen to put its time, money, its expertise and its technology into the family farm, rather than into corporate pockets, then rural America today would be a place where millions could live and work in dignity.

The colleges have mistaken corporate need as "the changing needs of a changing nation." That is proving to be a fatal mistake—not fatal for the corporations or for the colleges, but for the people of America. It is time to correct that mistake, to reorient the colleges so that they will begin to act in the public interest. It is time that America issued an ultimatum to the land grant complex: "adapt or die."

RECOMMENDATIONS

The land grant college complex must adjust its focus to meet the needs of a rural America in crisis. The complex must be returned to the people, shifting the preponderance of its resources into activities that will make rural America a place where millions of families can both live and make a living.

It is possible to suggest substantive change in the work of the land grant complex. It seems obvious, for example, that there must be a major emphasis in such areas as cooperative marketing structures, access to credit, land reform, housing and community utility systems, technological displacement, food quality and taste, non-chemical pest control, cost of agricultural in-puts, rural health systems and non-farm employment.

But it is not the place of this Task Force to determine the agenda of the land grant complex. That is the proper role of constituencies with a direct interest in the work of the complex: farmers, farm workers, rural businessmen, non-farm laborers, small town officials, the rural poor, big city mayors, consumers, environmentalists and even agribusinessmen.

Today, the complex serves only one constituency: corporate agribusiness. Others must get into this public complex, and they must get in on an equal footing with corporate executives. But the land

[2]Oren Lee Staley quoted in Nick Kotz. "U.S. Policy Handcuffs Small Farmer," *The Washington Post*, October 5, 1971.

grant community will not break off its monogamous relationship with agribusiness simply because it ought to do so. Significant change will come only under pressure.

The recommendations of the Task Force, therefore, are directed toward opening this closed world to public view and to participation by constituencies that today are locked out.

First, the Task Force calls for a full-scale public inquiry into the land grant college complex. Congress immediately should initiate a thorough investigation into the impact of the land grant effort, into the relationships between agribusiness and the land grant community, into the policy-making apparatus, into disclosure requirements and into all other aspects of the comilex. Congress should take its investigation onto the campuses and into the rural areas, seeking testimony at the local level from all constituencies that ought to be served by the land grant complex. To assist this congressional inquiry, members of Congress should immediately initiate an audit of the land grant complex by the General Accounting Office.

In addition to a national investigation by Congress, state legislatures should undertake investigations of the agricultural complex in their land grant institutions.

Second, the Task Force calls on the House and Senate agricultural appropriations subcommittees:

(1) to re-open this year's hearings on the agricultural research budgets in order to conduct a serious and meaningful examination of those budgets, including a detailed look at the exact nature of the land grant research now underway and proposed for fy 1973;

(2) to invite witnesses from constituencies and organizations that now stand outside the land grant-agribusiness community; and,

(3) to write into the committee reports on this year's agricultural appropriation a requirement that the Secretary of Agriculture establish a Research Review Committee that would develop broad research goals for the next decade. The RRC would evaluate current research policy and procedure, and it would recommend allocations of money and man years for a new, national research policy for agriculture and rural America.

This was attempted in a joint USDA-NASULGC study in 1966, but both the general and specific recommendations reflected the narrow focus of the closed community chosen to participate in that study. Unlike the 1966 study, the Research Review Committee would be required to include not only USDA,

the land grant community and agribusiness, but also representatives of urban and urban constituencies directly affected by
research policy.

Third, the Task Force calls on the Secretary of Agriculture
immediately to restructure the national advisory and policy-making
apparatus so that there is broadened in-put for research planning.
Both the National Agricultural Research Advisory Committee and the
Agricultural Research Policy Advisory Committee of USDA should
immediately be restructured to include a majority membership representing legitimate spokesmen for consumers, environmentalists, independent family farmers, farm workers, minorities, small town
businessmen, rural public officials and other interests directly affected
by the work of the land grant complex.

In addition, the Secretary of Agriculture, in cooperation with the
land grant community, should conduct a public review of advisory
structures at the campus level of the land grant complex. Out of that
review should come a restructuring and a formalizing of those advisory
committees, including procedural assurances that all constituencies
with a legitimate interest in the work of the land grant complex will
be represented.

Fourth, the Task Force calls on the Secretary of Agriculture, in
cooperation with the land grant community, immediately to initiate
public negotiations with "outside" constituencies to develop and pro-
mulgate procedures that will allow these interests, as well as
agribusiness, to initiate research requests and otherwise make use
of this public resource. All research requests should come through
these channels and should be public information.

Fifth, the Task Force calls for an immediate end to racial discrimination within the land grant complex. Research and extension money
should be allocated directly to the black land grant colleges on the
same basis as it is allocated to the white colleges. Federal money
should be withheld from any state land grant complex that does not
place its black institution on an equal footing with the white college.
Also, federal money should be withheld from the Extension Service
until that agency complies with the civil rights legislation of this country.

Sixth, the Task Force calls for legislation or regulations that would:

(1) prohibit land grant officials and other personnel from receiving
remuneration in conflict of interest, including compensation
for service on corporate boards of directors, retainers and other
fees for agribusiness consultations and private research grants
to test corporate products;

(2) prevent corporations from earmarking contributions to the land

grant complex for specific research that is proprietary in nature; and

(3) ensure that land grant patenting practices do not allow private gain from public expenditures without adequate, financial compensation to the public. Where exclusive licenses are necessary, an open bidding system should be employed.

Seventh, the Task Force calls for full public disclosure from the land grant complex. Specifically, legislation should be enacted to require an annual report from each land grant complex. The annual report should be filed at the end of each fiscal year; it should be filed with the Secretary of Agriculture and with the House and Senate agricultural appropriations subcommittees; and it should be public information, readily available. Information in annual reports should be detailed, complete and uniform. A national report, compiled from the state reports, should be prepared annually by the Secretary of Agriculture and distributed to the public.

Each annual report from the state land grant complexes should include the following:

(1) Deans' Narrative—an interpretation of the focus of teaching, research and extension during the past year and plans for the next year;

(2) Financial Report—detailed statement of receipts, expenditures and assets;

(3) Research Report—detailed listing of all research projects conducted and underway during the year, categorized under USDA's Research Problem Areas

(4) Patent Report—summary of all patents held or applied for, including:
   • patents licensed (to whom and terms of the agreement)
   • patent income received, by patent;

(5) Advisory Committees—listing of each committee, including its purpose, members and their affiliation; and,

(6) Research Foundation Report—detailed statement of the land grant complex's relationship to its foundation, including:

   • staff, officials and resources shared
   • money received from the foundation, including original source of the money, amount and purposes for which it is given
   • services or products delivered to the foundation
   • receipts, expenditures and assets of the foundation.

The USDA: A Fertile Field for "Deadwood"

by Karen Elliott House

Dalton Wilson has a nice salary, a long title and a clean desk.

Wilson, 52, is an assistant to an assistant administrator for management in the Foreign Agricultural Service of the Agriculture Department. The other day, when a reporter dropped in to chat, Wilson's desk top held a candy bar, a pack of cigarettes — and Wilson's feet. He was tilted back in his chair reading real-estate ads in The Washington Post.

Exactly what, the reporter asked, does a man with that title do?

"You mean, what am I *supposed* to do?" said Wilson with a chuckle. "Let me tell you what I did last year." It turns out that Wilson, whose annual pay is more than $28,000, spent the entire year trying to assess the adequacy and timeliness of the department's fats and oils publications. He says 1977 is shaping up as another slow year; he is planning another study, this one designed to justify the use of satellites to forecast crop production.

Wilson's pace is typical of the life at the Agriculture Department. With 80,000 full-time employees, the department has one bureaucrat for every 34 American farmers. Now that President Carter is setting out to reorganize the government to make it more efficient, a close look at the Agriculture Department provides a vivid picture of the problems he faces.

As the number of farmers has declined in recent years, the Agriculture Department has turned increasingly to self-promotion and has adroitly managed to continue doing outdated jobs while thinking up new jobs to do. The result is a huge bureaucracy engaged in scores of dubious tasks and seemingly beyond direction.

"No Secretary of Agriculture runs the department," says Rep.

Thomas Foley (D-Wash.), chairman of the House Agriculture Committee. "It's too big."

The department's full-time employees, plus 45,000 part-time helpers, occupy five buildings in Washington and spill out across the country into 16,000 others. Its employees direct self-awareness programs for women, write standards for watermelons and measure planted acreage for a dozen crops — even though governmental limitations on planting no longer exist.

The department is the government's biggest moneylender (it will lend $9 billion in 1977). It has also built more dams — two million so far — than any other government agency. And it is one of the government's top three publishers, with a $16 million annual printing bill. Part of that goes to print 28,000 types of forms used internally to keep track of department activities.

Agriculture Secretary Bob Bergland says he soon will ask every employee to furnish a written justification for his job. Bergland, who worked at the department in the 1960s, says it is distinguished by inefficiency and a lack of clear goals. "I intend to find out what's really necessary and eliminate the rest," he says.

But employees don't seem worried. "He'll never do it," says a young statistician, heaving his feet onto his desk. "He wouldn't have time to read them," a second man adds. A third man says, "Don't worry, guys — those with the least work to do will have the most time to justify their jobs."

Even a casual stroll through the department suggests something is awry. Throughout the main office building, old clocks are stopped at various hours as if time, too, had stopped. At all hours, hundreds of people mill about the corridors or linger in the large, sunny cafeteria.

Loafing became such a problem last year that the secretary's office sent a memo to supervisors requesting a crackdown on "significant problems of attendance in the Washington, D.C., complex." A second memo went to all employees warning that "tardiness, eating breakfast immediately after reporting for work, extended coffee breaks, excessive lunch periods and early departures" convey a "poor image to the public."

Today, laziness is still apparent and is a standard source of humor. Says a young man resting on a bench outside the cafeteria, "My only concern about work is breakfast, lunch, two coffee breaks, and being the first one out the door each evening." Sometimes the humor is unintentional. "I'd like to be sick tomorrow," a woman tells her ele-

vator companion, "but I can't. The woman I work with plans to be."
This lackadasical attitude irks J. P. Bolduc, the department's top management official. "There's too much deadwood around here," he says. "The answer is for every administrator to get rid of that in his agency, even if it causes a stink."

But instead of getting rid of the dead weight, the department rewards it. An internal memo shows that of the 45,000 employees eligible last year for merit pay increases, 44,956 received them. "We don't have that many super performers," Bolduc concedes when asked about the memo.

Motivation is difficult for many employees because their tasks seem pointless. Paul Beattie in the Agriculture Marketing Service spent much of last year drafting a standard for watermelons, including sketches illustrating a good one. He concedes that the standard which defines a bad melon in terms of its deformities and disfiguring spots, is rarely used by growers or retailers. Anyway, he says, most consumers know a good watermelon when they see one.

Ava Rodgers, the department's deputy assistant administrator for home economics, says she spends half her time traveling the country to coordinate activities of 4,000 home economists. Asked to describe a typical day in her office, Rodgers says, "I've answered the phone a couple of times this morning. That's about it. It's a normal day." She is paid $33,700 a year.

Elsewhere in the department, 2,000 people are busily planning new dam projects even though there is a 10-year backlog of such projects already planned and awaiting construction. Secretary Bergland says he issued an order several weeks ago halting further dam-construction planning, but Joe Haas, assistant administrator for water resources, says he hasn't heard of such an order. So the planning continues. "You need new planning to have a continuous workload," Haas explains.

One reason the department remains so big is that it continues to perform outdated tasks. A notable example is the Rural Electrification Administration, begun in 1935 to provide electricity to rural America. Today, 99 per cent of the rural homes have electricity, but the REA is still around and is getting bigger.

No longer does it simply lend money to build electricity lines. This year the agency will guarantee $3.5 billion in government loans for generating electricity, up from $1.2 billion last year. "We make a $40 million loan before lunch and never think a thing about it," says David Askegaard, deputy REA administrator.

An amazing ability of officials to dream up new tasks also contributes to the department's size. During the Depression, President Roosevelt created the Resettlement Administration, currently known as the Farmers Home Administration, to make loans to help farm families remain on their land. To qualify, a farmer could have no more than one hired hand, two mules and two cows. Today, he doesn't even have to be a farmer.

The department and Congress have expanded the program to permit loans to any poor person in a community of fewer than 50,000 residents. And loans may be used to finance sewer and water systems, recreational centers, and business and industrial construction. These low-interest Farmers Home Administration loans this year are expected to total $6.7 billion.

"Now the rural areas have everything town's got but grime and crime," says Mississippi Democrat Jamie Whitten, chairman of the House Agriculture Appropriations Subcommittee since 1949.

Having powerful congressional friends like Whitten is a big reason some of these outdated programs survive and grow. Every president since Harry Truman has tried to curtail conservation payments to farmers, who often use the money to enhance production rather than preserve their land. But Whitten always blocks such cutbacks. This year, farmers will receive $190 million in conservation payments. These payments help keep the 13,500 Soil Conservation Service employees busy.

Congress also strongly influences where the department spends its research funds — $592 million this year. Largely because southern lawmakers are prominent on the agriculture committees, the department spends twice as much — about $22 million a year — on cotton research as it does on corn, wheat or soybean research, even though the latter crops are more important to farm income.

There are other contradictions. The department will spend $4 million this year on peanut research, including efforts to increase yields; at the same time it doles out $188 million in payments for surplus peanuts.

Another questionable activity is the department's market research. A typical project is aimed at producing oranges of uniform size to make packing easier. Recently the department spent $45,000 on a study to determine for the food industry how long Americans commonly take to cook breakfast. Similar research projects are planned for cooking lunch and dinner.

The department also spends considerable time and money on self-promotion. With a $16 million annual public-relations budget, the department's 600 publicists crank out 2,500 press releases a year and about 70 television films. Another $16 million a year is spent printing an estimated 54 million books, brochures and pamphlets to distribute to the public.

A large portion of the publications are distributed on behalf of Congressmen — a practice that publicity-conscious lawmakers remember when voting on the department's appropriations. Each member of Congress is entitled to 10,000 agriculture publications a year for his constituents.

The department maintains six full-time employees to mail the requested brochures for each congressman and to keep track of how many remain in his "bank." Those who run the "bank" say that some senators save their annual allotment to blitz constituents in an election year and that other urban congressmen trade the brochures to rural colleagues for football tickets. By law, the records of all these transactions must be kept secret.

Overall, the department hasn't any resemblance to the nine-employee agency created 105 years ago. That department's goals were limited and clear: "to procure, propagate and distribute among the people new and valuable seeds and plants."

Bergland wants to streamline the department and focus its resources on rural development. He says he won't fight if President Carter moves the 45,000-employee Forest Service, which grows and cuts timber in national forests, to the Interior Department. And he would accept a decision to move $7 billion in feeding programs to the Health, Education and Welfare Department. These two moves would eliminate half of Bergland's full-time employees and about half of the department's $15 billion annual budget.

Those familiar with the department are highly skeptical, however, that Carter and Bergland will be able to do much about the scores of programs that have outlived their usefulness. "Survival is the strongest urge in Washington," says former Agriculture Secretary Earl Butz, currently a professor at Purdue University. "Carter and Bergland are going to find it difficult to reorganize because Congress won't go along with much. You can move the boxes around, but then all you have is the new program plus the old one."

ADDITIONAL VIEWS

AGRICULTURE AND RELATED AGENCIES APPROPRIATIONS FOR 1978

HEARINGS

BEFORE A

SUBCOMMITTEE OF THE COMMITTEE ON APPROPRIATIONS HOUSE OF REPRESENTATIVES

NINETY-FIFTH CONGRESS

FIRST SESSION

SUBCOMMITTEE ON AGRICULTURE AND RELATED AGENCIES

JAMIE L. WHITTEN, Mississippi, *Chairman*

FRANK E. EVANS, Colorado
BILL D. BURLISON, Missouri
MAX BAUCUS, Montana
BOB TRAXLER, Michigan
BILL ALEXANDER, Arkansas
ROBERT L. F. SIKES, Florida
WILLIAM H. NATCHER, Kentucky

MARK ANDREWS, North Dakota
J. KENNETH ROBINSON, Virginia
JOHN T. MYERS, Indiana

ROBERT B. FOSTER and CHARLES G. HARDIN, *Staff Assistants*

APRIL 20, 1977.

POLICY OFFICIALS OF UNITED STATES DEPARTMENT OF AGRICULTURE AND THE FOOD AND DRUG ADMINISTRATION

WITNESSES

JOHN COYLE WHITE, DEPUTY SECRETARY OF AGRICULTURE

M. RUPERT CUTLER, ASSISTANT SECRETARY FOR CONSERVATION, RESEARCH, AND EDUCATION

DALE HATHAWAY, ASSISTANT SECRETARY FOR INTERNATIONAL AFFAIRS AND COMMODITY PROGRAMS

ROBERT H. MEYER, ASSISTANT SECRETARY FOR MARKETING SERVICES

CAROL TUCKER FOREMAN, ASSISTANT SECRETARY FOR FOOD AND CONSUMER SERVICES

ALEX MERCURE, ASSISTANT SECRETARY FOR RURAL DEVELOPMENT

HOWARD W. HJORT, DIRECTOR, AGRICULTURAL ECONOMICS

JEROME A. MILES, DIRECTOR OF FINANCE, DEPARTMENT OF AGRICULTURE

DEPARTMENT OF HEALTH, EDUCATION, AND WELFARE, FOOD AND DRUG ADMINISTRATION, DONALD KENNEDY, COMMISSIONER OF FOOD AND DRUGS

PURPOSE OF THE COMMITTEE HEARING

Mr. WHITTEN. The subcommittee will please come to order.

Gentlemen, the committee has been faced with quite an unusual year, and the committee is holding this special hearing as a result.

I do not know how long we should continue this hearing, because I have felt it somewhat unfair to quiz too much those who have just been appointed to a job.

On the other hand, as you know, we must go to the House floor with a bill on appropriations, and to do that after not even having met you, or given you a chance to be heard, would just not do. We have done the very best we could.

I think to some degree that problems may result from the delay in your appointments—problems for the Nation, for the committee, and for the Department.

TOP POLICY LEADERSHIP

In the years I have been here, we have established a policy that we do not have any hearings with the civil service people unless we also have somebody here from the Department, at the top level, who can speak to policy.

That came because of the experience we have had with civil service people who attempted to handle the policy questions, and not only crossed it up, but frequently spoke contrary to the policy of the top people involved. Here we are past the middle of April, and we have had a Department that has been virtually leaderless.

I was one of those who had the privilege of recommending Bob Bergland, the Secretary. I know him to be a very good man.

RECENT NEWS ARTICLES

The Wall Street Journal wrote up a deplorable situation in the Department.

Now, the young lady who wrote this talked to me at great length, and I explained the part that agriculture played in our standard of living. At least I tried to, although I see no reference to that in her article. I find she talked to folks in the Department, who also explained the interrelationships of the various aspects of the Agriculture Department, the part it plays in the economy, and our standard of living. I am told she did not follow any of that, so she might have intended to write the kind of article she did. If so, she certainly found what she was looking for, because there has been nobody running around telling the people down there what to do. I do hope we can see you get behind those doors and get the Department operating.

IMPORTANCE OF AGRICULTURE

Less than 5 percent of the American people—those who engage in agriculture—free the rest of us to do something else. And in order to start out in farming today they must invest a great deal of money; an average of around $200,000, which is far more than it takes to start some other kind of business. Today, to start out in farming it almost takes enough money to start a bank, and enough nerve to rob one. With those conditions facing us, we need to get this Department off the ground.

About 85 percent of the United States is not in the major cities, but in smaller cities and in rural areas.

In going over the list of experiences that all of you have had, with some exception, of course, everybody seems to have had a whole lot more experience in protecting the consumer instead of promoting the production comparatively.

Today we now have a lot of hamstringing in connection with restricting the use of the tools that are so essential to agriculture. I was with a dealer recently who handles farm equipment. He said that about $2,400 of the cost of the average tractor is now the result of requirements through various Government regulations. It just adds to the cost. When you look through all of this, it is frightening. I look forward to meeting with all of you, and getting some reassurance that there is an appreciation of agriculture as the backbone of the United States.

May I say that I am a lawyer. I found out long ago that the best way to farm was to get a salary on the side. I am proud of those who are in agriculture. But a few years ago in the Department, there was a new farm program that was thought up by the young executives.

I told the Secretary of Agriculture that he had better study history, or he will have to relive it. Unless we study the mistakes of the past, and the reasons for them, we will be in for trouble. As for the young lady who wrote that article, I would say that she probably had not read anything and has had no experience. The article shows that she has not had any time to study what went on before.

NEED FOR AGRICULTURAL CONSERVATION

Now, for the record, growing crops is what has made this country great for many years. But in the process, we wore out about 40 percent of our land and we used up about 60 percent of our timber. These various Government programs we have had, the agricultural conservation programs, for instance, where the landowner puts up about 50 percent of the cash money, and his labor, which amounts to about two-thirds of the costs, have resulted in having had over 1 million Americans engaged in restoring the environment over the years. In recent years, we have seen that program largely strangled by the attitude of its administrator in the Department.

We have had any number of pools, as we call them in some places, ponds in others, tanks in others, which have contributed greatly to the food supply. Cattle will not go so far, as some of you know, for water. So if you do not have water, you are limited in grazing, and so forth.

In the dust bowl days of the early 1930's we recognized that we had to do something and so we started out on these programs. But the thing I do not find in much of what I read today, particularly by these newer people dealing with agriculture, is the realization that agriculture is the biggest market for industry and labor.

AGRICULTURAL PROGRAMS IN GOVERNMENT

I have heard two Secretaries of Agriculture who said that agriculture is largely taken for granted, even in top Government circles.

In the period I have been here, I have dealt with a whole lot of different subjects. Next to Mr. Mahon, I have been on the committee longer than anyone else, and in that period, I have been on a number of subcommittees—Defense, Military Construction, Public Works, Interior, you name it.

I have stayed with this subcommittee because I think it is basic.

If you study the depression, you will see that it started with a breakdown in agricultural income. The farm program, contrary to many people today think, was not started as a program for farmers. It was to restore purchasing power and get the strength back up.

STATEMENT OF T. W. EDMINSTER
ADMINISTRATOR, AGRICULTURAL RESEARCH SERVICE

As we put the 1978 budget together, it addressed the high priority research problems facing the United States and world agriculture. U.S. food policy and the role agricultural science and technology play in that policy have been expressed through the International Food Conference in Rome, Italy, the Kansas City Food Conference, congressional oversight hearings, world food and nutrition reports of the National Academy of Sciences, and countless other reviews and articles published over the past several years.

The budget request is being made with an awareness that, as America looks ahead to its third century, an ever-expanding, interdependent world population will look to America for more food, more fiber and more agricultural technology. Further, the proposed research will contribute to energy conservation. The proposed research on nitrogen fixation will reduce our dependence on fertilizer nitrogen manufactured with fossil fuels.   ·

Expanding world food requirements and changing agricultural policies are placing added pressures on the U.S. agricultural research capacity which has been on a resource plateau for well over 10 years. That is, our research dollars currently have a purchasing power about equivalent to our appropriations in 1966 and we have 890 fewer scientists and support staff. Past research funding and staffing levels stand challenged as insufficient to sustain an aggressive export-oriented agriculture, to supply the increasing food production, transportation, storage, processing, and dietary demands of a world population that will nearly double in 25 years. In brief, the research community is being called upon to provide the technology that will permit the production, 25 years from now, of twice as much food and fiber as we have learned to produce since the dawn of history. We believe the current proposals for expanded Federal research programs together with the new competitive research grant programs will enable us to meet these urgent needs for agricultural research.

PROPOSALS

The fiscal year 1978 budget provides for an appropriation of $319,-719.000.

Within the agency proposal is a request of $27,600,000 to initiate a new departmental competitive grants program with an estimated cost of $150 million over a 5-year period. This program will involve competitive grants to universities, private organizations, and other governmental agencies. Research to be undertaken will initially concentrate on improving crop production through research on photosynthesis, nitrogen fixation, genetic engineering, and plant protection with emphasis on selected biological stress areas through mission-oriented basic research. Competitive grant research will complement the ongoing efforts of the USDA agencies land grant universities, and private organizations. Not only will it accelerate this high priority research but also will draw from a larger group of capable scientists in helping to solve these problems. In developing such a program, it is imperative that current base and in-house programs be continued and strengthened to assure core leadership in national planning efforts and to provide effective national coordination for the total research community. To meet projected 21st century world food needs, food production and energy conservation will require support from the entire research community. The U.S. Department of Agriculture must supply leadership to this endeavor. The proposed grant program is recognition of the need and a clear signal that the Department accepts that responsibility.

MANAGEMENT OF GRANT PROGRAM

I think it important to note that in our testimony last year we described in considerable detail this new management and planning system which ties together all ongoing ARS research efforts into nationally planned and coordinated programs. Our national research programs have now been formulated and documented. They form the basis for managing research programs financed by appropriations made available to this Service. The Department now envisions that these national research programs will provide the base for coordination and effective management of the mission-oriented program. The national research programs can help provide the framework for coordinating currently fragmented research done at several locations outside the traditional agricultural research community and can identify areas of research that can contribute toward meeting our national priorities.

CURRENT STATUS REPORT

Ample evidence exists that we are concentrating our research efforts in priority areas. Public and scientific debate at various forums have identified many of the national priority agricultural research needs. We are pleased to report that programs of this Service are addressing these priorities as effectively as possible.

The infusion of additional resources appropriated for fiscal year 1977, particularly the $3,312,000 for repairing and maintaining existing facilities has helped to meet some of the fiscal emergencies faced this agency in previous years. We have had to make some adjustments to accommodate unfunded congressional priorities. For example, the industrial fats research at Wyndmoor, Pa. has been continued in part, as directed, by making adjustments in other work including termination of the contract work on cottonseed protein.

CHALLENGES

Currently, we are in the process of determining how best to maintain flexibility in responding quickly to unexpected and emerging research needs. Almost daily new and unexpected needs for research are brought to my attention by various segments of the agricultural community. Recently, emergency situations have occurred that required strengthened research efforts for brucellosis, bluetongue, cattle fever ticks, mediterranean fruit fly, and citrus black fly. Pressure is mounting from other sources as we see the industrial private sector support of agricultural research being increasingly redirected to defensive activities to cope with the growing intensity of regulatory pressures. This is particularly true in the food safety and environmental areas. Research needs of our sister action agencies continue to expand. The Agricultural Marketing Service, Federal Grain Inspection Service, Animal and Plant Health Inspection Service, Food and Nutrition Service, and others are having to undertake added work to meet issues in environmental protection, food safety, and related areas. The challenge for the Agricultural Research Service is to sort out the first priority research needs of the entire research community, and, if necessary, adjust our ongoing programs as required. To do so effectively requires a continuing assessment of our efforts and the determination to terminate, if necessary, programs not of a first priority nature.

Available Funds and Man-Years
1976 and Estimated, 1977 and 1978

Item	Actual 1976		Estimated 1977		Estimated 1978	
	Amount	Man-Years	Amount	Man-Years	Amount	Man-Years
Agricultural Research: Service:	a/		a/			
Regular appropriation:	$281,839,000	9,060	$280,589,000	9,474	$319,719,000	9,484
Scientific activities overseas (Special Foreign Currency Program) ....:	7,500,000	15	7,500,000	15	7,500,000	15
Total ....:	289,339,000	9,075	288,089,000	9,489	327,219,000	9,499
Deduct allotments to other agencies .....:	-827,912	-15	-1,757,000	-15	-1,926,000	-25
Net ....:	288,511,088	9,060	286,332,000	9,474	325,293,000	9,474
Obligations under other USDA appropriations:						
Animal and Plant Health Inspection Service--emergency programs and field station services ..:	3,905,518	115	3,981,947	120	3,981,947	120
Food and Nutrition Service--improved dietary nutrition .:	296,005	17	348,898	17	348,898	17
National Agricultural Library-- various services ..:	303,467	- -	348,293	- -	348,293	- -
Soil Conservation Service--field station services ..:	235,109	2	196,129		196,129	2
Economic Research Service--including P.A.S.A. and training of foreign nationals ....:	825,660	29	3,032,446	60	3,032,446	60
Agricultural Marketing Service--field station services ..:	129,399	- -	111,199	- -	111,199	- -
Coordinated Departmental Services ....:	152,186	6	137,369	6	137,369	6
Miscellaneous reimbursements ....:	7,582	- -	34,325	2	34,325	2
Total Other USDA Appropriations ..:	5,854,926	169	8,190,606	207	8,190,606	207
Total, Agricultural Appropriation ......:	294,366,014	9,229	294,522,606	9,681	333,483,606	9,681
Other Federal Funds .:	7,379,175	116	9,378,427	115	9,378,427	115
Non-Federal Funds ...:	1,503,766	35	1,230,967	34	1,230,967	34
Total, Agricultural Research Service ....:	$303,248,955	9,380	$305,132,000	9,830	$344,093,000	9,830

	1976 Actual	1977 Estimated	1978 Estimated
End-of-Year Employment:			
Permanent full-time	8,383	8,403	8,423
Other	1,436	1,350	1,350
Total included in ceilings ....,	9,819	9,753	9,773
Number of disadvantaged youth	456	600	600
TOTAL	10,275	10,353	10,373

a/ Excludes $1,000,000 reappropriation.

(a) Agricultural Research Service

Appropriation Act, 1977	$270,576,000 a/
Budget Estimates, 1978	319,719,000
Increase in appropriation	+49,143,000

Adjustments in 1977:
Appropriation Act, 1977	$270,576,000	
Supplemental Appropriations:		
Pay Costs	+10,013,000	
Adjusted base for 1978		280,589,000
Budget Estimate, 1978		319,719,000
Increase over adjusted 1977		$+39,130,000

a/ Excludes reappropriation of $1,000,000 of prior year funds for additional labor, subprofessional and junior scientific help in the field.

SUMMARY OF INCREASES AND DECREASES
(on basis of adjusted appropriation)

	1977	Increase or Decrease	1978 Estimate
Program Changes:			
Providing for food needs in the third century	$ 9,418,000	$+5,250,000(1)	$ 14,668,000
Competitive Grant Research Fund		+27,600,000(2)	27,600,000
Repair and Maintenance	3,312,000	+3,904,000(3)	7,216,000
Pesticide Impact Assessment Program	a/	+1,020,000(4)	1,020,000
Annualization of pay increases effective FY 1977	10,013,000	+1,012,000(5)	11,025,000
GSA Space Rental	1,758,000	+258,000(6)	2,016,000
USDA Working Capital Fund Services	(4,515,000)	+536,000(7)	536,000
All Other	255,638,000	- - -	255,638,000
Total, Program Changes	$280,139,000	$+39,580,000	$319,719,000
Facility Changes:			
Elimination of non-recurring facility items	450,000	-450,000(8)	
TOTAL AVAILABLE	$280,589,000	$+39,130,000	$319,719,000

a/ Excludes proposed supplemental of $1,020,000.

PROJECT STATEMENT
(on basis of adjusted appropriation)

	1976	1977 (Estimated)	Increase or Decrease	1978 (Estimated)
1. Research on animal production:				
(a) Animal production efficiency research ...:	$ 48,638,068:	$ 56,246,000:	$ +1,180,000:	$ 57,426,000
(b) Research on housing ....:	377,017:	368,000:	+13,000:	381,000
Total, Research on animal production ....:	49,015,085:	56,614,000:	+1,193,000:	57,807,000
2. Research on plant production:				
(a) Crop production efficiency research ...:	90,041,144:	105,496,000:	+7,665,000:	113,161,000
(b) Tropical and subtropical agricultural research .:	508,533:	679,000:	+11,000:	690,000
Total, Research on plant production ....:	90,549,677:	106,175,000:	+7,676,000:	113,851,000
3. Research on the use and improvement of soil, water, and air:				
(a) Research on conservation and use of land and water resources and maintaining environmental quality ....:	21,670,876:	24,892,000:	+1,389,000:	26,281,000
(b) Research on watershed development ....:	8,324,400:	10,123,000:	+230,000:	10,353,000
Total, Research on the use and improvement of soil, water & air ....:	29,995,276:	35,015,000:	+1,619,000:	36,634,000
4. Processing, storage, distribution, nutrition and food safety, and consumer services research:				
(a) Processing, storage and distribution efficiency research ....:	50,343,957:	53,249,000:	+565,000:	53,814,000
(b) Research to expand agricultural exports ......:	2,114,232:	2,254,000:	+51,000:	2,305,000
(c) Food & nutrition research ....:	9,179,039:	13,969,000:	+409,000:	14,378,000
(d) Research to improve human health and safety:	11,125,047:	12,127,000:	+447,000:	12,574,000
(e) Research on consumer services ....:	473,730:	593,000:	+20,000:	613,000
Total, Processing, storage and distribution, nutrition and food safety, and consumer services research ....:	73,236,005:	82,192,000:	+1,492,000:	83,684,000
5. Competitive grant research fund ....:	- -	- -	+27,600,000:	27,600,000
6. Support services for other USDA Agencies ....:	135,000:	143,000:	- -	143,000
7. Construction of facilities:	29,930,000:	450,000:	-450,000:	- -
8. Contingency research fund :	a/	1,000,000:	- -	1,000,000
Unobligated balance ....:	9,977,957:	- -	- -	- -
Subtotal ....:	282,839,000:	281,589,000:	+39,130,000:	320,719,000
Deduct reappropriation for Special Fund ....:	-1,000,000:	-1,000,000:	- -	-1,000,000
Total, Available or estimate :	281,839,000:	280,589,000:	+39,130,000:	319,719,000

EXPLANATION OF PROGRAM

Under the Agriculture and Related Agencies Appropriation Act of 1977, the
Agricultural Research Service carries out the following activities:

1. Research on animal production.--Research is conducted to improve livestock
    productivity (including poultry) through improved breeding, feeding, and
    management practices and to develop methods for controlling diseases, para-
    sites, and insect pests affecting them. Research is also conducted on
    improved rural housing.

2. Research on plant production.--Research is conducted to improve plant producti-
    vity through improved varieties of food, feed, fiber, and other plants; develop
    new crop resources; and improve crop production practices, including methods
    to control plant diseases, nematodes, insects, and weeds.

3. Research on the use and improvement of soil, air, and water.--Research is
    conducted to improve the management of natural resources, including investiga-
    tions to improve soil and water management, irrigation and conservation
    practices; to protect natural resources from harmful effects of soil, water,
    and air pollutants and to minimize certain agricultural pollution problems,
    and to determine the relation of soil types and water to plant, animal, and
    human nutrition. The research includes studies on hydrologic problems of
    agricultural watersheds. Research is also conducted on the application of
    remote sensing techniques in meeting agricultural problems and on effects of
    the reduction of ozone.

4. Processing, storage, distribution, nutrition and food safety and consumer
    services research.--Research is conducted to develop new and improved foods,
    feeds, fabrics and industrial products and processes for agricultural commodi-
    ties for domestic and foreign markets, including ways to minimize processing
    wastes. Research is conducted on the processing, transportation, storage,
    wholesaling and retailing of products; on human nutritional requirements; and
    the composition and nutritive value of food as needed by consumers and by
    Federal, State and local agencies administering food and nutrition programs.

    Research is conducted on problems of human health and safety, including means
    to insure the safety of food and feed supplies; control insect pests of man
    and his belongings; reduce the hazards to human life resulting from pesticide
    residues, tobacco, and other causes, and on consumer services.

5. Competitive grant research fund.--These funds will support competitive research
    grants to complement the efforts of USDA agencies, universities, and private
    research organizations. The objectives of this program are to emphasize basic
    research critical to food production and to obtain the participation of out-
    standing researchers in the entire U.S. scientific community.

The research performed by the Agricultural Research Service is authorized by the
Department of Agriculture Organic Act of 1862 (5 U.S.C. 511) and the Research and
Marketing Act of 1946, as amended (7 U.S.C. 427, 427i).

STATUS OF THE SPECIAL FOREIGN CURRENCY RESEARCH PROGRAM (SFCRP)

In Fiscal year 1958, the Department initiated a research grant program abroad utilizing foreign currencies from the sale of surplus agricultural commodities under Title I of Public Law 480. Originally confined to market development research authorized by Section 104(b) (1) of P.L. 480, as amended, the program was subsequently expanded to include agricultural and forestry research under Section 104(b) (3) of the law, as amended. In fiscal year 1966, the authorization changed to permit the use of all excess currencies for work performed under the Special Foreign Currency Program. Activities sponsored fall into the following general areas:

1. <u>Agricultural research</u>, including research on plant and animal production; use and improvement of soil, water and air; and research on marketing, use and effects of agricultural products.

2. <u>Forestry research</u>, including research on the protection of forests from fires, diseases and insects; on methods and procedures for increasing the growth of managed forests, and on properties and uses of forest products.

3. <u>Agricultural economics research</u>, including farm and market economics research and foreign trade analysis.

Dollar-financed research in these areas is conducted by the Agricultural Research Service, the Forest Service, and the Economic Research Service in their respective areas of functional and subject-matter responsibilities. Research under this program is designed to complement and not to duplicate or displace the dollar-financed research activities of these agencies.

Within the Department, primary responsibility for administration of this program is assigned to the Agricultural Research Service. The activities are coordinated with operations in the Forest Service, Economic Research Service, and the Foreign Agricultural Service by the Director, International Programs Division, ARS. The Director coordinates development of broad policies for operations of the program and coordinates the activities of the various Department agencies in carrying out research financed by foreign currencies. Initial arrangements and budget clearances for the research in foreign countries are made through the Department of State as required by Executive Order 10900, Section 3(b) and (c), and through the Agricultural Attaches of the Foreign Agricultural Service of the Department.

Prior to executing any research agreement with a foreign institution, the Department again consults with the Agricultural Attaches and Heads of Missions to insure that the proposed projects would be consonant with the foreign policy of the United States.

Care is exercised to make certain that research projects undertaken benefit American agriculture and do not develop undesirable competition for American agricultural products abroad. Careful attention is given to the type of institution conducting research under this program to make certain it has the facilities, equipment, and personnel to carry out sound and productive research. Because of these high standards, about 58 percent of the proposals received from foreign institutions have been rejected by the Department; 41 percent of the proposals have been accepted, and the agreements have been executed or are awaiting execution. Final determination has not yet been made on acceptance or rejection of the remaining 1 percent.

U.S. research priorities, as well as foreign country participant priorities, are constantly updated and publicized through personal contacts and written communications. Consequently, the bulk of the proposals currently submitted for consideration are generally of the highest interest to U.S. agriculture.

Selected Examples of Recent Progress: Through September 30, 1976, a total of 1,705 research agreements have been obligated with foreign research institutions. In fiscal year 1976, 64 new agreements were obligated. Agreements vary in total amount for the life of the project from approximately $12,000 to slightly over $475,000 dollar equivalent. Recent examples of research progress under these agreements follow:

1. New Techniques Found for Producing Virus-Free Citrus Seedlings. One of the research frontiers in plant science is producing new plants from old through tissue culture techniques. Research in India has produced virus-free citrus plants from infected stocks and is accelerating multiplication of virus-free rootstocks for citrus orchards.

2. Nutritious Low-Cost Meals Developed for Young Children. Studies in India demonstrated ways of supplementing cereals to supply sufficient protein and other nutrients or maintaining adequate nutrition without adding large amounts of animal products. The diets formulated in these studies could be modified using foods available in the United States or in any other country to provide adequate nutrition at low cost.

3. Yugoslavia Blackberries have Potential for U.S. Research in Yugoslavia identified four blackberry lines with outstanding hardiness and resistance to pests and diseases. Another line was found to be outstanding in producing multiple berry clusters. Use of the native Yugoslavian blackberry material has been initiated in the U.S. to develop the type of coldhardiness required for the mid-Atlantic States.

4. New Techniques Developed for Crop Improvement. Scientists in Israel working with peanuts developed techniques for detecting natural-occuring differences in the non-chromosomal inheritance of plant cells. They also discovered several new methods for producing these unique mutations. This project has generated some 51 cross-combinations that are now being used to improve domestic peanuts and the techniques are being applied in breeding improved corn and pearl millet.

5. Biological Control Found for Tea Scale Insect. The tea scale is a serious pest of ornamental plants in the South, and of mango orchards in Florida. A small wasp which parasitizes this scale insect was imported into Florida from India. Information after the first release of the parasite in the Gainesville, Florida, area have confirmed its potential as an effective method for control of the scale insect.

6. New Control Developed for Khapra Beetle. The khapra beetle is a major destroyer of stored grains and food products in many countries. Research in Pakistan has established several methods that improve the effectiveness of eight insecticides and combinations of insecticides for controlling khapra beetle. Results from this project help lessen the hazards of costly reinfestations of stored grain in the U.S.

7. Polish Researchers Demonstrate Efficiency of Ultra Low-Volume (ULV) Spray Systems to Protect Apple Trees. With the (ULV) system, apple trees are protected using half as much pesticide. With low volume requirements, the likelihood of environmental hazards are reduced. The use of lighter equipment causes less soil compaction. Also hazards for the operators are reduced since mixing and washing stations at the orchards are eliminated.

Special Foreign Currency Program
Research Proposals and Agreements by Subject Matter
(Cumulative: Through September 30, 1976)

	Number of Proposals				Total Number of Agreements Obligated		Total Number of Agreements Currently Active	
	Received	Rejected	Awaiting Modification Negotiation or Review	Approved (Proposals) Awaiting Obligation	Number	Dollar Equivalent	Number	Dollar Equivalent
Agricultural Research Service	3,958	2,310	57	160	1,431	$ 95,267,938	324	$28,906,667
Forestry Research	499	250	6	17	226	14,926,311	53	5,162,802
Agricultural Economics Research	163	108	7	4	44	2,460,664	9	947,220
Statistical Reporting Service	3	2	-	-	1	32,073	-	- 1,467
Animal & Plant Health Ins. Service	1	-	-	-	1	136,806	1	136,806
TOTALS	4,624	2,670	70	181	1,703	$112,823,792	387	$35,152,028

Obligations, Expenditures and Conversions of Foreign Currencies

Obligations: Through September 30, 1976, a total of $120,287,021 (including $5,068,131 for administrative expenses) has been obligated for activities under the Special Foreign Currency Program. In fiscal year 1977, an additional $8,904,632 will be used. These obligations are summarized as follows:

Cumulative Obligations through F.Y. 1977
(Dollars in Thousands)

Fiscal Year	Market Development Research (Sec. 104(b)(1))	Agricultural and Forestry Research (Sec. 104(b)(3))	Translations of Publications and Scientific Cooperation, Executive Office of the President a/	Total
1958	$ 371.5	$ --	$ --	$ 371.5
1959	1,651.8	--	1.7	1,653.5
1960	2,230.5	--	793.2	3,023.7
1961	1,893.2	1,832.4	1,565.2	5,290.8
1962	2,859.0	5,294.6	595.8	8,749.4
1963	2,566.3	5,000.7	248.6	7,815.6
1964	3,214.8	4,466.6	555.5	8,236.7
1965	3,485.8	5,408.1	72.2	8,966.1
1966	703.7	3,877.4	-199.5	4,381.6
1967	1,620.6	7,953.2	114.5	9,688.3
1968	991.9	6,317.0	- 44.1	7,264.8
1969	971.9	4,733.2	--	5,705.1
1970	790.5	4,076.0	--	4,866.5
1971	654.0	4,171.8	--	4,823.8
1972	840.4	5,853.6	--	6,694.0
1973	1,026.1	7,995.8	--	9,021.9
1974	195.9	7,551.5	--	7,747.4
1975	349.2	6,263.6	--	6,612.8
1976 b/	326.6	9,044.7	--	9,371.3
1977 (Est'd.)	1,000.0	7,904.6	--	8,904.6
Total	$27,741.7	$97,744.6	$3,703.1	$129,191.4

a/ This fund merged with Special Foreign Currency Program by the Department of Agriculture and Related Agencies Appropriation Act, 1969. b/ Includes Transitional Quarter.

The following tables present a more detailed picture of the $9,371.3 obligated in 1976 and the $8,904.6 estimated to be obligated in 1977 for the Special Foreign Currency Program.

Special Foreign Currency Program, July 1, 1975 - September 30, 1976 Obligations
(In Thousands)

Country	Market Development Research Section 104(b)(1)	Agricultural and Forestry Research Section 104(b)(3)				Total
	Agricultural Research	Agricultural Research	Agricultural Economics Research	Forestry Research	Animal and Plant Health Inspection Service	
Burma	$ --	$ .1	$ --	$ --	$ --	$ .1
Colombia	--	--	--	- .1	--	- .1
Egypt	110.2	2,940.6	--	166.0	--	3,216.8
Germany	3.5	--	--	--	--	3.5
Guinea	--	.2	--	--	--	.2
India	- 13.1	151.2	--	--	--	138.1
Israel	- 6.2	- 28.5	- 1.6	- 2.3	--	- 38.6
Italy	34.2	- .3	--	- .2	--	33.7
Morocco	--	- 16.4	--	--	--	- 16.4
Pakistan	- 1.5	2,627.6	6.8	166.2	137.2	2,936.3
Poland	215.5	1,518.9	--	588.8	--	2,323.2
Sri Lanka	--	- 13.8	- 2.3	- 2.3	--	- 18.4
Tunisia	--	9.8	--	--	--	9.8
Turkey	--	.2	--	--	--	.2
United Kingdom	- 2.0	--	--	--	--	- 2.0
Yugoslavia	- 14.0	- 41.0	- .6	- 9.1	--	- 64.7
Total	$ 326.6	$7,148.2	$ 2.3	$ 907.0	$137.2	$8,521.3

Transfer to National Science Foundation for translation of scientific publications 850.0

GRAND TOTAL $9,371.3

Special Foreign Currency Program, Estimated FY 1977 Obligations
(In Thousands)

Country	Market Development Research Section 104(b)(1) Agricultural Research	Agricultural and Forestry Research Section 104(b)(1) Agricultural Research	Agricultural Economics Research	Forestry Research	Total
Egypt	$ 515.0	$1,962.9	$301.0	$ - -	$2,778.9
India	200.0	960.0	- -	215.0	1,375.0
Italy	25.0	15.0	- -	- -	40.0
Pakistan	260.0	1,935.0	- -	65.0	2,260.0
Poland	- -	934.0	- -	166.0	1,100.0
Tunisia	- -	149.0	- -	- -	149.0
Total	$1,000.0	$5,955.9	$301.0	$446.0	$7,702.9

Transfer to National Science Foundation for translation to scientific publications 1,201.7

GRAND TOTAL $8,904.6

Expenditures: Expenditures of foreign currencies, from the inception of the program through September 30, 1976, totaled $101,093,015. In addition, the Department plans to expend $9,067,000 in fiscal year 1977. These expenditures may be summarized as follows:

Cumulative Expenditures through F.Y. 1977
(In Thousands)

Fiscal Year	Market Development Research	Agricultural and Forestry Research	Translation of Publications and Scientific Cooperation Executive Office of the President a/	Total
1959	$ 195.1	$ --	$ 0.1	$ 195.2
1960	654.6	--	75.1	729.7
1961	1,254.9	350.2	495.2	2,100.3
1962	1,735.8	1,351.8	425.6	3,513.2
1963	2,136.8	2,071.7	590.9	4,799.4
1964	2,292.9	2,514.9	655.5	5,463.3
1965	2,816.3	3,724.6	616.0	7,156.9
1966	2,435.2	4,113.9	211.2	6,760.3
1967	2,487.0	4,754.6	224.7	7,466.3
1968	1,951.0	5,028.8	200.5	7,180.3
1969	1,598.9	5,454.6	--	7,053.5
1970	1,092.6	4,863.4	--	5,956.0
1971	955.9	4,753.1	--	5,709.0
1972	884.2	5,337.3	--	6,221.5
1973	704.1	4,644.0	--	5,348.1
1974	731.2	7,052.9	--	7,784.1
1975	783.6	6,491.7	--	7,275.3
1976 b/	902.9	9,477.8	--	10,380.7
1977 (est'd.)	901.8	8,165.2	--	9,067.0
Total	$26,514.8	$80,150.5	$3,494.8	$110,160.1

| Location | Estimated 1978 | |
Financial Project	Dollars	Man-Years
Alabama, Auburn		
Research on animal production; plant production; and the use and improvement of soil, water and air	$ 1,611,800	61
Alaska, Palmer		
Research on animal production; plant production; the use and improvement of soil, water and air; and on processing, storage, distribution, nutrition and food safety, and consumer services research	482,900	9
Arizona		
Flagstaff – Research on plant production	93,200	4
Phoenix – Research on plant production; the use and improvement of soil, water and air	2,815,200	118
Tucson – Research on plant production; and the use and improvement of soil, water and air	2,311,800	88
Total, Arizona	5,220,200	210
Arkansas, Stuttgart		
Research on plant production	151,200	2
California		
Albany – Research on animal production; on plant production; processing, storage, distribution, nutrition and food safety, and consumer services research	12,784,900	444
Brawley – Research on plant production; and the use and improvement of soil; water and air	737,900	31
Davis – Plant production	611,200	17
Fresno – Research on animal production; plant production; the use and improvement of soil, water and air; and processing, storage, distribution, nutrition and food safety, and consumer services research	1,672,300	61
Indio – Research on plant production	230,000	12
Pasadena – Research on processing, storage, distribution, nutrition and food safety, and consumer services research	503,900	16
Riverside – Research on plant production; the use and improvement of soil, water and air; and processing, storage, distribution, nutrition and food safety, and consumer services research	1,952,200	67
Salinas – Research on plant production	783,100	33
Shafter – Research on plant production	560,200	20
Total, California	19,835,700	701
Colorado		
Akron – Research on the use and improvement of soil, water and air	210,500	9
Denver – Research on animal production and plant production	1,188,000	44
Fort Collins – Research on plant production; and the use and improvement of soil, water and air ..	2,548,900	100
Total, Colorado	3,947,400	153

ARS OBLIGATIONS AND MAN-YEARS BY LOCATION AND FINANCIAL PROJECTS

Mr. WHITTEN. Would you please update for the record the table on ARS locations and man-years by location as well as the principal types of research at those locations?

[The information follows:]

Location Financial Project	Estimated 1978 Dollars	Man-Years
District of Columbia		
Program - Research on plant production	$ 1,587,400	89
Headquarters		
Agency Management Services	22,632,800	542
Centrally Financed Programs	14,105,100	5
Repair and Maintenance	7,216,000	- -
Subtotal	43,953,900	547
Total	45,541,300	636
Delaware		
Georgetown - Research on animal production	257,300	10
Newark - Research on plant production	294,100	12
Total, Delaware	551,400	22
Florida		
Belle Glade - Research on plant production	151,700	6
Bradenton - Research on processing, storage, distribution, nutrition and food safety, and consumer services research	39,100	1
Brooksville - Research on animal production	141,900	3
Canal Point - Research on plant production	346,500	15
Fort Lauderdale - Research on plant production	103,500	3
Gainesville - Research on animal production; plant production; the use and improvement of soil, water and air; and processing, storage, distribution, nutrition and food safety, and consumer services research	4,455,900	139
Lake Alfred - Research on plant production	102,500	5
Miami - Research on plant production; and processing, storage, distribution, nutrition and food safety, and consumer services research	791,900	27
Orlando - Research on plant production; and processing, storage, distribution, nutrition and food safety, and consumer services research	1,950,100	67
Winter Haven - Research on processing, storage, distribution, nutrition and food safety, and consumer services research	574,800	23
Total, Florida	8,657,900	289
Georgia		
Athens - Research on animal production; plant production; the use and improvement of soil, water and air; and processing, storage, distribution, nutrition and food safety, and consumer services research	6,043,500	262
Byron - Research on plant production; the use and improvement of soil, water and air; and processing, storage, distribution, nutrition and food safety, and consumer services research	1,522,300	62
Dawson - Research on processing, storage, distribution, nutrition and food safety, and consumer services research	519,900	23
Experiment - Research on animal and plant production	228,400	6
Savannah - Research on plant production; processing, storage, distribution, nutrition and food safety, and consumer services research	1,793,400	76
Tifton - Research on animal production; plant production; the use and improvement of soil, water and air; and processing, storage, distribution, nutrition and food safety, and consumer services research	3,110,700	100
Watkinsville - Research on plant production; and the use and improvement of soil, water and air	1,080,400	38
Total, Georgia	14,298,600	567

Location Financial Project	Estimated 1978	
	Dollars	Man-Years
Hawaii		
Hilo - Research on plant production .... $	246,600	5
Honolulu - Research on plant production; and process- ing, storage, distribution, nutrition and food safety, and consumer services research	994,800	26
Total, Hawaii	1,241,400	31
Idaho		
Aberdeen - Research on plant production	277,500	7
Boise - Research on the use and improvement of soil, water and air	490,900	19
Dubois - Research on animal production; and plant production	738,000	20
Twin Falls - Research on plant production; and the use and improvement of soil, water and air	1,260,300	50
Total, Idaho	2,766,700	96
Illinois		
Chicago - Research on processing, storage, distribu- tion, nutrition and food safety, and consumer ser- vices research	139,700	4
Peoria - Research on animal production; plant prod- uction; the use and improvement of soil, water and air; and processing, storage, distribution, nutri- tion and food safety, and consumer services research	12,117,000	455
Urbana - Research on animal production; plant prod- uction; and the use and improvement of soil, water and air	1,357,000	46
Total, Illinois	13,613,700	505
Indiana		
Lafayette - Research on animal production; plant production; and the use and improvement of soil, water and air	1,410,100	37
Vincennes - Research on plant production	209,300	8
Total, Indiana	1,619,400	45
Iowa		
Ames - Research on animal production; plant produc- tion; the use and improvement of soil, water and air; and processing, storage, distribution, nutri- tion and food safety, and consumer services research	8,360,300	304
Ankeny - Research on plant production	332,900	8
Total, Iowa	8,693,200	312
Kansas, Manhattan		
Research on plant production; the use and improvement of soil, water and air; and processing, storage, distribution, nutrition and food safety, and con- sumer services research	2,564,400	71
Kentucky, Lexington		
Research on plant production	723,600	28
Louisiana		
Baton Rouge - Research on plant production; and the use and improvement of soil, water and air	1,118,800	47
Crowley - Research on plant production	48,500	2
Houma - Research on plant production	722,700	32
Jeanerette - Research on animal production	119,500	4
Lake Charles - Research on animal production; and processing, storage, distribution, nutrition and food safety, and consumer services research	196,200	7

Location Financial Project	Estimated 1978	
	Dollars	Man-Years
Louisiana - Cont'd.		
New Orleans - Research on plant production; and processing, storage, distribution, nutrition and food safety, and consumer services research	$ 13,086,600	500
Total, Louisiana	15,292,300	592
Maine, Orono		
Research on plant production; the use and improvement of soil, water and air; and processing, storage, distribution, nutrition and food safety, and consumer services research	407,500	17
Maryland		
Beltsville - Research on animal production; plant production; the use and improvement of soil, water and air; and processing, storage, distribution, nutrition and food safety, and consumer servcies research	44,862,800	1,723
Frederick - Research on plant production	1,401,200	41
Glenn Dale - Research on plant production	264,700	12
Hyattsville - Research on processing, storage, distribution, nutrition and food safety, and consumer services research	4,708,200	89
Total, Maryland	51,236,900	1,865
Michigan, East Lansing		
Research on animal production; plant production; and processing, storage, distribution, nutrition and food safety, and consumer services research	1,866,800	72
Minnesota		
East Grand Forks - Research on processing, storage, distribution, nutrition and food safety, and consumer services research	290,300	10
Minneapolis - Research on the use and improvement of soil, water and air	132,600	4
Morris - Research on the use and improvement of soil, water and air	833,000	38
St. Paul - Research on animal production; plant production; and the use and improvement of soil, water and air	1,386,300	38
Total, Minnesota	2,642,200	90
Mississippi		
Gulfport - Research on processing, storage, distribution, nutrition and food safety, and consumer services research	248,800	8
Meridian - Research on plant production	307,800	11
Oxford - Research on the use and improvement of soil, water and air	1,393,600	59
Poplarville - Research on plant production	73,100	3
Mississippi State - Research on animal production; plant production; and the use and improvement of soil, water and air	3,052,300	107
Stoneville - Research on plant production; the use and improvement of soil, water and air; and processing, storage, distribution, nutrition and food safety, and consumer services research	4,011,600	157
Total, Mississippi	9,087,200	345

Location Financial Project	Estimated 1978	
	Dollars	Man-Years
Missouri, Columbia		
Research on animal production; plant production; the use and improvement of soil, water and air; and processing, storage, distribution, nutrition and food safety, and consumer services research	$ 2,724,900	96
Montana		
Bozeman – Research on plant production	528,600	17
Miles City – Research on animal and plant production	744,600	11
Sidney – Research on the use and improvement of soil, water and air	677,800	28
Total, Montana	1,951,000	56
Nebraska		
Clay Center – Research on animal production	5,089,300	64
Lincoln – Research on plant production; and the use and improvement of soil, water and air	1,055,000	32
Total, Nebraska	6,144,300	96
Nevada, Reno		
Research on plant production	467,400	12
New Jersey, New Brunswick		
Research on plant production; and processing, storage, distribution, nutrition and food safety, and consumer services research	360,000	10
New Mexico, Las Cruces		
Research on plant production; and on processing, storage, distribution, nutrition and food safety, and consumer services research	820,200	32
New York		
Geneva – Research on plant production	157,300	6
Ithaca – Research on animal production; plant production; and the use and improvement of soil, water and air; and processing, storage, distribution, nutrition and food safety, and consumer services research	1,657,200	44
Plum Island – Research on animal production	8,746,900	346
Total, New York	10,561,400	396
North Carolina		
Oxford – Research on plant production	871,700	35
Raleigh – Research on plant production; the use and improvement of soil, water and air; and processing, storage, distribution, nutrition and food safety, and consumer services research	2,258,800	56
Total, North Carolina	3,130,500	91
North Dakota		
Fargo – Research on animal production; research on plant production	3,695,500	123
Grand Forks – Research on processing, storage, distribution, nutrition and food safety, and consumer services research	1,396,600	38
Mandan – Research on plant production; and the use and improvement of soil, water and air	1,432,800	48
Total, North Dakota	6,524,900	209
Ohio		
Columbus – Research on the use and improvement of soil, water and air	162,400	4

Location Financial Project	Estimated 1978	
	Dollars	Man-Years
Ohio — Cont'd.		
Coshocton — Research on the use and improvement of		
soil, water and air .... $	468,200	18
Delaware — Research on plant production	395,600	15
Wooster — Research on plant production	818,700	33
Total, Ohio	1,844,900	70
Oklahoma		
Chickasha — Research on the use and improvement of		
soil, water and air	742,900	37
Durant — Research on the use and improvement of soil,		
water and air	566,700	21
El Reno — Research on animal production	291,600	7
Stillwater — Research on plant production; and the		
use and improvement of soil, water and air	824,000	22
Woodward — Research on plant production	323,600	16
Total, Oklahoma	2,748,800	103
Oregon		
Burns — Research on plant production ....,...	75,600	2
Corvallis — Research on plant production; and the use		
and improvement of soil, water and air	1,360,900	42
Pendleton — Research on the use and improvement of		
soil, water and air	546,400	21
Total, Oregon	1,982,900	65
Pennsylvania		
University Park — Research on plant production; and		
the use and improvement of soil, water and air	1,528,000	50
Wyndmoor — Research on plant production; and process-		
ing, storage, distribution, nutrition and food		
safety, and consumer services research	8,276,500	340
Total, Pennsylvania	9,804,500	390
South Carolina		
Charleston — Research on plant production	787,100	35
Clemson — Research on animal and plant production;		
and processing, storage, distribution, nutrition		
and food safety, and consumer services research ...	1,049,300	38
Florence — Research on plant production; and the use		
and improvement of soil, water and air	821,300	34
Total, South Carolina	2,657,700	107
South Dakota		
Brookings-Madison — Research on plant production	938,800	36
Tennessee		
Greenville — Research on plant production	136,200	7
Jackson — Research on plant production	95,900	4
Knoxville — Research on animal production; plant		
production; and processing, storage, distribution,		
nutrition and food safety, and consumer services		
research	777,600	29
Lewisburg — Research on animal production	87,300	4
Total, Tennessee	1,097,000	44
Texas		
Beaumont — Research on plant production; and process-		
ing, storage, distribution, nutrition and food		
safety, and consumer services research	375,200	12
Big Spring — Research on the use and improvement of		
soil, water and air	156,200	5
Brownsville — Research on plant production	1,124,300	45

Location Financial Project	Estimated 1978 Dollars	Man-Years
Texas – Cont'd.		
Brownwood – Research on plant production .... $	303,000	12
Bushland – Research on animal production; plant production; and the use and improvement of soil, water and air	1,044,600	38
College Station – Research on animal production; plant production; and processing, storage, distribution, nutrition and food safety, and consumer services research	4,228,200	147
El Paso – Research on plant production	47,900	2
Kerrville – Research on animal production; research on plant production	1,699,000	60
Lubbock – Research on plant production; and processing, storage, distribution, nutrition and food safety, and consumer services research	668,400	25
Mission – Research on animal production	688,100	17
Temple – Research on plant production; and the use and improvement of soil, water and air	1,464,000	46
Vernon (Chillicothe) – Research on plant production	58,600	3
Weslaco – Research on plant production; the use and improvement of soil, water and air; and processing, storage, distribution, nutrition and food safety, and consumer services research	2,496,000	95
Total, Texas	14,353,500	507
Utah, Logan		
Research on animal production; plant production; and processing, storage, distribution, nutrition and food safety, and consumer services research	1,670,400	56
Virginia		
Blacksburg – Research on plant production; and the use and improvement of soil, water and air	103,700	4
Richmond – Research on processing, storage, distribution, nutrition and food safety, and consumer services research	144,400	5
Suffolk (Holland) – Research on plant production; processing, storage, distribution, nutrition and food safety, and consumer services research	323,900	13
Total, Virginia	572,000	22
Washington		
Prosser – Research on plant production; and the use and improvement of soil, water and air; and processing, storage, distribution, nutrition and food safety, and consumer services research	965,800	37
Pullman – Research on animal production; plant production; the use and improvement of soil, water and air	1,777,300	67
Wenatchee – Research on plant production; and processing, storage, distribution, nutrition and food safety, and consumer services research	582,500	21
Yakima – Research on plant production; and processing, storage, distribution, nutrition and food safety, and consumer services research	1,109,800	46
Total, Washington	4,435,400	171
West Virginia, Morgantown		
Research on the use and improvement of soil, water and air	395,700	16

Location Financial Project	Estimated 1978	
	Dollars	Man-Years
Wisconsin, Madison		
Research on plant production; and processing, storage, distribution, nutrition and food safety, and consumer services research	$ 1,337,400	44
Wyoming		
Cheyenne – Research on plant production; and the use and improvement of soil, water and air	453,500	16
Laramie – Research on plant production; and the use and improvement of soil, water and air	295,600	11
Total, Wyoming	749,100	27
Puerto Rico		
Mayaguez – Research on plant production	904,600	39
Rio Piedras – Research on the use and improvement of soil, water and air	299,700	9
Total, Puerto Rico	1,204,300	48
Virgin Islands, St. Croix		
Research on processing, storage, distribution, nutrition and food safety, and consumer services research	195,600	10
Other Foreign Countries		
Argentina – Research on plant production	54,100	– –
El Salvadore – Research on processing, storage, distribution, nutrition and food safety, and consumer services research	179,000	2
France, Paris – Research on plant production	219,700	9
Italy, Rome – Research on plant production	106,200	4
Kenya – Research on animal production	99,800	2
Netherlands, Rotterdam – Research on processing, storage, distribution, nutrition and food safety, and consumer services research	239,800	5
Pakistan – Research on plant production	55,200	2
Thailand – Research on plant production	62,900	2
Total, Other Foreign Countries	1,016,700	26
Construction of Facilities	– –	– –
Contingency Research Fund	1,000,000	– –
Competitive Grant Research Fund	27,000,000	– –
Allotment to:		
Forest Service – Research on plant production	376,000	10
Cooperative State Research Service – Competitive Grant Research Fund ....…..	600,000	15
TOTAL, Budget Estimate	$320,719,000	9,484

Status of Staffing of Agricultural Research Service Facilities
Projected September 30, 1977

(Expressed in terms of scientific personnel)

Location	Total Capacity (Scientists)	Total in Use (Scientists)	Percent Staffed
Alabama:			
Auburn	16	14	88
Arizona:			
Phoenix	40	37	93
Tucson	39	28	72
California:			
Albany	210	181	86
Fresno	35	24	69
Pasadena	14	14	100
Riverside	37	29	78
Salinas	16	12	75
Colorado:			
Denver	11	11	100
Ft. Collins	36	36	100
District of Columbia	35	33	94
Florida:			
Gainesville	63	57	90
Miami	11	7	64
Orlando	26	26	100
Winter Haven	16	14	88
Georgia:			
Athens	118	113	96
Byron	24	19	79
Dawson	15	9	60
Savannah	29	27	93
Tifton	22	20	91
Watkinsville	18	13	72
Hawaii:			
Honolulu	10	9	90
Idaho:			
Kimberly	25	25	100
Illinois:			
Peoria	236	224	95
Iowa:			
Ames	132	132	100
Kansas:			
Manhattan	47	33	70
Louisiana:			
Baton Rouge	22	21	95
Houma	13	13	100
New Orleans	185	178	96
Maryland:			
Beltsville	579	523	90
Frederick	26	20	77
Hyattsville	49	42	86
Michigan:			
East Lansing	11	10	91
Minnesota:			
Morris	15	10	67
St. Paul	12	9	75
Mississippi:			
Oxford	36	36	100
State College	38	37	97
Stoneville	78	44	56

Status of Staffing--Continued

Location	Total Capacity (Scientists)	Total in Use (Scientists)	Percent Staffed
Missouri:			
Columbia	17	17	100
Montana:			
Sidney	10	9	90
Nebraska:			
Clay Center	44	29	66
New Mexico:			
Las Cruces	11	10	91
New York:			
Greenport	51	45	88
Ithaca	16	12	75
North Carolina:			
Oxford	16	11	69
North Dakota:			
Fargo	39	37	95
Grand Forks	14	14	100
Mandan	20	19	95
Oklahoma:			
Chickasha	10	9	90
Durant	12	11	92
El Reno	20	5	25
Woodward	10	4	40
Oregon:			
Pendleton	13	13	100
Pennsylvania:			
University Park	14	14	100
Wyndmoor	182	169	93
Puerto Rico:			
Mayaguez	15	8	53
South Carolina:			
Charleston	14	14	100
South Dakota:			
Brookings	17	15	88
Texas:			
Brownsville	15	10	67
Bushland	22	22	100
College Station	64	55	86
Kerrville	22	15	68
Temple	20	20	100
Weslaco	36	36	100
Utah:			
Logan	21	19	90
Washington:			
Wenatchee	11	8	73
Yakima	27	22	81
Subtotal, (67 locations with capacity of 10 or more scientists)	3,128	2,762	88
All other locations (42 with capacity of less than 10 scientists)	231	190	82
Total, Federal Facilities	3,359	2,952	88
Number of Non-ARS scientists included above		341	
Number of ARS scientists included above:			
ARS Junior scientists (Below GS-11)		182	
ARS Senior scientists (GS-11 and above)		2,429	
Total		2,952	

STATEMENT AND QUESTIONS OF HON. ROBERT L.F. SIKES

BUDGETARY HISTORY

Mr. Administrator, your statement has some very apt observations. You say that "Expanding world food requirements and changing agricultural policies are placing added pressures on the U.S. agricultural research capacity which has been on a resource plateau for well over 10 years."

Are you saying that you tried to get increased budgets but they have not been made available to your department for the last 10 years?

Mr. EDMINSTER. Mr. Sikes, the budgetary history that we have had over the past 10 years is that we have had some increases in appropriations essentially every year, except one or two occasions when it was either static or a slight reduction. However, the rate of inflation has been greater than the rate of increase of the budgets, so consequently, as I indicated in my statement, the purchasing power on the basis of constant dollars today, using the 1977 appropriation, is approximately the same as it was in 1966.

Mr. SIKES. You also say that you have 890 fewer scientists and support staff. Did you attempt to obtain sufficient funds to retain those 890 scientists and support staff?

Mr. EDMINSTER. Yes, sir, Mr. Sikes. Each year we develop a program that we hope will at least retain the level of research and strengthen it at any point of weakness. In those requests we attempt to not only fund the necessary programs, but also indicate the needs for staff to accomplish this.

Mr. SIKES. You are doing very important work, and everyone recognizes that, and it appears that you have been severely limited in funds with which to do the job that you see you have to do; is that correct?

Mr. EDMINSTER. We have been severely limited because not only do these records show this, but there is another element that also should be in the record. During the same 10-year period it has been necessary for us to reduce many of the very basic lines of research and divert the manpower and the funds to meet some of the new environmental issues. This involves finding answers to meet the regulatory constraints that some of our farmers and ranchers will be facing. We have been having to look into more problems on nutrition, food quality, and food safety. Each of these things has diverted some of our base toward these new requirements and new thrusts.

The field of agricultural research today is much broader and more complex than it was 10 years ago because of these new elements.

BUDGET REQUESTS

Mr. SIKES. Would you tell us what your budget estimate is for fiscal 1978, and the amount which you requested initially for fiscal 1978?

Mr. EDMINSTER. The President's budget is $319,719,000. The agency request was $409,786,000 for fiscal year 1978.

Mr. SIKES. I think it would be useful if you would provide for the record a breakout of your initial request and the actual budgeted amount that you received for the past 10 years when you have been on a resource plateau, including the number of people you were denied each of those years.

Mr. EDMINSTER. We would be glad to supply that for the record, sir.

[The information follows:]

HISTORY OF BUDGET REQUESTS

	Agency estimate		Budget estimate	
	Budget authority	Permanent full-time employment	Budget authority	Permanent full-time employment
Fiscal year:				
1978	$409,786,000	9,747	$319,719,000	8,423
1977	312,682,000	9,653	263,202,000	8,331
1976	267,608,000	9,173	241,130,000	8,475
1975	231,772,400	8,677	219,994,000	8,275
1974	211,986,600	8,659	185,790,000	8,170
1973	230,806,500	9,806	192,814,000	8,732
1972	213,855,200	10,282	184,422,000	8,759
1971	197,787,000	10,160	156,437,200	9,241
1970	202,856,100	11,494	145,631,300	9,653
1969	200,260,830	12,641	151,273,100	10,628

REDIRECTIONS TO ENVIRONMENTAL RESEARCH

Mr. SIKES. And if you would provide more detail on the amount of funds and the number of people diverted from pure research of the type you were doing and into the environmental area, it would be useful.

Mr. EDMINSTER. We can provide a reasonable estimate on that. In many instances there is a man working in two fields instead of one. It would be a little hard to get a very precise estimate on that shifting, but I think we can give a reasonable estimate.

[The information follows:]

RESOURCES SHIFTED TO ENVIRONMENTAL RESEARCH

In fiscal 1966 ARS had 43 scientist-years and $1.3 million devoted to pollution-related research. In fiscal 1975 the respective values were 211 and $14.2 million. During this 10-year period, the number of scientists in ARS increased by 36, so most of the additional scientists came from other programs, principally marketing research and soil and water conservation research. Similarly, the number of scientists working on human health and safety increased by 125, most of them coming from the marketing research program.

RESEARCH NEED PRIORITIES

Mr. SIKES. Would you provide for the record the areas in one, two, three order which you consider most important in your fiscal 1978 budget in which you were denied additional funds but which you felt should have been provided in the budget? Include the amounts involved.

Mr. EDMINSTER. We will do that, sir.

[The information follows:]

MOST IMPORTANT AREAS OF RESEARCH

The most important areas of research not being funded in this budget would be the development of new and improved practices for increased protection of animals from parasites and diseases including fundamental research to develop new technology for immunizing against diseases and biological control of pests. This would be followed by research to increase livestock production efficiency through improved management systems, structures, facilities, and equipment; to improve safety and quality of animal products; and to recover energy now lost in animal waste products. The estimate for this area is approximately $3 million.

The next most important area of research would be in increasing plant production efficiency through development of new or improved equipment to detect and track insect pest populations, biological control agents for plant pests, disease resistant grain crops, improved harvesting equipment, and chemicals for minor use. This would be followed by research to improve the quality of agricultural products shipped overseas. The estimate for this area is approximately $3 million.

The next most important area of research would be on evaluating the nutritive value and natural toxicant content of perishable commodities and on the development of methods to reduce losses of nutrients and other quality factors of such commodities during their distribution in the marketing process; research on stored agricultural commodities to maintain their quality and protect against attack by insects and microorganisms; and research to assess hazards arising from the presence of natural toxicants, toxigenic fungi, and pesticides. The estimate for this area is approximately $3 million.

Further research would be undertaken on water quality with special emphasis on municipal wastes, agricultural chemicals, and sediments; on conservation tillage to reduce erosion and sedimentation; and improved irrigation and drainage to conserve water, energy, and nutrients. The estimate for this area is approximately $3 million.

Additional production and protection efficiency research to increase agricultural production would be undertaken. Basic studies would be undertaken on improving biological efficiency of plants; maximizing utilization of grazing lands for livestock production; developing methods for future insect, disease, and weed control technologies; and enhancing the use of superior genetic breeding stock. Fundamental research would be undertaken in subparticle vaccines and in respiratory and foreign animal diseases. The estimate for this area is approximately $12 million.

AGRICULTURAL RESEARCH SERVICE 1978

Mr. EDMINSTER. We have also provided for the use of the committee a series of visual materials pointing to some 32 key areas of research, providing background material which we hope will be of assistance to the committee in its deliberations. I would ask these be added to the record in support of our testimony.

CONTENTS

PHOTOSYNTHESIS -- KEY TO LIFE

Problem

- Low crop yields caused by low photosynthetic efficiency

Research Goals

- Better understanding of basic processes
- Develop varieties with higher photosynthetic efficiency
- Higher yielding varieties
- Improved management practices

Benefits

- More efficient photosynthesis will provide better production potential to feed, clothe and warm an ever increasing population

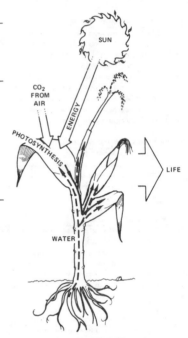

WATER AND NUTRIENTS

RESEARCH NEEDS:

We must continue to rapidly increase our basic knowledge of photosynthesis and related processes if U.S. agricultural scientists are to attain breakthroughs necessary to increase food, feed, fiber, and fuel production. Expanded research is needed to:

--Exploit genetic differences in light reactions and carbon metabolism to increase the efficiency of photosynthetic processes.
--Develop varieties and management practices for higher yields and better use of the growing season.
--Reduce the effects of environmental stress on photosynthesis and on yield of major crops.
--Identify specific growth regulators, natural and synthetic, that improve photosynthetic capability and increase yield.
--Make photosynthesis research more efficient and yield forecasting more accurate by improving systems analyses and simulation models.

BENEFITS:

Basic research on major plant processes is an essential forerunner of developmental and applied research. Photosynthesis, the primary solar-energy conversion process, is singularly important in the production of useable energy for all life. Improving photosynthesis and allied plant processes will increase crop yield and quality. Also, greater efficiency in converting solar energy to crop matter will conserve fossil fuel.

BASIC RESEARCH

can help alleviate our heavy dependence on fossil fuel

Biological nitrogen fixation by crop legumes now produces 12 mil. tons of nitrogen annually, equivalent to 83 mil. barrels of oil

Soybean legume crop

Root nodules -- nature's nitrogen factory

Problem

- Today's production of synthetic nitrogen fertilizer uses 72 million barrels of oil equivalents annually
- Higher cost of fossil fuel increases food production costs
- Biological nitrogen fixation must be adapted to many other field crops

Research Needs

- Improve biological nitrogen fixation in legume crops and extend it to other major crops
- More knowledge to improve biological nitrogen fixation efficiency
- Develop cell and tissue culture methods to identify, isolate, and transfer the genetic capability to enhance nitrogen fixation

Benefits

- Reduce agriculture's dependence on fossil fuels
- Reduce cost of food production
- A 10 percent increase would provide an additional $300 million worth of nitrogen to crops

RESEARCH PROGRESS:

We have recently created hybrids of nitrogen-fixing bacteria. The ability to fix Nitrogen independently of the legume host has been induced in Rhizobium bacteria. Some biochemical and genetic control mechanisms that regulate nitrogen fixation in bacteria have been identified. Nitrogen-fixing Spirillum and other bacteria can form close associations with roots of various crops. More efficient strains of rhizobia have been added to the Rhizobium Culture Collection maintained by USDA-ARS. The collection supports nitrogen fixation research by providing rhizobia for research purposes to scientists and industry in the United States and many foreign countries. New approaches to improving the efficiency of biological nitrogen fixation are now possible.

INTEGRATED WEED CONTROL
now effective on difficult weeds in wheat, corn and sorghum

Herbicide mixtures control weeds in corn and increase yields 25 percent (right).

Problem

- Wild oats, Canada thistle and other weeds reduce potential yields of wheat, corn, and sorghum more than 10 percent

Research Progress

- New integrated systems of control have been developed in the last decade that reduce yield losses in wheat, corn, and sorghum. As a result crop yields have been increased up to 25 percent

Research Needs

- Develop new and better total farm systems of weed control
- Develop a better basic understanding of the ecology, physiology, and biochemistry of weeds, and determine their vulnerability to control
- Determine the behavior, fate, and effects of chemical and nonchemical methods of control on crops, soils, and the environment

Benefits of improved weed control

- Increased grain crop yields
- Reduced crop production costs
- Increased crop quality
- Improved mechanization
- Reduced tillage and soil erosion
- Better use of fertilizer and water
- Optimum crop plant populations for maximum yields

PLANT TOLERANCE FOUND
to adverse soil conditions

WHEAT   ALFALFA

Plants tolerant to aluminum toxicity (at right in photographs) show increased yield.

Problem

- Adverse soil conditions exist in much of the U.S.
    Examples of soil toxicity:
        Aluminum
        Manganese
        Salinity
        Heavy Metal

Research Progress

- Plants developed with tolerance to aluminum toxicity include:
        Wheat
        Barley
        Alfalfa
        Soybeans

Benefits

- Increase crop yields and quality on current cropland acreage
- Expand cropland acreages using tolerant species
- New and profitable species can be introduced
  on marginal lands
- Reduce use of lime and fertilizer
- Increase efficient use of water

IMPROVED URBAN MARKETING, NUTRITION AND FOOD SAFETY

Crowded, antiquated conditions in the Faneuil Hall market area where much of food in Boston was handled

New, modern facilities for marketing produce

Problem

- High food distribution costs in urban areas
- Inadequate, antiquated wholesale and retail markets
- Food spoilage and decay
- Serious food quality deterioration
- Traffic management

Research Results

- New city food markets
- Improved inner-city retailing
- Improved transportation and delivery
- Better refrigeration and product protection
- Improved sanitary and food safety practices

Benefits

- Lower food costs
- Increased competition
- Safer food products
- More nutrients retained in food
- Reduced food losses

STATEMENT OF HON. JOHN B. BRECKINRIDGE

I would like to preface my remarks, if I might, Mr. Chairman, by just observing that much of what I have to say this morning is "old hat" to the chairman who was here when the Rural Development Act was developed in 1972 but not implemented. I am aware of the outstanding leadership he accorded the Congress at that time which is the primary reason for our meeting here this morning to hopefully implement the Rural Development Act. The chairman is also a member of the rural caucus so there is nothing I am going to say here today that he is not already privy to.

Mr. Chairman and members of the Subcommittee on Agriculture and related agencies. I want to thank you for extending me the opportunity to present to you the proposals for the congressional rural caucus (CRC) for fiscal 1978 for rural development and job creation.

Th CRC has, during the past year, conducted extensive research and thoroughly examined a broad range of problems confronting rural America. The results of this investigation have been compiled into a 65-page report which includes a $16.4 billion rural development proposal, the bulk of which would come from guaranteed loan programs financed off the Federal budget through the private sector, and which is the subject of these hearings today. This proposal is also under study by the White House and the interested executive agencies.

If implemented, the CRC program, along with a comparable expansion of the SBA loan programs, would have a significant impact on revitalizing the economy of rural America and could additionally create as many as 3 million private-sector jobs across the country—jobs that could be targeted to areas of high unemployment. Also, because these would be private sector jobs that create rather than consume revenues, these proposals could be implemented at a net profit to the taxpayer at the Federal, State, and local level in the shortest possible time.

Before going further, I think it would be appropriate at this point to relate for the record, and for the benefit of those who are unfamiliar with the work of the CRC, a brief history of the organization and the processes by which we arrived at the proposal we are discussing today.

The congressional rural caucus is a bipartisan group composed of approximately 100 members of the House of Representatives from some 38 States and two territories, who share a common concern for the orderly growth, development, and quality of life in rural America. In addition to its congressional membership, the caucus has established what we call our off-Hill advisory team (CRCAT) which, in turn, is made up of over 50 organizations representing various interests such as: agriculture, energy, financial resources business and labor, health, housing, public works, rural development and other areas, all of which are of the utmost importance to the farmers and nonfarmers who constitute nonmetropolitan America. The team includes both the public and private sectors, States, counties, and municipalities, producers and consumers, employers and employees. At this point I ask for unanimous consent that a list of the membership of the caucus, the advisory team, and the committee structure be placed in the record.

During 1976, at the request of the CRC, the Congresional Research Service prepared 10 basic background reports on rural America, including: "Community Facilities in Rural Areas: The Federal Role," by Philip Winters; "Financing Rural Development: Credit Needs and Resources," by F. Jean Wells; "Report on Rural America: Transportation," by Leon H. Cole and Stephen J. Thompson; "Federally Assisted Housing in Rural America," by Richard L. Wellons; "Local Implementation of National Rural Development Programs and Policies," by Sandra S. Osbourn; "Trends in Rural Employment," by Jeffrey H. Burton; "Educational Problems and Federal Alternatives," by Paul M. Irwin; "Health of and Health Services for Rural America," by Herman Schmidt; "Some Economic and Social Trends in Non-Metropolitan America," by Anne M. Smith; and "Environmental Protection and Rural Development," by Susan R. Abbasi and W. Wendell Fletcher.

The budget proposal we submit to you calls for the maximum utilization of already existing and proven loan and grant programs under Farmers Home Administration (FmHA) and the Small Business Administration (SBA), where applicable, making financial resources available to accommodate America's rapidly expanding credit needs. It also is directed at stimulating the economy through the protection of existing jobs, plus the creation of new and additional jobs, with private funds in the private sector. This results in tax revenues from wages and salaries as well as profits for farm and nonfarm enterprises. Under the proposal jobs will be created at a profit to the taxpayer without deficit financing, utilizing existing and experienced Federal and private resources already in place throughout the country, in urban as well as rural areas. This program could potentially produce in the neighborhood of 2 to 3 million private-sector jobs. Most importantly, it is more than 95 percent privately, non-tax-dollar funded.

Specifically, the report includes recommendation for selected FmHA program funding levels of $557 million for grant appropriations, and $15.9 billion for loan level authorizations by the appropriations committees, totaling $16.4 billion.

The proposed $557 million grant appropriations include $85 million for rural housing programs, $397 million for community programs, and $75 million for business and industrial programs, all of which are appropriated items. These grants would provide the infrastructure necessary for full and effective implementation of the increased loan authority we are seeking.

The recommended $15.9 billion loan authorization levels include $2.3 billion for farmers programs, $6.6 billion for rural housing programs, $4 billion for rural community programs, and $3 billion for rural business and industrial programs. All of these do not directly add to Federal budget outlays inasmuch as, with the exception of certain interest subsidies and losses, insured loans are not paid out of the Federal Treasury. These loans are resold through the Federal financing bank, and guaranteed loans do not appear in the Federal budget except as losses occur. The subsidies or losses are offset by more than 100-percent return on the taxpayers investment.

The existing authorities of the Secretary of Agriculture and Small Business Administration constitute two of the most economical, effective, expeditious and beneficial vehicles available to alleviate and eliminate underemployment and unemployment throughout the Nation, including our rural areas. Their agencies are capable of providing the long-sought-for job-creation stimulus for continuing farm and nonfarm employment, including the rural disadvantaged. These proposals can also save the lives of many operations currently facing disastrous financial crisis or possible bankruptcy for reasons beyond their control resulting from last year's calamitous weather conditions in both the Eastern and Western portions of the country.

The CRC also recommends that Federal agencies with established and proven loan programs should place greater responsibility for these loans on the regulated financial institutions. Those banks which exercise good credit judgment and maintain satisfactory records of loan repayment should have discretionary authority to fund loans on an automatic or semiautomatic basis, thus expediting and helping to eliminate the heavy burden of unnecessary Federal paperwork and personnel. Adequate monitoring will assure public accountability.

You have been listening to me for several minutes talk about creating private sector jobs at a profit to the taxpayers, and doing it without constructing another enormous Federal bureaucracy. This is not pie in the sky dreaming. In this country we already have in place an organization that last year alone created nearly 300,000 private sector jobs and reaped a neat $2 billion profit for the American taxpayer.

In my March 1976 Separate Views to the House Agriculture budget, and in testimony before the House Small Business Committee in March and April of 1976, I noted the jobs-creation effect of expanding the loan authority of the SBA and FmHA. Since that time I have, with the assistance of the Economics Division of the Congressional Research Service, explored these programs extensively—especially their relation to the problem areas of employment and inflation, and have prepared a brief outline of their present and potential cost and benefits to the American taxpayer.

In 1976 the SBA loaned approximately $2 billion private dollars to various enterprises throughout the Nation, creating approximately 288,000 jobs in the private sector. SBA's 4,200 employees cost $200 million in administrative costs. Based on a 5-percent loan-loss ratio (or 10 percent, if one prefers), ($2 billion times 5 percent), $100 million ($200) will not be recovered. Thus $1.9 billion ($1.8) will be repaid to taxpayers with principal and interest. The estimated 288,000 jobs created by SBA in the private sector cost approximately $200 million for administration and $100 ($200) million for loan losses, for a total cost of $300 ($400) million.

Because these 288,000 jobs are private sector jobs—that pay rather than absorb taxes—the CRC estimates that the total benefit to the taxpayer is as follows:

1976 TAX REVENUE AND SAVINGS FOR 288,000 SBA PROGRAM-CREATED JOBS

	Per job	Total
Federal individual income tax	$2, 300	$662, 000, 000
Federal corporation tax	1, 134	326, 000, 000
Federal welfare savings	2, 500	720, 000, 000
State and local tax	2, 114	609, 000, 000
Total	8, 048	2, 317, 000, 000

Simply stated, the total $2.3 billion in benefits, less the $300 ($400) million in SBA costs, leaves a total net benefit of $2 ($1.4) billion to the taxpayers annually thereafter; for every taxpayer's dollar put out by SBA, the taxpayers receive a return of $7, or $1 cost for $7 benefits received.

It is significant to note that with nine-plus million small businesses in the United States, the SBA was able to help less than 30,000. Of the 370,000 new businesses incorporated in 1976, SBA will only be able to help 8,000. Many of these are in small towns and rural communities as well as center cities. Obviously, legitimate credit demand is there for a major expansion of the FmHA and SBA programs, and I trust that some of our other witnesses will address themselves to this aspect of our proposal. A major advantage in the expansion of FmHA and SBA programs is that they are not pilot programs. They are highly successful, existing programs which are known to the President, the Congress, the business and financial communities. By increasing the current average loan from $100,000 to $1 million for instance, SBA could increase the number of jobs tenfold without significantly increasing administration costs, as will appear elsewhere in today's testimony. Especially important is the fact that by using existing FmHA and SBA offices the towns, cities, counties, States, and regions of high unemployment could be targeted for their fair share of the increased employment activity.

On February 24 I was privileged to meet with President Carter at the White House, and one of the subjects of our discussion was the CRC package we have before us today. As you would expect, the President displayed complete familiarity with both the Rural Development Act of 1972 and the SBA programs. In fact, in 1972 then Governor Carter testified in favor of the act at hearings held by Senator Talmadge in Georgia. Jimmy Carter knows first hand the needs of rural America. His background, inter alia, is that of both a farmer and a small businessman. The President indicated a keen interest in our proposal and has directed its study internally by his administration. Since my meeting with President Carter I have also visited with OMB Director Bert Lance and others in his office about the caucus proposals. Mr. Lance expressed both understanding and interest in our recommendations and I, along with members of the CRC executive committee and advisory team have also met with members of his staff to open a dialog which has as its primary purpose the development procedures whereby the rural development and job creations aspects of the proposal, as well as such administrative problems as exist within the responsible public and private sector delivery systems can be both explored and resolved.

On March 3 and 4 the CRC, in conjunction with the House Agriculture Committee's Subcommittees on Conservation and Credit, and Family Farms, Rural Development and Special Studies, and the Small Business Committee's Subcommittee on Antitrust, Consumers and Employment, held joint hearings with the caucus on the CRC 1978 recommendations for rural development and anti-inflationary job creation. These hearings produced testimony from a wide variety of interested individuals and groups representing a broad spectrum of American society, among which groups were out farmers, financial institutions, professional engineers, contractors, consumer groups, and other segments of both the public and private sectors, including a panel from the Department of Agriculture led by Alex Mercure, Special Assistant to Secretary Bergland.

A transcript of those hearings has been produced in limited quantity and, without objection, I would like to introduce a copy for the record of this hearing. In addition I would like to submit a copy of a special order which I took on March 10 to explain the CRC program to the Congress. Included in that special order is a summary report of the testimony to be found in the transcript. This summary report contains a brief outline of the CRC program as well as a summary of the highlights of the testimony received. Without objection, I would like to introduce a copy for the record. You will note that the testimony was virtually unanimous in its support of the caucus proposal.

The primary purpose of our hearings was to prepare a record on the caucus program for presentation to the Agriculture Committee during deliberations on its budget recommendations which, as you know, had to be submitted by March 15. In a meeting on March 10 the Agriculture Committee, by a division vote of 21–6 approved with minor changes the entire caucus grant request of $492 million—CRC recommendation $492 Million—and $195.8 million for FmHA salaries and expenses—CRC recommendation $225 million—for inclusion in its budget report. As the loan authorization levels which comprise the bulk of the caucus' $16.4 billion program are guaranteed and insured loan programs, financed off the Federal budget, the committee did not consider the loan aspects of the CRC proposal as part of its budget recommendations at that time.

On Tuesday of this week, March 22, at a special meeting called to consider the loan authorization levels contained in the CRC proposal, the Agriculture Committee by a recorded vote of 34 to 3 endorsed a resolution calling on the Appropriations Committee to raise FmHA ceilings to the levels recommended by the CRC; that is, $2.316 billion for farmer programs, $4 billion for community facilities programs, and $3 billion for business and industrial programs for a total loan authorization level of $9.316 billion. This did not include $6.565 billion for rural housing programs which do not come under the jurisdiction of the Committee on Agriculture, but which are before this subcommittee today.

Earlier this week, members of the executive committee met with Chairman Bob Giaimo, of the House Budget Committee, who advised us that his committee would begin markup Thursday on the fiscal 1978 budget resolution, and may complete action next week. The chairman also discussed with us a proposal which he planned to submit to his committee, which would identify a certain amount of funds for new and expanded programs under budget function 450—community and regional development. These funds would become the subject of competition from several sources, including the programs espoused by the rural caucus.

The next step is, of course, up to your subcommittee and the full Appropriations Committee. The century-old migration from rural areas to the metropolitan centers has stopped and has begun to reverse itself. People are moving back into our nonmetropolitan areas in unprecedented numbers. Small communities are not prepared for this influx of population and attendant problems which it entails.

These towns and counties need planning assistance, water, waste disposal, fire stations, and other community facilities; our farmers need loans to keep them on the land producing food and fibers for America and the world; our young would-be farmers need credit, if the next generation is to feed the world; and most of all, we need jobs, new nondeficit private sector jobs that provide a permanent and growing economic and revenue base for our communities. Adoption of the CRC recommendations would significantly contribute to meeting these needs.

We are not asking for handouts. FmHA and SBA are already in place, established, and successful programs. The loss ratio on the loans they make is insignificant. For SBA, it is in the neighborhood of 5 to 6 percent, and for FmHA it has historically been between 1 and 2 percent for all of the programs they administer. The jobs these programs create, the revenues they produce dwarf these miniscule outlays.

In 1968, the Agriculture Committee, in H.R. 18209, which later became Public Law 90–488, removed limitations on the aggregate amount of loans which may be insured—this includes guarantees—under the FmHA in any 1 year. Since the adoption of Public Law 90–488, ceilings on loan levels have been established solely by the members of the Appropriations Committee. Today, we are requesting this committee to increase loan programs to a level more commensurate with the demand, if not remove them entirely. As testimony at our hearings indicates, the backlog of qualified loan applicants remains substantial and could easily accommodate the significant increases in the loan authorizations ceilings that the CRC advocates. FmHA and SBA, with the help of trained people in our private financial institutions, will oversee these increases and bring about new jobs while fighting inflation and helping us to balance our budget—goals which all support. We ask for your assistance.

STATEMENT OF NATIONAL RURAL ELECTRIC COOPERATIVE ASSOCIATION ON
RURAL DEVELOPMENT BUDGET PROPOSED BY CONGRESSIONAL RURAL CAUCUS
BEFORE JOINT SUBCOMMITTEE HEARINGS MARCH 3, 4, and 5, 1977

Mr. Chairman and Members of the House Subcommittees on Rural Development, Conservation and Credit, and Small Business.

My name is William E. Murray. I am legislative specialist for rural
area development of the National Rural Electric Cooperative Association.
The national service organization of nearly 1,000 rural electric systems
operating in 46 states. These systems bring central electricity to
approximately 25-million farm and rural people over lines in 2,600 of the
nations 3,100 counties.

NRECA and its member systems have long been active in rural development. Rural electrification is one aspect of that interest and certainly
one of the most successful rural development programs in the history of
the nation.

We appreciate the opportunity to make our views known in regard to
the proposed Congressional Rural Caucus rural development budget which is
the subject of these hearings.

We feel that the Congressional Rural Caucus, made up of a hundred
members of the House of Representatives of both parties, is to be commended
for its proposal which at long last would make it possible to fully implement
the Rural Development Act of 1972, which NRECA has advocated for several years.

While we are confinding our comments to the part of the CRC budget
dealing with USDA rural development programs -- a total of $14.1-billion -- we
hope that Congress sees fit to also approve the $2.3-billion for farmer

programs. Thousands of our consumers are engaged in farming and it should
go without saying that a healthy, prosperous agriculture is basic to the
economy of rural America. Further, we would point out that there is a strong
interdependence between the non-farm and farm sectors so that it is important
that both the farm and non-farm economies are strong and growing. Some 40
to 45-million rural Americans depend on non-farm jobs for their livelihoods.
Over 50 per cent of farm families obtain more than half their incomes from
non-farm jobs.

The CRC budget, it seems to us, fulfills the commitment that Congress
made in Title IX of the Agriculture Act of 1970 when it stated: "The Congress
commits itself to a sound balance between rural and urban America. The
Congress considers this balance so essential to the peace, prosperity, and
welfare of all our citizens that the highest priority must be given to the
revitalization and development of rural areas."

The manifestation of this commitment was in the Rural Development Act
of 1972. Unfortunately, however, this act has yet to be fully implemented.
We believe the CRC budget would make it possible to do just this.

Moreover, we believe that the Rural Development Act could achieve all
the objectives Congress intended for it assuming the Executive Branch would
implement it on a scale commensurate with the need. We are encouraged to
think that the new administration will use the broad rural development
authorities which Congress provided in that legislation, not only to help
stabilize the populations and economies of rural communities, but as a part
of its priority commitment to reduce unemployment.

Rural development authorities, which have been successfully applied to halting rural outmigration, can now be directed to creating hundreds of thousands of new jobs for unemployed and underemployed in rural areas where unemployment rates often exceed the national average.

In a resolution which is attached, the membership of NRECA at its recent Annual Meeting in Atlanta, Georgia urged the USDA to use the authorities of the Rural Development Act and other legislation which supplements these authorities to launch a national effort "aimed toward substantial reduction of unemployment."

The resolution pointed out that "under the Rural Development Act of 1972 and other legislation, USDA has the potential for unlimited financing of a broad range of job creating enterprises including housing, community facilities of all kinds, business and industry, farming, electrification, telephony, health centers, telecommunications, conservation, and others."

It is obvious, however, that it will require a sizeable increase in the rural development budget to have the kind of impact on unemployment that is necessary. And that, it seems to us, is another justification for accepting the CRC proposal.

Our membership pointed out in their resolution that "most of this financing would be in the form of guaranteed or insured loans with minimal impact on the federal budget. This appears to us as the most cost effective manner of stimulating the economy which the government could choose."

We would add that of the $14.1-billion in the CRC proposal for rural development, $13.5-billion would be in the form of loan authorizations and only $557-million in grants. This could stimulate both the private and public sector to create permanent jobs which as CRC Chairman Rep. John Breckinridge pointed out in his statement would stimulate "the economy with protection of existing jobs plus the creation of new and additional jobs, resulting in tax revenues from wages and salaries as well as profitability potential for farm and non-farm enterprises." He added that the proposed budget "might well produce in the neighborhood of two to three million private sector jobs" and would be "more than 95 per cent privately, non-taxed dollar funded."

RESOLUTION ADOPTED BY MEMBERSHIP OF NATIONAL RURAL ELECTRIC
COOPERATIVE ASSOCIATION AT THEIR ANNUAL MEETING IN
ATLANTA, GEORGIA, FEBRUARY 24, 1977

Rural Jobs Creation

The President has assigned top priority to the critical national problem of unemployment which will require millions of new jobs.

We believe that the rural development authorities of the U.S. Department
of Agriculture could contribute significantly to reducing unemployment and
underemployment in rural areas and thereby help the President achieve his
goal.

USDA's rural development authorities, which have been successfully
directed to halting rural outmigration, could now be focused on the creation
of hundreds of thousands of jobs in rural areas where the unemployment rate
often exceeds the national average. This could benefit urban areas as well
since many rural people in search of employment migrate to the cities.

Under the Rural Development Act of 1972 and other legislation, USDA
has the potential for unlimited financing of a broad range of job-creating
enterprises including housing, community facilities of all kinds, business
and industry, farming, electrification, telephony, health centers, telecommunications, conservation, and others. Most of this financing would be
in the form of guaranteed or insured loans with minimal impact on the
federal budget. This appears to us as the most cost-effective manner of
stimulating the economy which the government could choose.

We urge the President and Secretary of Agriculture to develop a plan
to mobilize and coordinate the resources of the USDA and its constituencies
in a national effort aimed toward substantial reduction of unemployment.
Moreover, USDA could enlist the assistance of other federal agencies under
its authorities to provide leadership and coordination for all federal rural
development.

The rural electric systems pledge their full cooperation in such an
undertaking recognizing as they do its importance to the lives of millions
of Americans and to our nation's future.

STATEMENT OF EMBREE K. EASTERLY, PRESIDENT, CAPITAL BANK & TRUST CO.

Mr. Chairman and members of the subcommittee my name is Embree Easterly and I am president of the Capital Bank & Trust Co., a $170 million deposit institution located in Baton Rouge, La. I have been an officer of Capital Bank since it was organized in 1955 and its chief executive officer the past 15 years. I am past president of the Independent Bankers Association of America (IBAA) and serve at the present time on its administrative committee.

We are delighted to have this opportunity to appear before this distinguished committee to discuss the budget proposals for the Farmers Home Administration (FmHA) which will have far reaching impact upon life in many rural areas. IBAA is deeply concerned with these proposals since our membership is an integral part of the rural economy. Approximately one-half of our 7,300 member banks are located in towns of 2,000 or less. The average assets of our member banks is between $10 million and $15 million. Banks in this size category are keenly aware of the need for adequate funding of the FmHA loan programs and the full implementation of the Rural Development Act. Our testimony before the joint public hearings of the Subcommittee on Conservation and Credit, Subcommittee on Family Farms, Rural Development and Special Studies and the Subcommittee on Anti-trust, Capital and Employment on March 4, 1977, evidenced our concern in these areas and the continuing interest on the part of the IBAA.

On several occasions we have pointed out the need for additional capital to carry on meaningful rural development. In our opinion one of the best vehicles available for infusing massive doses of credit into rural areas through private lenders is the guaranteed loan. Under the FmHA program the lending institution may receive a guarantee of payment of principal and interest up to 90 percent of the original face value of the loan. The commercial bank benefits through broadened lending activities, increased earnings, and approved customer service capabilities and at the same time can maintain a high degree of liquidity. The Comptroller of the Currency has ruled that only the nonguaranteed portion of these loans counts against a national bank's legal lending limit. Bank regulatory agencies in most States have adopted the same rule for State banks under their jurisdiction.

Applicants for commercial and industrial loans with maturities usually exceeding 10 years frequently find that long-term credit is not available on a conventional basis in a small community. Such loan applicants can, however, be accommodated by a bank if guaranteed loans are available through the FmHA or other Government agencies. The guaranteed portion of such loans can be carried by the banking institution as a nonrisk asset and only that portion of the loan which is not guaranteed would be charged against the bank's legal lending limit.

In a typical situation a bank which may budget $500,000 for real estate loans could expand its loanable resources to $5 million with the benefit of a 90-percent guarantee. Furthermore, the guaranteed portion of such loans, which carries the full faith and credit of the U.S. Government, can be assigned to an outside investor, thereby bringing new capital into the bank and at the same time relieving the lending institution of the long-term investment which may present liquidity problems. The guarantee instruments offered by the FmHA in connection with the business and industry loans have been perfected to permit such assignments. As a consequence, a bank looks favorably upon this loan program in meeting its responsibility to its community.

Many banks are now utilizing the guaranteed loan programs effectively in rural areas and others will soon become involved in such lending. Our association recognizes the growing interest on the part of commercial banks and has recently conducted a seminar for banks to acquaint them with the procedures to be followed in processing guaranteed loans and the steps to be taken in selling of the guaranteed portion to institutional investors. The response of our banks has been encouraging and we look forward to additional seminars in the future to familiarize other banks with the guaranteed loan programs and marketing techniques.

It is our opinion that the guaranteed loan programs available through the FmHA and the SBA could stimulate business and industry in rural areas to the same extent that FHA and VA insured loans stimulated the housing industry. The guaranteed loan programs benefit the rural community, the business entrepreneur that frequently is unable to obtain conventional financing, and the banking institution which is confronted with capital shortages in meeting the seasonal demand in most rural communities. From our experience, these programs have created additional business for our bank and generated additional tax revenues for the Federal, State, and local governments.

I should point out that it takes a lot of hard work to get a program of this type moving. We now have over $30 million in loans that are being processed through the Capital Bank and its rural correspondent. These loans will create many new jobs. We expect to do three times as large a volume in 1977 as we have done in the past 6 years, and we are just getting started.

These programs are limited of course by the amount of guarantees made available by our Congress. From the banker's point of view a guarantee fills the capital void which has become critical in many sections of the country. With the contemplated growth of the guaranteed lending programs, it is obvious that commercial lending institutions will have to think of ways of improving the delivery system. We intend to work very closely with the FmHA personnel as well as other government agencies in bringing about a more efficient method of credit analysis and reduction in paperwork which becomes extremely burdensome for the country banker.

We feel confident that the potential for creating jobs and for expansion of rural economies through utilization of the guaranteed loan is almost unlimited. Futhermore, with the benefit of sound credit judgment on the part of the commercial banks, such programs can be made available with limited Federal outlays. At the present time the loss ratio on FmHA B. & I. loans is one-tenth of 1 percent. The average loss ratio for commercial bank mortgage loans is approximately one-half of 1 percent.

As bankers we feel that the guarantee fees which are charged by the guaranteeing agency should be based upon the best possible loss experience. In other words, these programs should be self-sustaining. The fees paid by banks should fund the Government's losses.

Under the 1977 budget, FmHA allocated $350 million for B. & I. loans. As of February 28 the agency had a backlog of 891 applications exceeding $991 million. The average loan is $654,000 which would only provide for 535 projects in the current fiscal year. During the current fiscal year guaranty loan allocations have already been exhausted in many States.

We would also like to call your attention to the fact that the farmer programs, that is the farm operating loans and farm ownership loans, for the most part have been financed directly by the FmHA under their insured loan program. At such time that the loan guarantee instruments are perfected to permit the sale to secondary market investors we can look forward to increased activity from commercial banking institutions in these areas as well.

Our association will continue to do all it can to encourage its members to utilize the guaranteed loan programs in achieving the objectives of the Rural Development Act. We respectfully urge your favorable consideration of the budget recommendations before you today.

Statement in Support of the Fiscal 1978 Appropriations for the Cooperative
State Research Service and the Extension Service of the U.S. Depart-
ment of Agriculture Cooperative State Research and Education Programs
by Dr. Kenneth A. Gilles, Chairman, Legislative Committee for USDA
Budget, Division of Agriculture, National Association of State
Universities and Land Grant Colleges and Vice President for Agriculture,
North Dakota State University, Fargo, North Dakota.

Mr. Chairman and members of the subcommittee: As representatives of
the National Association of State Universities and Land Grant Colleges,
we are truly appreciative of the opportunity to present this statement
concerning support for appropriations of the cooperative land-grant univer-
sity/USDA research and educational system in agriculture, home economics,
forestry, rural life and industry, and human welfare.

We wish to express our sincerest thanks and appreciation for the
positive support and understanding that you have given our programs. The
federal support for the agricultural research and experiment station programs at the various land grant colleges throughout the United States has
been a cornerstone of the financial support so essential for the continued
operation of these institutions which have become recognized worldwide
for their contributions to the improvement of agricultural technology,
agricultural systems and rural life. We pledge our fullest efforts to
give this country the best kind of effort and performance which fully
meets the expectations placed upon us.

We represent the state agricultural experiment stations, the state
cooperative extension services, the land grant institutions created by the
Act of 1890, as well as those created by the original Morrill Act, and the
state forestry research organizations. This is an integrated system and
our presentation today is one made in unity. We work together as a group;
our institutions are mutually supportive and function in close cooperation.
Those members of the Legislative Committee for USDA Budget who appear
before you today represent these several organizations.

During last year's presentation, we stressed that the uncertainty
about world food and fiber supplies for the short term as well as the long
term has kindled a renewed interest in agricultural research and extension
programs and that proper financial support and necessary attitude of
urgency for these programs must be recognized. However, during the past
year, peculiar and favorable weather conditions throughout the world
have created short-term food and fiber supplies and quality conditions
which suggest that, in the short term, basic needs in the developed
countries are being met. However, as quantities of various agricultural
commodities attain different marketing positions, interest in specialty
crops, particularly, take on new and important significance and the need
for agricultural research, education and extension programs remains as one
of the paramount issues.

If projections of the demographers are correct, world population will
approximately double shortly after the turn of the next century. This
will mean that to meet the level of nutrition that the world currently
enjoys, we must double food production worldwide; and if we wish to
overcome some of the deficiencies and concerns about malnutrition, food
production, distribution and processing systems must more than double
their capacity to create, to transport and to process food for the populations of the future.

We must take full cognizance of the fact that food research is a slow
process because it deals with life cycles of plants and animals. Frequently, several life cycles must be studied before one can conclude, with
certainty, that new and improved varieties of plants and animals have
indeed been created or modified for the well-being of mankind. We must

also take full cognizance of the fact that there are a number of immediate issues that must be evaluated as we plan for the future. One is that arable land resources are continually diminishing placing an increased pressure on the remaining land for increased production potential. Two, while the most valuable resource that much of our agricultural sector has is land, adequate sources of water of adequate quality to support plant and animal life must also be husbanded very carefully. The weather patterns of the western part of the United States during the past calendar year have reaffirmed the need for research in these areas of natural resources.

While we point with pride to the increased productivity of the agricultural sector, we must also recognize that because the innovative farmer has drawn heavily on science and technology to increase food and fiber productive capacity of the United States, the demands for an improved quality of life, concern about the environment, conservation of natural resources, and conservation of energy have necessitated re-evaluation and exploration of a number of agricultural processes. These current concerns have created a need to reassess old technology, evaluate current applications of science and technology and to strike out in new areas for the future. It is essential that we re-evaluate and exhibit vigorous leadership for the entire area of food and agricultural research. Within the structure of the land grant college system, we have the capabilities of providing this stimulating leadership; our greatest need is recognition and reaffirmation of federal financial support for these endeavors.

My colleagues who represent the agricultural research and extension organizations who are present today will expand on specific programs. My comments have been rather general; however, I believe they have emphasized two very important elements: One, there is a great need to recognize and to provide continual funding for agricultural research and extension programs at the individual land grant universities where factors such as local conditions of climate, soil, disease, plant pests, marketing, natural resources, and people can be accommodated into the research program. Secondly, there is need to expand research and extension programs in areas of current significance.

The budget requests which we present today are based on program needs as perceived by the research and extension leaders of the various states and territories. We are strongly committed to the system of research, extension and education which is currently being conducted and which has been recognized for its unique contributions to the improvement of the quality of life both in the United States and in its various foreign assistance programs. We support the concept of the land grant university system and appeal to you to provide continual federal support necessary for stability and growth for the food and fiber research, extension, youth and home economics programs.

FISCAL YEAR 1978 BUDGET RECOMMENDATIONS

for the

STATE AGRICULTURAL EXPERIMENT STATIONS
COLLEGES OF 1890 AND TUSKEGEE
ASSOCIATION OF STATE COLLEGES AND UNIVERSITIES' FORESTRY
RESEARCH ORGANIZATION

Presented by Dr. James H. Anderson, Director, Mississippi Agricultural and Forestry
Experiment Station, and Chairman, Legislative Subcommittee of the Experiment Station
Committee on Organization and Policy; with auxiliary statements by: Dr. Donald P.
Duncan (Missouri) for ASCUFRO; Dr. Edward M. Wilson (Missouri), Representative,
Division of Agriculture Legislative Committee, 1890 Institutions and Tuskegee.

RATIONALE

Wide recognition of the importance of agriculture to mankind's future is developing rapidly,
not only in the field row but in the city streets. Much less recognized are the problems of and
limitations to substantially increasing output of agricultural products. We cannot increase output
in the ways of the past. We must concentrate on efficiency of agriculture. We must find new ways
to get more from each acre at less cost—whether measured in dollars, energy, or some other method.
Simply put, we must make significant additional investments in research so that major breakthroughs
can be made.

Agricultural research needs are of a magnitude to tax the capabilities of federal (primarily
USDA) and state agricultural research institutions. The needs have been identified by a number
of national study groups as well as by administrators in the USDA and the SAES. Even though the
different study groups used different formats in outlining critical needs, there is general agreement
on research priorities. Some problems lend themselves ideally to the national and regional capabilities of the USDA. Others, and many of the really critical ones, are more appropriately the
domain of the state institutions, with their "grass roots" orientation that places them near where
"much of the action is."

As this nation enters its third century, it is evident that agriculture will continue to contribute greatly to the economic stability of the nation. By the turn of the century we will have less
prime agricultural land available, the same amount of fresh water will fall from the skies, yet we
will need to produce a third more food for our domestic needs, find ways to dispose of millions of
tons of solid waste each year and conserve the natural resources at our disposal. Furthermore,
burgeoning world populations and rising affluence will create opportunities for increased agricultural
export. Therefore, we must improve the efficiency of American agriculture if we expect to meet
our needs and capitalize on the opportunities available to us. Obviously, this will demand that we
make additional investments in agricultural research and education programs.

In order to point out the magnitude and complexity of the problem facing us, I am summarizing
below several items for your information and consideration.

1.   Federal Research Expenditure for the Period 1967-77.

        Federal expenditures for research increased between the period 1960-67
        and then leveled off. The total USDA research investment in 1967 was
        250.1 million dollars. In 1977, the USDA research investment is 250
        million in terms of 1967 dollars. During the 10-year period, the CSRS payment
        going to the states and the in-house research conducted by ARS decreased
        by approximately 8 percent. During the period 1967-75, non-federal
        funding in SAES increased by 42 percent but has leveled off during the
        past two years. Presently, federal funds account for only 17 percent of the
        funds in SAES. What was once a state/federal partnership in the SAES
        is now largely a state supported effort.

2.   The Research Agenda.

The research agenda consists of two items: a mission-oriented thrust designed
to serve the existing agricultural industry and a long-range dimension designed
to develop the technology base upon which to build the agricultural industry of
the future. Both are absolutely essential and present funding levels are not
adequate to support both. In times of limited resources, immediate problems
take priority and long-range efforts are delayed. Results: we are running out of
basic technology and can expect only marginal increases in productivity by
further massaging or fine tuning existing technology. Consequence: we will
not increase productivity to any great extent without major research breakthroughs
in several fundamental areas. Additional investments in long-range research
and a strengthening of basic mission-oriented research to exploit breakthrough
are an absolute necessity.

3.   The Payoff of Investment in Research.

Investments in agricultural research return large dividends to people in all walks
of life. A recent study made by the National Association of State Universities
and Land-Grant Colleges shows that society received an annual rate of return of
26.5 percent on investments in research on production agriculture during the
period 1939-72. Further, the study estimates that for additional investments in
research during the period 1978-85, the following annual returns (percentage) can
be expected: corn--32.0; soybeans--31.0; wheat--46.0; beef-forages--16.5;
swine--50.0; dairy--38.0.

4.   Research Priorities.

The high priority areas which have been identified as needing immediate attention
are:
   -Upgraded protein-rich cereals and other crops similar to high lysine corn.
   -Hybridization of additional crops, including wide crosses such as triticale.
   -Soil management techniques which would permit agricultural use of many of
      the low productive soils.
   -Biological rather than chemical control of harmful insects and diseases.
   -Extension of the principle of nitrogen fixation to new groups of plants in addition
      to legumes, thus cutting down the need for commercial fertilizer.
   -Greater environmental control for both plants and animals, providing more
      economical production and high, more standardized quality.
   -Improved biological efficiency of plants and animals in the use of plant and feed
      nutrients.
   -Improved production management systems for converting agricultural resources
      into useable plant and animal products.
   -Improved photosynthetic efficiency.
   -Expanded studies in tissue and cell culture.
   -Improved food safety and reduced loss of food in the production system.

-Improved fiber production to meet human needs for clothing, lumber and paper.
-Broadened studies of nutrient functions as reliable indicators of requirement and
  deficiency states for humans.
-Enlarged interdisciplinary longitudinal studies of consumer expenditures and
  resource use.
-Reduction of energy consumption and improved efficiency of energy use in
  agricultural production, processing, transportation and marketing.

It is evident that many of the high priority research areas outlined above are directly
related to energy efficiency in agriculture. Furthermore, breakthroughs in some of these areas will
result in large increases in production for a given set of resource inputs. This will not only increase
the direct on-the-farm efficiency of energy utilization but also the overall energy efficiency of the
total agricultural industry.

It is clearly in the interest of individual consumers (particularly those with lower incomes)
and in the national interest for the federal and state governments to make significant increases in
investment in agricultural research. Since we no longer have a backlog of agricultural technology,
time is of the essence because the scientific time lag is real. The longer increased support is
delayed, the longer we will have to wait for results. It is imperative that we begin immediately
to strengthen the research capability in both the USDA and SAES so maximum pressure can be
brought to bear on research problems in both the plant and animal sciences. This is the only way
to improve the efficiency of agricultural production.

Supplying an abundance of food at reasonable prices is not enough. Our national interest
in a healthy and productive society dictates that we achieve and maintain high standards of nutrition
despite changes in work habits, in family living patterns, in food pricing structures and in the use
of new food processing techniques. It simply is not enough to state that we have the safest, most
wholesome food to be found anywhere in the world. The accuracy and authenticity of that statement
must be examined and reexamined by our food and nutrition scientists to the end that continuing
wholesomeness and maximum nutritional value can be assured.

Individuals and families at all economic levels are faced not only with problems of obtaining
adequate nutrition but also with problems of money management and food preservation and
preparation, with concerns about health care, with the need for information about clothing, textiles
and housing and with great need to help to improve family living and child development.

The flow of residents from rural areas to urban areas has created significant problems both
for rural communities and for urban communities. Only token appropriations have been made to
support programs specific to rural development. We badly need a research effort designed to
further our understanding of the economic and social problems of our stagnating and deteriorating
rural communities. Only by such research will we be able to identify alternative programs that
hold promise for improvement of rural communities, and of urban communities insofar as problems
of the two are interrelated.

FISCAL 1978 BUDGET REQUEST

The FY 78 Budget Request has been authorized by the Agricultural Research Policy Advisory Committee (ARPAC) and the National Association of State Universities and Land-Grant Colleges. In addition, it has been discussed and approved by the Experiment Station Directors in the four regions, the Home Economic Subcommittee of ESCOP, and by the Association of State Colleges and University Forestry Research Organization, and the Colleges of 1890. The budget reflects what we believe are the most pressing research needs.

The FY 77 Budget increased the funds available to the Cooperative State Research Service for distribution to the states by $12,192,000 (Total FY 77 Budget -- $126,765,000). The FY 78 Budget Request outlines the need for an additional increase of $45,442,930 (36 percent increase in federal funds) to offset the increased cost of doing business, to undergird the present research effort and to expand the effort in selected critical areas (See Table 1). The total FY 78 Budget Request amounts to $172,207,930 for FY 78 (See Table 2, appendix). Admittedly, this is a large increase; however, we believe it is justified when one considers the magnitude and complexity of the research problems and the small increases in federal support over the past several years.

This statement is designed to give an óverview of the entire budget request and covers eight major items with brief justification of each item. The request covers a broad array of problems and time did not allow us to develop analytical data to justify the entire request. We have prepared a detail analysis on $10,100,000 or 22 percent of the requested increase. This material is presented in supplemental statements.

1.   Increased Operating Costs - $7,071,940

Inflation continues to severely erode the ability to adequately support the efforts of scientists in the State Agricultural Research Institutions. Numerous examples of increases in operating costs during the period July, 1975 - December, 1976 can be cited. Costs of natural gas and electricity have increased more than 26 percent; truck and automobile costs are up by 20 percent; public transportation costs are almost 18 percent higher. An increase in financial support is imperative if we are to cope with inflation, revitalize our research base, and maintain the level of agricultural research required for the solution of the complex problems facing our Nation.

Inflation is not the only culprit responsible for the erosion of support of agricultural research base. The kinds of research problems we are now required to address, their complexities, interrelationships, and impacts throughout our society, demand that we provide more sophisticated, costly laboratories; that our field experiments be conducted on a larger scale; and that in general we spend considerably more money to support the same relative level of scientific inquiry. Failure to address these complex problems facing agriculture and to be innovative and financially supportive of efforts to obtain solutions will be an abdication of our responsibilities in the SAES, but more importantly, the research base for the expanded food and fiber production required for our national growth and development will not be provided.

TABLE 1

Increase In Funds Requested for Support of Research Programs
in the States from Federal Sources (CSRS), FY '78

Component	Hatch	Mc-St	Specific Grants	1890 & Tuskegee	Rural Development	Total
Increased Operating Costs	5,688,100	492,720	--	801,120	90,000	7,071,940
Improved Productivity of Crops	6,900,000	--	2,000,000	650,000	--	9,550,000
Improved Productivity of Livestock and Poultry	5,300,000	--	--	350,000	--	5,650,000
Improved Environmental Quality and Conservation of Natural Resources	5,000,000	--	500,000	200,000	--	5,700,000
Food and Human Nutrition	3,000,000	--	500,000	1,200,000	--	4,700,000
Consumer Competence and Family Resource Use	1,700,000	--	500,000	--	--	2,200,000
Improved Timber Supply and Use of Forest Land	--	4,000,000	--	--	--	4,000,000
Rural Development	--	--	--	1,200,000	4,000,000	5,200,000
CSRS Administration	827,600	379,790	--	--	163,600	1,370,990
TOTAL	28,415,700	4,872,510	3,500,000	4,401,120	4,253,600	45,442,930

The cost of conducting all kinds of research has increased phenomenally. The laboratory equipment to support basic research has changed both in kind and in value. Electron microscopes, satellite observations, computers and other electronic devices are essential for the solution of the basic problems related to energy use and, indeed, almost all significant problems facing agriculture and forestry.

Developing and analyzing innovative, efficient systems for utilization of basic discoveries in the production, processing, financing, distributing and marketing of our food and fiber products are much more expensive. Systems are much more complex and experiments are more involved as additional concerns for environmental and social impacts have to be evaluated. The technological and managerial packages required by decision-makers in the food and fiber system cannot be developed with the present level of support for applied research.

Our research productivity is almost totally dependent upon the extent to which we adequately support our research scientists. An increase of $5,688,100 for Hatch programs and $90,000 for Rural Development programs is requested for the State Agricultural Experiment Stations, $492,720 for McIntire-Stennis Forestry programs, and $801,120 for programs of the Colleges of 1890 and Tuskegee.

2. Improved Productivity of Crops - $9,550,000

All of agriculture is directly dependent upon photosynthesis. While there have been continuous investments in photosynthetic research, there has been limited support for it within agriculture, and consequently, its relationship to increased yields has not been explored. The path of carbon is well defined but the enzymology of the process, the mechanism of photosynthesis, the nature of the light reactions, and the regulatory processes that control the chemistry of the products are still not sufficiently understood to permit rational application in improving crop performance. Likewise, the translocation of natural products and herbicides in crops and weeds is not adequately understood.

It is abundantly clear from a great deal of research that the chemical composition of row crops and forage crops is amenable to change through genetic manipulation. Plant breeders have traditionally been most concerned with yield and stability. Little attention has been paid to biochemical properties. Increased concern about the chemical and nutritional composition of our crops makes it mandatory that we give increased attention to genetic modifications of nutritional value, natural products for specific industrial uses, and the regulation of naturally occurring toxins in our food and fiber crops.

It has long been estimated that three times as much nitrogen is fixed by legume Rhizobium symbiosis as is produced by the chemical industry. Since there are genetic differences in Rhizobia, it is possible to identify strains which are more efficient in nitrogen fixation. There appears to be tremendous opportunities for increasing nitrogen fixation in soybeans, forage legumes and even extending the process to the grasses and cereals.

Techniques and procedures for accurately appraising crop losses due to pests need to be developed so that present losses can be accurately estimated. Basic studies to determine mechanisms of resistance to diseases and insects need to be intensified. A knowledge of biochemical defense systems in insects is vital in at least four major aspects of entomology: pest resistance to insecticides, insecticide synergism, host selection and host plant resistance. It is well documented that most resistance of insects to pesticides can be attributed to an increase in the insect's capability to detoxify the insecticide. Detailed information on the precise mechanisms involved could give valuable clues to reducing insecticide use and also to developing more effective insecticides.

Practically every aspect of the life of an insect necessary for its survival depends upon its uniquely keen sense of smell and taste. Well over 300 species detect and recognize potential mates by specific odors called pheromones. Others detect the plants on which they feed by specific odors and tastes, while still others identify their prey or hosts which they parasitize by specific chemical cues. The isolation, identification, and formulation of these specific chemicals into traps and baits for use in insect control represents one of the most rapidly expanding areas of a combined basic-applied research effort in today's agriculture. Our complete lack of understanding of how the insect's chemoreceptive system works severely limits our efforts to solve existing problems of pheromone and plant attractant use.

The amount of $6,900,000 for Hatch programs, $2,000,000 for Specific Grants and $650,000 for the Colleges of 1890 and Tuskegee is requested for research in Improved Productivity of Crops.

3.   Improved Production of Livestock and Poultry - $5,650,000

The animal industries are a large and dynamic part of the nation's agriculture. They perhaps have changed more in the past and will change more in the future than other segments of agriculture. The development of animal industries has been an exciting chapter in the history of agriculture. The beef business has come a long way from the scrawny woods cattle of a few decades ago to the modern pure-bred and cross-bred herds now seen on pastures and ranges throughout the nation. The dairy business has changed from the farmer milking by hand a few head of low-producing cows in an open corral to the large-scale modern dairies of today. The poultry business has come a long way from the barnyard flocks to the current egg and broiler factories.

The stories of success are legend--success in overcoming problems of breeding, nutrition, diseases, parasites, and management of animals under a wide range of environmental conditions. Today, livestock and poultry products play a key role in meeting the nutritional needs of the nation's people. They also are a major contributor to farm income, accounting for almost 43 billion dollars in farm income in 1975, or about 48 percent of total cash receipts from farming. But the animal industries still have a long way to go.

More efficient livestock and poultry production techniques as well as improvements in processing and marketing systems for these products are essential if an abundance of high quality animal protein is to be continually made available to consumers. Disease, insect and parasite losses; efficiency in meat, milk and egg production from available feedstuffs; and improvement in product quality and safety----all of these represent existing challenges to scientists engaged in livestock and poultry research. Much costly research must be undertaken if reproductive efficiency in beef is to be improved, if reproductive diseases are to be conquered, ova transplants are to become a reality, and if improved growth rates in beef are to be found. Similarly, these are great challenges for improving the reproductive efficiency in swine and for further improving the efficiency of feed conversion in swine and poultry.

Concern has been expressed about the inefficiencies of livestock and poultry as converters of feed to human food. The future of these animals in the food-producing chain has been questioned. The ruminant animals----beef cattle, dairy cattle and sheep----need not compete with man for sources of food. They rank high among the animal species that can convert materials unsuitable for human consumption into human foods. If it were not for the unique digestive processes of the ruminants, millions of acres of grasslands and many byproduct feeds would go largely unused in the production of human food----a waste that is hardly consistent with the critically increasing need for food. The transformation of the carbohydrates and proteins of forages, range and pastures into edible meat and milk products would be extremely costly to duplicate by any chemical-synthesis method yet devised.

Dynamic and profitable livestock and poultry industries are important to both the consuming public and the agricultural industry. In order to assure a continuous supply of meat, milk and egg products at reasonable prices to consumers, public support for an expanded and productive research program in the high priority problem areas identified above is essential. An amount of $5,300,000 for the State Agricultural Research Stations and $350,000 for the Colleges of 1890 and Tuskegee i requested for research on improved productivity of livestock and poultry.

4.   Improved Environmental Quality and Conservation of Natural Resources - $5,700,000

We are dependent upon natural resources for the production of food and fiber to sustain life for the present, and to ensure it for future generations. Concern with the conservation of our lands and waters is basic to all citizens. Past prosperity has been accomplished often at the expense of seemingly boundless natural resources, including many non-renewable ones. New land frontiers have essentially vanished. Yet, a burgeoning population demands higher food production while maintaining a quality environment. World population has increased about 50 percent in merely two decades. The costs of cleaning and maintaining a quality environment are all too evident in the absence of commensurate basic conservation knowledge.

Diminishing prime agricultural lands and the constant depletion of natural resources are stark realities. Resource inventory and monitoring programs identify the numerous problems and areas of concern, but they do not solve basic conservation dilemmas. Basic research efforts are necessary to understand the complex interactions of increased pressures on soil and water resources. Basic answers are needed to enable proper restoration of millions of acres of barren, nonproductive former agricultural areas. Factual data are needed to minimize increasing soil erosion and sedimentation, and the resultant costly stream eutrophication. Facts are required to minimize land waste and reduced agronomic production resulting from improper soil utilization.

Critical conservation choices require factual data bases for decision making. Intensive conservation and resource utilization methodologies must be developed, implied by high levels of technology capacity to support the present and future populace. An amount of $5,000,000 for the State Agricultural Research Stations, $500,000 for Specific Grants, and $200,000 for the Colleges of 1890 and Tuskegee is requested for research in the essential problem areas identified above.

5.   Food and Human Nutrition - $4,700,000

Although the primary objective of production - oriented agricultural research may be to expand food production, such an objective may be viewed as a means to reach one of several final goals - improved human nutrition. Research in human nutrition in the Experiment Station environment facilitates close coordination of research with disciplines involved in food production. Home economists have been active in food and nutrition research in the State Agricultural Experiment Stations since early in this century. Achievements over the past fifty years have included the application of knowledge to measure the nutritional status and needs of various age groups; the utilization of nutrients from a variety of food sources; interrelations among nutrients, food intake habits. Home economists are particularly concerned about the need for research in nutritional requirements of people in the face of restrictive resources and possible changing food

supplies. Nutritional status varies among different economic, ethnic, sex, and age groups. In order to make recommendations for improving the nutritional status of a population, it is necessary to learn how food patterns are developed. Additional information is needed on how ethnic background, income, nutrition knowledge, and level of education influence food choices. We can most effectively change food habits when we have a better understanding of the meaning of food and its significance and relationship to the total life styles of individuals and groups. Home economics focuses on determining the optimal nutrient requirements of healthy human beings, to discover the sources of these nutrients in food; and to evaluate the dietary habits and nutritional value of foods consumed by the nation's households. An amount of $3,000,000 for the State Stations, $500,000 for Specific Grants and $1,200,000 for the Colleges of 1890 and Tuskegee is being requested in Food and Human Nutrition.

6.   Consumer Competence and Family Resource Use - $2,200,000

While the nature of the field of Home Economics has evolved, its basic mission remains essentially the same, a concern for family and the quality of home and family life. The management of resources has become a national concern as well as a crucial concern for individuals and families. The effects of unemployment, underemployment, and inflation on the management of resources is not fully understood. It is essential that studies of the strategies which help families adjust and work out their problems be undertaken. Changes in family life style via the way they buy and use material resources such as food, clothing, and housing appears to be linked with the competence of family members as consumers. Both rural and urban families make purchase and use decisions which affect the environment.

Families with limited resources, particularly our senior citizens, would be important research populations since their purchasing power has been eroded severely. Research should be expanded on delineating the factors contributing to the deterioration or enhancement of the quality of home and family life. Understanding of how family interaction affects and is affected by various social institutions and programs is relatively meager. Home economics is an applied and integrative field, so we are accustomed to working across a variety of fields to incorporate useful information and techniques from many different areas. Such an approach is essential to assess throughout the life cycle the achievements of families in relation to their resource adjustments in periods of transition. An amount of $1,700,000 for the State Stations and $500,000 for Specific Grants is requested in the area discussed above.

7.   Improved Timber Supply and Use of Forest Lands - $4,000,000

An increase of $4,000,000 for the McIntire-Stennis Cooperative Forestry Research program is requested to expand research by the 62 cooperating institutions to improve timber and wood products supply and to improve decision making and management in managing forest and related resources for multiple benefits and in land use planning and allocation. Dr. Don Duncan, President, The Association of State Colleges and Forestry Research Organization, has prepared an auxiliary statement outlining the justification of the McIntire-Stennis Request. A copy of this statement is submitted with this request.

8.   Rural Development - $5,200,000

Rapid changes in technology, shifts in population concentrations, changes in the price and availability of resources and changes in institutions and organizations providing goods and services have resulted in a geographical redistribution of population and economic activity in this nation. The aged, small farmers and low-skilled nonfarm rural residents who were unable to, or who chose not to, migrate from their communities have long been a neglected strata from the standpoint of public policy research and public expenditures. They, more than any other demographic group, have borne the costs of both national economic growth and farm technological advance. There have been relatively few specific policies for these groups even though rural communities have the greatest relative concentration of persons disadvantaged by age, low income, underemployment, and inadequate health, education, recreational and housing facilities. Rural communities have not received an equitable share of the income and capital values generated by growth of our national economy over the past few decades.

Basic challenges to rural development researchers are the identification of the nature, location and extent of the inequities falling on these rural communities and their various population strata; the evaluation of alternatives for alleviating these inequities; and the provision of the necessary knowledge base for formulating public policy and program assistance to accomplish the task of improving rural communities. Central to these research challenges is the need to evaluate alternatives for the elimination of inequities in income, underemployment, human services, unfavorable living conditions and welfare conditions in rural areas. Alternatives for job creation and job training must receive high priority in the research agenda. Effective methods are needed to train the nonfarm work force in rural areas and to provide jobs for them there, or in nearby communities. Improvements in rural labor markets call for both types of programs--alternatives for the moving of people to jobs and the moving of jobs to people are required.

We believe the FY 78 Budget Request for $172,207,930 is necessary if the State Agricultural Experiment Stations are to meet the research challenges facing them. We are convinced that significant investments in agricultural research must be made if we are to make major increases in agricultural and forestry productivity. The budget outlines the critical areas needing attention in both agriculture and forestry.

The budget also outlines research needs in environmental quality and conservation of natural resources, food and human nutrition, consumer competence and family resource use and rural development. The solution to problems in these areas is imperative if we are to maintain a competitive agriculture and improve productivity.

A detailed breakdown of the budget request is shown in Table 3 in the appendix.

APPENDIX

Table 2
Appropriations for FY 77, Increases Requested, and Total FY 78 Requested by the States from Federal Sources (CSRS) for FY 78

Program	Appropriations FY 77	Increase Requested FY 78	Total Requested FY 78
Hatch			
To maintain program at current level	$	$ 5,688,100	$ 5,688,100
Payment to states	94,801,701	21,900,000	116,701,701
CSRS Administration	2,695,299	827,600	3,522,899
Penalty Mail	476,000		476,000
TOTAL Hatch	$ 97,973,000	$ 28,415,700	$ 126,388,700

McIntire-Stennis

To maintain program at current level	$	$ 492,720[1]	$ 492,720
Payment to states	8,212,000	4,000,000	12,212,000
CSRS administration		379,790	379,790
TOTAL McIntire-Stennis	$ 8,212,000	$ 4,872,510	$ 13,084,510

Specific Grants to Further USDA Programs

Environmental quality	$	$	$
Food and nutrition		500,000	500,000
Beef and pork production	400,000		400,000
Soybeans	500,000		500,000
Pest management	500,000		500,000
Rural development centers	300,000		300,000
Transportation and storage	500,000		500,000
Forage and range	400,000		400,000
Genetic vulnerability	300,000	1,000,000	1,300,000
Pesticide clearance	1,000,000		1,000,000
Land use		500,000	500,000
Crop loss appraisal		1,000,000	1,000,000
Family resource use		500,000	500,000
Food and agriculture policy	150,000		150,000
Soil erosion in the Pacific Northwest	350,000		350,000
Environmental plants in Hawaii	75,000		75,000
Dried bean research in North Dakota	25,000		25,000
TOTAL Specific Grants	$ 4,500,000	$ 3,500,000	$ 8,000,000

Program	Appropriations FY 77	Increase Requested FY 78	Total Requested FY 78
Special Grants to Colleges 1890 & Tuskegee			
To maintain program at current level	$	$ 801,120[1]	$ 801,120
Payment to states	13,352,000	3,600,000	16,952,000
TOTAL Colleges 1890 & Tuskegee	13,352,000	4,401,120	17,753,120
Rural Development, Title V, P. L. 92-419			
To maintain programs at current level	$	$ 90,000	$ 90,000
Payment to states	1,440,000	4,000,000	5,440,000
CSRS Administration	60,000	163,600	223,600
TOTAL Rural Development	$ 1,500,000	$ 4,253,600	$ 5,753,600
CSRS Administration--Direct Appropriation	1,228,000		1,228,000
TOTAL CSRS	$ 126,765,000	$ 45,442,930	$ 172,207,930

[1] 6% of FY Appropriations

March, 1977

STATEMENT OF DAVID L. HUME, ADMINISTRATOR

Mr. Chairman, the Department has estimated agricultural exports in the current fiscal year at around $23 billion—near last year's $22.8 billion. In both instances, I refer to October–September fiscal years. In the first 3 months of fiscal 1977, export value has been running above the preceding year—by nearly 4 percent.

In any case, it is believed likely that in fiscal 1977 the value of U.S. farm product exports will be slightly above last year's all-time record. This will be the fourth consecutive year that agricultural exports have exceeded $21 billion. In 3 of those years, including this year, export volume will have been at the level of about 100 million tons.

Without detailing the growth that these figures represent, I would like to make a point that seems most central to our whole export effort. It is the fact that, to a degree never before known, the export trade is now built in to the entire production and marketing structure of American agriculture.

In 1976, American farmers harvested 337 million acres—the largest harvested acreage in two decades. According to our projections, we will export the production from about 100 million of those acres. That is almost 1 acre in every 3 acres harvested. It is double the number of acres producing for export in the late 1950's and half again the number of acres producing for export in the late 1960's.

Meanwhile, the farmer's costs have continued to rise in this country. His investment and his equipment are geared to a planted acreage some 45 million acres greater than the area planted 7 or 8 years ago. Most of this additional acreage is being planted for export purposes, and it is very clear that farmers must export at today's higher level or face serious adjustment problems. Such problems would also affect government, business, working people, and consumers throughout the Nation.

With the overseas market having become such a vested part of our production and marketing system, a high level of farm exports becomes increasingly important to the entire economic complex related to food and agriculture. Agriculture employs 3.4 million workers. The food and fiber complex as a whole is believed to employ about 15 million. This is almost one American worker out of every six.

The high level of U.S. agricultural trade is also crucial to economies throughout the world. The United States is the world's largest agricultural exporter and the second largest agricultural importer. One-half or more of the grains in world trade and two-thirds of the soybeans in world trade originate on American farms.

Nations of the world have become increasingly interdependent and this affects our political and diplomatic relations with other nations—opening new avenues of communication with some countries where we had little or no economic relations a half dozen years ago. So it is evident that we are in a new era of global agriculture, a time in which nations are more sensitive to the need for each other, more aware of the long-term food problems presented by population growth, and more inclined to seek stability in world supplies and prices.

There is no agency of government upon which these new dimensions bear more heavily than they do upon the Foreign Agricultural Service. The FAS response to these developments has, of necessity, been carried on with little change in the basic resources of money and people that have been available to us.

The need to respond most effectively to new demands and responsibilities—and particularly to anticipate and plan—led us in 1976 to undertake a resource study examining the Agency in greater depth and detail than had ever been attempted before. We determined that we needed to go more deeply into our objectives and the resources available to us—to make a detailed review of programs and needs not just with reference to the coming year but to the longer term. We have now assembled the results of this review in a document that we are already finding very useful as a management tool.

We started out by asking ourselves a series of very basic questions: What should FAS be doing? What should FAS not be doing? What resources are at hand for the work we should be doing? What shifts in resources are possible to better meet our work objectives? What additional resources will be needed to do the additional work that we perceive as necessary?

We sought to answer these questions through a planned procedure—a disciplined sequence involving everyone in FAS down through the level of branch chiefs within divisions.

First, we defined more precisely than ever before the major objectives of FAS as they apply to the new global agriculture—the new era that is upon us these past 5 or 6 years. These objectives are:

(1) To achieve maximum foreign market access for American agriculture.

(2) To provide information to assist U.S. agriculture's adjustment to short-term changes in world supply and demand.

(3) To expand long-term foreign commercial markets for U.S. agricultural products.

(4) To safeguard American farmers and farm programs against unfair or injurious import competition.

Once these objectives were defined, we determined those activities and programs most needed to accomplish these objectives. We did not permit ourselves to mention or think about numbers of people or amounts of money in the resource review. We did not limit our thinking to ceilings or floors, but rather proceeded with minds as open as possible to those activities and programs, which, when carried out, would assure the most effective and economic achievement of the Agency objectives. These activities would be those which, in our collective judgment, would maximize the FAS contribution to USDA farm and food policies.

Only after going through this process did the Administrator and his immediate staff determine priorities and the numbers of people and amounts of money needed to do the job—that is, to mount and operate the programs needed to accomplish the Agency's objectives.

As Secretary Bergland has said, the next few years will place enormous new pressures on American agriculture and the Department of Agriculture. With completion of the resource review, we believe that FAS is in a position to perform more effectively its job of representing the Secretary abroad and furthering the interests of American farmers in the world economy, as well as to assure agriculture's very important role in keeping the U.S. national economy in good health.

Mr. Chairman, the budget request for the Foreign Agricultural Service in fiscal year 1978 is for $43,040,000—a net increase of $1,967,000 over this year's adjusted appropriation. Sixty-two percent or $1,213,000 of the requested increase consists of nondiscretionary items, the largest being overseas inflation, payments to the State Department for administrative support, and space rental costs paid to the General Services Administration. The remaining $754,000 of the requested increase is for additional program effort.

The largest program increase is $450,000 requested for the Large Area Crop Inventory Experiment (LACIE). This will provide the system with software packages applicable to crop forecasts in large geographical regions not yet surveyed. It will also provide the technological components for additional analyst stations to analyze and disseminate reported data. This software-hardware combination will permit LACIE to begin transition from an experiment to an operational system within USDA.

The other large item is $388,000 requested for new and expanded post coverage by the Agricultural Attachés. Specifically, it will provide for new posts in the German Democratic Republic, the U.S.S.R. (at the U.S. Consulate in Kiev), Singapore, and the Arabian Peninsula. Funding is requested for additional staff at existing posts in Indonesia and New Zealand.

In addition, an increase is requested to strengthen the U.S.–U.S.S.R. Secretariat, which administers and coordinates the U.S. part of the 1973 U.S.–U.S.S R. Agreement on Agricultural Cooperation.

Statement

By A. Harold Peterson
Executive Director and Counsel
National REA Telephone Association
March 29, 1977

INTRODUCTION

The telephone amendment to the REA Act was signed into law
in October, 1949. On February 24, 1950, the first REA
Telephone loan was made to Florala Telephone Company at
Florala, Alabama. In the twenty-seven years since, and
through January 31, 1977, loans totalling over $4 billion
dollars have been made to 923 borrowers. In all the history
of this program there has never been a default on a loan.
This outstanding financial record tells only part of the
story.

The hundreds of old, worn-out telephone systems that
existed in 1949 have been transformed into the most modern
telephone systems in our country. The state of the art in
this industry is improving each year. REA, through the
leadership and ability of its fine technical staff, has led
the industry in accomplishing many of these improvements.

The extent to which development has been achieved in Rural
America would not have been possible without the REA electric
and telephone program. It is most gratifying to witness the
large number of people who have moved and continue to move
into rural areas. This is good from the sociological as
well as the economic viewpoint.

CONGRESS CORRECTS UNINTENDED INEQUITIES

Three years operation after the major 1973 amendments to the REA Act showed that too many companies were eligible for the two percent "special rate" of interest. This result was neither intended by the Congress nor expected by the borrowers. Both the electric and telephone borrowers acted in a responsible manner and recommended that this situation be corrected. Congress responded and new criteria was adopted late in the 94th Congress. As a result the number of borrowers who qualify for the two percent "special rate" financing for the telephone program was reduced substantially to the number originally intended in 1973. The step-by-step ability to pay basis concerning rate of interest was restored and the integrity of the program preserved. Borrowers' interest rates on loans range from insured loans at 2% and 5%, Rural Telephone Bank loans (now 6.5%), and guaranteed loans at the market rate of interest.

BACKLOG OF UNAPPROVED LOANS IS $725.9 MILLION

In spite of the higher loan levels of the past three years, the backlog of unapproved loan applications on hand remains relatively high.

On February 28, 1977, the amount of unapproved telephone loan applications on hand was $725.9 million.

Testimony of Hon. Teno Roncalio

Mr. Roncalio. Mr. Chairman, thank you for the opportunity to appear today to present the interests and concerns of my Wyoming constituents in regard to the fiscal year 1978 budget requests of the Department of Agriculture. My testimony today concerns various programs in the following areas: The Agricultural Research Service, the Extension Service, the Farmers Home Administration, the Soil Conservation Service, the agricultural conservation program, and finally, the Food and Nutrition Service.

AGRICULTURAL PROGRAMS

I am pleased to note that President Carter increased the request for the Agricultural Research Service by $37.1 million for fiscal year 1978. I heartily endorse this increase. I would like to request that the subcommittee earmark a portion of this increase to be used for research in agricultural pharmacology. Agricultural pharmacology involves the use of chemicals and drugs to enhance the production and to maintain the health of livestock. Not only will the utilization of agricultural pharmacology have benefits for livestock, it will also benefit consumers through increased food and fiber production and better nutrition.

There are two items under the Extension Service that I would like to address. I am pleased to see a $1-million increase in fiscal year 1978 for activities of the Extension Service. However, I am concerned over the decision to eliminate $1 million for community resources development programs. I would also like to take this opportunity to express my sincere support for the nutrition education program and hope that the subcommittee will again approve $50.5 million.

RURAL DEVELOPMENT AND ASSISTANCE PROGRAMS

I would like to express my elation over the fact that the administration has seen fit to include $190 million in its fiscal year 1978 budget requests for the agricultural conservation program in the Agricultural Stabilization and Conservation Service. I am sure that all of the members of the subcommittee are pleased that they will not have to restore this valuable program in fiscal year 1978, for the first time in nearly 22 years. It is my sincere hope the subcommittee will support this $190 million request.

The Farmers Home Administration has been an effective and important institution in our State of Wyoming. I am pleased that President Carter has increased the request for the FmHA to $961.8 million. However, I am concerned that three FmHA programs have been scheduled for elimination in fiscal year 1978. These are: The mutual and self-help housing program, community fire protection grants, and finally, rural development grants. It is my hope that the subcommittee will take positive action by restoring these programs to their fiscal year 1977 levels. The State of Wyoming could be adversely affected if these programs were discontinued.

A final area of concern under rural development and assistance is the Soil Conservation Service. Decreases have been proposed for several programs in SCS. At a time when the entire Western United States faces a serious and severe drought, the decision to decrease funds for watershed planning and construction, for river basin surveys, and for resource conservation and development, is untimely. I respectfully request that the subcommittee increase funds for these programs, at the very least to their fiscal year 1977 levels of $1 million for watershed planning; $21 million for watershed construction; $356,000 for river basin surveys; and $7.3 million for resource conservation and development. The consequences of the drought in the West are frightening enough, without having to deal with substantial decreases in watershed planning and construction.

DOMESTIC FOOD PROGRAMS

Agriculture's Food and Nutrition Service performs one of the most important functions in the Nation: It is involved in assuring and maintaining the health of this Nation's most important resource: Children, by providing adequate nutrition. At the present time, the Elementary, Secondary and Vocational Education Subcommittee is considering authorizing legislation for several child nutrition programs, and it is difficult, therefore, to speak of hard facts and figures with regard to these programs. I ask that the subcommittee make every effort to see that these child nutrition programs are funded at adequate and realistic levels in fiscal year 1978.

I am pleased to note that President Carter increased the funding level for the child nutrition program to $2.5 billion. Unfortunately, this falls far short of the fiscal year 1977 funding level of $2.8 billion. I hope that the subcommittee will increase this item to its fiscal year 1977 level. It is also disheartening to see a substantial cut in the special milk program, and hope the subcommittee will increase this program to its fiscal year 1977 level of $154.1 million. Finally, I am pleased to see that the special food supplemental program for women and infants has been maintained at its fiscal year 1977 level of $247 million. All of these programs are vital to assure that our children have adequate nutrition.

Mr. Chairman, I want to thank you and the members of the subcommittee for your kind attention to these remarks.

Mr. Chairman, I would hope that you could at least consider the present drought, and restore the funds to the fiscal 1977 levels, and that is $1 million for watershed planning, and $20 million for watershed construction, and $256,000 for river basin surveys, and $7 million for resource conservation development, especially in lieu of the fact that there will be some changes somewhere on the Rocky Mountain West, either the Colorado River, maybe in your area, Mr. Andrews, but we will not win them all.

We hope that the more valuable ones will survive.

In any event, it would make it doubly important in my opinion to continue the resource conservation and development program, in spite of the drought, in spite of the arid conditions of the West, and the inevitable cuts on the water programs that seem to be the result of the administration.

Mr. WHITTEN. We appreciate your appearance and your support for these valuable programs.

This committee has a long record of support in that area, and we expect to do the very best we can. We are glad to see that the new President has recognized the value some of these programs that have suffered in the past.

TUESDAY, APRIL 5, 1977.

TESTIMONY OF HON. FRED RICHMOND, CONGRESSMAN FROM THE STATE OF NEW YORK

Mr. WHITTEN. Gentlemen, the subcommittee will please come to order.

I remember back in my high school days having had what was called a declaration of interdependence. At that time we had competition in public speaking and debating.

I think as you gain experience in life, you get to where you have a realization of the interdependence in a community, and in a State and in a country and throughout the world. The members of this subcommittee realize that as our society has become more and more urban, that it becomes more essential that we have this awareness of our interdependence on one another.

We have written reports through the years showing the fact that our whole standard of living is based on the fact that so few of us provide food, clothing, and shelter for all of us. As a result the rest of us can do whatever we may wish to. Our agricultural production is a key to our standard of living.

The press, the news media, and those running for public office usually give attention to the numbers. In this case it is the 95 percent of our people who are not in family. We have fewer and fewer rural people and fewer and fewer farmers, those that actually produce food and fiber for the rest of us. Naturally, magazines, newspapers, politicians, and everybody else is going where the numbers are primarily, and pretty much ignore the 5 percent who produce our food. Whether they intend to or not, it ends up that way.

I have been very proud that this subcommittee with the help of my friend, Fred Richmond from downtown New York City, who is before us today, and other Members of Congress, have recognized that the programs that we have had in rural areas are ultimately of benefit to the people in the cities. The votes that the rural people need are in the cities also, so it has been a 2-way street.

I am also very proud in what we have done in the way of spreading 4-H Club work. About 6 months ago, I spoke to 4-H leaders from throughout the country, and it developed as it is shown in the record, that the biggest 4-H Club in the United States is in downtown Indianapolis, Ind.

We on this committee also sponsored the nutrition aides program. We have provided human nutrition aides to people in urban areas, assistance from people they knew and liked and in turn who knew what they were doing. Prior to that, we on this committee had sponsored and had approved by Congress funds to provide for studies of the wholesale marketing facilities in the various large cities. Funds to draw up plans which would improve the distribution of food, and to reduce the cost of food distribution.

These plans have been adopted in the city of New York, the city of Detroit, the city of Philadelphia, the city of Baltimore and many, many other large cities throughout the country. In recent years, at our suggestion and through some pressure on the Department, we have stressed home gardening. I believe a report stated last year over 51 percent of the American people had a garden.

Fred, we are proud to have you with us today, and I want to say for the record that your interest in agriculture and in the basic things is not only a credit to you, but very helpful to the Congress and to this subcommittee.

We appreciate the way you have worked for all of us, and we just hope we can contribute a little on our part.

We are glad to hear from you.

Mr. RICHMOND. Mr. Chairman, thank you.

I thank you for those remarks, and they make me feel like doing more.

Mr. Chairman, I appreciate this opportunity to appear before you and express my continued support for the Department of Agriculture's urban-oriented programs.

As an urban Representative, I am constantly aware of the value and impact of such programs. Those which I will discuss today are not only vital to urbanites, but to every American.

These programs are becoming a vital link between urban and rural America, and must be given serious consideration by those of us who can provide for their effective implementation.

URBAN GARDENING

Urban gardening and food preservation programs in our large cities are essential if we are to have well-educated consumers.

I believe that urban residents should be made aware of how their food is grown.

Two years ago, as you well know, Mr. Chairman, I proposed such educational programs; action was taken to investigate the possibilities and a pilot program was initiated.

The New York State Cooperative Extension Service at Cornell University has developed an urban gardening proposal for New York City during these past 2 years.

Through the generous funding of this committee, the service is literally reaching into the inner city and is finding a receptive and anxious group of city gardeners.

There will be 19 full-time experts implementing the program in New York City this year when staffing is completed.

Agriculture students from Rutgers and Cornell Universities will assist the experts this summer as the program gets underway.

The level of enthusiasm is high among the many groups who are starting community-wide programs. Senior citizen homes, drug rehabilitation centers, church groups, environmental groups, and others are swinging into action.

Orientation has begun and planting will soon begin. "Home grown," fresh, nutritious vegetables will soon be popping up throughout the city—on rooftops, on patios, on vacant lots—everywhere.

Urban agriculture, thanks to this committee, is taking root.

The level of excitement is high. Many are harboring dreams of a green, vital, and growing city where abandoned buildings will be torn down to provide more gardening space.

Soon, after the planning is finished, nutrition education programs will begin. Extension program directors are already planning for summer nutrition workshops and similar related activities.

New York is only one of six cities in the United States chosen for this program. Other participating cities include Philadelphia, Detroit, Chicago, Los Angeles, and Houston.

Each has submitted an urban gardening plan during the past year, and all have been approved. These cities are now also staffing and gearing up for the coming activities.

However, I now believe that organizational change is necessary if the program is to totally succeed.

I believe that urban gardening should be funded separately under the Extension Service, rather than as a unit of the expanded food and nutrition education program.

This change would give the urban gardening program more flexibility in designing its programs because it would no longer financially deplete funds of the nutrition aides program.

It would also allow the principles and techniques of urban gardening to reach an enormous number of city-dwelling gardeners throughout the Nation.

Rural gardening programs could be brought to the city, utilizing the same types of service that are now offered to farmers.

These would include meetings for discussion of new gardening practices, energy-saving measures and economic considerations.

Educational newsletters could be started and urban farmers could begin to draw upon the agricultural expertise of the entire Extension Service.

Also, Mr. Chairman, by allowing the current urban gardening program to expand, we would also help our Nation's farmers, who often complain that urban consumers don't understand their situation.

Expansion of this program would give city dwellers the opportunity to understand how difficult it is for a farmer to cope with environmental problems, including pest and disease control, soil conservation and the vagaries of weather.

It would give them grassroots knowledge of their food source and act as an important element in expanding a necessary urban/rural understanding.

The New York City program has served as a model for cities throughout the country. With a funding level of $1.5 million and establishment as a separate functional unit of the extension service, urban gardening would be well on its way to setting an impressive precedent for future urban programs.

DIRECT MARKETING

As this committee considers funding for other USDA programs that affect our Nation's urban citizens, it has the opportunity to begin to share the fruits of agriculture directly to provide a comprehensive and vitally needed direct marketing program.

The Farmer-to-Consumer Direct Marketing Act of 1976 authorizes $1.5 million for fiscal years 1977 and 1978 for the Extension Service and the various State departments of agriculture to encourage direct farmer-to-consumer marketing.

These funds would help farmers identify consumer groups that are interested in direct marketing techniques, such as co-ops, farmers' markets, "pick your own" farms, roadside markets and other numerous possibilities.

Farmers and consumers would begin working more closely together in developing direct economic ties. A basis for a true understanding of each other's problems would be provided upon which farmers and consumers could build.

In addition to this essential grassroots knowledge these two groups would gain about one another in economic terms, I strongly believe both would gain closer social ties that would help bring the entire Nation closer together.

As yet, these funds have not been appropriated. I hope this committee will see fit to appropriate the $1.5 million in needed funds to get this program rolling.

The USDA has expressed interest in using its expertise to implement this act and both consumers and farmers are ready and waiting.

EXPANDED FOOD AND NUTRITION EDUCATION PROGRAMS

I also urge this committee to examine the positive social impact of the expanded food and nutrition education program.

Funding of this program at approximately $50.5 million has been maintained for the past 4 years.

I thank the committee for realizing the worth of this vital arm of the Extension Service.

However, during the past 4 years, the program's purchasing power has decreased from $34,654,000 in 1973 to $24,237,000 at present. As a result, the program is only reaching about 255,000 families or only 20 percent of the eligible population.

As you know, this program involves direct, personal contact between nutrition aides and low-income families.

Adequate funding is necessary to provide wages and training for these nutrition aides, who themselves come from low-income families.

In order for it to start effectively reaching at least 80 percent of our in or near poverty level population, I recommend a funding level of $60 million.

This will insure nutrition education for food stamp recipients and for those participating in the women and infant children's program.

Additionally, I am pleased at President Carter's proposal to maintain the funding of the youth conservation program of the Forest Service at last year's level.

The program, which employs high school age students during the summer months in forest areas, is an excellent way to bring our urban, inner-city youth closer to forestry so they may have a better understanding and appreciation of our shared environment.

Mr. Chairman, last year I arranged for 10 youths from my district to spend 2 weeks on Minnesota farms with the help and coordinating efforts of Congressman Richard Nolan.

I visited the children on the farms at the end of their stay and was truly impressed with how much their understanding of agriculture had increased.

They returned home and told their friends about their trip and enthusiasm has developed to a point where we are arranging for 50 young students to visit farms this summer.

DEPARTMENT OF AGRICULTURE AND RELATED AGENCIES APPROPRIATIONS FOR FISCAL YEAR 1978

TUESDAY, APRIL 5, 1977.

SELECTED URBAN PROGRAMS

WITNESS

M. J. PALLANSCH, ASSISTANT ADMINISTRATOR, MARKETING, NUTRITION, AND ENGINEERING SCIENCES, AGRICULTURAL RESEARCH SERVICE

OPENING REMARKS

Mr. WHITTEN. The subcommittee will please come to order.

Gentlemen, we will today discuss some selected urban programs with two groups' programs which we have sponsored through the years. In recent years we have not had them appear together. I think we need to continue to stress and recognize the desirability of their work. That is why we have scheduled this appearance.

One of the groups has to do with marketing and the other has to do with nutrition aid.

Dr. Pallansch

URBAN PROGRAMS OF THE AGRICULTURAL RESEARCH SERVICE

With the growth of the cities, Congress recognized the growing problem encountered in providing food and fiber to urban areas and passed legislation to authorize the USDA to conduct research directed toward increasing marketing efficiency.

One phase of USDA marketing research that has had a relatively large but unrecognized impact upon urban populations is our studies of the wholesale food marketing facilities.

Many of the wholesale food marketing facilities have become outdated, inadequate, and inefficient to use.

The Agricultural Research Service of the USDA has the only fulltime research program in the United States on improving the facilities and methods for marketing food.

Through this program, ARS has gained knowledge, rapport, respect, and expertise that has given it a worldwide reputation as the leading authority in food marketing facility planning.

Facilities patterned after concepts ARS has developed have been built in cities all over the country and the world.

Upon request, ARS provides technical assistance and guidance to cities that want new food facilities and to private consulting, engineering, construction, architectural, and food industry firms who actually plan and build them.

Urban wholesale markets have been built or are under construction in 40 of the 70 cities where ARS studies have been completed.

The new markets that have been built as a result of this program have demonstrated the far-reaching effects of such developments. These include, but are not limited to: (1) more efficient food handling;

(2) redevelopment of blighted communities; (3) better local employ-ment opportunities; (4) better services by food distributors; (5) more orderly food distribution; (6) upgrading of the local food industry in·the local communities; and (7) improved sanitation, food safety, and reduced food losses.

All these result directly or indirectly in benefits to the city dweller.

URBAN GARDENING

Many people in urban areas are well aware of their vulnerability in regard to the food supply and higher costs for food and attempt to circumvent this to some extent by gardening at home.

It has been estimated that in 1977, slightly more than 50 percent of the U.S. families will have home gardens.

A considerable amount of the information developed by USDA farm research is directly applicable to the solution of problems en-countered by the home gardener.

Home gardeners usually have to work with poor soil, polluted air, and temperatures, humidities, and levels of sunlight that are quite different from those found on the typical farm.

In consideration of this, the Department has conducted and supported research on home gardening.

The beneficial results of this effort have been numerous.

During the last 5 years, ARS scientists have released or participated with the State agricultural experiment stations in the release of 41 varieties and 62 breeding lines involving 18 vegetable crops.

These new varieties are better producers, more disease resistant and capable of surviving better in smog-polluted air.

Today ARS scientists are conducting research with over 20 different vegetable crops. Such research will result in a continuing progression of improved varieties ready for immediate use by small farmers and home gardeners, as well as valuable breeding lines for release to seed companies to use in their own breeding work in the production of garden seed.

Other USDA research is being conducted on landscape plants suit-able for urban and suburban areas.

Such crops are widely grown in nurseries operated by urban garden-ers and small- and part-time farmers in all parts of the country.

New varieties of fruit and nut trees having higher yields, better quality, greater consumer acceptance, and greater resistance to disease and insects have been developed by USDA scientists for the home garden.

The Department is continuing its efforts to develop more efficient and safer pesticides for use by small farmers and home gardeners.

In consideration of the need to preserve the successful harvest of the home gardener, the Department also conducts research to develop improved methods for home canning.

The research results that are useful to the home gardener have been printed in pamphlet form.

The Department's instruction booklet describing proper methods for home canning has been issued at the rate of 1 million copies per year for the past 5 years.

STATEMENT OF DR. AUGUST E. KEHR, STAFF SCIENTIST, VEGETABLES AND FLORIST
AND NURSERY CROPS, NATIONAL PROGRAM STAFF, ARS.

Mr. Chairman and members of the committee, with rising food costs, more and
more Ameicans are producing homegrown food. Recent surveys results by the
U.S. Department of Agriculture indicate there has been a steady increase in urban
gardening in the last 5 years.

Predominant reasons for homegrowing of vegetables and fruits were a desire
to reduce food costs for the family, a preference for the taste of freshly harvested
produce, and for the pleasure and recreation. Tomatoes are the most popular
vegetable for fresh use and canning; green beans are most popular for fresh use
and freezing.

ARS RESEARCH FOR URBAN GARDENERS

Recent research by ARS scientists has had significant application and use by
urban gardeners. The major contributions have been in the development and dissemination of new varieties that are disease and insect resistant, high quality,
and adapted to urban environments. ARS research has also contributed to new
and improved cultural practices, and disease and insect control.

During the last 5 years, ARS scientists have released or participated with State
agricultural experiment stations in the release of 41 varieties and 62 breeding
lines involving 18 vegetable crops. Specific examples of research developed in
the last year include the following:

Tomatoes

Development of resistance to verticillium and of fusarium resistant lines—
these two diseases are found throughout the United States and most urban gardens carry the disease indefinitely from year to year in the soils. No home gardener could grow tomatoes without this deveopment unless his garden soil is
fumigated.

Release of Roza, Columbia, Rowpac, and Saladmaster—four curly top resistant
tomatoes for home gardens in Western States where this disease is a hazard to
home production.

Development of tomato breeding lines with resistance to early blight, septoria
leaf spot, and anthracnose fruit rots, all of which are diseases difficult or impossible to control by urban gardeners.

Development of tomatoes resistant to spider mites, flea beetles, aphids, and
fruit worms—all serious tomato insects.

Nematode resistance.

High color factors (genes) to give brighter red fruits.

Potatoes

Parental development. Parental combinations are being developed combining
wide adaptability, resistance to leafroll, tuber net-necrosis, golden nematode,
scab, late blight, immunity to virus Y and resistance to the leafhopper in both
white and russet skin clones. Approximately 250 selections were evaluated for
resistance to viruses A, X, and Y. B6987–56, a widely adapted high quality, pest-
resistant clone, is being named as variety Atlantic.

Insect resistance. Breeding clones were field tested for resistance to potato
leafhoppers and potato flea beetles. Consistent with previous tests, B6712–9,
B6761–11, B6558–2, and BR7103–7 exhibited low leafhopper infestation and
hopperburn levels.

Vitamin C. There were highly significant differences between families in
tuber ascorbic acid (Vitamin C) content, indicating good potential for increasing contents of this vitamin through breeding and selection.

Close spacing increases yield. Yield increases of potatoes over conventional
3-foot row spacing were as great as 40 percent when the crop is planted in rows
18 inches apart in a home garden.

Pumpkins

Insect resistance. Sixty-seven pumpkin cultivars/lines were screened in cage houses for resistance to the red pumpkin beetle. One accession showed no feeding damage while all others showed varying degrees of susceptibility.

Edible seed. Pumpkin seed with no seed coat were developed for ease of eating, and a variety released and named "Lady Godiva." This variety has seed with 35-percent protein and 45-percent high quality fat—comparable to peanuts in food value.

Bunch types. To save space in a home garden, nonvining or bunch type pumpkins are being developed.

Onions

Long-storage inbreds developed. New inbred lines with the long-dormant characteristic, tested in storage trials, proved superior to those previously tested. After 11 months of nonrefrigerated home-type storage with no sprout inhibitor, the best lines had less than 15-percent loss from sprouting while all currently used cultivars were over 90-percent sprouted.

Air pollution resistance

Germplasm has been found in beans, tomatoes, spinach, lima beans, and potatoes with high tolerance or resistance to air pollution. The germplasm will be used to develop varieties adapted for growing in urban environments and in areas with high levels of air pollution.

Melons

Pest resistant lines developed. About 1,000 varieties, plant introductions, new crosses, and breeding lines were evaluated for disease resistance. Fifty-seven lines were found that retained good foliage under severe incidence of downy mildew, powdery mildew, alternaria, and gummy stem blight.

One selection of breeding lines 63–4–M1–18–M8 remained free of aphids in a heavily infested field. It produced a high yield of fruit with good levels of ascorbic acid and soluble solids.

Sweet Corn

High sugar types. Work has continued toward the development of high-sugar genotypes using the endosperm mutant genes amylose extender (ae), dull (du), and waxy (wx). Sweet corn with these new genes are sweeter at harvest and retain their sugar content longer than do commonly grown sweet corns with the sugary genes.

Sweetpotato

Breeding for resistance to grubs and wireworms.

ARS has accelerated its research program to clear many pesticides for crops grown by urban gardeners.

Today, ARS scientists are conducting research with over 20 vegetable crops. ARS undertakes research that vegetable seed companies cannot afford because they will be unlikely to recoup their investment. This includes searching for new sources of genetic resistance to diseases and insects, identifying factors responsible for high quality, and identifying the basic factors responsible for high yield and adaptability to a wide range of cultural and climatic conditions. Such research will result in a continuing progression of improved varieties ready for immediate use by small farmers and gardeners as well as valuable breeding lines for release to seed companies to use in their own breeding work in production of garden seed. As a result, ARS research reduces the need for small farmers and gardeners to concern themselves with identifying and controlling diseases and insects and provides them with greater certainty of producing high-quality crops, even in areas of the country with less than ideal growing condition and during seasons of adverse weather.

LANDSCAPE PLANTS AND VEGETABLE BEDDING PLANTS

ARS scientists have been working directly with producers of bedding plants, foliage plants, and ornamentals for use by urban gardeners. ARS research has studied the effects of light sources, controlled environment, and growth hormones on plant response and has developed the equipment and facilities necessary to produce plants under controlled conditions. This research has improved the technology to grow vegetable plants and flowers in urban gardens, small acreages, or in greenhouses. Hobbyists also are using this research and technology to enhance the growth of plants at home.

Other ARS research is being conducted on landscape plants, especially developing plants suitable for urban, suburban, and rural areas. Such plants are usually disease resistant, tolerant of air pollution and low growing in order to correspond with modern home architecture. ARS has released improved cultivars of camellias, hollies, pyracantha, crepe myrtles, magnolias, shade trees, azaleas, and similar nursery crops. Such crops are widely grown in nurseries operated by urban gardeners and small part-time farmers in all parts of the country.

SMALL FRUITS

The ARS fruit and nut research programs provide excellent examples of research to help the small farmer. Such research includes breeding programs for strawberries, blueberries, raspberries, blackberries, grapes, cherries, peaches, plums, apples, pears, citrus, and pecans. During the last 20 years, 37 new varieties of small fruits have been introduced, including 18 strawberries, 10 grapes, and 9 blueberries. Newer varieties also have higher yields, better quality, greater consumer acceptance, and greater resistance to diseases and insects. Strawberries, for example, could not be grown in most Eastern States if ARS–SAES breeders had not developed varieties resistant to *Phytophthora fragaria*, a root disease organism. The newer introductions have resistance to five races of the disease. In Illinois, for example, 65 percent of the strawberry acreage is in ARS varieties.

Development of thornless blackberries has made this fruit especially suitable to home gardens. Recently introduced strawberries were tailored to resist disease problems common to home gardens. There varieties are also especially suitable for home freezing.

Pest control in horticultural crops

ARS work on pest control provides a number of examples of benefit to home gardeners. Improved pesticide application equipment has resulted from ARS research on the use of various pesticide formulations such as granules, foams, invert emulsions, and devices to control spray droplet formation. Small pesticide application equipment is available to homeowners. ARS is continuing its efforts to develop more efficient and safer pesticides for use by homeowners. ARS is now collecting data that will help obtain registration of certain pesticides for so-called minor uses on several commodities including fruits and vegetables. This will fill a gap in control measures resulting from pesticide regulations.

The Department is now in final stages of preparing the 1977 Yearbook of Agriculture aimed specifically at the urban gardener. It contains 52 chapters on subjects such as where to garden, equipment and supplies, climate, structures, pest control, organic gardening, how to grow individual vegetables, herbs, fruits, and nuts, and information on food preservation and storage including canning, freezing, jams, pickles, and drying.

ARS also publishes over 100 bulletins, leaflets, and information sheets useful to urban gardeners.

RESEARCH NEEDS

The home gardener needs research to increase crop production efficiency by such methods as intensive intercropping where many varieties of plants are grown in a small area, and multiple cropping where two or more crops are grown in sequence on the same plot in one season. Such practices pose special cultural management problems that only research can solve. These include development of new and inexpensive cultural methods including watering, fertilizing, mulching, land preparation, and even selection of planting methods to maximize use of the limited gardening space. Publications describing such new techniques must be prepared. Research to develop and improve simple, inexpensive equipment necessary for all gardening activities and procedures for their most effective use should also be initiated. There is need for further development of varieties adapted specifically for homeowners and small-acreage farmers. For example, where the home gardener grows one crop per season, he needs varieties that can be harvested over a longer period than the varieties available to him today.

Agricultural Research Service

WITNESSES

GARY R. RASOR, PICKLE PACKERS INTERNATIONAL, INC.
DALE CRANFIELD, CHAIRMAN, RESEARCH AND DEVELOPMENT COMMITTEE

We are requesting that the Subcommittee on Agriculture and the Appropriations Committee of the Senate and the House give consideration to the funds requested, to increase the technical staff, the laboratory equipment for agriculture in total.

Carrots represent an income of over $124 million at the farm level and are a major crop in California, Colorado, Florida, Michigan, Oregon, New York, Texas, Washington, and Wisconsin. Carrots are an important processing crop of importance to the members of the National Canners Association.

Onions have a farm value of $160 million, primarily in the States of Arizona, California, Colorado, Idaho, Michigan, Minnesota, New Jersey, New Mexico, New York, Oregon, Texas, and Wisconsin. This crop is important to the dehydration industry, retail and wholesale grocery trade, and to the freezing industry. A total of over 25 million pounds of onion rings and chopped onions are frozen annually.

These crops are now provided to the National Research Organization through the U.S. Department of Agriculture, but are operating with limited manpower and facilities.

We feel research is the key to productivity, and the economics of food production, and we have identified several priority areas requiring research, and these are explained in detail in our statement.

Most importantly, we feel there is a need to process quality and to broaden the genetic base, to develop more effective and safe chemicals, to develop nonchemical methods for pest control, new cultural methods, new concepts of plant disease control, and more vigorous seed are needed to insure high plant establishment under precision planting.

Solutions are required, therefore we urge that the laboratory staff be increased by additional skills in plant genetics, pathology, and chemistry.

We are requesting a total of five technical man-years per year to accomplish this. We feel, with more emphasis on the basic sciences, new principles may be discovered to maintain and increase the efficiency of production.

As a result, we feel very strongly that this will be of benefit to both the producer and the consumer.

STATEMENT OF THE ASSISTANT SECRETARY FOR RURAL DEVELOPMENT,
ALEX P. MERCURE

Mr. Chairman and members of the committee, I appreciate this opportunity to appear before you for the first time as Assistant Secretary of Agriculture for Rural Development. I'd like to briefly try to put the rural development challenge into perspective as I see it. I would like to begin with a brief report on life in rural America.

First, rural America is no longer a zone of population outmigraton. Since 1970, nonmetropolitan population has grown more rapidly than metropolitan population for the first time in this century. Since 1970, there has been a net migration of 1.8 million people into nonmetro areas. Three million people left nonmetro America in the 1960's, to give just one example of the great contrast between past and present.

Also heartening, the net movement of people into rural areas is not just a continuation of urban sprawl. Even nonmetro counties not adjacent to metro areas are now showing net movement of people after several decades of rapid outmigration.

This population progress has been paralleled by substantial progress in three other crucial areas: employment, income, and housing. In fact, since 1970, these three indicators have all increased faster in nonmetros areas than in metro areas.

In employment, nonmetro areas had an average growth of 15.9 percent for nonfarm wage and salary employment from March 1970 to March 1976. In metro areas, the rate was less than half that.

By the measure of unemployment, nonmetro areas have also fared much better—compared with the past and compared with metro areas. During all of 1974, most of 1975, and all of 1976, nonmetro unemployment was less severe than metro unemployment.

Progress has also been evident in agricultural employment: in the 1970's, this has remained fairly stable at around 4.5 million. About 3.5 million are people who depend on farm employment as their major source of income. Also encouraging is the fact that the farm population is younger.

In income, rural areas have shown encouraging trends since 1970. From that year through 1975 (the last year for which we have data), median family income rose faster in nonmetro areas than metro areas.

By the important measure of decline in poverty, rural areas are also making substantial progress. In 1970, 49.1 percent of poor families lived in nonmetro areas, while only 35.6 percent of total families lived there. By 1975, the poverty share had dropped to 40.9 percent (versus 32.7 percent of total families).

By four measures of housing improvement, nonmetro areas have also shown substantial progress. Since 1970, nonmetro areas have shown growth in occupied housing, homeownership, and value of housing, plus reduction in substandard housing all at rates faster than those in metro areas.

In the important measure of decline in substandard housing, by 1976 only 8 percent of occupied nonmetro housing was substandard. The rate was 15 percent in 1970. Also, the share of the Nation's occupied substandard housing that is in nonmetro areas has declined continually since 1950. In 1976, 51 percent of the substandard housing was in nonmetro areas compared with 60 percent in 1950.

Unfortunately, we do not have national data available to detail trends in other critical areas such as water and sewer services, public transportation, solid waste management, and employment and training services. However, the relative inferiority of rural community facilities and services can be asserted even in the absence of good data. On the other hand, it is almost certain that some progress would be apparent at least for nonmetro counties as a class, were adequate data for measuring this available.

The progress outlined above is gratifying, but it is only progress starting from a very low base. For example, although 1,836 nonmetro counties are growing in population, 633 are continuing to decline. Although employment is is growing faster than in metro areas, job opportunities are more limited and wages and labor force participation rates are lower. Median family incomes, although rising faster in nonmetro areas, remain below the metro level. The gap is a substantial one. In 1975, nonmetro median family income was only $11,600 versus $14,909 in metro areas. Lower costs in many nonmetro areas, however, counter some of the gap. So does some nonmonetary income benefits for the fairly small share of the nonmetro population that produces its own food or gets other necessities from the land.

Although rural poverty is declining, the gap between rural America and urban America is still there. In 1975, 12.1 percent of nonmetro families were poor, compared with 8.5 percent metro.

Housing shows the same picture. Although improving rapidly by a number of measurements, it continues to be relatively inferior. Only 33 percent of the Nation's housing stock is in nonmetro areas but 51 percent of the substandard housing is there.

Thus, in all four of the crucial progress areas there has been substantial improvement but in no case have the gaps and differentials been eliminated. The years of outmigration and consequent decline and neglect left deep and cumulative scars on rural society and these have yet to be erased.

This mixed picture of good overall progress since 1970 but a continuation of residual problems poses three broad challenges for the future of rural development.

First, we must direct our development efforts to those of the 633 declining nonmetro counties and other rural areas losing population when stablization or economic development is feasible and sought by the local people.

Second, we must focus our efforts on the thousands of growing communities that need help in accommodating the growth, in meeting the greatly increased demands for housing, facilities, and services. Some 300 counties have grown by 15 percent since 1970, a rate almost impossible for a community to sustain without severe problems. Communities growing more moderately are also facing stresses as the composition of their population changes. For example, areas growing through an influx of retired people can expect the demand for health services and public transportation to increase. Growing towns with an increasing share of young adults face rising demands for education, new housing, fuel, water, sewer, and other housing-associated services.

Third, we must focus on the residual problems that are everywhere in rural America, in growing counties as well as declining counties. Some especially affect minority groups, the poor, and the elderly while others affect rural residents in general. Even in growing counties, I am sure that many, many communities and entire population groups are being bypassed by rural development. The progress picture I have summarized is based on national data only and for nonmetro counties as a class. But the poverty figures alone tell us that there are thousands who are not benefitting from rural development. There is still chronic, lifelong poverty in rural areas, something we must not forget. There are still the rural ghettos of poverty which exist unseen. We need to return these problems more to the forefront of our attention. When we talk about comprehensive rural development—and that is something I believe in—we should always include those who are most in need of its benefits.

I have mentioned the overall challenges that confront us in the face of this mixture of progress with continued gaps in opportunities in rural America. I would like now to discuss some of my specific concerns.

For one thing, a primary goal of rural development as I see it is to help young farmers establish farm enterprises and to help keep farm families on the land. There are several reasons why I hope to help bring about a renewed USDA commitment to family farms. Direct ownership is the most powerful incentive to effective management and the family farm has served this Nation effectively, we all know, for 200 years. Also, we want to see family farming preserved as a way of life. With the changing face of American agriculture, it is possible that labor-intense family-operated farms may be able to slow the increase in the price we all pay for food. Rural development's purpose, after all, is to help provide for alternative life styles, for freedom to pursue opportunity to work and live where and how one would like to. The family farm system must be preserved as part of this option.

Another thing that I believe: If we were able to get electricity to all of rural America we can get pure water to rural families and effective means of waste disposal for them. It is time for this. And it is time for us to try to make more progreses on feasible and affordable alternatives to central systems when these are the only answer because of the nature of the area. Also, it is not unreasonable to design sewer systems which have the capability to reclaim and recycle the waste, yielding methane gas and a very high quality fertilizer. The diverse benefits of such a simple process are strong incentives for us to proceed with this approach.

I believe we must meet our responsibilities as stewards of the land. I am not reluctant to talk in those terms. There are encouraging signs that people now want to see some sense and order to land use decisions. Some rural communities have lost things of value beyond estimate because short term profits were the sole determining factor in land-use decisionmaking, decisionmaking done by a very narrow group of people.

Development involves the gain and the loss of tangible and intangible values, and local people must be willing to do the hard work—physically and emotionally hard work—of using democratic formulas for determining the pace and type of development they want.

Except in the clear case of preservation of prime agricultural and forest land in the national interest, where USDA must have a prominent role, the rural development policy that we hope to develop will stress locally controlled, State-assisted identification of land use options. This should be supported by technical and educational assistance from Federal agencies, as it is now.

Too often rural development has meant disappointment to the long time residents, costly strip development, and overtaxed community services because of a lack of alternatives.

A letter in Time magazine last April stays in my mind. A woman wrote from a small town in Florida: I have seen what this migration has done to beautiful, little towns and lovely forests, and it breaks my heart. These people must realize that they are destroying rural happiness by bringing their industries, crime, hate, and other city "advantages" with them.

This woman and probably a number of other rural residents feel they are helpless objects of blind economic forces. In many cases, of course, such residents do not need the new jobs the industries bring and so they see only the change that they don't like.

It is true that it is very difficult to overcome the lack of jobs and social and cultural facilities in rural America without sacrificing the values of rural living. It can't be done completely. But it can be done at the least cost if the fast-receding value of "growth at any cost" is properly buried, if community residents will try to nourish even a minimum concern for the common good, and if residents will get involved in good old local issues and local politics and be prepared for hard work.

This land use planning concern and citizen involvement lead me to mention another issue. One of my primary concerns will be to work to help improve the capacity of people to work with their neighbors and their local institutions to achieve the improvements they want. I wish that the Rural Development Service's National Rural Development Leaders School could train people in every town in rural America. It can't but the spinoff efforts planned for it should result in a good expansion of this very necessary type of assistance.

According to a Rural Development Act-financed study in Kentucky, government-citizen relations is the most important community problem in the State—more serious even than employment or housing problems. Over three-fourths of 3,500 people polled said that not enough people are taking part in community decisions. I feel sure that if local people worked harder at democratic involvement in development decisions the type of letter I quoted from Time would not have to be written.

There are many other concerns that I wish I could enlarge upon here but that would require too much of your time at this particular hearing. I do want to address the rural elderly for a moment. There are signs that our country is finally recognizing its responsibilities to the aging. The same will be true in my office to the extent that I and the appropriate USDA agencies are involved in coordinated efforts involving Federal agencies with resources that can help. The over 65 group is the fastest growing segment of our Nation's population and already more heavily represented in rural America than urban America. On top of this, retirement communities are the fastest growing type of area in nonmetro

America. We are aware of this and we know that senior citizens in rural areas have more problems than others. With lower incomes, greater health care needs, less access to transportation to areas providing basic services, the rural elderly must be in the forefront of our attention when we work to identify and address the needs of those whom we want to make sure rural development does not bypass.

There are two remaining issues that I want to address, and both of these are very crucial.

First, although the Rural Development Act of 1972 required it, there has to date been no national rural development policy and no explicit national rural development strategy. There has been a national rural development goal of improving rural conditions so that Americans will have reasonable freedom of choice as to where they will live and our country will have a greater chance for optimum health by experiencing more rational balanced growth.

Not only has there been no comprehensive rural development strategy but also separate departments have begun to seriously try to develop their own rural policies but they are having to do this in the vacuum of no overall comprehensive national policy on rural development. The fragmentation concerns me deeply. So do the difficulties involved in developing a coordinated strategy with measurable goals.

Our numerous definitions of rural—10 to 20,000 at last count—are hindering us. We cannot institute a consistent overall national rural development policy with the contradictory terms and definitions of rural now in legislation and program guidelines. I know the Congress is equally concerned about this very difficult problem and has initiated work on some potential resolution of it. It may be easier for community residents as well as for administrative simplicity, to develop arbitrary definitions of the size determinants for rural and urban areas.

We have great problems with a lack of information on who is being bypassed by rural development, what are the unmet needs, where are they, how do they vary regionally, what community services are most deficient, what is the private sector share in the current inventory and what should it be in the future, what is the qaulity of the existing facilities and services once we are able to quantify them? We are now evaluating the National Rural Development Information System proposed for the Rural Development Service, explained earlier before this committee which should help us in this serious problem area.

And of course, we have problems with efficient delivery of services. Farmers Home Administration—which I feel has done an excellent job in the face of vastly increasing responsibilities for widely varying client groups—is still at 1971 staffing levels. In addition to improving staffing, I want to help find the key to improving the Farmers Home Administration's delivery of services. This is a challenge we in the Department are determined to meet. The scope and size of the FmHA program and the rural need for this program deserve no less.

It is also desirable as we try to improve the delivery of services to rural America to expand the Rural Development Leaders School concept to include updated training for USDA employees as well as for community leaders. The rural Development Act of 1972 amended the Organic Act of the Department to include rural development as one of the primary responsibilities of USDA. A good way to begin making this a reality would be to provide this training, and not just in operational and program areas. It should also include the broader area of rural development philosophy and rural development as a procees.

The rural development strategy that I envision will also emphasize reliance on cooperation and self-help in rural America. Once in rural America there was a time when cooperation and self-help were the only ways to survive. Now as the population influx increases demand for housing and utilities there are new opportunities and pressures for a renewed spirit of cooperation.

I am impressed by some examples from our Rural Electrification in this regard. As the availability of electric and telephone services helps attract people to the countryside, the influx of more and more people then places increasing demands on these services. But even in the face of this increased pressure, REA-financed co-ops are deeply involved in cooperating with newer groups in developing areas of the country. For example, in many cases the electric co-ops are helping new water co-ops and water associations with billing and accounting, providing them with meeting space and secretarial help, helping solicit members, and providing publicity. They are also providing invaluable assistance with our new weatherization program. This type of local cooperation is very much related to the essential local participation in rural development that I stressed earlier. It comes from a healthy self-reliance and the mature acceptance of the challenging fact that to a large extent, we make our own environment, it is not imposed on us.

I hope it has been clear that the approach will be to help establish a comprehensive and coordinated approach to the development of rural America which builds on a foundation of local decisions and resources. I share the strong commitment of President Carter and Secretary Bergland to such an approach. I agree that we will give top emphasis to the input of States and localities, drawing on the great expertise that is available in the rural-related private and public nonprofit groups in Washington and elsewhere and on the great knowledge of the representatives of rural citizens.

We will also work to change the attitude that there must be a natural and unhealthy competition between rural and urban areas. This is a belief that is harmful although it is not difficult to understand how it could arise in the arena of intense competition for limited funds.

In the Washington Post last November, the mayor of one of our largest, oldest, and most troubled cities commented on the economic development program of a certain agency that he said—and I quote—"lured industry away from cities." He ended with a plea that we work to make our cities—and again I quote—"better places for all Americans."

Well, you know, for years now, the rural development goal has been to make rural America a better place to live and work. I am so struck by the similarity between the plea of that city mayor and the plea implicit in the rural development goal. Isn't it so obvious that it almost doesn't bear explaining, that we all want the same thing for all our towns and cities and villages?

The facts are that many Americans prefer a smaller scale environment, and improving conditions in rural areas are now allowing them to act on that preference. But it is surely true that this preference can be met in neighborhoods of cities also. In revitalized neighborhoods that I have known in large cities the attachment and loyalty and sense of community could not be surpassed by any in the villages. I hope and I believe that the cities will be able to redevelop neighborhoods—without displacing longtime residents—and that these neighborhoods will satisfy many, many people who yearn for a spirit of community and yet have the big city in their bones.

We all want our settlements to be livable, enjoyable, and nurturing, and all sectors of our country are interdependent. One piece of evidence for this is the burdensome effect that rural outmigration had on our cities for so many years and that still is making its mark. A very prime goal will be to help expand all our citizen's understanding that rural development is in the best interest of the entire country, and that we share our common humanity and common problems and needs. Our goal is equity—quantitatively proportionate and qualitatively equal. Whether it be in the share and kinds of funds that go to rural America or the kinds and number of services and facilities we have. The purpose is to allow Americans to have a choice as to where they will live and try to pursue their dreams. I am concerned that the rural/urban division is perhaps encouraged when we have separate goals reports and separate national growth reports and hearings on urban development policy and a number of other separate approaches that are not integrated into a rational national policy. At the same time, I know that to be manageable, the problems also must be dealt with on a rural or urban basis.

Working within the structure, it seems necessary to demonstrate to all Americans that rural development is good for the Nation because it is a movement to support of our most basic values.

March 25, 1977

The Honorable George H. Mahon, Chairman
House Appropriations Committee
House of Representatives
Washington, D. C. 20001

Dear Mr. Mahon:

The new labeling laws scheduled to go into effect in January, 1978 will create some problems and concerns, greater than those which they are designed to solve. As a processor of meat fat making shortening for the food industry, we are concerned about regulations that would require shortening be designated as either animal or vegetable fat.

Because of the tremendous propaganda program backed by the vegetable oil people, the reputation of animal fat as a food substance has been blackened. Their hue and cry has been that animal fat "is dangerous to your health" and that vegetable oils "are good for you". Little scientific or medical research has been done to prove these contentions one way or another.

Primarily, the "natural" edible fat from our cattle and hogs, to a large part, is being converted to inedible for use in animal feeds, soap, chemicals, and much export. Of the more than five billion pounds of tallow produced in the United States, approximately 90% goes to inedible uses. If only 20% of this fat were rendered as edible, the consumer would pay $100 million less than we are now paying for imported vegetable oil. Under existing conditions, those who stand to benefit most are the foreign producers of vegetable oils: South American soybean interests and Malasian and Indonesian palm oil processors.

In brief, the point we wish to make is that the cattle raising industry is suffering enough from other economic problems than to be further handicapped by regulations calling attention to shallow and unfounded fears of the consumer and, at the same time, fostering prosperity for foreign entities.

Additionally, Ex-President Ford's budget for research in FY 1978 included no increases in spite of a number of critical problem areas identified by the USDA and supported by the food and fiber industry. Research labs have been cut back for 10 to 15 years and funds are needed to overcome these past program cuts. We are seeking·

1. Increased funds for human nutrition research.

2. Increased funds for research on post harvest physiology and food technology and to reduce food loses.

3. Increased effort on the use of renewable agricultural resources, conservation of energy and improved efficiency of processing.

4. Research on increased efficiency of farmers markets, direct marketing and consumer food marketing problems.

As I am sure you can see from this letter, we are vitally concerned about the survival of our industry, consumer awareness, and conservation of our natural resources. Research and publication of data from the USDA research centers can provide this necessary service to us all IF properly supported.

I ask that you introduce this information and our proposals of support of pending legislations into the Committee record. Our industry groups greatly appreciate what you are doing and I wish to thank you for your assistance.

Respectfully yours,
RUST SALES COMPANY

STATEMENT OF M. RUPERT CUTLER

In the relatively short time I have been in Washington, I have been impressed with the degree to which the activities and responsibilities of other agencies and congressional committees have a direct bearing on the Department and on agriculture. A short list of such matters in which Agriculture has a vital interest includes: Energy policy, surface mining, pesticide registration, and wetlands preservation. It is important that when decisions are made on such matters that they are made with good information on their ramifications on agriculture.

CONSERVATION

The ongoing drought in the Great Plains and the loss of 1 million acres of prime farm land each year underscore the importance of having a sound conservation policy. Several policy reviews, as you know, are underway.

The Senate Committee on Agriculture, Nutrition, and Forestry has requested our assistance in carrying out a major oversight study of the Federal role and effectiveness in preventing degradation of our natural resource base over the past 30 years. We have developed a set of proposed plans for carrrying out such a study and the Senate committee is reviewing them at this time. We hope this study will provide current data on which to base our future soil and water conservation program.

Finally, Secretary Bergland has committed us to a Blue Ribbon Conservation Review to be directed by recognized conservation experts in an effort to insure that USDA's programs and efforts are properly directed now so that we will maintain our agricultural productive capacity for the next 50 years. We are currently planning the best way to establish and organize such a Blue Ribbon Review Commission. We intend to make sure that the Blue Ribbon Commission is representative of people fully knowledgeable about SCS and its programs, and the related programs of ASCS, such as the ACP and ECM programs, so as to insure that the review has credibility with this committee, and others.

RESEARCH

Agricultural research has implications much broader than just the agricultural sector. Accordingly, small and part-time farmers as well as large farm operators, consumers as well as producers, and the larger scientific community ought to have input into the agricultural research policymaking process.

We intend to consult the chief science advisor to the President for guidance on potentially fruitful directions for our research efforts. We are establishing a competitive research grant program which will draw upon the expertise in research that exists both in the agricultural research community and the larger scientific community. At the same time USDA will continue to provide leadership and coordination in its role as lead agency in agricultural research.

We look forward to working with the Congress in the drafting of this year's agricultural research legislation to embody these ideas.

As you pointed out at the ARS hearings this committee has supported human nutrition research for the past 30 years. This work has not been underfunded, and the USDA can point to a good record of achievement in this area. As the hearing record shows we are now spending about $14 million on this work; but there is much that we still do not know. This administration is taking a hard look at human nutrition research. The National Academy of Sciences will complete in June a study of the Federal role in human nutrition research. In addition, the Office of Science and Technology Policy will work with OMB to consider recommendations of the study on both USDA and other agencies' roles and the coordination of Federal activity in this area. At that time we will be prepared to consider in what directions USDA's human nutrition research effort ought to move.

EDUCATION

Because of my close association with extension programs at the State level, I have firsthand knowledge of the important role extension can perform in disseminating timely information to a broad spectrum of society. Although things have changed since passage of the Smith-Lever Act in 1914, the extension concept is as relevant today as it was then. As with any long-established program, periodic examination is necessary to ensure that the highest priority needs are being effectively met. In this connection, I have asked the Extension Service to thoroughly review their programs to determine:

The relevance and effectiveness of ongoing programs; and

The opportunity for program initiatives to meet new needs.

Specific areas and issues I have identified for special attention include forestry; urban gardening; information needs of consumers; and small and part-time farmers. At the same time, I need to be convinced that all current extension programs are of sufficient value to be continued at current funding levels and without modification in terms of program goals and clientele served.

While I do not anticipate recommending drastic changes in funding or focus of extension programs, I would not hesitate to recommend significant, long-run changes if convincing evidence is presented to me that improvements would result.

One issue, with which I am particularly concerned, is the actual and potential establishment of extension-type agencies or programs to disseminate information on specific subject areas. I believe that the current extension system is effective and efficient and should be utilized by other Federal agencies to disseminate information relevant to their programs.

It would also be appropriate to mention the administration's concern about the condition and productivity of the Nation's small, private forest land holdings. These forests are mostly in sadly neglected small tracts. The production of wood and other resources from these lands is far below potential. Assessments of future needs for lumber show that we need to count on these lands for a much greater share of the Nation's future lumber supply.

The Department offers a number of programs under which we provide assistance to private landowners on forestry and related matters. The list of programs includes: the State and private forestry programs of the Forest Service which are handled by the Interior Appropriations Subcommittee, the agricultural conservation program under which cost-share payments are made for tree planting and stand improvement, the conservation technical assistance, and soil survey work done on forested lands by the Soil Conservation Service, the work of Extension Service agents, and the McIntire-Stennis research work of the Cooperative State Research Service.

These programs of assistance to State and private forest landowners need to be improved. National direction can be clarified. Federal funds can be utilized more effectively. The Department plans to undertake a comprehensive review of these programs with a view toward developing a comprehensive proposal for improvements. We will be working with representatives of State and local governments, and the private sector, and other Federal agencies as the review is carried out.

Finally, I would like to add my endorsement to the President's and Secretary's intention to carry out a comprehensive, zero-based budget analysis. There is a danger that those involved in exercises such as this become overwhelmed with the sheer magnitude of the task and lose sight of their real purpose—to identify opportunities for making positive improvements in Federal programs.

My interest will be to make sure that we do not lose sight of our purpose. In fiscal year 1979, as a result of our efforts, we will have budget recommendations that reflect our best judgment as to what the Federal Government ought to be doing, and how it can most effectively and efficiently proceed in meeting its goals and objectives.

MAN'S WASTE OF HIS NATURAL RESOURCES

Perhaps the greatest single fault of mankind through the annals of recorded history has been his failure to preserve and protect the natural resources which provide him with his basic necessities of life—food, clothing, and shelter. History indicates that each civilization developed by mankind through the course of the centuries, regardless of the degree of sophistication and advancement attained, has disappeared from the earth because of man's abuse of the soil, water, forests, and other basic resources passed on to him for his use and custodianship.

One of the most serious questions facing our highly developed civilization of the 20th century is whether or not, through more intelligent use of our natural resources and more advanced agricultural technology, we can meet the ever-increasing demands of rapidly expanding populations for food, clothing, and shelter.

A review of the earlier civilizations of the wornout and food-deficient areas of the world indicates what has resulted from the failure of man through the ages to apply an adequate portion of his wealth to the protection of the soil, the forests, the rivers, and lakes, and other resources as he used them to feed and clothe himself.

In 3500 B.C. the valleys of the Tigris and Euphrates Rivers supported a large and prosperous civilization. By the year 2000 B.C. great irrigation developments had turned this part of the Middle East into the granary of the great Babylonian Empire. Today, however, less than 20 percent of this area is cultivated because, as they became urbanized, the people of that civilization failed to continue to preserve the productive capacity of the land, according to LaMont C. Cole of Cornell University:

The landscape is dotted with mounds, the remains of forgotten towns; the ancient irrigation works are filled with silt, the end product of soil erosion; and the ancient seaport of Ur is now 150 miles from the sea, its buildings buried under as much as 35 feet of silt.

Extensive irrigation systems were established in the Valley of the Nile before 2000 B.C. to create the granary for the Roman Empire. This land, which is made fertile by the annual overflowing of the Nile, continued to be productive for many centuries. However, in recent years, as the result of more intensive use of the land and inadequate attention to conservation measures, the soils have deteriorated and salinization has decreased the productivity in the valley to the point where this area is now largely dependent on food shipments from other parts of the world to feed its people.

Ancient Greece had forested hills, ample water supplies, and productive soil. In parts of this area today, the old erosion-proof Roman roads stand several feet above a barren desert. Ancient irrigation systems in many parts of China and India are abandoned today and filled with silt. Most of India's present land problems are due to excessive deforestation, erosion, and siltation made necessary by tremendous population growth during the past two centuries.

The highly developed civilizations of ancient Guatemala and Yucatan are merely history today. Archeologists believe that they exploited their land as intensively as possible until its fertility was gone and their prosperous civilizations vanished.

The city-states throughout history have failed to realize that the cost of food, clothing, and shelter is going to be paid, either by the consumer or by the land from which they come. They have ignored the fact that soil cannot be cultivated year after year unless as much fertility is put back each year as is taken out.

WASTE OF NATURAL RESOURCES IN THE UNITED STATES

The United States is still a young country in relation to the ancient civilizations referred to above. During our short history, however, we have used up and destroyed vast amounts of the plentiful supply of natural resources which were here when the Pilgrims landed at Plymouth Rock. The continuation of such abuse could eventually reduce this country to a barren wasteland with the low standard of living found in much of Asia and the Middle East.

This country had 8,000 billion board feet of timber about 150 years ago. Today we have around 1,600 billion board feet left—only 20 percent of the original stand. This terrible waste of timber resources points up the extent to which our highly competitive economy can deplete a national asset in the generation of new wealth. It points up the need for continuing and expanding conservation efforts on a national basis.

Only 175 years ago we had 500 million acres of fertile soil in this Nation. We have already wasted 200 million acres—40 percent—and another 100 million acres—20 percent—is washing away today. It has been estimated that an average of 40 acres of top soil flows down the Mississippi River each day of the year. Also, estimates are that more than 1 million acres of arable land are lost to residential areas, highways, and other urban developments each year.

COMMITTEE CONCERNS

Mr. WHITTEN. I would like to make two or three comments. This committee has a long record in connection with the environment. We feel that the producer has to stay in business, because if he quits, then we all go hungry. All of the food stamps in the world will not save us if there is no food on the shelves. You can't eat food stamps.

Obviously, a farmer cannot stay in business if he goes broke. And it seems to me there is something wrong when the commercial lending agencies write trying to get the Farmers Home Administration to guarantee farm loans and provide money, so that they will not have to run the risk of proper financing. As I said, it takes at least $200,000 to start out in farming today, and you could lose it all the first year.

Being somewhat of an economic background, I asked the Secretary of the Treasury when we had the overview hearings earlier in the year to supply for the record the obligations of the Federal Government in retirement alone.

That is Federal employees, Congressmen, and all of the rest. It exceeded $8 trillion. That is $8 million millions, and we have no gold and silver to pay for it.

We do not have gold and silver behind our money. If the Congress can just provide it by ink and paper, it is hard to hold back, which means more and more inflation.

According to simple arithmetic, if the present rate of inflation continues, by the year 2000, our dollar will be worth a nickle.

That is on that side of money. Now, let us go to the other side. No nation in the history ever had it so good in material wealth—more cars, more televisions, more everything. So if you do not reform the world, if you just keep me like I am doing now, I will be thankful, and the American people will be the same. So let us not forget to look back and see what a great job we have done insofar as producing food for the purpose of keeping our international payments up. And let us realize what went on before.

What does bother me is that being here a considerable length of time, I can remember many things that went on a few years back. The farm bill that was eventually passed was not a relief program for those in agriculture, it was to restore the purchasing power of those engaged in agriculture, and thereby protect the purchasing power of the people in other segments of our economy.

Now, when that law was passed, it made a whole lot of sense, because it meant that if you had a tremendous crop of basics or storables in 1 year which could be in the way of the next year's crop, you could agree to limit your production the next year in line with needed supplies for domestic use and exports.

Back when people farmed with a mule and a plow, they were pretty well limited to what you could plant. Then they learned to plant the crops close to each other in rows, and put on more fertilizer, and the new methods developed by research. Then they found they could plant eight rows where they had only four before. So we started getting into quantity, and the problems resulting therefrom.

For basics, any excess production could be stored so as to eliminate market saturation. For perishable crops, however, this was not possible.

So Congress passed the law known as section 32 to buy up surpluses of perishables to prevent market gluts and resulting reductions in market prices.

However, to enable section 32 to work, we have got to have the money to be able to announce a program to buy up the surplus. Otherwise, it won't work. Unless the Department of Agriculture is in a position to take the entire surplus off the market, the remaining amount, no matter how small, will break the market and the price.

Now, the dairy people want Congress to provide section 32 funds every year as a part of the regular milk purchase program for feeding programs, which deprives us of the benefits of being able to use section 32 to buy up surplus, protect the market, and keep farmers producing.

The food stamp program was started by a gentlewoman from Missouri. It was intended to go to people that had a need, so they could buy the food they needed for a balanced diet. Then it got to where agencies put ads in the paper asking people if they wanted food stamps. This year we have a request for over $5.6 billion for food stamps. We recently were told that about 18 percent of those getting food stamps are ineligible.

When former Secretary Butz criticized Congress for not changing the law, I got the law and read it to him. He agreed that he had the authority to make the needed changes, and he acted on it. Then somebody went into court, and the court stopped him. Now our new Secretary of Agriculture has set aside the regulations—but the law still says the Secretary can make the changes needed to correct the abuses in the program.

The point is when you got away from giving commodities, instead of food stamps, you really did it to strengthen the market for the producer, so he could stay producing. Then the wholesalers wanted to get cut in on it, and they did. Then the retailers wanted to get cut in on it, and they did.

They did not want any commodity distribution, because it did not go through them. Now we have to not only have problems with the person who is the recipient, but we have to contend with the wholesaler and the retailer who gets a cut.

We have got to do something in my opinion to correct these things. But the one thing we cannot afford to do, is to get rid of the money in section 32 which can be used when needed to buy up perishables. Frequently the Department does not have to hardly buy anything to support the market.

STATEMENT OF DALE N. ANDERSON, STAFF SCIENTIST

Mr. ANDERSON. In the mid-1960's, when some of these research and extension programs began to fall off, food distribution and productivity also began to change. The costs of wholesalers and retailers escalated; the cost of energy, and the cost of things they use and their labor rates went up rapidly.

About 1970, productivity also began to drop off at a very rapid rate. As a consequence, in food retailing, the best from productivity declined from 1970 to 1975, at the rate of 1 percent per year.

RISING COST OF FOOD

These things are beginning to impinge upon the prices that people pay, particularly in the city, and for the first time in 60 years, the percentage of disposable income spent for food did not decline, but began to go up. For the first time in a 60-year period, what the consumer is spending for food has gone up, and 80 percent of that increase is in the marketing sector, and not because of agricultural production shortage.

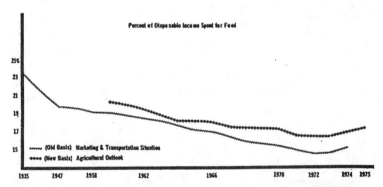

Percent of Disposable Income Spent for Food

•••••• (Old Basis) Marketing & Transportation Situation
•••••• (New Basis) Agricultural Outlook

Mr. ANDERSON. Because of these rising costs and the difficulty of doing business in old facilities, the study and development of new wholesale markets have been extremely important to these independent wholesalers.

We have calculated in six cities, where we have records and where we have new wholesale markets, there was a savings of about $13 million per year. If this is projected to the 40 markets, which have been built, we think we have provided a savings in the order of $400 million over the last 5 years from this type of research, and that savings will directly benefit urban consumers.

I will be glad to submit some of this information.

[The information follows:]

STATEMENT ON WHOLESALE FOOD MARKETS

This research is part of an Agricultural Research Service program that has direct benefit to urban and other consumers. It includes transportation of the food to the cities, storage and wholesale facilities, delivery, retail and institutional food service, consumer food economics and household budgets, food

safety and human nutrition. The research seeks to cut costs and improve relia-
bility of the service and the product.

The marketing bill, estimated at $104 billion in 1975, continues to comprise
approximately two-thirds of the consumers' expenditure for food. Wholesaling, retailing, and food service now comprise 72 percent of the marketing
bill with retailing surpassing processing as the costliest marketing function.
The largest cost component is labor and labor productivity has been declining
recently in this industry. While productivity in farming has risen at a steady
3 percent to 4 percent per year, productivity in food retailing has declined an
average of 1 percent per year over the last 5 years, according to the Bureau
of Labor Statistics. This food wholesaling research is directed at cutting these
escalating distribution costs.

FOOD WHOLESALE RESEARCH

The work is divided into urban and rural sections. The Urban unit conducts
research studies necessary (1) to determine the needs and to develop the plans
for more effective wholesale food marketing facilities, and (2) to evaluate alternative methods of getting food delivered from wholesale terminal markets to
consumers in urban areas. These include studies of the supply delivery system
and evaluating methods to improve the operational efficiency of food wholesale,
retail and food service firms.

The rural unit conducts research studies to develop improved guidelines and
procedures for operating assembly and processing facilities to handle locally
produced agricultural products and to help guide in the planning and development of effective farmers' marketing faciltities.

Many of the wholesale food marketing facilities in cities have become outdated, inadequate, and inefficient to use. This obsolescence is costing millions of
dollars each year in excessive handling, waste, deterioration, and spoilage. Obsolescence in city wholesale food distribution facilities has been a problem for
years. It is even more of a problem today as urban areas and urban populations
grow still larger. Distributing the required quantities of food efficiently becomes
a national problem of serious concern.

Using inadequate, outdated, and inefficient facilities causes unnecessarily high
handling costs which, of course, adds to the cost of marketing food and increases
the spread between the price received by the farmer and the price paid by the
consumer.

Many urban areas are becoming increasingly concerned about the decline in
the number of supermarkets in urban areas, making it increasingly difficult and
costly for consumers to shop for food. Conferences have been held and task forces
have been established to try and resolve this problem, but they have met with
little success because of a lack of understanding about food distribution. Alternatives are needed to assist the low-income poor, which includes many of our
elder citizens and minority groups.

Urban wholesale markets have been build or are under construction in 40 of
the 70 cities where ARS studies have been completed. In Boston a savings of $6
a ton was projected in the 1962 study. In a follow-up study in 1971 actual savings were found to be $5.93 per ton, but with an added volume of 75 percent
total savings were greater than estimated, and totaled $1,768,000 per year for
10 wholesalers studied. Savings projected for consolidated delivery of bakery
and biscuit goods amounted to $134 a week per store and consolidation of all
vendor products could save up to 60 percent of total delivery costs. Similar savings in warehouse, retail and restaurant operations have been achieved. These
savings are largely reflected through competition to holding down prices to the
consumer or better services and in the long run to farmers in increased markets.
Poor assembly market facilities often cause product losses or damage which are
deducted from prices paid to farmers in cooperative or commission sales. Similar
results for improved assembly marketing facilities in rural areas are therefore
frequently reflected back to farmers in higher prices for farm products.

ARS studies have conservatively estimated that savings of 25 percent can be
realized in the cost of receiving, handling, and distributing food at the wholesale level by providing improved facilities and handling methods. New markets
that have been built as a result of this program in cities such as Boston, Atlanta,
New York, Philadelphia, San Antonio, and many others, have demonstrated the
far reaching benefits of such developments. These include, but are not limited to:
(1) more efficient food handling; (2) redevelopment of blighted communities;
(3) better local employment opportunities; (4) better services by food distribu-

tors; (5) more orderly food distribution; (6) improved sanitation, food safety, and reduced food losses; and (7) upgrading of the local food industry in the local community.

Holding down the costs of getting food to the people in urban areas, reducing the number of delivery vehicles on city streets, developing alternative methods of handling food to either make the supermarket viable in urban areas or else to encourage establishment of other alternative food facilities represent additional opportunities. Incremental savings achieved in the food marketing sector have high benefit-to-cost ratio due to the magnitude of the dollar costs.

ARS has the only full-time research program in the United States on improving the facilities and methods for marketing food. Through this program, ARS has gained the knowledge, rapport, respect, and expertise that has given it a worldwide reputation as the leading authority in food marketing facility planning. Facilities patterned after concepts ARS has developed have been built in cities all over the country and the world. Upon request, ARS provides technical assistance and guidance to cities that want new food facilities and to the private consulting, engineering, construction, architectural, and food industry firms who actually plan and build them.

Most firms lack the expertise and operating margins to conduct their own research. The only research they could do would be internal because they cannot change the operations of other firms in the marketing channel. Also, Federal laws inhibit firms from getting together to develop new technology for fear of possible collusion. The Congressional Office of Technology Assessment indicates the level of R. & D. in this segment of the food industry is very low.

ARS research in marketing has served traditionally as a catalyst to spur adoption of new technology. It serves an important role in providing an objective analysis of the marketing system. Most research work that is presently being done is by equipment or supplies manufacturers with vested interests, or by consultants who draw upon ARS research and industry practices for their basic information. Government can bring together firms within the marketing system to discuss system-related problems, to help smooth out the flow of foods by providing both a forum and a research data base to get man-made barriers removed.

This work complements much of the work of HUD and some of the work of DOT. Urban food market plans often become part of urban development projects. State departments of agriculture participate with us in studies, as do local governmental and private organizations and groups. In many cases, the studies are requested by these agencies and groups. DOT is very much interested in our approach to urban distribution work since it involves a micro rather than a macro approach. They tend to look at aggregate goods movement problems, recognizing that their recommendations are more difficult to get implemented. They think we may have a much better chance of successful adoption of improvements with our commodity approach. The DOD is also interested in this ARS research, especially for communities where large defense facilities have been closed.

IMPACT OF MARKETING RESEARCH ON MARKETING FACILITIES

Over 70 studies have been conducted in cities throughout the United States to develop plans to improve the facilities and methods used for the wholesale distribution of food. As a result of these studies, improved food distribution facilities have been constructed or are now under construction in over half of these cities. Followup studies of new facilities which were built have shown that food distribution costs would have been about $6 per ton higher if the wholesale operations were still being carried out in the old facilities. Eighty-one percent of the increased costs would have been borne by wholesalers and 19 percent by shippers, transportation companies, and retailers. These increased costs, in all probability, would have been passed on in the form of lower prices paid to farmers and of higher prices paid by consumers. Savings in the wholesale costs of distributing food over the past 5 years due to these new markets is estimated to be over $400 million. These savings are of direct benefit to urban consumers.

STATEMENT OF DALE E. HATHAWAY, ASSISTANT SECRETARY FOR INTERNATIONAL
AFFAIRS AND COMMODITY PROGRAMS

Mr. Chairman and members of the committee, I am please to appear before
your committee as you consider the fiscal year 1978 budget.

Your committee and the Department of Agriculture share strong concern for
maintaining a vigorous agricultural economy in the United States and around
the world. I am grateful for the opportunity to work with you and with Secretary Bergland as his Assistant Secretary for International Affairs and Commodity Programs. My 30 years of professional experience has involved me in the
operations of domestic farm programs, internatonal trade, food aid, and international agricultural development.

My responsibilities in the Department include the Agricultural Stabilization
and Conservation Service, the Federal Crop Insurance Corporation, the Foreign
Agricultural Service, and the Office of the General Sales Manager. I serve as a
member of the boards of directors of the Commodity Credit Corporation and the
FCIC. I am the Secretary's designee for the Department's participation in international trade negotiations and international organizations.

I will speak briefly about several tasks which lie ahead of us in international
affairs and commodity programs. Except to respond to any questions you might
have, I won't discuss the details of the farm bill now being considered by the
Congress.

The agenda of international negotiations involving food and agriculture will
be a heavy one during the next several years. Negotiations toward an international sugar agreement have begun this week in Geneva. Discussions regarding a
wheat agreement will be resumed in a few weeks. The United States has the opportunity to exercise new initiatives in the international community. I hope that,
through cooperation between the Congress and the executive branch and in consultation with groups here in the United States affected by international trade
in agricultural products—and virtually everyone is—we will develop a pattern
of international agreements which serves the interests of producers and consumers in this Nation and the interests of people of other countries, especially
the poor, food-deficit countries.

Part and parcel of our concern in these international argeements is, of course,
an expanding market for commercial exports of American agricultural products.
Agricultural exports now are valued at $23 billion and account for 20 percent of
the value of total exports (fiscal year 1976), and we need to expand our agricultural exports as one important means of improving farm income and for improving our balance of payments situation.

These matters relating to expanded trade, increasing exports of farm products,
and food aid are now in several parts of the Department of Agriculture and involve the working with several other parts of the executive branch. I have placed
a high priority on a review of these activities within and outside the Department
with a view to increasing their effectiveness and the speed with which we can
respond to changing needs.

On a related matter, President Carter has directed that the Public Law 480
programs be reviewed this year. Proposals now being considered by the Congress
would expand Public Law 480 programs and improve the quality of these programs. In the Department of Agriculture we think more can be done to make
these programs effective as means both for transferring resources to poor countries and for helping poor, food-deficit countries improve their own production
of food while at the same time they contribute to an expanded use of U.S. farm
products.

Domestically, we need to revitalize the Agricultural Stabilization and Conservation Service, which has declined sharply both in numbers and morale during recent years. While general budgetary constraints may now allow much
leeway for increasing numbers, we must restore the effectiveness of the ASCS
so it can deliver the services and support farmers require and the Congress
authorizes.

Through the Federal Crop Insurance Corporation we intend to develop a crop
insurance program which will be an alternative to disaster payments. Recent
visitors from around the country have told me disaster payments are a disaster.
While strengthening its programs, we also need to bring the FCIC closer to the
ASCS, especially so that the FCIC uses the field organization and information of
the ASCS.

IMPORTANCE OF URBAN ACTIVITIES

Mr. WHITTEN. Thank you very much.

As I listened to your presentation, it made me realize how important it is that we have this special hearing on these activities, as we used to have. We have greatly increased in recent years the amount of money available to the Department for the purpose of getting this message over. I think that it would be well for Mr. Gifford with the USDA Office of Communications to give thought to this.

I recognize as a lawyer, and as a practical Member in Congress, that we have to have the city votes in Congress to carry on these programs which are essential to all of the people of the United States.

I recognize that we need the benefits of what you are able to do for the American people as a whole. When I was in New York City, for instance, they had an old market where you could bring a big truck in, back it up in a certain way, so that one man could block out all of his competitors from receiving delivery of food.

I have also seen in some of our major cities where the meat had been handled strictly in accordance with the Departments of Health—national and local. But when it got to the big cities it had to be laid out on the sidewalk, because there were no facilities to handle it. Then once it got out to the retailer, once again it goes under the supervision of the Department of Health. So in between the livestock producer and the consumer, the meat was frequently open to all sorts of filth, insects, and heat, without any degree of protection.

Based on such observations as those, we have been taking pride in the improved new markets of San Francisco, New York, and many other areas.

PERISHABLE COMMODITIES

Also, I would point out that historically, it was next to impossible to deal with perishables.

Take the poultry business, for instance. If a man producing broilers had to keep them 2 extra days, there went his profit. When they reach a certain age, you have to kill them or move them. So they are absolutely at the mercy of the buyers. Given this timing situation, we found that many fruits and vegetables went to New York all at one time. At that end they had no means to sell them quickly. But now we have a means whereby they can do a whole lot of other things, including refrigeration.

All of this is fine, but we are not getting the message over, in my opinion, to the urban Members of Congress and to the urban press.

DIFFICULTY IN COMMUNICATING THE IMPORTANCE OF AGRICULTURE

It is mighty hard. Some years ago, I was asked to speak to a national agricultural organization out in San Diego. About 3,000 people were to be there at the meeting.

At that time I was also on the Appropriations Subcommittee for Defense. San Diego, as you know, is pretty much a Navy base, so, of course, I did not have to send word to the military that I was going to be out there. They already knew about it.

When I got off the plane, there were two people there to interview me with regard to my speech to the agriculture group. I went into great detail for them to be able to cover my speech on an agricultural subject. As one of them left, he said, "I see you are also on the Defense Appropriations Subcommittee."

I said, "Yes." He said "We had another failure of a missile launch at Cape Kennedy." I said, "Yes, we advertise our failures. Russia only advertises their successes." So the next day, after this long interview about my speech to an agricultural group, the news story and my picture came out: "Congressman says when we make mistakes we advertise our failures."

I mentioned this in my speech. So another paper was going to be sure they treated agriculture fairly. So the next day, when that paper came out, not only did they kill the story, but they had an editorial that San Diego was not getting its fare share of Federal money.

That is the truth, so help me. The news media just will not report on the importance of agriculture to the American people.

Now, the point is that you have a great story. I do not think the people in New York City know what agriculture does for New York. I do not believe they know it in San Francisco, and so forth. So I would hope in your report, you can see that these things are carried.

Any questions?

Mr. BURLISON. No questions.

Mr. ANDREWS. No questions.

You are looking at the man who has the longest voting record in the House.

Mr. NATCHER. Mr. Andrews, if you just say back to March 4, 1789, I would appreciate it.

Mr. ANDREWS. The longest since March 4, 1789.

I do not know what happened before that.

Mr. WHITTEN. Thank you very much.

Dr. PALLANSCH. Thank you. It has been a pleasure being here.

Mr. WHITTEN. The subcommittee will stand in short recess.

APPENDICES
AS GIVEN
IN ORIGINAL
HARD TOMATOES

LEGISLATION CREATING THE LAND GRANT COLLEGE COMPLEX

The land grant college complex, including the agricultural extension services and the agricultural experiment stations were created and are now governed by various laws codified at 7 U.S.C. sections 301-390. The establishment of the land grant colleges is covered by sections 301-331; cooperative extension work is governed by sections 341-349; and the agricultural experiment stations and research facilities are governed by sections 361-390.

The major legislation creating the land grant complex as it exists today is summarized below under the three functions of teaching, research and extension.

EDUCATION

The Morrill Act: Act of July 2, 1862, which provided for the original grant of land to the various states for the endowment, support and maintenance of agriculture and mechanical arts, and established the formulas for appropriations. Public lands were granted to the states in a quantity equal to 30,000 acres for each senator and representative in Congress, determined under the census of 1860. There were strictures placed on the States' management of that land in order to ensure that the entire proceeds from the land grants would be applied, without any dimunition whatever to the purposes of the Act. In this regard, the state was to replace any of the capital of the fund should it be diminished or lost. The Act was amended in 1866 to allow for an extension of time for states to comply with the provisions of the Morrill Act by either establishing new colleges with the donation of public lands, or to grant such benefits to existing colleges, and to clarify that when new states were admitted to the Union they would be entitled to the benefits of the Morrill Act by expressing their acceptance within three years from their date of admission into the Union.

The Second Morrill Act: Act of August 30, 1890, with the stated purpose of providing further for the endowment of colleges of agriculture and the mechanical arts. The Act increased the appropriations to endow and support colleges of agriculture and mechanical arts, with the specific proviso:

> That no money shall be paid out under this Act to any State or Territory for the support and maintenance of a college where a distinction of race or color is made in the admission of students shall be held to be a compliance with the provisions of this Act if the funds received in such State or Territory be equitably divided as hereinafter set forth.

The black land grant colleges are governed by the same administration procedures as the 1862 colleges. The express creation of separate colleges for white and black students has never been amended by Congress.

The Nelson Amendment: Amendment of March 4, 1907, granted a further appropriation for the endowment and maintenance of land grant colleges, with the proviso that a portion of this money could be spent in providing courses for the special preparation of instructors for teaching the elements of agriculture and the mechanic arts.

The Purnell Act of 1925 authorized the more complete endowment of the agricultural experiment stations, and stated, "funds . . . shall be applied to . . . such economic and sociological investigations as have for their purpose the development and improvement of the rural home and rural life . . ."

The Bankhead-Jones Act of June 29, 1935 (subsequently amended June 1952 and July 14, 1960) provided additional funds for basic research into the laws and principles relating to agriculture, the further development of cooperative extension work and the more complete endowment and support of the land grant colleges. In writing up the act in 1950, USDA issued a monograph, which stated:

> *The Bankhead-Jones Farm Tenant Act* may be said to have had its origin in a national tradition. That tradition is a belief in the economic and social values of owner operated family farms. To such farms in no small measure the great middle class in American society owes its origin. Upon such farms in no small measure the middle class must depend for continued influence in shaping the destinies of our democracy.
>
> Among the founding fathers Thomas Jefferson was an outstanding exponent of the virtues of family farms. He was expressing the prevailing views of his time when he said "the small land holders are the most precious part of a State."
>
> A resolution adopted by the American Farm Bureau Federation at its annual meeting in Chicago in December 1935 contained the following statement: "We recognize the tremendous importance of home ownership in agriculture . . ."
>
> The National Grange in 1943 stated, "The best interests of our Nation will be served if a higher percent of our farms are owner operated."
>
> In a report dated October 1944 a Committee of the Association of Land-Grant Colleges and Universities said: "The family type farm should remain the basis on which American agriculture typically is organized."

RESEARCH

The Hatch Act of 1887 authorized federal grant funds for direct payment to each state that would establish an agricultrual experiment station in connection with the land grant college established under the provisions of the *First Morrill Act.* Section 2 of the *Hatch Act* states the purpose of the Federal-grant research program as follows:

> It is the policy of Congress to promote the efficient production, marketing, distribution and utilization of farm products as essential to the health and welfare of our people. . . . It shall be the object and duty of the State agricultural experiment stations through the expenditure of the appropriations hereinafter authorized to conduct original and other researches, investigations and experiments bearing

directly on and contributing to the establishment and maintenance of a permanent and effective agriculture industry of the United States, including researches basic to the problems of agriculture in its broadest aspects, and such investigations as have for their purpose the development and improvement of the rural home and rural life and the maximum contribution by agriculture to the welfare of the consumer.

With the passage of the *Hatch Act* and the act raising the Department of Agriculture to cabinet level, the organized system of agricultural research in the United States was put on a permanent and nationwide basis.

What developed was a movement for more funds to fulfill the goal of advanced research and experimentation in agriculture. In many states, so much of the *Hatch Act* funds were being used for administrative purposes, the preparation and distribution of publications, and the more superficial experiments that little was left for thorough research. There were 52 experiment stations in 1902 when the Adams Act was passed "to be applied only to paying the necessary expenses of conducting original researches or experiments bearing directly on the agricultural industry of the United States. . . ."

The Adams Act funds were always administered separately by the USDA. Each station was required to keep a separate account of *Adams Act* funds and a financial report of each investigation and problem studied to be made on a form provided by USDA. The work of experiment stations thus proceeded along the basis of explicity well-defined projects to strengthen their scientific work, with the following policy stated by the Office of Experiment Stations in its report for 1906:

> In passing upon these projects the Office has undertaken to determine only their suitability and appropriateness under the terms of the act. It has left to the individual initiative of the station workers the planning of the investigations and the selection of the topics most important to their localities. The Office has insisted only that the projects as outlined should be such as to characterize them as scientific investigations embracing some original features. . . . Research is worthy of its name only as it is directed to the answering of definite problems by scientific methods of procedure. This will involve a definite plan of operation and thorough consideration of what is known of the subject and its bearing, and should lead to a knowledge of the reasons for the results secured. Again, research presupposes a definite aim and a definite problem to be solved, a specific end to be attained rather than the mere accumulation of data. . . .

Agricultural Marketing Act of 1946 provided for extensive research in conjunction with the experiment stations and cooperative extension services on a state matching fund basis, to provide for "an integrated administration of all laws so that marketing is improved, costs reduced, dietary and nutritional standards improved, and wider markets developed resulting in the full production of American farms being disposed of usefully, economically, profitably, and in an orderly manner."

The 1955 Amendments further restated the policy of Congress with respect to the experiment stations, as follows (7 U.S.C. 361c):

It is further the policy of Congress to promote the efficient production, marketing, distribution, and utilization of products of the farm as essential to the health and welfare of our peoples and to promote a sound and prosperous agriculture and rural life as indispensable to the maintenance of maximum employment and national prosperity and security. . . .

The McIntyre-Stennis Bill passed October 10, 1962 and provided for the funding of forestry research through the land grant colleges and experiment stations.

EXTENSION

The Smith-Lever Act of May 1914 established the agricultural extension services for "aid in diffusing among the people of the United States useful and practical home economics, and to encourage application of the same" in connection with the *First Morrill Act* colleges. As further defined in section 2 of the Act,

cooperative extension work shall consist of the giving of instruction and practical demonstrations in agricultural and home economics and subjects relating thereto to persons not attending or resident in said colleges in the several communities, and imparting information on said subjects through demonstrations, publications and otherwise . . . and this work shall be carried on in such manner as may be mutually agreed upon by the Secretary of Agriculture and the State agricultural college or colleges receiving the benefits of the Act.

Added to the *Hatch Act* with the 1955 amendments was the following "Special Needs" section, which authorizes up to 10% of the total appropriation for extension work to be allocated over and above the annual appropriation to the "Disadvantaged Agricultural Areas". This is codified at 7 U.S.C., sections 347a:

Disadvantaged Agricultural Areas—Congressional Findings

(a) The Congress finds that there exist special circumstance in certain agricultural areas which cause such areas to be at a disadvantage insofar as agricultural development is concerned, which circumstances include the following: (1) There is concentration of farm families on farms either too small or too unproductive or both; (2) such farm operators because of limited productivity are unable to make adjustments and investments required to establish profitable operations; (3) the productive capacity of the existing farm unit does not permit profitable employment of available labor; (4) because of limited resources, many of these farm families are not able to make full use of current extension programs designed for families operating economic units nor are extension facilities adequate to provide the assistance needed to produce desirable results.

No funds have ever been allocated under this section. State extension directors are the only ones authorized to submit projects under this section, and USDA has not revealed whether any plans have ever been submitted.

LAND GRANT COLLEGES AND UNIVERSITIES

Land Grant Instituton	Location	Date Est. as a Land-Grant College
Alabama:		
1. Auburn University	Auburn	1872
*1. Alabama Agricultural & Mechanical College	Normal	1891
Alaska:		
3. University of Alaska	College	1922
Arizona:		
4. University of Arizona	Tucson	1885
Arkansas:		
5. University of Arkansas	Fayetteville	1871
*6. Agricultural, Mechanical and Normal College	Pine Bluff	1875
California:		
7. University of California	Berkeley	1866
Colorado:		
8. Colorado State University	Fort Collins	1879
Connecticut:		
9. University of Connecticut	Storrs	1862
Delaware:		
10. University of Delaware	Newark	1867
*11. Delaware State College	Dover	1891
District of Columbia:		
12. Federal City College	Washington, D.C.	1968
Florida:		
13. University of Florida	Gainesville	1870
*14. Florida Agricultural & Mechanical University	Tallahassee	1893
Georgia:		
15. University of Georgia	Athens	1866
*16. Fort Valley State College	Fort Valley	1874
Hawaii:		
17. University of Hawaii	Honolulu	1907
Idaho:		
18. University of Idaho	Moscow	1890
Illinois:		
19. University of Illinois	Urbana	1867

	Land Grant Instituton	*Location*	*Date Est. as a Land-Grant College*
Indiana:			
20.	Purdue University	Lafayette	1865
Iowa:			
21.	Iowa State University	Ames	1862
Kansas:			
22.	Kansas State University	Manhatten	1863
Kentucky:			
23.	University of Kentucky	Lexington	1863
*24.	Kentucky State College	Frankfort	1893
Louisiana:			
25.	Louisiana State University	Baton Rouge	1869
*26.	Southern University & Agricultural & Mechanical College	Baton Rouge	1890
Maine:			
27.	University of Maine	Orono	1863
Maryland:			
28.	University of Maryland	College Park	1864
*29.	Maryland State College	Princess Anne	1890
Massachusetts:			
30.	University of Massachusetts	Amherst	1863
31.	Massachusetts Institute of Technology	Cambridge	1863
Michigan:			
32.	Michigan State University	East Lansing	1863
Minnesota:			
33.	University of Minnesota	Minneapolis	1863
Mississippi:			
34.	Mississippi State University	State College	1866
*35.	Alcorn Agricultural and Mechanical College	Alcorn	1871
Missouri:			
36.	University of Missouri	Columbia	1863
*37.	Lincoln University	Jefferson City	1891
Montana:			
38.	Montana State University	Bozeman	1889
Nebraska:			
39.	University of Nebraska	Lincoln	1869
Nevada:			
40.	University of Nevada	Reno	1866

Land Grant Instituton	Location	Date Est. as a Land-Grant College
New Hampshire:		
41. University of New Hampshire	Durham	1866
New Jersey:		
42. Rutgers, The State University	New Brunswick	1863
NewMexico:		
43. New Mexico State University	University Park	1889
New York:		
44. Cornell University	Ithaca	1863
North Carolina:		
45. North Carolina State University	Raleigh	1866
*46. Agricultural and Technical College of North Carolina	Greensboro	1891
NorthDakota:		
47. North Dakota State University	Fargo	1889
Ohio:		
48. Ohio State Univeristy	Columbus	1864
Oklahoma:		
49. Oklahoma State University	Stillwater	1890
*50. Langston University	Langston	1897
Oregon:		
51. Oregon State University	Corvallis	1868
Pennsylvania:		
52. The Pennsylvania State University	University Park	1863
PuertoRico:		
53. University of Puerto Rico	Mayaguez	1908
Rhode Island:		
54. University of Rhode Island	Kingston	1863
South Carolina:		
55. Clemson University	Clemson	1893
*56. South Carolina State University	Orangeburg	1896
South Dakota:		
57. South Dakota State University	Brookings	1883
Tennessee:		
58. The University of Tennessee	Knoxville	1868
*59. Tennessee Agricultural and Industrial State University	Nashville	1891

	Land Grant Instituton	*Location*	*Date Est. as a Land-Grant College*
Texas:			
60.	Texas Agricultural and Mechanical University	College Station	1866
*61.	Prairie View Agricultural and Mechanical College	Prairie View	1891
Utah:			
62.	Utah State University	Logan	1888
Vermont:			
63.	University of Vermont	Burlington	1862
Virginia:			
64.	Virginia Polytechnic Institute	Blacksburg	1870
*65.	Virginia State College	Petersburg	1872
Washington:			
66.	Washington State University	Pullman	1889
West Virginia:			
67.	West Virginia University	Morgantown	1867
Wisconsin:			
68.	University of Wisconsin	Madison	1863
Wyoming:			
69.	University of Wyoming	Laramie	1889

*Black Land Grant Colleges created under the Morrill Act of 1890.

APPENDIX C
NATIONAL TOTAL SAES

Table IV-D-9 Summary by Problem Area of 1969 Funds by Source — In Thousands of Dollars

Classification Category	No. of Proj	SMY	HATH	RRF	MCIN STEN	SP GT	Oth CSRS	Tot CSRS	USDA CGCA	Other Fed	State Appro	Prod Sales	Indus-try	Other	Total
00-0001 Administration															
001 Administration	480	273.4	0	0	0	0	0	0	0	0	0	10	7	0	17
Subtotal	480	273.4	0	0	0	0	0	0	0	0	0	10	7	0	17
11-6030 Eval Imp Farm Inc															
506 Sply Demand & Pri	164	30.4	438	181	0	0	0	619	11	2	437	16	28	11	1123
507 Comp Rel in Agric	102	20.9	258	116	0	0	0	374	18	0	231	9	8	84	724
510 Farmer Bargaing Pow	10	2.3	17	3	0	0	0	20	2	12	47	0	0	1	82
807 Agric Economic Chan	70	15.8	113	10	0	0	0	123	25	0	382	1	28	21	581
808 Gov't Programs	52	10.5	75	0	0	0	0	75	.23	67	156	2	27	10	360
Subtotal	398	79.9	900	310	0	0	0	1210	79	81	1253	29	91	127	2869
12-6121 Frt & Veg Prod Ef															
204 Cntr Pests Frt & Ve	486	135.3	686	64	7	0	0	757	280	500	3595	93	263	53	5540
205 Cntr Dise Frt & Ve	663	214.6	1418	317	0	0	0	1735	278	565	5722	155	473	138	9066
206 Cntr Weeds Frt & Ve	182	49.3	371	86	0	26	0	482	53	80	961	32	166	24	1800
304 Imp Bio Eff Frt & V	1334	423.4	2203	315	0	0	0	2517	256	1368	12767	488	460	241	18097
305 Mech Prod Frt & Veg	190	64.1	332	71	0	18	0	421	24	22	1765	44	82	27	2384
306 Sys Anal F&V Prod	32	5.7	19	0	0	0	0	19	6	1	181	8	9	2	226
402 Imp Accept Ft & Veg	211	40.1	221	3	0	2	0	226	30	86	1086	47	54	16	1545
Subtotal	3098	932.6	5249	856	7	46	0	6157	926	2622	26078	867	1508	502	38659

Classification Category	No. of Proj	SMY	HATH	RRF	MCIN STEN	SP GT	Oth CSRS	Tot CSRS	USDA CGCA	Other Fed	State Appro	Prod Sales	Indus-try	Other	Total
12-6122 Field Crops Prod															
207 Cntr Pests Fld Crop	606	165.9	1245	318	0	178	0	1741	672	468	3346	139	383	382	7131
208 Cntr Dis Field Crop	669	192.5	1425	295	0	184	0	1904	464	622	4127	223	396	281	8017
209 Cntr Weeds Fld Crop	324	84.8	854	238	15	39	0	1146	104	114	1542	189	445	122	3663
307 Imp Bio Eff Fld Crp	2090	705.6	4667	756	4	216	0	5643	1069	2236	17659	2534	1816	901	31858
308 Mech Prod Field Cro	199	47.3	334	115	0	86	0	535	73	0	1045	47	112	133	1945
309 Sys Anal Fld Crop P	101	18.1	132	45	0	20	0	197	27	1	286	97	12	13	633
405 Imp Accept Fld Cr	125	29.1	207	38	0	4	0	248	32	35	600	112	86	50	1163
Subtotal	4114	1243.1	8865	1805	19	727	0	11416	2441	3476	28605	341	3249	1883	54410
12-6123 Livestock Prod Ef															
210 Contr Pests Animals	167	32.9	250	24	0	0	0	274	97	195	711	21	34	19	1352
211 Contr Dis Animals	513	225.6	1491	533	0	139	0	2163	632	2376	5412	307	353	330	11572
212 Cntr Inter Parasite	121	41.0	292	71	0	0	0	363	32	213	897	45	136	62	1747
213 Prot Anmls from Tox	41	9.0	62	16	0	0	0	78	27	131	271	15	31	51	604
310 Animal Reproduction	504	162.0	1418	426	0	5	0	1849	140	2043	5030	1303	408	225	10999
311 Nutri Eff Anml Pr	1371	443.0	4500	925	0	50	0	5475	289	1972	14392	5198	958	955	29241
312 Env Stress in Anml	255	77.0	611	153	0	0	0	764	31	970	1660	260	102	103	3891
313 Imp Mgt Sys Anml Pr	371	87.8	644	171	0	0	0	816	54	79	2617	1260	197	68	5091
409 Imp Cons Accp Anml	194	33.6	382	118	0	0	0	500	121	116	1083	644	108	18	2590
Subtotal	3537	1111.9	9651	2438	0	194	0	12282	1422	8095	32074	9054	2327	1832	67086
12-6124 Genl Purpose Prod															
109 Weather Effects	93	27.5	151	169	30	0	0	350	14	173	509	27	16	44	1132
112 Range Management	230	55.4	290	94	16	1	0	401	35	254	1035	67	90	38	1920
314 Insct as Pollinator	35	13.5	46	0	0	0	0	46	31	65	404	5	13	12	576
315 Imp Farm Supp & Fac	168	50.3	290	71	0	8	0	369	65	95	992	242	121	77	1961
316 Farm Adjust & Mgt	191	50.4	468	56	0	0	0	525	69	16	961	38	62	28	1699
Subtotal	717	197.2	1245	390	47	9	0	1690	215	603	3902	378	302	199	7289

Table IV-D-9 Summary by Problem Area of 1969 Funds by Source — in Thousands of Dollars (continued)

Classification Category	No. of Proj	SMY	HATH	RRF	MCIN STEN	SP GT	Oth CSRS	Tot CSRS	USDA CCCA	Other Fed	State Appro	Prod Sales	Indus-try	Other	Total
12-6125 Soil & Water Cons															
101 Apprais of Soil Res	289	121.5	584	138	8	20	0	751	25	182	2417	133	355	246	4108
102 Soil Struct & Nutri	433	115.5	700	137	42	27	0	906	59	531	2646	248	169	109	4667
103 Saline Soils	21	7.3	29	0	0	0	0	29	0	28	137	0	26	2	222
104 Altern Use of Land	68	11.5	62	8	16	0	0	86	11	14	284	48	10	5	457
105 Conserv Use of Wate	272	64.3	322	109	23	53	12	519	49	268	1528	116	179	31	2690
106 Drain & Irrigation	87	26.0	144	46	0	11	0	201	9	231	681	26	47	25	1221
Subtotal	1170	346.0	1841	440	89	111	12	2492	154	1253	7694	571	785	418	13365
12-6240 Remote Sensing															
113 Remote Sensing	7	9.3	13	0	3	0	0	16	193	157	93	6	5	8	478
Subtotal	7	9.3	13	0	3	0	0	16	193	157	93	6	5	8	478
13-6151 Frt & Veg Mktg Ef															
403 New & Imp F&V Prod	281	102.1	706	63	0	36	0	805	93	441	2390	55	251	29	4063
404 Mkt Qual Frts & Veg	161	53.3	514	183	0	0	0	698	54	218	1181	22	79	50	2303
503 Mktg Eff Fts & Vg	80	18.0	220	108	0	0	0	328	30	6	223	1	31	26	645
Subtotal	522	173.3	1440	355	0	36	0	1831	177	665	3794	79	361	104	7011
13-6152 Field Crops Mktg															
406 Imp Food Prod Fld C	154	33.0	189	11	0	28	0	228	87	338	589	61	298	33	1634
407 Imp Non Food Fld Cr	74	21.7	167	31	0	15	0	213	70	210	408	20	67	25	1012
408 Mkt Qual Field Crop	100	24.7	224	87	0	0	0	311	61	18	442	45	57	37	970
504 Mktg Eff Field Crop	88	14.3	206	139	0	0	0	345	29	11	149	6	17	1	559
Subtotal	416	93.8	786	268	0	43	0	1096	247	577	1587	132	439	97	4175

Classification Category	No. of Proj	SMY	HATH	RRF	MCIN STEN	SP GT	Oth CSRS	Tot CSRS	USDA CGCA	Other Fed	State Appro	Prod Sales	Indus try	Other	Total
13-6153 Livestock Mktg Ef															
410 Imp Meat Milk Egg P	373	107.9	1161	148	0	0	0	1309	154	611	2155	337	348	116	5030
411 Imp Wool Hde Skn Fa	15	1.0	7	0	0	0	0	7	0	12	34	3	0	0	56
412 Mkt Qual Animal Pro	160	38.4	576	74	0	0	0	651	46	162	596	123	81	21	1680
505 Mktg Eff Livestock	188	48.0	585	437	0	0	0	1021	59	12	392	17	17	3	1520
Subtotal	736	195.2	2329	639	0	0	0	2988	260	797	3177	478	446	140	8286
13-6154 Mktg Firms & Sys															
501 Imp Grades & Stands	59	12.8	96	45	0	0	0	141	20	30	267	16	7	20	502
508 Domestic Mkt Develp	78	18.8	266	78	0	0	0	344	0	0	241	10	3	10	609
509 Mktg Firms & Sys Ef	122	35.2	409	105	0	30	0	544	49	19	410	11	27	20	1080
Subtotal	259	66.7	771	229	0	30	0	1030	69	49	919	37	38	50	2191
13-6180 Imp Agric Statist															
511 Imp Agric Statistic	21	4.9	74	2	0	0	0	75	6	15	99	0	17	2	215
Subtotal	21	4.9	74	2	0	0	0	75	6	15	99	0	17	2	215
21-6350 Food Aid Programs															
602 Eval Food Aid Progr	1	2.0	0	0	0	0	0	0	0	0	0	0	0	0	0
Subtotal	1	2.0	0	0	0	0	0	0	0	0	0	0	0	0	0
22-6360 Foreign Mkt Devel															
601 Frgn Mkts for US Pr	62	13.3	141	45	0	0	0	186	35	0	185	2	3	74	485
Subtotal	62	13.3	141	45	0	0	0	186	35	0	185	2	3	74	485
23-6410 Foreign Agric Dev															
603 Tech Aid Dev Crty	36	14.7	6	0	0	0	0	6	4	23	104	2	40	108	287
Subtotal	36	14.7	6	0	0	0	0	6	4	23	104	2	40	108	287
31-6460 Food & Nutrition															
703 Food Consump Habits	52	11.5	121	49	0	0	0	169	3	5	151	7	14	11	361
704 Food Preparation	51	12.4	104	2	0	0	0	106	2	55	206	13	63	2	446
708 Human Nutrition	241	93.5	473	350	0	23	0	846	127	1251	1577	25	117	125	4069
Subtotal	344	117.3	698	401	0	23	0	1121	132	1310	1935	45	195	138	4876

Table IV-D-9 Summary by Problem Area of 1969 Funds by Source — in Thousands of Dollars *(continued)*

Classification Category	No. of Proj	SMY	HATH	RRF	MCIN STEN	SP CT	Oth CSRS	Tot CSRS	USDA CGCA	Other Fed	State Appro	Prod Sales	Indus-try	Other	Total
32-6480 Human Health & Sa															
701 Tox Res in Food	229	94.5	570	511	0	19	0	1100	241	1058	1854	35	106	103	4497
702 Food Prot from Tox	41	9.8	65	5	0	0	0	70	99	218	177	3	42	7	616
706 Contr Insects Aff M	126	30.8	151	4	0	0	0	155	48	199	838	3	38	50	1331
707 Trans Animal Man Di	34	13.4	60	0	0	7	0	67	33	361	64	4	56	23	608
709 Hlth Haz Non Food P	11	4.0	38	0	0	0	0	38	45	0	102	3	0	4	191
Subtotal	441	152.6	883	521	0	25	0	1430	466	1836	3035	48	242	187	7243
34-6500 Imp Levels of Liv															
705 Cloth and Textl Car	82	15.0	158	96	0	0	0	254	0	27	277	4	1	1	565
802 Family Finance Mgmt	55	16.0	124	52	0	0	0	176	15	1	291	3	0	2	488
Subtotal	137	31.0	282	148	0	0	0	431	15	28	567	7	1	3	1053
41-6670 Community Improve															
803 Rural Poverty	81	17.1	199	55	0	10	0	265	27	41	273	10	0	32	649
804 Econ Potent Rurl Pe	47	9.8	82	21	0	2	0	104	7	521	118	0	3	16	768
805 Communicat Rural Pe	60	18.3	71	28	2	2	0	103	2	270	458	8	47	18	904
806 Adjustment to Chang	102	25.6	97	69	0	2	0	168	11	205	1590	9	13	63	2060
907 Rural Income Imp	90	17.9	239	38	0	8	6	291	55	621	365	18	21	25	1396
908 Rural Institut Imp	203	45.3	262	89	0	3	0	353	41	267	864	6	102	126	1760
Subtotal	583	134.0	950	300	2	24	6	1284	143	1926	3668	51	186	279	7537
42-6690 Housing															
801 Rural Housing	39	6.5	29	31	9	0	0	70	12	20	102	3	0	2	209
Subtotal	39	6.5	29	31	9	0	0	70	12	20	102	3	0	2	209

Classification Category	No. of Proj	SMY	HATH	RRF	MCIN STEN	SP GT	Oth CSRS	Tot CSRS	USDA CGCA	Other Fed	State Appro	Prod Sales	Indus try	Other	Total
44-6730 Pollution															
214 Air Pollution Prote	24	8.1	54	20	0	0	0	74	0	190	120	7	36	0	427
901 Pollution Control	265	86.9	483	355	0	4	0	842	183	1412	1673	36	449	108	4703
Subtotal	289	95.0	537	375	0	4	0	916	183	1602	1793	43	485	108	5130
44-6870 Watershed Develop															
107 Watershed Conserv M	109	22.4	85	30	69	3	0	187	47	105	565	32	16	11	964
108 Econ Leg Prob of Wa	70	15.1	91	85	1	0	0	177	18	122	252	7	23	9	608
Subtotal	179	37.5	176	115	70	3	0	364	65	227	817	39	39	20	1572
44-6890 Fire Prevention															
203 Forest Fire Protect	5	0.6	0	0	1	0	0	2	9	1	5	0	0	0	17
Subtotal	5	0.6	0	0	1	0	0	2	9	1	5	0	0	0	17
45-6710 Natural Beauty															
905 Trees Beautification	99	22.0	82	22	27	0	0	132	22	175	512	16	50	30	937
906 Ornament &Turf Dev	613	177.9	889	130	8	0	0	1026	33	145	4355	187	322	226	6293
Subtotal	712	199.9	971	152	35	0	0	1158	55	320	4867	203	372	256	7230
45-6980 Outdoor Recreation															
902 Forestland Recreation	134	21.8	106	95	143	0	0	344	53	57	343	7	27	64	895
Subtotal	134	21.8	106	95	143	0	0	344	53	57	343	7	27	64	895
45-6990 Wildlife & Fish															
904 Wldlfe & Fish Eco	380	99.6	280	32	132	0	0	444	66	963	1947	73	733	386	4612
Subtotal	380	99.6	280	32	132	0	0	444	66	963	1947	73	733	386	4612
46-6910 Forest Insects															
201 Cntrl Forst Insects	85	31.4	112	9	194	0	0	315	36	84	520	12	43	45	1055
202 Control Forest Dis	82	21.3	90	12	197	0	0	229	29	41	420	7	11	26	832
Subtotal	167	52.7	202	21	391	0	0	615	65	125	949	19	54	71	1887

Table IV-D-9 Summary by Problem Area of 1969 Funds by Source — in Thousands of Dollars (continued)

Classification Category	No. of Proj	SMY	HATH	RRF	MCIN STEN	SP GT	Oth CSRS	Tot CSRS	USDA CGCA	Other Fed	State Appro	Prod Sales	Industry	Other	Total
46-6930 Timber Production:															
110 Apprais Forst & Ran	84	18.1	37	24	162	0	0	224	34	50	226	7	18	99	698
111 Timber Management	228	53.9	170	17	382	0	0	570	26	31	1004	31	57	158	1877
301 Imp Bio Eff of Tree	216	60.6	163	124	709	0	0	996	29	28	1205	45	61	35	2397
302 Imp Forest Eng Sys	13	6.4	5	0	65	0	0	70	0	0	130	0	7	1	209
303 Econ Timber Product	18	4.8	12	0	53	0	0	65	0	0	64	5	0	6	140
903 Multi-Use-Forst Pot	31	5.2	13	0	15	0	0	28	2	0	97	5	2	7	141
Subtotal	590	149.0	400	166	1387	0	0	1953	91	109	2766	93	145	306	5463
46-6950 Forest Products M															
502 Mktg Timber Product	42	8.3	68	14	32	0	0	114	35	1	93	0	1	0	244
512 Imp Grades Frst Prd	11	3.0	7	0	19	0	0	26	4	2	54	0	0	0	87
513 Price Anal Frst Pro	19	3.7	34	7	36	0	0	76	4	3	32	0	0	0	115
Subtotal	72	15.0	109	21	87	0	0	217	42	6	179	1	1	0	446
49-6970 Forest Prod Utli															
401 New Imp Forest Prod	102	41.5	125	6	403	42	0	576	42	25	620	16	42	76	1396
Subtotal	102	41.5	125	6	403	42	0	576	42	25	620	16	42	76	1396
99-9900 Unclassified															
990 Unclassified	217	44.5	188	103	0	0	0	291	83	608	1108	84	98	77	2350
Subtotal	217	44.5	188	103	0	0	0	291	83	608	1108	84	98	77	2350
Science in Serv of Man Grand Total	19965	5955.9	39248	10282	2825	1316	18	53688	7749	27576	134253	15718	12236	7519	58739

SOURCE: USDA, Science and Education Staff. "Inventory of Agricultural Research FY 1969 and 1970," vol. II, table IV-D-9, pp. 247-248.

APPENDIX D

COOPERATIVE STATE RESEARCH SERVICE

PURPOSE STATEMENT

The Cooperative State Research Service was established by Secretary's Memorandum No. 1462 dated July 19, 1961 and Supplement 1, dated August 31, 1961 under Reorganization Plan No. 2 of 1953. The primary function of the Service is to administer acts of Congress that authorize federal appropriations for agricultural research carried on by the state agricultural experiment stations of the 50 states and Puerto Rico, by approved schools of forestry and nonprofit institutions.

Acts under which payments to states may be made include:

1. Agricultural Experiment Stations Act of August 11, 1955 (Hatch Act of 1887, as amended: 7 U.S.C., 361a-361i).

2. Cooperative Forestry Research Act of October 10, 1962 (16 U.S.C., 582a-582a-7).

3. Act of September 6, 1958 (42 U.S.C., 1891-1893) and the Act of August 4, 1965 (7 U.S.C., 450b), authorizing grants for support of scientific research.

4. Research Facilities Act of July 22, 1963 (7 U.S.C., 390-390k)

Administration of payments and grants involves the review and approval in advance of each individual research proposal submitted by a state agricultural experiment station or other institution to be financed in whole or in part from federal grant funds, the disbursement of the funds, and the continuous review and evaluation of research programs and expenditures thereunder. The service also encourages and assists in the establishment and maintenance of cooperation within and between the states, and participates in the planning and coordination of research programs between the states and the U.S. Department of Agriculture.

The program coordination and planning is carried out by a Cooperative State Research Service staff located entirely in Washington, D.C.

SOURCE: U.S. House of Representatives, Committee on Appropriations. "Agriculture-Environmental and Consumer Protection Appropriations for 1972," *Hearings*, 92nd Congress, 1st Session, part 2, p. 512.

APPENDIX E

AGRICULTURAL RESEARCH SERVICE

PURPOSE STATEMENT

The Agricultural Research Service was established by the secretary of agriculture on November 2, 1953, under the authority of the *Reorganization Act of 1949* (5 U.S.C. 133z-15), *Reorganization Plan No. 2 of 1953*, and other authorities. It conducts farm, utilization, marketing, and nutrition and consumer use research, and plant and animal disease and pest control and eradication activities.

The program of the Agricultural Research Service is organized under two major areas of activity as follows:

1. *Research* is conducted under four major categories: (a) farm research (research on crops and livestock and their diseases and pests, soil and water conservation, and agricultural engineering); (b) utilization research and development; (c) nutrition and consumer use research; (d) marketing research.

2. *Regulatory activities* are conducted under two major categories: (a) plant disease and pest control; (b) animal disease and pest control.

The Service carries out emergency programs, when necessary, for the control and eradication of animal diseases, such as foot-and-mouth disease, and for the control of emergency outbreaks of insects and diseases.

The Service directs research mutually beneficial to the United States and the host country which can be advantageously conducted in foreign countries through agreements with the foreign research institutions and universities. This program is carried out under the authority of section 104(b) (1) and (3) of Public Law 480, *the Agricultural Trade Development and Assistance Act of 1954,* as amended.

The Service maintains central offices in the Washington metropolitan area, and operates the 10,311 acres Agricultural Research Center at Beltsville, Maryland. However, most of the Service's work is conducted at numerous field locations in the 50 States, Puerto Rico, the Virgin Islands, and in several foreign countries. Much of the work is conducted in cooperation, or under contracts and grants, with the state agricultural experiment stations, state departments of agriculture and with other agencies, both public and private.

SOURCE: U.S. House of Representatives, Committee on Appropriations. "Agriculture-Environmental and Consumer Protection Appropriations for 1972," *Hearings,* 92nd Congress, 1st session, part 2, p. 147.

APPENDIX F

PRIVATE FINANCIAL SUPPORT FOR RESEARCH
PURDUE UNIVERSITY AGRICULTURAL EXPERIMENT STATION

July 1, 1969 to June 30, 1970

Title	Department	Principal Investigator	Amount
ABBOTT LABORATORIES:			
Virus respiratory diseases of poultry	Vet. Sci.	R. W. Winterfield	$ 4,500.00
AGRICULTURAL BUSINESS SERVICE COMPANY			
Electronic farm accounting and analysis	Ag. Econ.	R. J. Rades	7,000.00
AMERICAN CANCER SOCIETY			
Changes in transfer RNA species in viral infected plant cells	Hort.	R. Venkataraman P. De Leo	3,750.00
AMERICAN CYANAMID COMPANY			
Studies with antibacterial drugs and their effect on growth of cattle during the early feeding period	An. Sci.	W. M. Beeson	4,000.00
AMERICAN OIL COMPANY			
Utilization of weed oils for control of weeds in corn and soybeans	Bot. Pl. Pth.	J. L. Williams M. A. Ross	1,000.00
Evaluation of oils for use in alfalfa weevil management	Entomol.	M. C. Wilson	2,000.00
AMCHEM PRODUCTS, INC.			
Herbicide research	Bot. Pl. Pth.	J. L. Williams M. A. Ross	750.00

Appendix F (continued)

Title	Department	Principal Investigator	Amount
ARKANSAS VALLEY INDUSTRIES			
Quality of poultry meat	An. Sci.	W. J. Stadelman	$ 1,000.00
ARMOUR PHARMACEUTICAL COMPANY			
Hypocholesteremic agents	Biochem.	F. W. Quackenbush	20,000.00
THE BEACON MILLING COMPANY, INC.			
Management science research	Ag. Econ.	J. C. Snyder	12,000.00
BEECH-NUT, INC.			
Insect problems in processed foods and insecticide residue studies	Entomol.	J. V. Osmun	3,000.00
BOMARKO, INC.			
Effects of soya additives on the chemical and physical properties of ground meat	An. Sci.	M. D. Judge	1,250.00
BURNS PHARMACEUTICALS, INC.			
Selenium responsive diseases in swine	Vet. Sci.	K. B. Meyer	1,000.00
CASTER AND FLOOR TRUCK MANUFACTURER'S ASSOCIATION			
An evaluation of the effect of floor surface texture and other variables upon the performance and endurance characteristics of furniture and industrial casters	For. Cons.	C. A. Eckelman	6,000.00

Title	Department	Principal Investigator	Amount
CHEMAGRO CORPORATION			
Chemical weed control	Bot. P.L. Pth. Hort.	M. M. Schreiber	$ 200.00
		G. F. Warren	
Use of Bay 79770 and ®Morestan for control of	Bot. Pl. Pth.	G. E. Shaner	500.00
powdery mildew on wheat			
Baygon use for alfalfa weevil control	Entomol.	M. C. Wilson	350.00
Corn and soybean insect control	Entomol.	D. B. Broersma	350.00
Anthelmintic efficiency of Trichlorofon in swine	Vet. Sci.	D. G. Bennett	1,825.00
CHEVRON CHEMICAL COMPANY			
Research dealing with grain storage	Bot. Pl. Pth.	J. F. Tuite	500.00
Vegetation control for legume und corn production	Bot. Pl. Pth.	J. L. Williams	500.00
in established sod and weed control in soybeans		M. A. Ross	
CONTINENTAL OIL CO., AGRICO CHEMICAL CO.			
Plant analysis as an aid on soybean and corn production	Agron.	A. J. Ohlrogge	600.00
CORN PRODUCTS FOOD TECHNOLOGY INSTITUTE			
Meat to bone ratios in chicken roasters	An. Sci.	W. J. Stadelman	1,200.00
CORN REFINERS ASSOCIATION, INC.			
Dr. Whistler's research	Biochem.	R. L. Whistler	8,500.00
CPC INTERNATIONAL AND FUNK BROTHERS SEED COMPANY			
Basic biochemical research on high lysine corn	Biochem.	E. T. Mertz	5,000.00
CUSTOM FARM SERVICES, INC.			
Sub-soil fertility	Agron.	D. R. Griffith	1,000.00

Appendix F (continued)

Title	Department	Principal Investigator	Amount
DAIRY TRAINING AND MERCHANDISING INSTITUTE			
Improved merchandising of milk and dairy products in supermarket dairies	Ag. Econ.	E. C. Oesterle	$22,300.00
DeKALB AG RESEARCH, INC.			
Inheritance of important agronomic characters in corn and breeding methods	Agron.	J. B. Peterson	3,500.00
DISTILLERS FEED RESEARCH COUNCIL			
Nutritional factors in distillers dried grains with solubles affecting the bacterial synthesis of protein form ureal in cattle	Am. Sci.	W. M. Beeson	4,000.00
DOW CHEMICAL COMPANY			
Weed control for soybeans and corn utilizing pre-emergence, post-emergence, and directed post-emergence herbicides	Bot. Pl. Pth.	J. L. Williams M. A. Ross	1,500.00
DUVAL SALES CORPORATION			
Sulfur and magnesium levels for Indiana	Agron.	E. L. Hood	500.00
ESSO RESEARCH AND ENGINEERING COMPANY			
Studies of pesticide activity of pesticides formulated in synthetic hydrocarbons	Hort.	G. F. Warren	1,500.00
Utilization of Esso herbicides, ER-5461, ER-9061, and ER-9063 for control of weeds in soybeans and corn	Bot. Pl. Pth.	J. L. Williams M. A. Ross	1,000.00
FATS AND PROTEINS RESEARCH FOUNDATION, INC.			
Effect of different levels of fat on the utilization of urea, digestibility of nutrients, and feedlot performance of steers	An. Sci.	W. M. Beeson	6,000.00

Title	Department	Principal Investigator	Amount
FMC CORPORATION, NIAGARA CHEMICAL DIVISION			
Studies relating to integrated control of insects in corn	Entomol.	R. T. Huber	900.00
Insecticidal research in connection with corn and soybean production	Entomol.	D. B. Broersma	500.00
Studying chemical control of insects affecting alfalfa	Entomol.	M. C. Wilson	750.00
GEIGY AGRICULTURAL CHEMICALS			
Herbicide research/corn, soybeans, alfalfa minimum tillage	Bot. Pl. Pth.	J. L. Williams M. A. Ross	1,000.00
Integrated control of alfalfa weevil	Entomol.	M. C. Wilson	500.00
GENERAL FOODS CORPORATION, IGLEHEART OPERATIONS			
Improvement of soft red winter wheat in Indiana	Bot. Pl. Pth.	R. M. Caldwell	20,000.00
W. R. GRACE AND COMPANY, CONSTRUCTION PRODUCTS DIVISION			
Potential nutritional effect of verxite grits as a roughage extender for ruminant animals	An. Sci.	T. W. Perry	2,500.00
GULF RESEARCH AND DEVELOPMENT COMPANY			
Weed control in turf	Agron.	W H. Daniel	250.00
HALE AND HUNTER COMPANY			
Profit planning and control system research	Ag. Econ.	J. C. Snyder	4,500.00
HOFFMAN-LA ROCHE, INC.			
Effect of vitamin E and selenium on performance of beef cattle	An. Sci.	W. M. Beeson	5,000.00

Appendix F (continued)

Title	Department	Principal Investigator	Amount
INDIANA CANNERS ASSOCIATION			
Improvement in producing and handling raw products for the canning industry	Hort. Bot. Pl. Pth. Ag. Eng.	H. T. Erickson M. L. Tomes G. W. Isaacs	$12,500.00
THE INDIANA CROP IMPROVEMENT ASSOCIATION, INC.			
Seed quality investigations with soybeans	Bot. Pl. Pth.	M. L. Tomes	15,000.00
INDIANA DEPARTMENT OF NATURAL RESOURCES			
Cooperative relationships in wildlife research	Forestry	C. M. Kirkpatrick	15,000.00
INDIANA ELKS			
Genesis and transformation of the cytokinetic apparatus	Bot. Pl. Pth.	C. E. Bracker	2,000.00
Induction and regulation of DNA polymerase and RNA polymerase associated with induced cell division of 2,4-dichlorophenoxy-acid treated soybean seedlings	Hort.	T. J. O'Brien	2,000.00
Biochemical and genetic studies on DAHP-synthetase of Escherichia coli K12.	Biochem.	K. Herrmann	3,000.00
INDIANA HEART ASSOCIATION			
Enzyme repression and control of cholesterol synthesis	Biochem.	V. W. Rodwell	4,500.00
Role of cholesterol esters in milk lipid formation	An. Sci.	T. W. Keenan	6,000.00
INDIANA PORK PRODUCERS ASSOCIATION			
Hormone levels in stress-susceptible pigs	An. Sci.	M. D. Judge	1,500.00
INDIANA TUBERCULOSIS ASSOCIATION			
Levels of biologically active amines in brains of ducks undergoing isoniazid toxicosis	Vet. Sci.	W. W. Carlton	6,384.00

Title	Department	Principal Investigator	Amount
INTERNATIONAL MINERALS AND CHEMICAL CORPORATION			
Use of growth regulators in field crop production	Agron.	A. J. Ohlrogge	15,495.00
Evaluation of Thuricide-Pyrethrin mixture in pressurized sprays	Entomol.	D. E. Schuder	550.00
JACOBSEN MANUFACTURING CORPORATION			
Effects of shatter cultivation on water infiltration	Agron.	W. H. Daniel	1,000.00
Establishment and survival of seedlings following vertical grooving	Agron.	W. H. Daniel	1,000.00
ELI LILLY AND COMPANY			
Diagnosis and immunology of hog cholera	Vet. Sci.	D. P. Gustafson	3,400.00
Critical evaluation of the anthelmintic EL-974 in dogs	Vet. Sci.	S. M. Gaafar	1,100.00
Evaluation of Treflam and Ryzelan for weed control in soybeans	Bot. Pl. Pth.	J. L. Williams M. A. Ross	750.00
MALLINCKRODT CHEMICAL WORKS			
Seedhead inhibition of *Poa annua*	Agron.	W. H. Daniel	500.00
Growth retardants for control of *Poa annua*	Agron.	W. H. Daniel	500.00
MIX-MILL, INC.			
Effect of heat treating livestock feeds	An. Sci.	T. W. Perry	3,000.00
MONSANTO CHEMICAL COMPANY			
Herbicide research	Bot. Pl. Pth.	J. L. Williams M. A. Ross	1,250.00
Integrated control research using methyl parathion	Entomol.	M. C. Wilson	500.00
JOHN MORRELL AND COMPANY			
Management science research	Ag. Econ.	J. C. Snyder	16,133.37

Appendix F (continued)

Title	Department	Principal Investigator	Amount
MORTON SALT COMPANY Quality of turkey meat	An. Sci.	W. J. Stadelman	$ 500.00
THE NATIONAL BANK OF LOGANSPORT Electronic farm accounting	Ag. Econ.	R. J. Rades	225.00
NATIONAL MOLASSES COMPANY Energy value of molasses and its effect on urea utilization in beef steers	An. Sci.	W. M. Beeson	5,000.00
NATIONAL SOYBEAN PROCESSORS ASSN., CROP IMPROVEMENT COUNCIL Physiological barriers to yield improvement in soybeans	Agron.	H. R. Koller	15,000.00
THE NATIONAL TURKEY FEDERATION Predicting tenderness of turkey meat	An. Sci.	W. J. Stadelman	1,000.00
S. B. PENICK AND COMPANY Insecticide evaluation and phytotoxicity studies of SBP 1382	Entomol.	D. E. Schuder	550.00
PIONEER CORN COMPANY, INC. The effect of potassium fertility upon the yield and nutritive value of corn silage	An. Sci.	T. W. Perry	2,500.00
THE POPCORN INSTITUTE Combine harvesting of popcorn	Bot. Pl. Pth. Ag. Eng.	R. B. Ashman C. G. Haugh	2,000.00
PORTLAND CEMENT ASSOCIATION Effects of soil applications of Portland-type cement materials on crop yield and soil properties	Agron.	D. Swartzendruber	22,400.00

Title	Department	Principal Investigator	Amount
QUAKER OATS COMPANY Research and breeding for high protein in oats	Agron.	F. L. Patterson	3,500.00
RHODIA, INC., CHIPMAN DIVISION Selective weed control in turf	Agron.	W. H. Daniel	1,000.00
ROHM AND HAAS COMPANY Herbicide research	Hort.	G. F. Warren	500.00
JOSEPH E. SEAGRAMS AND SONS, INC. Ethiopian national pre-doctoral fellowship in the field of corn genetics	Agron.	J. B. Peterson	6,500.00
THE SEEING EYE, INC. A study of osteoarthritis of the canine shoulder	Vet. Sci.	D. C. Van Sickle	21,560.00
SHELL CHEMICAL COMPANY Efficiency of DDVP taste against ascarids, pinworms, and bots in horses and selected toxicology studies	Vet. Sci.	D. G. Bennett	4,000.00
Bladex and Planavin weed control test program on soybeans, vegetables, and corn	Bot. Pl. Pth.	J. L. Williams M. A. Ross	500.00
SHELL DEVELOPMENT COMPANY Herbicide studies under Indiana conditions	Bot. Pl. Pth.	J. L. Williams M. A. Ross	1,000.00
Herbicide research	Bot. Pl. Pth.	J. L. Williams M. A. Ross	500.00
Insecticide research	Entomol.	G. E. Gould D. B. Broersma	1,250.00

Appendix F (continued)

Title	Department	Principal Investigator	Amount
SOUTHWEST POTASH CORPORATION			
Response and tolerance to turf to varying applications of potassium nitrate	Agron.	W. H. Daniel	$1,500.00
STAUFFER CHEMICAL COMPANY			
Chemical weed control research	Bot. Pl. Pth.	J. L. Williams	600.00
Alfalfa weevil insecticide research	Entomol.	M. A. Ross	500.00
To obtain additional insect species for Dyfonate 20G	Entomol.	M. C. Wilson	300.00
		D. B. Broersma	
SWIFT AGRICULTURAL CHEMICALS CORPORATION			
Research on slow release nitrogen sources	Agron.	W. H. Daniel	1,000.00
A. M. TODD COMPANY			
Research on mint diseases	Bot. Pl. Pth.	R. J. Green, Jr. •	1,900.00
	Hort.	G. F. Warren	750.00
UNION CARBIDE CORPORATION			
Alfalfa weevil research	Entomol.	M. C. Wilson	500.00
UNIROYAL CHEMICAL, DIVISION OF UNIROYAL, INC.			
Herbicide research	Bot. Pl. Pth.	J. J. Williams	1,500.00
		M. A. Ross	
Growth regulating chemicals research	Hort.	F. H. Emerson	2,000.00
VELSICOL CHEMICAL CORPORATION			
Selectivity of combined herbicides on weeds in turf	Agron.	W. H. Daniel	1,000.00

Title	Department	Principal Investigator	Amount
WILDLIFE MANAGEMENT INSTITUTE Wildlife studies	For. Cons.	D. L. Allen	$1,200.00
WINTHROP LABORATORIES Clinical evaluation of Winstrol-V in ponies	Vet. Sci.	W. W. Kirkham E. H. Page	2,750.00

SOURCE: Purdue University, *1970 annual report of Agricultural Experimental Station*, (Lafayette, Indiana), pp. 26-30.

APPENDIX G

BIOGRAPHICAL SKETCHES
MEMBERS OF
NATIONAL AGRICULTURAL RESEARCH ADVISORY COMMITTEE

DR. ORVILLE G. BENTLEY, DEAN, COLLEGE OF AGRICULTURE, UNIVERSITY OF ILLINOIS, URBANA, ILLINOIS

Dr. Bentley is dean of the College of Agriculture at the University of Illinois. He has a B.S. degree from the South Dakota State University at Brooking, South Dakota; M.S. and Ph.D. in biochemistry from the University of Wisconsin. He previously was dean of agriculture and director of the Experiment Station at South Dakota State College. Dr. Bentley is a member of the National Research Council, American Chemical Society, Society of Animal Science and the Nutrition Institute. He received the American Feed Manufacturers Association award in 1958. He served as a major in the Chemical Warfare Service from 1942 to 1946.

JOHN GAMMON, JR., ROUTE 1, BOX 252, MARION, ARKANSAS

Mr. Gammon operates a 1,000-acre cotton, rice, swine, and fish farm. He resigned from the Resettlement Administration to return home and take over the 200-acre family farm devoted mostly to cotton in 1936. Mr. Gammon is a graduate of Arkansas A.M. and N. College. He is president of the Negro Division of the Arkansas Farm Bureau Federation and manager of the cooperative cotton gin in his county.

DR. CHARLES E. GEISE, DIRECTOR OF AGRICULTURAL RESEARCH, DEL MONTE CORPORATION, SAN LEANDRO, CALIFORNIA

Dr. Geise is director of agricultural research for the Del Monte Corporation, processor of fruits and vegetables. He received a B.S. degree from Purdue University and an M.S. and Ph.D. in horticulture from Iowa State College. He previously was a sweet corn breeder, superintendent of the agricultural research and seed department, and manager of the research division of the California Packing Corporation. Dr. Geise is a member of the Society of Agronomy and the Society of Horticultural Science.

DR. PAUL B. PEARSON, PRESIDENT AND SCIENTIFIC DIRECTOR, THE NUTRITION FOUNDATION, INC., NEW YORK, NEW YORK

Dr. Pearson is a graduate of Brigham Young University, Montana State College and the University of Wisconsin. He holds a Ph.D. degree in biochemical nutrition from the latter Institution. He was formerly employed as a research associate, University of California; dean of the graduate school and head of the department of biochemistry and nutrition, Texas Agricultural and Mechanical College, chief, biological branch, United States Atomic Energy Commission, professor, Johns Hopkins University and science and engineering program of the Ford Foundation. He served on several committees of the National Research Council attending many international meetings as U.S. delegate. He is a member of many scientific organizations including the American Association for Advancement of Science, American Chemical Society, American Institute of Nutrition, London Biochemical Society, and American Society of Biological Chemists.

CLARENCE W. RICHEN, VICE PRESIDENT, NORTHWEST TIMBER OPERATIONS, CROWN ZELLERBACH CORPORATION, PORTLAND, OREGON

Mr. Richen was first employed by Crown Zellerbach in 1939 as forestry consultant, while he was on the faculty of the Oregon State University School of Forestry of which he is a graduate. In 1942 he joined the Company's Portland Timber Department, becoming chief forester in 1946. He is on the board of directors of the Industrial Forestry Association, a trustee and executive committee member of the Western Forestry Association; a member of the Pacific Northwest Forest Experiment Station Research Advisory Committee; member of the Committee on Forestry Research of the Agricultural Board of the National Academy of Sciences, and of the Cooperative Forestry Research Advisory Committee (established under the *McIntire-Stennis Act* of 1962).

CECIL H. ROBINSON, ROUTE 1, DELAWARE, OHIO

Mr. Robinson produces, processes, and markets hybrid seed corn, certified wheat, oats, and soybean seed. He also produces about 1000 hogs annually, mainly Yorkshires. He is past president, Ohio Seed Improvement Association; has served on Grain Advisory Committee, Farm Bureau; was chairman of County Agricultural Extension Committee; and member of the State Committee. In 1962 he served on the People-to-People Mission in Eastern Europe. Mr. Robinson is a graduate of Ohio State University where he majored in agricultural engineering and rural economics.

FRANK SCHUSTER, RT. 1, BOX 82, SAN JUAN, TEXAS

Mr. Schuster operates a 1400-acre farm in the lower Rio Grande Valley of Texas, of which about 50 percent is devoted to vegetable production. He specializes in spinach, turnip, mustard, kale, and collard greens and broccoli for freezing and canning, with smaller amounts of the same for the fresh market. He also grows about 150 acres of onions annually, with smaller acreages of tomatoes, cukes and peppers—all acreage under irrigation. Mr. Schuster is a strong supporter of research, and participates in the research programs of the Texas Agricultural Experiment Station by furnishing land and other production facilities and services. He is chairman of the Vegetable Subcommittee of the Agricultural Advisory Committee of the Texas A&M University; past president of Hidalgo County Farm Bureau; chairman of the Rio Grande Valley Farm Bureau's Fruit and Vegetable Committee; chairman of the Agricultural Committee of the Rio Grande Valley Chamber of Commerce; has been active in supporting the several marketing agreement and order programs now operating in the Lower Valley; and is a member of the Southern Texas Onion Committee. Mr. Schuster served in the U.S. Armed Forces 1943-1946. He was a member of the Horticultural Crops Research Advisory Committee, USDA.

ELTON R. SMITH, PRESIDENT, MICHIGAN FARM BUREAU, LANSING, MICHIGAN

Mr. Smith farms a 388 acre dairy farm in Kent County, Michigan. He is a prominent Guernsey breeder, president of the Michigan Guernsey Breeders Association, and in 1963 was named Michigan Dairyman of the Year. He received the Michigan State Distinguished Service to Agriculture award, and has been active in a variety of livestock organizations and for ten years, has been on his county Soil Conservation District Board. He has been very interested in research on pesticide problems and was helpful in establishing a pesticides research laboratory in Michigan State University. Mr. Smith has been president of Michigan's Farm Bureau since 1964, president of the Michigan Farm Bureau Services, and is a director of the American Farm Bureau Federation.

J. W. STILES, VICE PRESIDENT, DEVELOPMENT, AGWAY, SYRACUSE, NEW YORK

Mr. Stiles is vice president, development for AGWAY, a cooperative organization serving the eastern United States. He served for ten years as director of research for the Cooperative G.L.F. Exchange. Mr. Stiles is a graduate of Cornell University, a member of the American Society of Agricultural Engineers, American Grassland Council, and the Agricultural Research Institute.

DR. BETTY SULLIVAN, 4825 QUEEN AVENUE, SOUTH, MINNEAPOLIS, MINNESOTA

Dr. Sullivan is a graduate of the University of Minnesota and the University of Paris (France) where she majored in biochemistry. She was employed in 1924 in milling research by Russel Miller and served as director of research and vice president of the Peavey Company Flour Mills. Dr. Sullivan has been president of the American Association of Cereal Chemists, chairman of the Minnesota Section of the American Chemical Society and is a member of the Council of the American Chemical Society. She is a member of Societie Biologique de France, New York Academy of Science, American Association for the Advancement of Science, and the American Society of Bakery Engineers. She has served as chairman of the Technical Advisory Committee and is a member of the Flour Standards Committee of the Millers' National Federation.

PEDRO F. TIRADO, GPO BOX 2075, SAN JUAN, PUERTO RICO

Mr. Tirado is agricultural advisor (agrarian reform) to the Agricultural and Rural Development Office (ARDO) of the U.S. Agency for International Development. He previously served in a similar capacity with the U.S. AID Missions to Brazil, Costa Rico, Bolivia, and Guatemala. He also has been employed as regional director of agriculture, Department of Agriculture of

Puerto Rico at Ponce, P.R.; as a soil scientist and agronomist with the International Cooperation Administration, U.S. Department of State; and as acting chief USOM Agricultural Division in Honduras. He was a soil scientist with the Institute of Interamerican Affairs in Asuneion, Paraguay, and a soil conservationist (research) at the Puerto Rico Agricultural Experiment Station at Rio Piedras and Mayaguez.

Mr. Tirado has a B.S. degree in agronomy from the University of Puerto Rico and an M.S. in agronomy from the Texas A&M University. He also attended the USDA graduate school and the State Department Foreign Service Institute.

APPENDIX H

A STATISTICAL PROFILE OF IOWA STATE UNIVERSITY'S
AGRICULTURAL COMPLEX

Since national figures are sketchy, dated, unreported or non-existent, this short financial profile of one land grant college is offered for perspective. Iowa State University (ISU) is chosen for no more substantive reason than the fact that its financial report is (1) relatively detailed, (2) recent, and (3) available.

On September 11, 1862, the Iowa State legislature accepted the terms of the *Morrill Act* and ISU became the first land grant college in the country. ISU today is much more than the "agricultural college and farm" it was in 1862. As of June 30, 1971, the total university system had assets of $193,912,000 and annual expenditures of $106,347,606. There were 5,143 employees, ranging from 22 deans and directors to 701 clerical. The university enrolled 18,700 undergraduates and 4,849 graduate students, and through extension and short courses another 68,530 Iowans were reached by this educational facility. There is a graduate college, as well as undergraduate colleges of agriculture, home economics, education, engineering, science and humanities, and veterinary medicine.

Although it is separate at ISU, home economics usually is considered a function of colleges of agriculture, so the College of Home Economics will be figures in this profile as a part of ISU's agricultural complex.

That complex includes four components: College of Agriculture, College of Home Economics, Agricultural Experiment Station, and Agricultural and Home Economics Extension. Pages 181-183 show the divisions within each of those components and their expenditures for fiscal year 1971. In 1971, as shown on page 183, this complex had total expenditures of $22,091,792 (20 percent of the ISU total) and had assets worth $24,443,449 (13 percent of total assets of ISU):

SOURCE: All information used in the ISU profile is taken from: Iowa State University of Science and Technology. *Financial Report for the Year Ended June 30, 1971* (Ames, Iowa: November 1971).

276

IOWA STATE UNIVERSITY—AGRICULTURAL COMPLEX
STATEMENT OF CURRENT EXPENDITURES DISTRIBUTED
BY OBJECT FOR FISCAL YEAR 1971

COLLEGE OF AGRICULTURE

Administration	$ 178,917.26
Agriculture Economics	237,935.77
Agriculture Engineering	256,534.86
Agronomy	332,245.80
Animal Science	565,576.04
Animal Science—Dairy Science	282,811.02
Biochemistry and Biophysics	78,515.76
Dairy and Food Industry	138,736.18
Entomology	209,069.02
Forestry	184,514.37
Genetics	93,412.98
Horticulture	146,574.58
Landscape Architecture	182,494.60
Plant Pathology	44,247.29
Poultry Science	66,718.92
Sociology and Anthropology	50,558.29
Technical Journalism	321,189.40
Education	48,966.46
Computer Usage	3,027.99
Summer Quarter	83,260.82
Sub-Total	$3,505,307.41
Restricted Funds	444,908.84
Total	$3,950,216.25

COLLEGE OF HOME ECONOMICS

Administration	$ 206,899.10
Applied Art	401,471.61
Child Development	255,424.70
Family Environment	248,096.66
Food and Nutrition	277,132.20
Home Economics Education	119,284.96
Institutional Management	129,979.77
Physical Education for Women	268,199.63
Textiles and Clothing	256,686.97
Computer Usage	1,200.00
Summer Quarter	109,040.34
Sub-Total	$2,273,415.94
Restricted Funds	95,230.61
Total	$2,368,646.55

AGRICULTURAL EXPERIMENT STATION

Administration	$ 160,787.13
Agricultural Adjustment Center	564,556.07
Agricultural Economics	234,918.11
Agricultural Engineering	393,260.25
Agronomy	1,594,474.22
Animal Science	1,013,084.27
Annuity and Social Security	152,154.46
Bacteriology	32,076.54
Chemistry	339,473.40
Dairy and Food Industry	368,519.72
Dairy Science	241,954.16
Entomology and Wildlife	502,054.08
Forestry	151,652.47
Genetics	165,145.96
Home Economics	267,748.14
Horticulture	196,692.06
Information Service	136,350.52
Plant Pathology	333,842.82
Poultry Science	185,315.26
Sociology and Anthropology	308,377.48
Special Research and Development	1,229,872.55
Statistics	265,453.85
Veterinary Research	78,299.75
Vocational Education	19,220.63
Equipment	61,713.55
Total Agricultural Experiment Station	$8,996,997.45

AGRICULTURAL AND HOME ECONOMICS EXTENSION

Administration	$114,993.77
Agricultural Adjustment Center	58,280.85
Agricultural Economics	337,183.82
Agricultural Engineering	220,656.60
Agronomy	151,508.31
Animal Science—Dairy Science	241,100.21
County Agricultural Program—County Staff	3,467,522.36
County Youth Program—County	113,338.71
County Youth Program—State Staff	177,277.75
Dairy and Food Industry	57,286.01
Entomology and Wildlife	86,980.26
Family Arts and Science	281,829.41
Forestry	32,798.23
Horticulture	64,529.82
Information Service	309,469.51
Landscape Architecture	34,381.17

Plant Pathology	89,251.48
Poultry Science	53,229.05
Publications	176,285.75
Rural Sociology	60,078.46
Special Research and Development Unit	52,832.55
Staff Services	313,719.11
Veterinary Medicine	73,199.18
Equipment	17,445.16
Total Extension	$6,585,177.53

EXPENDITURES AND ASSETS
AGRICULTURAL COMPLEX FOR FY 1971

A. For Instruction, Research and Extension

College of Agriculture		$3,950,216	
College of Home Economics		2,368,647	
Agricultural Experiment Station:			
Federal	$1,284,449		
State	3,901,399		
Restricted	3,811,149*		
Total AES		8,996,997	
Agricultural and Home Ec. Extension:			
Federal	2,468,917		
State	3,037,467		
Restricted	1,078,793*		
Total A&HEE		6,585,177	
Total Instruction, Research and Extension			$21,901,037

B. For Purchase of Equipment

College of Agriculture	$ 25,659	
College of Home Economics	33,275	
Agricultural Experiment Station	61,464	
Agricultural and Home Ec. Extension	17,434	
Total Purchase of Equipment		$ 137,832

C. For Repairs, Replacements & Alterations:

Total	$ 52,923
Total Expenditures of ISU's Agricultural Complex	$22,091,792

ASSETS

A. Farmland
   58 farms (6,434 acres) $ 1,569,200
B. Investment in Farm Buildings   4,650,148
C. Investment in Buildings on Campus
      College of Agriculture $7,840,519
      College of Home
        Economics   2,478,334
        Total Campus
          Buildings   10,318,853
D. Investment in Improvements (other than buildings)   446,334
E. Investment in Equipment
      College of Agriculture $2,228,867
      College of Home Economics   725,440
      Agricultural Experiment Station   4,029,211
      Agricultural & Home Ec. Extension   465,396
      Total Equipment   7,448,914
Total Assets of ISU's Agricultural Complex $24,443,449

*Funds for research and extension given to ISU for specific purposes.
 Includes grants from governmental agencies, fundations and industry.

INTERNAL MEMORANDUM

Department of Entomology
University of California, Berkeley

"MEMO TO: Dr. R. F. Smith
"FROM: D. L. Dahlsten
"SUBJECT: Pesticide Companies and University Employees.

"I have become increasingly concerned about the roles that certain individuals are playing in the current fad on environmental pollution and ecology. Two recent events really brought this into focus for me and I want to address these problems to you as Department Chairman. The recent ranking of our Department as the number one entomological unit in the country has also caused me to reflect on this problem.

"First of all, I was ashamed of the letter that was published in *Science* magazine on 27 November, 1970 (vol. 170, no. 3961, p. 928) by Louis Lykken of our Department. This was a bitter letter and, as you will see when you read it, in it a total misunderstanding of the whole pollution, pest control issue is exhibited. When I think of the biological and ecological knowledge that has gone into the development of the integrated control concept in our own Department, I can't understand how one of our staff members can be so oblivious to the facts of life. There seems to be a trend developing that I don't think should continue.

"Men that retire from jobs with chemical corporations take jobs in universities if for no other reason than to give their ideas credence by using a university letterhead. Thomas Jukes, Guy MacLeod, and Louis Lykken fit this description. Jukes is continually writing letters; in fact, I think this is all he does. (See January 15, 1971, issue of *Science* for his most recent effort.) Lykken presumably sees this too. Next to Lykken's letter is another by Robert White Sevens of Rutgers in New Jersey. Isn't this the same person that worked or testified for the insecticide industry? You'll also note that he is in the Bureau of Conservation and Environmental Science. After reading his letter I couldn't believe his affiliation nor Lykken's either for that matter.

"I would like to know if these retired gentlemen have to go through the same hiring procedure as the rest of us. If not, why not? I would like to have something to say about this as one of the members of the staff, also, is Dr. Lykken on any committees? . . . I wonder which university will hire Louis McLean when he retires for Velsicol?

"The second item probably involves University Extension more than the Department but I want to air the matter with you first. I recently participated in a panel on pesticides at Modesto Junior College. The other members of the panel were Clark Ides, an attorney in Modesto, Roy Mansberry of Shell and M. E. 'Cane' Stevenson, a farm advisor in Stanislaus County. I was absolutely shocked by the farm advisor's behavior. Does this man represent the University or the chemical corporations? I found out later that he not only collaborated with Mansberry prior to the panel but that he and Mansberry do their defense of insecticides and ridicule of a biological and ecological approach to pest control regularly in the Central Valley. Isn't a farm advisor supposed to be the liaison between the researcher and the grower? Mr. Stevenson isn't pushing integrated control and this bothers me.

"I think that farm advisors should return to the University every three or four years for refresher courses. Also, shouldn't the farm advisor contact the University representative rather than the corporation representative? When Mr. Stevenson appeared on stage in the studio, he proceeded to place a series of chemicals in front of him. The brand names, incidentally, were clearly visible to the TV audience as I could see them on the monitor. He used the same old arguments supporting the use of chemical insecticides and he was certainly not aware of the new work on peaches which is one of his specialties. He was also misinformed on corporate farming in the Central Valley. Needless to say the experience was a disturbing one.

"I would like to talk with you sometime soon about these matters as I think they will have a great deal of influence on the development of the integrated control-pest management curriculum within our Department. I am fully aware that the National Agricultural Chemical Association is putting a large sum of money into their public relations program now. In fact, they must be spending more this year than they did right after the appearance of *Silent Spring* in 1962. I hope that those individuals with past industry ties who are working for the University will not become overly influenced by this increased activity. I am also concerned that increased efforts by the chemical corporations will overly influence certain individuals that are loyal to the insecticide companies than to the University or the growers."

NOTE: A zerox copy of this internal memorandum was obtained second-hand by the Agribusiness Accountability Project in January of 1972.

APPENDIX J
EXTENSION SERVICE

PURPOSE STATEMENT

Cooperative agricultural extension work was established by the *Smith-Lever Act* of May 8, 1914, as amended. The legislation authorizes the Department of Agriculture to give, through land grant colleges, instruction and practical demonstrations in agriculture and home economics and related subjects and to encourage the application of such information by means of demonstrations, publications, and otherwise to persons not attending or resident in the colleges. Extension educational work is also authorized under the *Agricultural Marketing Act* of 1946.

The basic job of the Cooperative Extension Service is to help people identify and solve their farm, home, and community problems through use of research findings of the Department of Agriculture and the state land grant colleges, and programs administered by the Department of Agriculture.

State and county extension work is financed from federal, state, county and local sources. These funds are used within the states for the employment of county agents, home economics agents, 4-H Club agents, state and area specialists and others who conduct the joint educational programs adapted to local problems and conditions.

The Extension Service, as a partner in the cooperative effort, has three major functions:

1. It serves as liaison between the Department of Agriculture and the states, provides program leadesrship and assistance to the states in the conduct of extension work.

2. It administers federal laws authorizing extension work and coordinates the work among the states.

3. It provides leadership in the coordination of the educational phases of all programs under the jurisdiction of the department.

This work is carried out through state and county Extension offices in each state, Puerto Rico, and the District of Columbia. This program is coordinated by an extension service staff located in Washington, D.C. In addition, the Extension Service has marketing specialists located at Clemson, South Carolina, Raleigh, North Carolina and Dallas, Texas, to provide special emphasis on cotton marketing and utilization and a grain marketing specialist in Peoria, Illinois.

SOURCE: U.S. House of Representatives, Committee on Appropriations. "Agriculture—Environmental and Consumer Protection Appropriations for 1972," *Hearings*, 92nd Congress, 1st session, part 2, p. 22.

APPENDIX K

DISTRIBUTION OF COOPERATIVE STATE RESEARCH SERVICE PAYMENTS AND NON-FEDERAL FUNDS FOR RESEARCH AT STATE AGRICULTURAL EXPERIMENT STATIONS AND OTHER STATE INSTITUTIONS
— Fiscal Year 1970 —

State	CSRS Funds	State and Private Funds	Total
Alabama	$ 1,741,388	$ 4,742,276	$ 6,485,664
Alaska	397,759	672,613	1,070,372
Arizona	784,555	3,840,284	4,624,839
Arkansas	1,365,763	3,879,136	5,244,899
California	1,924,934	25,295,872	27,220,806
Colorado	903,177	2,645,681	3,548,858
Connecticut	663,458	˙ 2,802,190	3,465,648
Delaware	496,086	814,191	1,310,277
Florida	963,421	12,466,308	13,429,729
Georgia	1,734,896	7,250,611	8,985,507
Hawaii	512,916	3,197,279	3,710,195
Idaho	735,022	2,738,036	3,473,058
Illinois	1,748,390	8,098,072	9,846,462
Indiana	1,568,281	5,080,916	6,649,197
Iowa	1,645,416	6,073,205	7,718,621
Kansas	1,062,095	5,824,235	6,886,330
Kentucky	1,624,169	4,251,644	5,879,813
Louisiana	1,232,704	6,310,886	7,543,590
Maine	736,189	1,192,390	1,928,579
Maryland	913,121	2,406,390	3,319,511
Massachusetts	795,618	1,446,804	2,242,422
Michigan	1,563,649	5,653,298	7,216,947
Minnesota	1,517,429	8,166,628	9,684,057
Mississippi	1,736,588	4,309,115	6,045,703
Missouri	1,603,306	6,059,461	7,662,767
Montana	768,270	3,013,327	3,781,597
Nebraska	1,008,517	7,722,523	8,731,040
Nevada	453,780	1,048,757	1,502,537
New Hampshire	557,097	471,934	1,029,031
New Jersey	839,919	5,206,691	6,046,610
New Mexico	714,027	1,333,165	2,047,192
New York	1,911,618	14,098,468	16,010,086
North Carolina	2,257,639	7,775,680	10,033,319
North Dakota	772,076	3,024,759	3,796,835
Ohio	1,767,011	5,424,293	7,191,304
Oklahoma	1,168,740	3,699,020	4,867,760

State	CSRS Funds	State and Private Funds	Total
Oregon	$ 1,080,037	$ 6,520,193	$ 7,600,230
Pennsylvania	1,970,710	4,455,471	6,426,181
Puerto Rico	1,535,208	3,873,209	5,408,417
Rhode Island	473,344	590,198	1,063,542
South Carolina	1,333,656	3,040,676	4,374,332
South Dakota	792,556	2,649,700	3,442,256
Tennessee	1,684,056	3,181,602	4,865,658
Texas	2,390,013	8,631,198	11,021,211
Utah	662,743	1,440,222	2,102,965
Vermont	551,426	648,400	1,199,826
Virginia	1,513,094	5,480,395	6,987,489
Washington	1,198,583	7,059,175	8,257,758
West Virginia	1,040,964	1,030,292	2,071,256
Wisconsin	1,505,188	8,211,957	9,717,145
Wyoming	565,220	1,313,175	1,878,395
Subtotal	$60,485,822*	$246,162,001	$306,647,823

*This is not total federal research funds to SAES. Excluded are research contracts made with SAES by other USDA offices and by other federal agencies. These funds would add approximately $35 million to the federal total.

SOURCE: U.S. House of Representatives Committee on Appropriations "Agriculture-Environmental and Consumer Protection Appropriations for 1972, *Hearings*, 92nd Congress, 1st session. part 2, pp. 520-521.

APPENDIX L

SOURCES OF FUNDS FOR COOPERATIVE EXTENSION WORK IN THE STATES AND PUERTO RICO FOR FISCAL YEAR ENDING JUNE 30, 1970

States	Total	Federal	State	County	Non-Tax
Alabama	$ 7,989,368	$ 3,702,786	$ 3,021,643	$ 1,154,389	$ 110,550
Alaska	721,801	330,515	382,286	—	—
Arizona	2,115,250	850,594	1,175,506	89,150	—
Arkansas	6,109,378	2,821,584	2,591,909	552,942	142,943
California	13,988,836	3,749,136	7,649,700	2,345,900	244,100
Colorado	3,632,100	1,202,125	1,580,203	790,000	59,772
Connecticut	1,939,858	735,082	1,204,776	—	—
Delaware	736,442	405,070	304,326	11,800	15,246
Florida	7,805,840	2,077,254	3,607,721	2,039,050	81,815
Georgia	10,951,447	3,940,450	4,759,700	1,546,080	705,217
Hawaii	1,783,214	538,145	1,245,069	—	—
Idaho	2,390,480	867,506	947,974	575,000	—
Illinois	9,211,561	3,673,058	4,334,135	547,746	656,622
Indiana	7,273,276	2,859,781	2,316,779	2,069,056	27,651
Iowa	7,830,175	2,856,256	3,000,000	1,850,000	123,919
Kansas	7,794,829	1,947,906	2,202,246	3,231,971	412,710
Kentucky	7,479,845	3,728,067	2,763,197	988,581	—
Louisiana	7,282,211	2,742,043	4,225,110	309,133	5,925
Maine	1,913,282	828,932	824,794	259,556	—
Maryland	4,337,420	1,319,452	2,559,913	458,055	—
Massachusetts	3,192,815	1,216,847	730,000	1,245,968	—
Michigan	9,519,542	3,388,754	4,049,231	1,536,788	544,769
Minnesota	6,719,691	2,769,345	2,544,259	1,376,762	29,325
Mississippi	7,005,370	3,754,336	2,266,397	967,487	17,150
Missouri	9,482,910	3,337,459	4,074,690	1,319,483	751,278
Montana	2,213,725	860,342	728,700	618,683	6,000
Nebraska	5,052,946	1,635,358	2,330,516	1,074,797	12,275
Nevada	1,215,722	386,622	587,074	242,026	—
New Hampshire	1,168,011	479,444	429,411	259,156	—
New Jersey	4,442,196	1,221,129	2,099,324	1,121,743	—
New Mexico	2,426,209	908,672	1,120,210	397,327	—
New York	14,278,630	4,012,931	3,959,784	5,824,274	481,641
North Carolina	14,243,964	5,274,497	5,776,346	3,193,121	—
North Dakota	2,690,708	1,165,349	767,137	680,222	78,000
Ohio	8,847,319	4,035,965	2,515,000	1,811,675	484,679
Oklahoma	$ 5,911,122	$ 2,403,140	$ 2,247,982	$ 1,100,000	$ 160,000
Oregon	5,223,627	1,221,014	3,136,164	866,448	—
Pennsylvania	7,381,783	4,285,998	2,203,285	885,000	7,500
Puerto Rico	5,344,582	3,216,123	2,045,600	—	82,859
Rhode Island	715,791	374,909	296,307	40,650	3,925
South Carolina	5,209,237	2,847,443	2,171,594	189,000	1,200
South Dakota	2,853,427	1,168,864	1,328,385	356,178	—
Tennessee	7,471,190	3,872,840	2,718,350	880,000	—
Texas	14,666,493	6,429,732	4,947,176	3,167,676	121,909
Utah	1,724,740	683,180	800,000	241,560	—
Vermont	1,537,186	567,233	817,953	152,000	—
Virginia	9,365,601	3,286,315	4,855,485	1,223,801	—
Washington	4,617,240	1,431,298	2,145,369	1,040,573	—

States	Total	Federal	State	County	Non-Tax
West Virginia	3,334,574	1,921,884	912,690	500,000	—
Wisconsin	8,043,800	2,746,993	3,200,549	2,096,258	—
Wyoming	1,442,884	551,883	613,500	257,501	—
Unallotted	37,319	37,319	—	—	—
AMA Contracts	50,000	50,000	—	—	—
Grand Total	290,687,967	112,718,960	119,115,452	53,484,575	5,368,980
District of Columbia	360,000	360,000			

SOURCE: F.E.S. "Sources of Funds for Cooperative Extension Work in the State and Puerto Rico for Fiscal Year Ending June 30, 1970.

APPENDIX M

SUPPLEMENTARY MORRILL APPROPRIATIONS AND ENDOWMENT INCOME FROM 1862 FUND BY STATE FOR FY 1970

State and Institution		Appropriation	Endowment
	Total All Land Grant	$14,720,000	$11,515,478
AL:	Alabama A&M U	94,572	0
	Auburn U	183,108	20,280
AK:	U of Alaska	205,378	0
AZ:	U of Arizona	230,964	47,308
AR:	Arkansas AM&N Col	66,130	0
	U of Arkansas	176,346	6,633
CA:	U of California	573,740	59,986
CO:	Colorado St U	241,707	43,238
CT:	U of Connecticut	260,285	9,069
DE:	Delaware St Col	42,122	0
	U of Delaware	168,490	2,505
DC:	Federal City Col	218,166	7,214,000
FL:	Florida A&M U	103,310	0
	U of Florida	214,433	0
GA:	Ft Valley St Col	83,519	0
	U of Georgia	210,244	9,364
HI:	U of Hawaii	215,047	236,028
ID:	U of Idaho	215,865	144,101
IL:	U of Illinois	439,721	32,451
IN:	Purdue U	310,870	16,041
IA:	Iowa St U	265,572	31,838
KS:	Kansas St U	251,805	33,001
KY:	Kentucky St Col	39,476	0
	U of Kentucky	232,768	8,645
LA:	Louisiana St U	188,943	9,115
	Southern U & A&M Col	88,506	0
ME:	U of Maine	223,048	5,915
MD:	U of Maryland	240,887	3,696
	U of MD, Princess Anne	32,844	0
MA:	MA Inst of Tech	16,667	3,650
	U of Massachusetts	305,761	7,300
MI:	Michigan St U	386,028	0
MN:	U of Minnesota	281,178	1,949,640
MS:	Alcorn A&M Col	124,280	12,592
	Mississippi St U	127,514	5,914
MO:	Lincoln U	18,920	0
	U of Missouri	283,801	29,694
MT:	Montana St U	216,045	97,136
NB:	U of Nebraska	233,560	36,735

State and Institution		Appropriation	Endowment
NV:	U of Nevada	$ 206,784	$ 7,994
NH:	U of New Hampshire	214,432	4,800
NJ:	Rutgers, the St U	344,262	5,800
NM:	New Mexico St U	222,614	227,735
NY:	Cornell U	599,067	34,429
NC:	North Carolina A&T St U	101,752	0
	North Carolina St U	206,589	0
ND:	North Dakota St U	215,039	147,672
OH:	Ohio St U	430,809	31,451
OK:	Langston U	25,536	0
	Oklahoma St U	229,828	0
OR:	Oregon St U	242,058	14,389
PA:	Pennsylvania St U	469,164	25,000
PR:	U of Puerto Rico	255,870	0
RI:	U of Rhode Island	220,438	4,059
SC:	Clemson U	128,328	5,754
	South Carolina St Col	128,328	5,754
SD:	South Dakota St U	216,182	202,489
TN:	Tennessee St U	51,524	0
	U of Tennessee	233,298	14,998
TX:	Prairie View S&M Col	106,948	0
	Texas A&M U, Col Sta	320,847	8,950
UT:	Utah St U	221,178	42,502
VT:	U of Vermont	209,271	7,320
VA:	Virginia Poly Inst	196,221	19,919
	Virginia St Col	98,109	7,030
WA:	Washington St U	267,847	517,222
WV:	West Virginia	244,239	5,029
WI:	U of Wisconsin System	293,969	10,925
WY:	U of Wyoming	207,849	88,382

SOURCE: H.E.W., Office of Education, Bureau of Higher Education, Division of College Support. "Statistics of Condition of Land-Grant Funds—1970 Report," August 31, 1971, tables 1 and 6.

Glossary and Abbreviations

Agribusiness. A corporate aggregation that includes: (1) agricultural in-put firms, (2) agricultural out-put firms, (3) corporations directly involved in farming and (4) corporations indirectly involved in farming.

Agricultural Efficiency. The concept of minimizing agricultural production costs by substituting capital, machinery, chemicals and other technological and financial in-puts for the more traditional farming in-puts.

Agricultural In-put Industry. An aggregation of firms that supply seed, feed, farm machinery, fertilizer, chemicals, credit, insurance and other factors of agricultural production.

Agricultural Out-put Industry. An aggregation of corporate middlemen between the farmer and the consumer, including those firms that pack, process, can, package, distribute, market, advertise, retail and otherwise handle food and fiber after it leaves the farm.

Agricultural Research Service (ARS). USDA's in-house research agency, conducting agricultural research at the federal level, based on USDA's perception of national and regional research needs.

Contracts, Grants and Cooperative Agreements (CGCA).

Cooperative Extension Service (CES). This is the usual designation of any state extension service.

Cooperative State Research Service (CSRS). The USDA agency that administers federal research money allocated to state agricultural experiment stations by statutory formula. In addition, CSRS administers a relatively small amount of non-formula funds, expending them through research contracts made with the stations.

Current Research Information System (CRIS). A USDA data bank containing computerized information on research projects conducted at state agricultural experiment stations.

Extension Service (ES). The national network of extension agents and administrators.

Family Farm. A farm that is controlled and worked by the family that lives on the farm. Financial risk, managerial decisions and work on the farm are direct responsibilities of the family, which exercises full, entrepreneural authority.

Federal Extension Service (FES). This is the USDA agency that administers national funds for extension work.

Fiscal Year (FY).

Hatch Act (HATH). See Appendix A, "Research".

Land Grant College Community. Includes people directly involved in the land grant college complex at the campus level, in government and in agribusiness. This is a community of shared interests, involving teachers, researchers, administrators, students, governmental officials relating to the complex and agribusiness organizations with a proprietary interest in the work of the complex.

Land Grant College Complex. The agricultural component of the land grant university system. The complex includes colleges of agriculture, agricultural experiment stations and extension services. Engaged in teaching, research and dissemination of knowledge in all 50 states, the complex accounts for an annual, public expenditure approaching $750 million.

Land Grant College System. The higher educational system created under the Morrill land grant act. It includes 69 land grant universities, ranging from M.I.T. to the University of California and teaching everything from nuclear physics to Chaucer. Included in this extensive, educational system is the land grant college complex, which is focused on agriculture.

McIntyre-Stennis (MCIN). This bill, passed October 10, 1962, provided for the funding of forestry research through the land grant colleges and experiment stations.

National Association of State Universities and Land Grant Colleges (NA-SULGC). A Washington-based organization representing 118 public institutions of higher education, including all 69 land grant colleges. NASULGC's Division of Agriculture represents agricultural college deans, heads of agricultural experiment stations and deans of extension. The division is operated by and for the land grant complex. The NASULGC division is a powerful spokesman for the complex and is directly involved in development of agricultural research priorities for the country.

People-Oriented Research. A USDA term referring to research focused directly on people, rather than on production, marketing, efficiency or some other aspect of agriculture. The term includes 12 research problem areas: food consumption habits, food preparation, human nutrition, clothing and textile care, family financial management, rural poverty, economic potential of rural people, communications among rural people, adjustment to change, rural income improvement, rural institutional improvement and rural housing.

Regional Research Fund (RRF).

Research Problem Areas (RPA). A series of USDA classifications for agricultural research projects. Allocations of money and scientific man years are categorized under these RPAs.

State Agricultural Experiment Stations (SAES). The agricultural research component of each land grant college.

Scientific Man Years (SMY).   A measurement of scientific, technical and other time expended on research projects. The measurement is based on a standardized formula, and allocations of SMY are reported through CRIS.

Special Grant (SPGT).

United States Department of Agriculture (USDA).   The department with primary federal responsibility for oversight of the land grant college complex.

Vertical Integration.   The movement of agricultural in-put and out-put firms into the production stage of food and fiber. The movement can be direct, as when processing plant buys or leases land to produce commodities for its processing operation. It can be indirect as when an agribusiness firm contracts with a farmer to produce a certain quantity and quality of a certain commodity at a certain time and for a certain price. In both cases, a degree of control over food and fiber production passes from farmers to agribusiness corporations.

FARMWORKERS IN RURAL AMERICA, 1971–1972

(The Role of Land-Grant Colleges)

MONDAY, JUNE 19, 1972

U.S. SENATE,
SUBCOMMITTEE ON MIGRATORY LABOR OF THE
COMMITTEE ON LABOR AND PUBLIC WELFARE,
Washington, D.C.

The subcommittee met pursuant to notice at 9:30 a.m. in room 1202, New Senate Office Building, Senator Adlai E. Stevenson III (chairman of the subcommittee) presiding.

Present: Senator Stevenson.

Staff members present: Boren Chertkov, subcommittee counsel; Basil Condos, professional staff member; and Eugene Mittelman, minority counsel.

Senator STEVENSON. The meeting of the subcommittee will come to order.

STATEMENT BY ADLAI E. STEVENSON III, A U.S. SENATOR FROM THE STATE OF ILLINOIS

For the past year, the Subcommittee on Migratory Labor has been conducting hearings into the continuing problem of poverty and deprivation among the Nation's farmworkers. In the course of our hearings, some striking facts have emerged:

We have learned that rural poverty, though it is largely invisible to the Nation's press and to the urban public, exists and persists. It is, in many areas, as deep and pervasive as it was 5, 10, or 20 years ago. The continuing flight of rural people to the cities, at a rate of 1 million a year, is only one dramatic sympton of shriveling opportunity in rural America—and it is one cause of crowding and crisis in urban America.

Through much of our history as a nation, rural poverty has been a melancholy recurring theme. Hunger among those who provide our food; poverty among those who create our abundance; dilapidated houses, rundown schools, dying towns—these depressing images of rural blight are not only pictures from the American past, they are contemporary scenes. And behind these images of decay are personal and human tragedies: families with little hope for success and independence; children with little future if they live their lives in rural America.

We have learned that, though rural poverty is nothing new, some of its causes are new.

While we in urban America have looked the other way, the face of rural America has been changed in the past few years—suddenly, violently, and with drastic consequences.

(2137)

In a few brief years, giant corporations have moved in on American agriculture. The aims of these giants are simple enough: to own or control the production, processing, and distribution of the Nation's food. Their slogans are appealing enough: "Progress," "Efficiency," "Economies of Scale."

But the human consequences of such progress and efficiency are often staggering: profit for the conglomerate farmers—but losses for farmworkers and farm families: losses not only of a livelihood, but of a way of life; the virtual death not only of the family farm as an enterprise in America, but of a whole fabric of institutions which once gave vitality to our Nation's rural communities.

And in the wake of all this devastating change, little has been created to replace what has been lost.

We have learned that the U.S. Department of Agriculture, though it invests some $6 billion in agriculture each year, has no clear and consistent policy for revitalizing rural America; no clear policy for reclaiming the lives that have been disrupted by the corporate advance into rural America; no policy for creating alternatives in the countryside which might help stem the crisis in the cities. Indeed, it is hard to distinguish the attitude of the Department of Agriculture from the attitude of the agribusiness giants; an attitude summed up in the heartless slogan, "Adapt or Die."

The farm policy—or nonpolicy—which now prevails in America, wittingly or unwittingly, is subsidizing the death of rural America as a place of opportunity for the farmworker and the enterprising small farmer and his family. A crazy quilt of unfair tax loopholes, crop subsidies, and cheap labor policies; our exclusion of farmworkers from the social programs and labor-protection laws which other citizens enjoy; our giveaway of federally funded irrigation waters—all these, it seems, work for the benefit of the giants. And they work against the rights and legitimate interests of farmworkers, family farmers, smalltown citizens, and by no means least, the American consumer.

The result is, in my judgment, both scandal and tragedy. And both the tragedy and scandal seem all the greater when we reflect that they need never have happened; they were not inevitable; they have occurred by default, if not by deliberate design. Why? Because all the while that rural America has been deteriorating we have had at our hands the resources to prevent this decline. What we have lacked has been a policy centered upon human beings and their well-being—and any strong will to implement such a policy. Even now we have the means to revitalize rural America: to make it a fit and promising place for families to live. But often it seems as if we prefer to watch as the rural landscape is reshaped in to a vast soulless, assembly line, and rural citizens are forced to become little more than cogs in the giant machine.

Our hearings today and tomorrow bring us to the Nation's land-grant colleges and their role in the life of rural America. The question before us is whether this vast system of education, research, and extension is working for or against the cause—livable communities in rural America. In short, our question is whether our land-grant colleges, with their great resources of manpower an dtalent; with their budgets totaling nearly three quarters of a billion dollars a year; with their far-flung network of research stations and educational services; with their almost unlimited potential for impact on our rural life—are part of the solution, or part of the problem.

In these 2 days, we will be asking some candid questions about the land-grant college system:

1. Who are the real beneficiaries of land-grant college efforts? Can we be satisfied that all those intended to be served are in fact served?

2. Have the land-grant colleges conspired, wittingly or unwittingly, in the displacement and impoverishment of farmworkers? Have they shown a sense of responsibility for solving the problems caused by mechanized and large-scale corporate farming?

3. Have the land-grant colleges lived up to their historic mission in rural America—to serve all the people of the Nation?

4. Should the land-grant colleges disclose publicly more details of their research projects, administrative operations, fiscal policies, industry contributions, and progress made toward their defined goals? What mechanisms are needed, if any, to make the land-grant college system more accountable and responsible to the public?

5. In view of the fact that less than 1 percent of all land-grant college money goes to the 17 land-grant colleges which are predominately black, what steps must be taken to eliminate racial discrimination where it exists in the system?

To some, notably the authors of the recent report on the system entitled "Hard Tomatoes, Hard Times," the answers to these questions constitute a sweeping indictment of the land-grant college system.

We will be hearing testimony on both sides of that issue. Throughout, our aim will be to be both positive and constructive: to learn whether changes are needed in our land-grant college system—and if so, whether they can be inspired by the Congress.

But certainly no apology is needed for holding the land-grant college system up to the light of congressional scrutiny. If we failed to assess the achievements and directions of a system so large, so expensive, and so important, we would be guilty of public neglect.

Statement by James A. McHale
Secretary of Agriculture, Commonwealth of Pennsylvania

Mr. Chairman, my name is James A. McHale, Secretary of Agriculture of the Commonwealth of Pennsylvania. I want to thank you for this opportunity to testify before your subcommittee on the value of agricultural research being done by the land grant colleges.

"The Hightower report, HARD TOMATOES, HARD TIMES, may be the catylyst that brings about something I have been calling for over many years: change in the agriculture establishment of our Nation." That establishment has been so long entrenched in power aided, knowingly or otherwise, by land grant colleges that it has now become petrified.

The biggest part of the problem as I see it is the tie-in between agri-business, the land grant colleges, and a great majority of state secretaries or commissioners of agriculture. Gentlemen, that's a pretty exclusive club and one in which I for one seek no membership.

Too often State Agriculture Secretaries who come from the academic community look on research as a tool designed to do one thing: help agri-business. Too often they share a view held by a powerful group in agriculture: get big or get out. Too often these land grant lend-lease secretaries choose to ignore the family farmer's needs and hopes. And much too often, blinding themselves to the obvious, they say that rural development and agriculture have separate futures when the fact is that the two are so inter-twined as to be inseparable. Let me read you a statement about rural development.

"Our cities have become too large and too congested, greatly increasing the cost of living and of doing business.

"The countryside is being depopulated; in some areas the population has fallen below the level at which needed public services can economically be provided.

Overcrowding in the great cities leads to lawlessness and disorder.

Considerations of equity argue for services to rural people that are comparable with those provided to people in the cities.

It is in the interest of national defense that the new increments of industry be located away from present manufacturing centers.

Excessive concentration of people in limited areas places great stress on the environment.

There are desirable non-economic qualities in rural living that would be lost if we were to continue the trend toward urbanization...

*   *   *

..."Rural development is a widening of the range of choice for rural people. So long as most of the increments of opportunity were built in the urban areas and farm jobs were diminishing, rural people had a very limited range of choice. If the various doors of opportunity are opened wider, the people themselves will select the door of their choice, and will choose wisely. The task of rural development is to help the people achieve the goals to which they themselves aspire.

We have in fact had, in the past, an implicit policy that drove rural people to the cities. What is now proposed is an explicit policy that gives them a choice.

"I do not believe that rural development is synonymous with economic development. The developmental process is not just economic, it is also social, political, and aesthetic. It is regrettable that the various social disciplines have contributed so unevenly to the understanding of this problem..."

*   *   *

That statement came from the United States Department of Agriculture's Director of Agriculture Economics, Don Paarlberg. Tomorrow you will hear from Secretary Earl Butz and I would hope that Dr. Butz would bear out Paarlberg's view.

Secretary Butz, a board member for Ralston-Purina and Stokely Van Camp, a speechmaker for General Motors and a faculty executive at Purdue has not often seen eye-to-eye with me on farm or rural development problems.

I have been pilloried in my state by entrenched interests for using minimal sums of money to build huge sums for a health care project in a rural area. My criteria for land grant college research will be detailed later but simply put, it comes to this. Let the land grant colleges answer the question, "Research for whom, research for what?"

The rural sector must recognize that when development monies become available the urban planners are right there with reasons why the monies should go to the cities. It is absolutely essential in my view that a substantial part of these monies must go for rural development to get at the root cause of the disease plaguing the inner core of our great urban areas. The sickness of the cities began years ago because this Nation saw fit to ignore the clear symptoms in the rural areas...the great outmigration that funneled millions of rural residents into a way of life they had no tools to cope with. The frustrations and fears of these people in a world they never made led to the freezing-in of the ghetto...eventually to Watts, to Newark, to anywhere the smoldering resentment of the displaced shot into flame.

Agricultural research has done nothing to stem the enormous outmigration in the past ten years in Pennsylvania of some 360,000 people from rural areas, who now glut our cities with an unskilled labor force that must depend on welfare. Research has done nothing to halt the disappearance of the small farmer. The number of farmers in Pennsylvania stands at about 63,000. There were twice as many 20 years ago.

My experience as a farmer and more recently as a member of Governor Milton Shapp's cabinet, leads me to conclude that research conducted at Pennsylvania State University — the land grant college in my state — has been of no benefit to family farmers and has done very little to help the plight of our rural communities.

I have no ties with Penn State, Mr. Chairman. I think I am one of the few or perhaps the only State Secretary of Agriculture who came to a cabinet post from the farm and not via the land grant college system route. That is why I am freer to criticize the evident partnership between academic research and big business interests. There is no job waiting for me at Penn State when my tenure with this administration ends. Nor, I am sure, will any large feed company draft me for a $100,000 job, playing the musical chairs game that goes on between USDA and private industry.

If I appear bitter about this situation, Mr. Chairman, please rest assured that I am. Rural America is being dried up by the unquenchable thirst of agribusiness, aided and abetted by the special interest research at land grant colleges.

The conclusion reached in "Hard Tomatoes, Hard Times," that the land grant college complex has hurt rather than helped rural people is fully applicalbe in Pennsylvania. We are also suffering from the social and economic upheaval occuring today in America's countryside.

When I began farming in 1946 in South Shenango Twp., Crawford County, there were 50 farmers. Now there are three.

I remember in the fall of 1959, when we dairy farmers were receiving $3.06 a hundredweight for milk, the extension agents had the nerve to come to Crawford County to hold educational seminars to improve our efficiency. They said we would have to become more efficient because milk prices would drop to $2.50 a hundredweight. I decided then that this system was killing us and would have to be fought.

Production efficiency research has driven us out of business because it plays right into the hands of the enormous inflationary rise of farm costs. Farmers were put on a treadmill and told that if they ran fast enough they could move ahead. Most of us have fallen off the treadmill and died of exhaustion.

It takes two and sometimes three or more times the bushels of grain to buy machinery and pay taxes today than 20 years ago. Here is a sample of what I mean:

ITEM		1952 BUSHELS	1971 BUSHELS
30-39 H P Tractor	Wheat	1,283	3,074
	Corn	1,659	3,291
12 self-propelled combine	Wheat	2,483	8,051
	Corn	3,210	8,622
½ ton pickup truck	Wheat	792	2,324
	Corn	1,024	2,488
4-door standard-size automobile	Wheat	943	2,882
	Corn	1,220	3,087
Real-estate taxes per 100-acres farm land	Wheat	36	195
	Corn	46	209
All machinery repairs per tractor on farm	Wheat	56	138
	Corn	72	148
Building repairs per farm	Wheat	68	191
	Corn	88	205
10-hour day of farm labor	Wheat	3	11
	Corn	4	12

Source: USDA

Economists have sought solutions by encouraging larger capitalization to support greater farm mechanization. This helped the large farmers and conglomerate agribusiness, but drove the small farmer off the land. With the rural countryside depopulating, it became impossible to sustain services for health, education, housing and transportation. Rural people sought these services in the cities and the vicious cycle of a degenerating money base in rural America continued.

As the Pennsylvania Secretary of Agriculture, I am empowered to determine how some $400,000 a year from state harness racing proceeds will be spent on agricultural research projects. This power derives from a state law passed in 1959 and amended in 1967.

The annual $400,000 appropriation is a drop in the bucket to do the job that is needed in Pennsylvania — to revitalize, recapitalize and repopulate

our rural communities. But when I joined Governor Shapp's cabinet in 1971, I
felt this could be a starting point at changing research priorities, at making
research people-oriented.

Most of the research money is spent on projects handled at Penn State's
College of Agriculture. The School of Veterinary Medicine of the University of
Pennsylvania also conducts projects financed by this allocation.

On reviewing various projects, I found that in the past five years
about $2.5 million had been spent without any appreciable benefit to the farmer's
economic condition.

I read about such projects as "Apple Harvesting Mechanization," a
three-year project begun in 1967 at Penn State at a cost of $78,500. The project
of this research, and I quote, was "to develop mechanical harvesting equipment and
harvest aids for tree fruits with special emphasis on apples"; and "to adapt and
develop trees for efficient mechanized harvesting of tree fruit." Gentlemen,
this could have been taken out of the "Hard Tomatoes, Hard Times" report.

Another project, the "Development of Mechanized Equipment for the Nursery
Industry, ran for three years at Penn State at a cost of $82,000. Researchers
found, and I quote, "Tools and machines developed on this project have shown promising potential. Based on present data, the machine and one operator can dig ten
times as many plants as one man can dig with a hand shovel in average soil conditions."
I can only ask, what is supposed to happen to the people displaced by this machinery?
What about research to keep these people employed? Apparently, nothing was being
done for them.

The selection of research projects funded by harness racing proceeds is recommended to me by an advisory committee, consisting of a cross section of farm interests, members of my department and the deans of both colleges mentioned. I gave them new guidelines for considering new research projects. They are to ask these questions of a project proposal in this order of importance: Does it benefit the family farmer? Make an economic contribution to Pennsylvania citizens: Revitalize rural Pennsylvania? Answer a current critical problem? Include cooperating funding sources? Indicate that scientific knowledge will be advanced? Fall within the realm of applied agricultural research, rural development, or market improvement and expansion?

We tried to do something about ongoing projects. For example, a 20-year project begun in 1967 at Penn State for a total cost of $402,000 involves the "Nutritional and Physiological Problems Encountered by Pennsylvania Mink Producers." Without going into details, I can tell you this project was churning out little more than incomplete progress reports while the number of mink producers declined in Pennsylvania. I conferred with some mink ranchers, banded them together into a special advisory committee and the ranchers informed me of their dissatisfaction with the results of Penn State's project. We advised the college to do some meaningful research on mink feed or else lose the project.

I believe the most significant thing we have done was to allocate $76,000 for a department-sponsored health demonstration project in Coudersport, Potter County. The pilot project provides 14 free health tests to rural residents in six northern tier counties. Results of these tests are sent to the patient's physicians for followup treatment. Many rural people have not seen doctors for years, and our project has uncovered a number of treatable diseases.

The health screening project has actually cost the Agriculture Department only $40,000, a sum which has served as seed for $500,000 in Federal funds. Other hospitals across the state have observed the clinic in the Cole Memorial Hospital at Coudersport and have expressed interest in starting such programs on their own.

My Department has also gotten together with the Pennsylvania Department of Community Affairs in launching what we hope will be a vast rural housing project. Each department put up $1,000. The Pennsylvania Rural Electric Association joined in with additional resources, enough to hire people to develop specifications to attract funds from HUD, FHA, and other Federal agencies. The package has grown to more than $100,000 and I hope will increase to $1 million. This money will permit us to form a rural housing cooperative, patterned after a successful one now operating in North Dakota, which will generate housing in rural Pennsylvania.

These are small, but we feel important steps in coping with the immense problems of providing an adequate rural health delivery system and housing. This is where I think agricultural research should be in 1972. Research must help the small farmer who in 1970 had to struggle with an average net income of $1,059. It must solve the pressing problems of rural transportation, rural housing, and rebuilding rural communities.

Let me add that for my efforts to change the direction of agricultural research, the special agri-business interests in my state rapped my knuckles by succeeding in having the legislature pass a bill stripping me of my powers to decide on how to spend the harness racing proceeds on research. That power would reside in a newly constituted committee that is heavily weighted with agri-business representatives. The bill was vetoed Thursday by the Governor.

I believe the Governor was motivated in my behalf by the "Hard Tomatoes, Hard Times" report and by an independent study he initiated early in his administration. Called, the "Governor's Review of Government Management," the study found that research at Penn State and the University of Pennsylvania had little to do with rural development and market expansion — priorities which the present agricultural advisory committee demanded as a basis for allocating harness racing proceeds.

The study found, and I quote, "that research projects submitted by these institutions for Fair Funds (derived from harness racing proceeds) are not necessarily their top priority projects. It would seem that Fair Funds are requested for these projects only when all other sources for funding have been exhausted.

The study cites no effort to eliminate research duplication, poor monitoring of contract progress, vague annual progress reports and sloppy cost-accounting techniques. A transcript of the review by Fidelco Associates Inc. is attached."

We are attempting to correct this situation by setting up advisory committees, such as the one of mink ranches I mentioned previously to make research accountable to the producers, the farmers themselves.

We have also revised our project proposal form to include such information as, sources of additional funds, biographies of researchers, and other agencies which may be cooperating.

We are also reforming patent regulations, an area of abuse cited in "Hard Tomatoes, Hard Times." Undre our old contracts, patents remained the property of the researching institution. They could benefit from royalties as they wished. I now plan to have any contracts signed by me provide that patent rights be granted to the State. In this way the taxpayer can benefit from the use of his money for research.

Mr. Chairman, on a national level I would recommend this general course of action:

1. Increase funding based upon total rural population rather than the importance of production of food and fiber. Specifically, in Pennsylvania we have 3,500,000 rural citizens requiring human services; our Agriculture appropriations must consider the total rural community and not just the top 10% of the farm community.

2. Create new job opportunities – such as Public Service Employment.

3. Increase the availability of equitable financing – professional and techincal assistance for the rural community.

4. Redistribute population by making our rural areas more attractive. This can be done by equalization of education

   opportunities, health care systems, transportation opportunities, improved utility systems, and general human services, all of which should be a prime concern of agriculture research.

5. De-emphasize the Land Grant College self-policing concept and involve the people for whom the research is intended.

Thank you, Mr. Chairman, for allowing me to present this statement.

The Honorable Adlai E. Stevenson, III, Chairman
Senate Subcommittee on Migratory Labor
United States Senate
June 19, 1972

Mr. Chairman and Members of the Committee:

I am Richard David Morrison, President of Alabama A&M University, one of
the 16 land-grant institutions which came into being as a result of the Second Morrill
Act, 1890. These institutions were supposed to serve as counterparts to the 1862 land-
grant institutions in states that insisted on a separation of races when it came to black
Americans.

Up to the present time, most of my life experiences have been in the south-
eastern states of the United States. I was born on a farm in Mississippi, and grew up
there until finishing high school. My undergraduate work was completed at Tuskegee
Institute in Alabama. My Master's degree was earned at Cornell University, Ithaca,
New York, and the Ph.D degree was earned at Michigan State University. Both universities,
I noticed, are known by the researchers of Hard Tomatoes, Hard Times.

My work experiences for 38 years have been in education — as a high school
teacher of vocational agriculture, as a director of agriculture at the college level, and
as president of a land-grant college.

The previous statements were intended to be brief documentation of some
credentials that may place my subsequent statements in a better position to claim your
favorable attention.

I wish to express my thanks to Senator Adlai Stevenson and his committee for
inviting me to testify before this committee. These words go deeper than a mere courtesy
statement. They are imbedded in an appreciation for having the opportunity as a black
man to speak at a Senate hearing on a matter of importance to people, and especially to
black people. Too often there is always someone else who thinks he is better qualified
to speak for us; therefore, we are not invited to speak on our own behalf.

Most recently, a report, Hard Tomatoes, Hard Times, seemingly has documented some facts which tend to question the wisdom of certain programs and the
expenditure of funds for these programs, especially as they pertain to the land-grant
college system. The implications are that the 1862 land-grant institutions have strayed
too far from the major intent of the land-grant system in the first place. These
accusations may prove to be advantageous to all who are concerned. Maybe it is time
for interested people to take a good hard look at how the land-grant system is meeting
its objectives.

More important is that some action should be taken to correct the agreed upon discrepancies and weaknesses when they are identified. Too often when such reports as Hard Tomatoes, Hard Times are fortunate enough to claim public attention, nothing is accomplished after the initial period of excitement is over.

At this point, I should like to discuss briefly one of my main concerns of interest in the whole package of the land-grant system — the 1890 black land-grant institutions. These institutions, in the 82 years of their existence, have never been accepted by the land-grant family as bona fide members. Even in Hard Tomatoes, Hard Times, the implications of a perpetual dichotomy is there when thoughts are in terms of 1862 and 1890 land-grant institutions. My question is why must there be this dichotomy in the minds of people about these institutions? Why can't the 1890 colleges just be good land-grant colleges in the system, respected and supported for their worth to society?

One of the focal points in the report hinges around the neglect of low-income groups, especially farm people, by the 1862 colleges. This is not true with the 1890 institutions. For 82 years, these institutions have devoted part of their meager general operation funds toward programs for poor people. Not until 1972 did these institutions receive any USDA funds for extension or research work. Moreover, the records will show that very little Morrill funds for instructional purposes were allocated to these institutions. (See Attachment A).

It is common knowledge that the 1890 colleges serve a clientele with an average income of less than $5,000 per year. The 50,000 plus students that the 1890 colleges enroll are, for the most part, from low-income families. If this is true, why then has it been so difficult for these colleges to share in funds that are purported to be available for programs designed to help people?

Hard Tomatoes, Hard Times has brought out into the open the kind of detailed information that can be helpful in appraising what is taking place in the land-grant system, as well as USDA. Regardless of how the tomatoes may be squeezed, there is a lot of meat in the report to be digested.

The statements in the book about the lack of support through the years for the 1890 land-grant institutions by USDA, through programs such as the Extension Service, CSRS, and other funded programs, are to the point. If there is a shortcoming in the section of the report on black land-grant colleges, it is that not much attention was given to efforts on the part of these colleges to participate in programs designed for low-income groups. These institutions have demonstrated their capability to work with such groups time and time again. A typical example of what I am talking about can be found in the language of the recent rural development program. The 1890 institutions were not included in this proposed bill — only the 1862 colleges. Past experience has taught us that 1862 colleges are not interested in sharing any funds with 1890 colleges. Putting it

another way, the law of gravity seems to work in the opposite direction when money
is in the hands of USDA and/or 1862 institutions. This is to say that funds gravitate
upward to those who are "well off," rather than downward to those who are "poor," be
this as it may, a person or an institution.

Some credit must be given to USDA for causing a slight modification in funding
patterns when, through some efforts on the part of the Department, plans were set in
motion for securing funds for extension and research work at the 1890 colleges. The
major efforts for these funds, 12.6 million dollars, took place in the Appropriations
Subcommittee on Agriculture–Environmental and Consumer Protection. A review of this
action may be found in Congressional Record Number 97, Page H5752, dated June 23, 1971.

It was implicit in the report, Hard Tomatoes, Hard Times, that the 1890 land–
grant colleges had always received next to nothing by way of sharing in Federal funds
appropriated for the land–grant system whether through USDA or otherwise. It was also
implicit that these colleges should be properly funded, else why mention the discrepancies in funding?

For too long, the 1890 land–grant colleges have been forced to deal with "Rotten
Tomatoes and Hard Times." Now that there seems to be come help on the way, certain
problems are coming up on the horizon. They are even being called segregated colleges,
although percentage–wise, they are more integrated than the 1862 colleges. They are
being called inferior, although they are educating more low–income black citizens than
all the major 1862 colleges combined. It is being said that there is no need for the
1890 institutions any longer since black students can attend the 1862 colleges. Maybe
it has never occurred to some people that all black students may not have a desire to
attend the 1862 institutions. Moreover, black students and black people, in general,
have black pride which makes it necessary for them to want a home base (an educational
institution of higher learning) from which to operate as their intellectual center.

These institutions also face the problem of those who would take them over
because they have grown to the extent that they are able to secure sizable grants that
make possible responsible jobs and attractive salaries. These institutions face the
problem of survival because there are those who would close them because it might mean
that more money would be available for their educational purposes if these institutions
did not exist.

Without a shadow of a doubt, the 1890 land–grant institutions, at present, know
better than any other group how to work with and get results from working with low–
income people. In the future, they should be given the opportunity to demonstrate this
ability under proper funding. This statement does not mean that these colleges do not
have other outstanding capabilities. They are capable of high quality achievements,
but like other good colleges, they must have funds capable of supporting high quality
work.

For a long time to come, these institutions will be needed to help overcome the cultural gap that exists in the United States. To some extent, this cultural gap can be attributed to the lack of educational opportunity for people with low incomes.

In order for the 1890 land-grant colleges to fulfill their educational commitment to their clientele, they need a substantial share of "hard money" — funds from existing acts that have been passed. If this is impossible because of the language of the acts, then the language should be changed or new legislation should be enacted. For example, I should like to see each 1890 college receive $500,000 (hard money) from the Morrill Act for instructional purposes rather than the small amount now allocated.

The 1890 institutions have never shared in the endowment money made available for 1862 colleges. I understand that the recently created land-grant colleges received $5,000,000 each for endowment purposes. Why cannot each of the 1890 colleges, after all these years of service, receive a $5,000,000 endowment?

A more substantial way of funding 1890 colleges for doing extension work and research should be found. The present funding level should be expanded from 12.6 million dollars in 1972 to 20.6 million dollars in 1973. Moreover, these institutions need money for educational facilities which they have never had. The 1862 institutions have used up all the facility funds and are now making preparation to ask for a new allocation.

The 1890 land-grant colleges can work effectively with low-income people. They have demonstrated their interest, capability, and achievements, through the years, in spite of the lack of adequate funds.

My final statement come by way of a request. For those of the committee who are vitally interested in the 1890 land-grant colleges, please read Pages   -   of the report, Hard Tomatoes, Hard Times, with a great deal of thought. (See Attachment A). Maybe the caption on Page   should read: "Colleges of 1890: The Deep, Dark <u>Truth</u>" instead of ". . The Deep, Dark Secret."

RECOMMENDATIONS

From time to time, the Presidents of the 1890 Land-Grant Colleges discuss the problems that face them. More recently, their thoughts have turned toward making suggestions that seem most appropriate if these institutions are to survive and make the kind of contribution to society that they are capable of making in the future.

To this end then, in order for the 1890 colleges to more adequately fulfill their commitment to the people they serve, it is recommended that the Federal Government:

1) Establish experiment stations on the campus of each 1890 college and give these colleges the freedom, encouragement, assistance and support to attack all areas which will result in improved life styles for people and communities.

2) Reestablish the Cooperative Extension Service as a meaningful part of each 1890 college.

Extension service was a vital part of all 1890 colleges. Under the guise of desegregation this important service was ripped out of the 1890 colleges and the type of services needed by the people is now missing in the areas where large numbers of blacks and browns reside. Active extension programs must be restored to 1890 colleges and they must be fully supported. The programs will not represent duplication.

The 1890 colleges, marching side by side with the 1862 colleges and other institutions, must be recognized as a legitimate part of the pluralism which is consistent with the American tradition. The question of duplication in America does not arise until its color is black or brown or its nature is poor. The 1890 colleges must be, once and forever, recognized as a pluralistic partner on the American higher education scene. Extension service must also be recognized as a pluralistic thrust from a most capable segment of the educational enterprise, namely the 1890 colleges.

The 1890 colleges can create innovative and meaningful approaches in a constructive extension service. It is imperative that this role be assigned to these colleges.

3) Establish data banks and retrieval systems at the 1890 colleges.

The 1890 colleges must be given financial support to establish contemporary data banks and information retrieval systems within each state and between each state, on all aspects of human needs and human technological factors. It is doubtful that there exists anywhere in the country the true facts on poverty-related consequences. It is doubtful that accurate data exist concerning the poor, unemployment, health, finance, jobs, etc. The 1890 colleges are capable of collecting and refining available data which will reveal a true picture. As a consequence, new solutions will be possible.

4) Reaffirm, recognize, establish, and support a moral commitment to the 1890 colleges as one of the principal educational agencies in each state as an aid to resolving people problems.

The problems facing our nation are so complex that they challenge the imagination and resources of all agencies interested in solutions. Rightly, the 1890 colleges should be designated to attack certain segments of these problems. It would be a tragedy and a sad commentary on higher education if the rich experiences, extensive expertise, great dedication, and positive commitment of these colleges are not used as principal resources in the solutions of problems facing our nation. One might be so bold as to predict that the problems will not be solved if the 1890

colleges are not a significant part of the action.

5) Make a financial commitment to fund the 1890 colleges as full
partners in the land-grant college system. This commitment
should include:

    a. The establishment of endowments, to which they are entitled,
but have never received, for each of the 1890 colleges.

    b. Full-funding of the annual Morrill-Nelson appropriations for
the 1890 colleges to provide needed teaching equipment.

    c. The establishment of "catch-up" funds to bring teaching
equipment at 1890 colleges up to a level consistent with
1862 colleges.

    d. Substantially increase the level of funds for state agricultural
experiment stations at 1890 colleges to permit them to work
on a greater portion of "people problems" in their respective
states.

    e. Substantially increase funding of cooperative extension work
at the 1890 colleges to enable them to deliver meaningful
services to rural people in terms of their immediate and
potential needs.

    f. To provide in each state a rural or people development center
under the direction of each of the 1890 colleges. These
centers will capitalize on present expertise of the 1890 colleges
as well as embark on new and different approaches in developing
meaningful solutions to the people problems.

    g. Funds must be proveded to construct adequate physical facilities
at the 1890 colleges comparable to those at 1862 colleges for
the proper conduct of teaching research and extension services.

    h. At least one USDA physical building and program should be
established on the campus of each 1890 college so as to demonstrate a commitment of true alliance between USDA and the 1890
colleges.

6) Make a moral commitment to eliminate all forms of racism and
discrimination in programs and resource allocation, especially
funds, from the land-grant system; to recognize as valid, the
pluralism of the 1890 and 1862 colleges and to develop this
pluralism into a meaningful system for delivering to the people
of our land, a life style which enhances them individually and
affords them life, liberty, and the pursuit of happiness.

A full study should be made of legislation governing the land-grant college

system. New legislation should be enacted and/or existing legislation should be

modified to guarantee full partnership and status of the 1890 colleges in the land-

grant system.

THE PERILS OF THE GREEN REVOLUTION*

We stand on the threshold of a new productivity of world agriculture, to be achieved by fertilizer, water control, genetic breeding, and pest control. The Green Revolution is the catch phrase. In effect it says that what we need is simply an intensified land use, which can be done by mobilizing all the modern scientific and industrial tools: improvement of genetic varieties of plants and animals, more efficient operation, capital investment, associated engineering works and industry, better storage, transportation, and distribution. In short, it advocates that the use of most of the earth's land surface (and large parts of its water area) be refashioned after Iowa pig farms or Texas cotton ranches. Until recently its advocates said that it would solve problems of poverty and starvation by increasing the world's food supply as rapidly as the world population grew. Until 1969 this was the official line of the World Food Organization of the United Nations. A tidal wave of scientific refutation and growing public awakening has at last caused some rethinking on the subject, which was as much a fabrication of vested interests and wishful thinking as it was the opinion of agricultural researchers.

It has been replaced by a slightly modified doctrine, that industrial agriculture will alleviate the effects of human density by reducing the magnitude of famine and postponing the crisis. It is argued indignantly that to do less is inhuman.

What, in fact, is the environmental effect of super-agriculture? In the United States land destruction is a matter of record. The erosion of large sections of the Southeast by tobacco and cotton in the seventeenth and eighteenth centuries and the dust bowls of the Great Plains in the twentieth are merely two of the many earlier examples. The combined effects of clearing, plowing, burning, overgrazing, ill-advised irrigation, breaking sods that should never be cultivated, removing timber from slopes that should remain in trees, draining marshes that served

*From THE TENDER CARNIVORE AND THE SACRED GAME
  ©1973 by Paul Sheppard

as uptakes for underground water supplies—all are documented in a vast literature. Explanations that it was a new continent with unfamiliar climate, that the frontier would always offer a fresh start, that methods were imperfect but would improve with new machines, have been belabored and accepted. A particular farmer in his time and place is not to be regarded as a greedy monster but only as a cog in the wheel of society.

The total damage to the continental environment has probably been underestimated. Much of it has been hidden by the buffering effect of long-accumulated reserves and the continued productivity of lands that are nevertheless losing their reserves of soil capital. The huge literature of lamentation and guilt has been countered by "practical" observations that, as long as productivity is high, losses are unimportant. It has been said that the rape of the continent was necessary to make us powerful and rich, that by being rich we are better able to solve problems caused by exploitation while at the same time living well. It can be convincingly shown that forest conservation will be practiced by forest industries and soil conservation by farmers as these become economically imperative; that the decline in natural resources will gradually be leveled by rising economic incentive.

Such arguments can be so neatly woven by professionals in the "resource field" that one is struck with awe and admiration at their beautiful simplicity. The way in which self-correcting means are built in, the aura of destiny and inevitability, the justification of past and present that relieves us of responsibility are more than seductive; they are ravishing.

For trapping the modern farmer and his wife within this dialectic we can thank academia—the land-grant universities and their affiliated state agricultural colleges. Wasteful and expensive even by modern American standards, most agricultural institutions cannot find applicants for all their fellowships, their proliferated courses are underenrolled, and their large faculties overpaid. The agriculture schools are carefully protected and fed by an industry grossing about fifty billion dollars a year in farm products alone (and some hundred billion in the making of agricultural supplies and equipment) and by the minions of that industry in government. Walk on the campus of any agricultural school. Look in the classrooms. Sit in on classes. Look in the libraries. Stroll through the model dairies. Count the students. You will see the most elaborate educational machinery for the education of the smallest group of professionals in academia. Compare what you see to the educational plant for biology or physics, or for history or literature.

Their bulk, duplication, and cost are not the worst. Home economics and agricultural training have from their inception been inimical to the creative wholeness of the family subsistence farm, in which those virtues of rural life which survive can be found. Among these are first-hand knowledge of weather, organisms, terrain, the development of manual skills in fashioning the crafts of rural life, knowledge of materials and textures in the making of things and of foods to be used.

Home economics, by its relentless advocacy of mechanization and consumerism, has sold the farm woman short. She no longer sews, churns, knits, bakes, preserves, works a garden, or participates in the care of animals. She is linked to the stores and to the society of the town. What is more, she will assure you that she likes it that way—though she may have simply escaped from the drudgery of the farm to a new set of equally pernicious stresses. I have no intention of arguing differently; as I have said, there is no reason, sentimental or rational, for perpetuating the hand toil of peasant life. Beyond her experience is the total price of continuing the farm at all, the cost to the land, to the biosphere, and to society as a whole (including the additional cost of urbanizing the farm family). The farm woman has been sold short because her instinctive concern for the organic and her womanly generosity and feeling for wholeness have been diverted into new social activities or de-fused by litter campaigns and beautification projects. She has been removed from the immediate scene of the farm. She is no longer a witness or participant. Her potential human and feminine reactions to the banality and monotonous horror of the new industrial farm are no longer a threat to its continuation. This is the Women's Auxiliary of the Green Revolution.

The Green Revolution is moving to complete the industrialization of the earth's land and sea surfaces. Its thrust will take two main directions, accompanied by chemical warfare on a scale precedented by the massive use of herbicides in the Vietnam war. The first is the genetic development of new super-strains of crop plants. The second is the irrigation and cultivation of the world's deserts. Neither can solve the world's food problems because of the exponential form of human population growth. Both are prescriptions for ecological disaster. They are the logical and final development of the poor ecology of agriculture that first ruined small areas and good soils, then extensive areas where the more vulnerable communities of natural life had less intrinsic stability. The principle is the same everywhere: the intensity of technique is commensurate with the rapidity and magnitude of potential calamity. By impoverishing an already fragile habitat with uniform crop plants and destroying its native life, the Green Revolution, in the name of a holy crusade, will create balances that cannot be kept, crops that cannot be protected, landscapes so foreign to the desert climate that their precarious existence will require ever-increasing inputs of chemical and mechanical control. When greenhouse projects the size of the Sahara desert topple, as they surely will, the consequences will make past famines in India look like minor incidents.

When the environmental crisis became a national preoccupation in 1970 attention was centered on pollution. The old conservation movement, with its gentlemanly voice of alarm over land, soil, and water, seemed almost obsolete. Neither the new radical youth element nor the establishment environmentalists had much good to say for it. Their dismissal of old-fashioned conservation of land and water as of no importance was shortsighted not only historically but ecologically as well. Pollution is only the debris resulting from mispractices and mis-policies relating people to the land.

Of course air pollution and water pollution have been the conspicuous aspects of the environmental situation, and to these the public could easily respond. More devastating, however, has been the destruction of soils and forests, which has been ignored —for an insidious reason: the harvest has been increasing. American economists and geographers, among others, have long boasted that American agriculture has been the most efficient on earth. When Premier Khrushchev of the Soviet Union visited the United States in 1956 it was an Iowa farm that he wanted to see and was pridefully shown. In the dust-bowl days of the 1930s, when farms were buried under suffocating layers of silt and abandoned, the lesson had seemed clear: land misuse led to economic failure. Since then, in Iowa as in other deep-soil Midwest states, land misuse has produced affluence. There are full barns, great rows of gleaming farm machinery, children in college, high land prices, and gross incomes for many farmers of more than a hundred thousand dollars per year. The lesson has been forgotten for the sake of economic gain.

To say that the most productive Iowa farms are among the most mismanaged lands in the world produces furious counter-claims. Nevertheless it is true. The Midwest cornfields, the cottonlands of Texas, the timberlands of the Northwest, the interior valleys of California—the most productive and "efficient" agriculture on the continent—are the homes of havoc. There the devastation, though invisible, sets the style for the Green Revolution.

The tools that keep the crops greening in Iowa, as elsewhere, are chemicals. In the past the one practice that has redeemed agriculture ecologically throughout the whole of its history has been the spreading of manure. Whenever this practice has been abandoned, cities, regions, even empires have obediently followed their soils into extinction. Everywhere that agriculture has endured, a suitable ratio of animals to cultivated land is found, and the deliberate and careful husbanding of human waste and other organic matter for fertilizer.

Organic matter does for a soil what no pure chemical elements can do. In addition to nutrients, it is a source of humus, essential for soil structure. Soils with adequate humus hold reserves of water and nutrient elements and therefore have the physical, chemical, thermic, and textural qualities that favor rich microbial life and the growth of plant roots, and produce nutritional balance in the harvest. If they are not impacted by the weight of heavy machines such soils withstand drought and storm, the plow and harrow, good years and bad. They remain intact and productive indefinitely if crops are properly rotated and occasionally rested.

Beginning with the mid-twentieth century, combinations of chemical nitrogen, potassium, and phosphorus have been increasingly used and sold as a "complete" fertilizer. Most farmers have used these together with calcium as a fertilizer program. Here and there, where other nutrient elements were lacking in particular soils, these too have been added. Coupled with chemical pesticides, herbicides, and the heavy planting of new strains of crop plants, crop yield has gone up. Meantime the soil has gone steadily down in structure and holding capacity. The massive doses of fertilizer have leached through, poisoning underground water and polluting by enrichment city reservoirs and lakes. One consequence of such pollution is heavy algal growth, which suffocates other life in lakes and is generally combated by another round of expensive chemical treatment.

The combination of crop strains that have been produced for characteristics other than nutritional value (uniformity, appearance, bulk, storing qualities, disease-resistance) and chemical fertilizing that omits organic matter and the two dozen other chemicals necessary to life has ruined the nutritional quality of soil and harvest. The complexity of a natural soil makes it comparable to a quasi-living being, an organism, or a kind of organ of the biosphere. It is also part of a larger ecosystem. The agronomists train the industrial farmer to sacrifice everything for crop productivity: fencerows, natural soil, trees, wildflowers, small mammals, insects, birds, natural brooks, and a truly quality product. As experts who also advise the powerful chemical companies, they permeate academia and dominate the theory if not the practice of commercial farming.

The travesty of chemical farming that engulfs the young farmer continues to enmesh him with its propaganda throughout his life. Mediated by the county agent, technicians of government agricultural agencies, the bureaucrats of subsidy and marketing programs, the industry-dominated farm media, and all the "agri-businessmen" together create rural Disneyland, a self-contained, self-explanatory, and self-judging sham.

No single farmer, no matter how educated his perception, or what his intuition with respect to the preservation of the soil and the natural community, can escape it. Surrounded by neighbors who compensate for the compacting of soil by their heavy machinery and for its functional failure by increasing the dosage of pure chemicals, he cannot reduce his harvest and still get the loans he needs; he cannot get sufficient manpower or animal power, reduce his field and farm size. He cannot survive economically if he allows space for wild creatures, or gives some of the harvest to pests, or uses varieties of crop plants with lower yield but higher food value. Indeed, he would be ostracized formally and informally. The system would crush him.

The successes and failures of chemical pesticides are well known. Their celebrated "control" of insect and fungal pests is conveyed in detail in advertising, textbooks, and "history" books. In time all target organisms become resistant by genetic selection, beneficial forms are harmed, and the biosphere is poisoned. The genetic response of pests is a fact that the industry is happy to admit in order to divert attention from the more serious effects of chemical pesticides and to justify the continued issuance of new compounds.

The replacement of one chemical pesticide with another, then another, and so on, not only works but is consumerism at its best. It is not only commercial but can be measured for success and progress. Ecologically, the swath of death cuts through the environment without reference to enemies or friends. Like using a cannon for surgery, it simply removes good and bad alike. In some places delicate species of insects and other invertebrates, in no way harmful to man, have been extinguished. As ecologists have pointed out for many years, some of these are parasites or predators on the pest organism.

Some pesticides, such as DDT, remain in the soil, air, and

water for many years, poisoning and repoisoning as they pass through food-chain systems in nature. They are stored in the fatty tissues of meat-eaters. The labor and expense it has taken to limit the use of DDT have been enormous. Yet how pathetic that effort seems when hundreds of substitutes are possible, many already in use, some better, some worse, all of which control by general destruction—the environmental equivalent of giving whole-body x-irradiation to control cancer.

Fortunately for man, his evolution toward carnivorousness over the past four million years progressed only to a point of eating around 30 per cent meat. Were he a true carnivore he would now be suffering far more DDT accumulation in his system. His tragedy would parallel that of peregrine falcons, brown pelicans, sea lions, and hundreds of other birds and mammals that live wholly on meat. As it is, every bite of meat from whatever source now carries its portion of DDT into the body, where part of it will be stored. Young adults have been accumulating DDT for more than twenty years, and will continue to accumulate it throughout their lives even if the use of DDT is eliminated. What this will mean to the health of the people now in their twenties as they approach their sixties cannot be foreseen, but the result will not be good. Nor is there any escape, since much DDT was applied by air and, instead of falling at once to the ground, entered the world's atmosphere and is falling slowly around the planet, a poisoned dew.

To expect contrition from agri-industry for the DDT episode would perhaps be too much. To expect intelligent reappraisal of the role of chemical pesticides is not too much. Nonetheless the chemical industries are fighting government regulation of DDT. Their answer to the problem is more research and more careful testing of substitute products. There is no evidence of redirection, only escalation of a chemical approach that will lead to catastrophe.

When the use of herbicides, hormones, and antibiotics in animal husbandry and seed and fruit treatment, and the use of disinfectants, preservatives, color and taste enhancers in food are objectively examined, the evidence is that we are poisoning and defrauding ourselves. To suppose that the damage done by each is an isolated instance or is caused by a transitory weakness in detail in the technology is delusion. Chemical agriculture fails because agriculture is an imperfect union of wild and tame.

The fate of domestic plants and animals now hangs in the balance. In peasant agriculture the selection for seed size or fruit color, for wool or milk production, was counteracted by hardiness or physical fitness, use qualities, and taste. Now industrial agriculture seeks mutations for extreme milk or beef production in cattle and ear size or position in corn, on the assumption that the weaknesses and unfitness that accompany them can always be countered by chemical disinfection, additives, and other substances that violate the organism and the environment.

Directly and indirectly these chemical poisons are passed on to us, either through our consumption of the farm product or through the environment. The modern creation of "animal machines" also changes the animals' tissues. The physiology and biochemistry of animals kept throughout their lives in cages are altered, adversely affecting the nutritive quality of such products as eggs and milk as well as the flesh itself.

The psychological effects, or life experience, of such captives must not be overlooked, not only for reasons of humane concern but because of their influence on body chemistry. Pigs that have been harshly treated in advance of slaughter undergo stress changes in their alimentary systems releasing a highly poisonous bacterium, *Salmonella,* into the gut from pouches along its wall. At butchering, *Salmonella* may then contaminate the meat. The toxins produced kill more people than any other kind of food poisoning. Recently new strains have been identified that are not susceptible to any known antibiotic treatment.

There is some evidence that the more industrialized agriculture becomes the less nutritious and delectable is its produce. Vegetables grown under irrigation or hydroponically (that is, in nutrient liquid) are notoriously tasteless. Where fowl are

kept in highly artificial and confined pens, egg quality is down
—by the industry's own standards, which are poor enough from
the consumer's point of view.

There is no doubt that modern agriculture is moving into
a new phase of animal husbandry that will fully justify the term
"industrial." No animal will have a life as it is ordinarily
thought of in the image of the barnyard community of the
subsistence farm. The animals will be contained and manipu-
lated only for their usefulness. Insofar as they are able to feel,
perceive, and respond, their experience will be limited to slings
or scaffolds in closed chambers, punctuated by the drone of
machines that castrate, inseminate, vaccinate, medicate, remove
excrement, extract by-products, and sluice a total-food-soup into
them, ending with the needle, gas jet, or knife.

This has been foreshadowed by the industrial slaughterhouse, a logical and necessary adjunct of scientific farming.
Every person in a developed nation should be required to tour
a slaughterhouse, and he should do so after learning any one of
the hundreds of ceremonies of apology, prayer, and symbolic
commitment to the prey that attend the hunt by cynegetic men.
As more is learned about the responses of plants and animals,
either the killing must increasingly be hidden from sight and
consciousness or it must be done in religious affirmation. By
"must" I do not mean courses of action to be taken. I mean that
we will be forced into one of two directions by the future.
Chemical agriculture, like chemical warfare, is slaughter at a
distance—death poorly directed and unseen battles won in a
war that will be lost—that is lost in the winning.

None of the fairy tales by which the war against nature is
described is more fanciful than that told by modern economics.
That one man with his machines can produce enough food and
fiber for one hundred people for a year from two hundred acres
is a typical example. It has been assumed that costs outside
capital investment and operational expenses, such as soil and
environmental deterioration, would show up eventually in his
accounting books. To a limited extent they do, as he piles more

and more chemicals onto the land and into his stock to compensate for what the soil no longer provides, as he builds dams and drills deeper wells for water the soil no longer holds, and as he enlarges and intensifies his operation in the face of an increasingly unstable ecosystem. These costs are measured in dollars, but the time lag is so great that many of the biological expenses have not yet materialized as cash losses.

The dollar calculations still look good in the farmer's own book, but his book includes public money in the debit column, which he has not earned. Some of this is clearly shown as subsidy in the form of government conservation payments; other items, like farm price supports, are not so marked because they are less direct—but no less real. The gross dollar value of farm crops in the United States in 1970 was about fifty billion dollars per year, expenses about thirty-five billion. Of the fifteen-billion-dollar profit, five billion came directly from government price and payment subsidies. If agricultural colleges with their scholarships, county, state and federal free services to the farmer, incentives, industrial handouts and favors to the farmer written off as tax-exempt expenses, adjusted land taxes, income-tax angles whose loopholes are second to none could all be taken into account, the ten-billion-dollar net would vanish like a dream. It is only fair to add that different types of farming vary in these respects. Some kinds feed less at the public trough than others. The point is that the total has never, to my knowledge, been calculated, but would probably run to a huge deficit. It has been called "the largest disguised income-transfer program in history."

In addition, agriculture is costly far beyond the boundaries of the farm. The pollution to the environment from the industries serving agriculture (and many other industries and services) begins with mining and smelting to get the ores to make farm machinery and strip mining for coal, and runs through the manufacturing processes, which are especially destructive and noxious among petro-chemical industries, to the final transporting of them to the farm. The boast that each acre of a modern farm can feed twenty or thirty times the number of men on it looks good when compared to peasant farming, but the calories of food energy produced per acre are fewer than the fuel energy put into the manufacture, transportation, and operation of the machinery.

Subsistence agriculture is directly based on photosynthesis. Solar energy is channeled to the consumer directly through the farm crops. Even the muscle energy from man and animal working the farm is derived from the crops themselves. When the energy from fossil fuels is added by mechanization the crop production is raised at an unseen expense to the whole biosphere. The input of fossil fuel raises the photosynthetic output slightly, but this is like running a huge generator in order to turn on a few more electric lights. The resulting pollution is not the only hidden cost. Petroleum is one of the richest potential sources of new food products on earth; the day may come when people will virtually weep to realize how much of it was squandered by burning. To argue that by then man will be able to replace it is fallacious because energy will be required to make the substitute for petroleum. It is like the argument that, having squandered rich soils, agricultural technology will make it possible to farm poor ones; the fallacy is that to do so will require an increased energy and materials input from the outside.

At the forefront of the Green Revolution is the genetic development of new crop varieties with higher yields. That some of these are less nourishing, and most poorer tasting, may be dismissed as the necessary price of more carbohydrates and fats for a growing population. Each new miracle plant does not simply replace a less efficient form; it replaces hundreds and hundreds of varieties. Originally domestication was a local affair. Plants adapted to the particular soils and climate were cultivated in each area. Hybrids of the domestic plant and its wild relatives sprang up along field boundaries, a rich reserve of genetic variability. Close to their wild origins, the native varieties were less productive than the new strains but more stable and resistant to local diseases.

In 1930, 80 per cent of the wheat grown in Greece was composed of scores of local varieties. By 1966, less than 10 per cent were native strains. The rest was a single imported super-plant. The biology of evolution, the principles of ecology, and the history of agriculture guarantee that sooner or later a disease will devastate that alien. Where previously diseases were local and food shortages in any year equally restricted, super-crops and massive famine are natural partners.

Though it was destructive enough in its own way, subsistence agriculture was broadly based, not only in diversity of crops, but in the closer-to-wild-type genetics of each. The inverted pyramid of super-strains must be propped up as each becomes weaker in vitality. Every year increased chemical and mechanical supports, infusions of capital and energy, must be added from the outside. The input to keep them alive increases until it surpasses the energy contained in the crop. The crop's vulnerability to disease increases with its increasing purity. The long-range virulence of the disease organism increases as it evolves by mutation and selection to counter the protective measures of the farmer. For every breed and variety a debacle is inevitable.

Agriculture works best where it is least perfect. Where the farmer still hunts and gathers and keeps many kinds of plants and animals; where he produces little surplus or cash crop, has wild lands and bushy fencerows on his farm, uses no chemical pesticides, fertilizers, or treatments, is minimally dependent on distant industries, and grows crops that are adapted to local conditions and correspond in structure to the wild types of the area (cereals in grasslands, orchards in forest lands), the enterprise will be more ecologically fit and durable.

This is the agriculture that the Third World seeks to escape. Though it is benign environmentally and efficient in its ecological accounting, it cannot support large populations, which already exist. It cannot support science, art, urban life, all the institutions that require leisure, education, and freedom to experiment. Man cannot go back to peasant mixed agriculture any more than he can turn time's arrow.

Nor can man continue to perfect industrial agriculture,

to maintain the idea of the farm at all. Life on the planet simply cannot afford more genetic narrowing. The moral and nutritional administration of domestic animals is failing. Forcing the soil with machines that pollute and that waste fossil fuels is catastrophic.

Progress in the efficiency of desalination of ocean water is rapidly bringing all the world's arid lands within reach of vast irrigation schemes. Unless our course is altered, the years from 1970 until the end of the century will see the construction of huge pipelines running thousands of miles into the interior of all the continents. Besides being irrigated by reactor-operated desalination processes, soils will be heated and fumigated. The night sky will be illuminated; gigantic electric-generating plants will empower fertilizer factories so that several multi-crops will be grown per year. On the surface this seems to be the epitome of progress and human betterment. However, a factory mono-culture—the dream of engineers and politicians—is a dependent enterprise, requiring heavy indutsrial support for sifting the planet for minerals and energy. As the Gobi, Sahara, Mohave, and Australian deserts are invaded, the natural buffers that have so far helped protect the planet will collapse. The dream of progress will become a nightmare.

The economic and social superiority of modern farming as a way of life is a fiction; as technology it is destructive; as a Green Revolution hopeless.

The New Cynegetics

The modern environmental crisis is a result of a state of consciousness as much as it is the outcome of bad technology. It may be infinitely more difficult to transform human sensibility than to pass laws and build new cities. Reordering our view of time, welcoming the dead as part of us, affirming a planetary ecology centered on food chains, extending the scope of history to the personal and to the cosmic—these are the essentials of the transformation. . . .

The Cultural Basis of Ecological Crisis

Insofar as farmers think of such matters, they are taken in by and gladly exploit the dream of rural virtue. All politicians, hucksters, farm magazines and other media directed to farmers deliberately foster this fantasy. The farmer is assured of his reverence for the soil, his knowledge of nature, his fondness for wild animals, his moral superiority, his political acumen, and so on. But if a farmer is asked what kind of place he likes or why he thinks nature is good, he will not be able to answer unless he is an educated man, a gentleman farmer—that is, a non-farmer who hires "hands."

The reason for this is not hard to find. Peasant existence is the dullest life man ever lived. Since the beginning of the modern world the brighter and more sensitive children have left the dawn-to-dusk toil of the farm to their duller brothers and sisters. Even for those who remain the routine must be leavened or it is intolerable. Rural peoples the world over have scores of holidays and festivals to alleviate their existence. The number of such occasions is proportional to the intensity and specialization of the agriculture. In a relatively diverse domestication there is less need for diversions.

A frontiersman or pioneer is self-sufficient in more than material needs. His subsistence farm is in closer ecological harmony with the natural environment; it might include a vegetable garden, hay and grain fields, fruit trees or bushes, bees, a fish pond, fowl, a variety of hooved animals, pasture, nut trees and other forest, and nearby natural vegetation from which mushrooms and other wild vegetables and wild game are taken.

Farmers in a cash crop, surplus food or fiber production, and monoculture setting, however, require constant social super-charging to remain sane and human. Their pastimes are often shocking and brutal, their religious observances noisy and dramatic. Cock-fighting, bull-fighting, bear-baiting, dog-fighting, men-fights, the debauchery of alcohol and drugs, socially sanctioned remission of standards of morality, public display and civil punishment, and sexual and religious frenzy and indulgence are social attempts to compensate for the nullity.

In the most extreme example of this vacuum, modern industrial irrigation monoculture, rural life is hopeless. The farmer lives in a town, which is socially and architecturally organized to provide a sensory barrage, and, like the peasant of the Old World, he commutes to the fields. This is the climax of ten millennia of separating work from leisure, depriving work of its redeeming, universalizing aspect, reducing leisure to idleness and whim, and separating both from the cultus, the social forms of divine activity. No margin for weeds and wild things is left; there is no recourse to hunting and gathering, no habitat in which man is in scale. It is not surprising that farmers the world over have always been ready to abandon these environments. Their eagerness to leave was implicit from the beginning. That modern farmers are becoming indistinguishable from city men, by place of residence as well as dress and habits, is the culmination of agri-culture with its pseudo-separation of urban and rural.

The depersonalizing and socially destructive forces of the city can be traced to their true origins: the country. If the city as we know it is unhealthy, a breeder of social and racial injustice, the wreck of human community, a sinkhole of crime, a failed complex of educational, religious, sanitary, and transportation facilities, then we have failed to design according to human need. Its rural foundation is no less defective. The country has fed the city with people whose ecological thought has been corrupted with delusions of mastery of nature, who have been trained to be stoic and stolid when the livable city demands sensitivity and creativity. The city has drawn from the hinterland materials and energy, fiber and food, forcing the escalation of monocultures and imposing chemical and industrial methods on agriculture.

The subsistence farmer invented security-mindedness. The money farmer outdid him with his seemingly insatiable desire for increasing productivity. That this led into slavery is more than metaphor. According to Daphne Prior, agriculture ceased to be voluntary and became coercive some six thousand years ago, with the emergence of the "autonomous, centralized political unit with the power to collect taxes, draft workers and soldiers and enforce law."